TAKING SIDES

Clashing Views on Controversial

Issues in Religion

TAKING SIDES

Clashing Views on Controversial

Issues in Religion

Selected, Edited, and with Introductions by

Daniel K. Judd
Brigham Young University

McGraw-Hill/Dushkin
A Division of The McGraw-Hill Companies

To My Grandfathers:
Daniel Knapp Judd and Frank Levi Farnsworth

Photo Acknowledgment
Cover image: © 2003 by PhotoDisc, Inc.

Cover Art Acknowledgment
Charles Vitelli

Library of Congress Cataloging-in-Publication Data
Main entry under title:
Taking sides: clashing views on controversial issues in religion/selected, edited, and with introductions by Daniel K. Judd.—1st ed.
Includes bibliographical references and index.
1. Religion. 2. Religion and science. 3. Philosophy and religion. 4. Religion and politics. I. Judd, Daniel K., *ed.* II. Series.
              200

0-07-255779-6
ISSN: 1541-8448

Printed on Recycled Paper

Preface

Philosopher and Christian apologist C. S. Lewis once described the importance of opposing views in scholarship when he wrote, "In such matters to find an opponent is almost to find a friend." It is in this spirit of dialectical camaraderie that this publication has been produced.

This volume contains 34 essays that are arranged in pro-con pairs, addressing 17 controversial issues in religion and theology. Many of the essays address theological questions that have been debated for thousands of years, while others comment on more current religious topics. Some of the essays are very provocative, others more "politically correct," but each addresses a question from the core of scholarship in religion.

Most of the essays in this text address the various issues from a Christian perspective, although Jewish, Islamic, and agnostic scholarship is represented as well. The preponderance of Christian writings should not be interpreted as a Christian bias but simply as a reflection of the major religious affiliation of the American public, as well as the religious scholarship with which I am most familiar. Well-written articles from non-Christian perspectives are welcome for inclusion in future editions. While I have attempted to reference the sacred texts of many different faith traditions, the majority of scriptural references are from the Hebrew Bible and the Christian New Testament. All references to Hebrew/Christian Scripture are taken from the King James version of Scripture unless otherwise noted.

A basic premise of the Taking Sides series is the idea that through the discussion of opposing ideas truth can be revealed and understood. One of the standards for this volume is that the article, while asserting a specific opinion, must not be polemic. Such a standard may sound contradictory, but I believe that it is possible to disagree on a particular issue without being disagreeable. In much the same way that satire differs from sarcasm, justice from revenge, and mercy from indulgence, this publication, *Taking Sides: Clashing Views on Controversial Issues in Religion*, is *dialectical* without being *polemic*. The etymological root of *dialectics* is tied to *language*, discourse, and conversation, while the root of the word *polemic* is connected to *war*. War may have its place in dialogue, but for the most part, the reader will find the articles in this volume reasonable and civil.

Plan of the book   Each of the 17 issues begins with a general *introduction* that sets the stage for the opposing essays and ends with a *postscript* that summarizes the arguments and considers other possible perspectives on the issue. Relevant Internet sites and addresses (URLs) are also included to assist the reader in learning more about the topic. The articles and books referenced in the introductions and postscripts will also serve as valuable resources to the reader.

Inasmuch as this is the first volume of Taking Sides to specifically address issues in religion, it is my desire that the readers will feel welcome to provide feedback concerning the publication. I am especially interested in other questions and/or essays that could be included in editions to follow. Please contact me at Daniel_Judd@byu.edu.

A word to the instructor   An *Instructor's Manual With Test Questions* (multiple-choice and essay) is available through the publisher for the instructor using Taking Sides in the classroom. A general guidebook, called *Using Taking Sides in the Classroom*, which discusses methods and techniques for integrating the pro-con approach into any classroom setting, is also available. An online version of *Using Taking Sides in the Classroom* and a correspondence service for Taking Sides adopters can be found at http://www.dushkin.com/usingts/.

Taking Sides: Clashing Views on Controversial Issues in Religion is only one of many titles in the Taking Sides series. If you are interested in seeing the table of contents for any of the other titles, please visit the Taking Sides Web site at http://www.dushkin.com/takingsides/.

Acknowledgments   I would like to acknowledge the assistance of the faculty and staff of the Department of Ancient Scripture at Brigham Young University. Special thanks also go to my secretaries Marianne Graf and Holly Rogers as well as my able research assistants Ben Rogers and Emily Halverson.

Finally, a special thanks to my beloved family—my wife, Kaye, and each of our children, Jacob, Jessica, Rachel, and Adam.

Daniel K. Judd
Brigham Young University

Contents In Brief

Contents

William Paley (1743–1805), Christian philosopher and archdeacon of the Anglican Church, concludes that just as an intelligent watchmaker is the only explanation for the existence of an intricate watch, only an intelligent creator could be responsible for the even more complex creation of humankind. Sally Morem, author and current president of Humanists of Minnesota, provides contemporary arguments against both "intelligent design" (like Paley's position) and the moral arguments for the existence of God. Morem asks, If an omniscient, omnipotent God is the creator, why is there so much of creation that is poorly constructed?

John Hick, theologian and philosopher at the University of Birmingham in the United Kingdom, asserts that God allows evil to exist as a means of enabling humankind to struggle in the process of gaining spiritual maturity. He argues that opposition, pain, and sorrow are all a necessary part of what he describes as "soul making." Author B. C. Johnson counters that the existence of evil proves the nonexistence of God—for if God exists and God is good, he would not allow evil to possess such a powerful influence.

Stephen N. Williams, professor of systematic theology at Union Theological College in Belfast, Northern Ireland, provides a defense *against* the theory of open theism, which proposes that God's knowledge of the future is limited. Williams defends the classical view of God's omniscience, stating that God's knowledge of the past, present, and future is absolute. John Sanders, associate professor of philosophy and religion at Huntington College in Huntington, Indiana, defends the "openness of God" theory, stating that God's knowledge is not omniscient in the traditional sense. Sanders asserts that while God does have complete knowledge of the past and present, his knowledge of the future is not complete because it is subject to humankind's exercise of free will.

Issue 4.   Can Morality Exist Without Religion?   50

John Arthur, professor of philosophy at the State University of New York at Binghamton asserts that religion is not necessary for a people to be moral. In addition to providing arguments against religion as a necessary "moral motivation" and as *the* source of truth, Arthur also asserts that morality is inherently social and is learned from interacting with others. Leo Tolstóy (1828–1910), moral philosopher and author of the classics *War and Peace* and *Anna Karenina,* argues for the necessity of God and religion in the existence of morality. Tolstóy contends that truth originates with God and that humankind must look to God (through religion) for continued guidance.

PART 2   DOCTRINAL ISSUES   73

Issue 5.   Is There Only One Way to Receive Salvation?   74

Keith E. Johnson, regional coordinator for *Ongoing Theological Education* with the Campus Ministry of City Colleges of Chicago, Illinois, asserts that while other religious traditions provide a supportive community and important ethical and moral teachings, salvation can only be found through faith in Jesus Christ. John Hick, theologian and philosopher of religion, is the author of what has come to be known as the pluralistic hypothesis. He argues that all religions are simply differing manifestations of the same ultimate reality. Hick maintains that salvation can be found through following God in whatever form we find him (or her).

Issue 6.   Is Acceptance of Christ Alone Sufficient for Salvation?   96

Charles C. Ryrie, former president and current professor at Philadelphia Biblical University, argues that "good works" are not in any way a part of salvation—salvation is obtained exclusively through the grace of Christ. While Ryrie believes that most people who accept Christ will manifest their acceptance of Him through good works, others will not. John F. MacArthur, Jr., president of The Master's College in Santa Clarita, California, and host of the *Grace to You* radio ministry, asserts that verbally accepting Christ is not sufficient for salvation. He believes that genuine acceptance of Christ is manifest through repentance and a sincere desire to live a moral life. MacArthur contends that those who have truly accepted Christ will manifest their commitment through their good works.

Issue 7.   Was Jesus Christ the Son of God?   118

N. T. Wright, canon theologian of Westminster Abbey and former dean of Lichfield Cathedral, argues for the divinity of Jesus. He maintains that faith and scholarship need not be mutually exclusive with respect to the debate over the divinity of Jesus Christ. Wright defends his position against the assertions of participants in the Jesus Seminar. Marcus J. Borg, professor of religion and culture at Oregon State University in Corvallis, Oregon, and a fellow of the Jesus Seminar, asserts that historical evidence does not support Jesus as being divine. A practicing Christian, Borg acknowledges Jesus as a great teacher and an embodiment of truth but not as the divine Son of God.

Issue 8.   Is the Family Primary in God's Plan?   138

Michael Gold, a Jewish rabbi who heads Temple Beth Torah in Tamarac, Florida, argues for the primacy of the traditional family in God's plan. Gold believes that the rescue of our decaying culture is dependent upon returning to the traditional family structure where moral values can be properly taught and modeled. Stanley Hauerwas, professor of theological ethics at Duke Divinity School in Durham, North Carolina, believes the family to be of great importance, but he states that it is not primary to God's plan. Hauerwas reasons from Scripture that it is the church that is primary and not the family. Putting the family first would be a form of idolatry, he concludes.

PART 3 SOCIAL ISSUES 161

This official "1974 Declaration on Procured Abortion" was written by the
Vatican and ratified by Pope Paul VI. The declaration is both a statement
of faith and reason for the Catholic Church's longstanding position against
abortion. It also addresses critics within the Catholic Church who assert
that abortion should be a personal decision based on conscience and not
obedience to authority. Daniel C. Maguire, Catholic professor of ethics at
Marquette University in Milwaukee, Wisconsin, argues for more flexibility in
the Catholic Church's stand on abortion. Maguire outlines the Catholic tradition of *probabilism*, which was originally designed to provide a legitimate
rationale for going against Church authority concerning moral issues.

Glen H. Stassen, professor of Christian ethics at the Fuller Theological
Seminary in Pasadena, California, argues that although the practice of
capital punishment has biblical roots, God does not intend the penalty of
death to be carried out in most cases. Former associate executive of the
United Presbyterian Church Jacob J. Vellenga provides an overview of the
scriptural teachings in favor of capital punishment from both Hebrew and
Christian Scriptures. He maintains that capital punishment is one of the
consequences God instituted to punish the perpetrator and prevent the
same kinds of acts among others.

Richard B. Hays, New Testament professor at the Duke Divinity School in
Durham, North Carolina, provides evidence from both Hebrew and Christian Scripture prohibiting the practice of homosexuality. Hays argues that
the prohibition against homosexual relations has continued from ancient
times to the present. Victor Paul Furnish, New Testament professor at

Southern Methodist University in Dallas, Texas, reasons that the arguments made against homosexual behavior found in the Bible are generally taken out of context and should not be interpreted as prohibitions against the practice.

Daniel C. Dennett, professor of arts and sciences at Tufts University in Medford, Massachusetts, argues against a God being involved in creation. He maintains that Darwin's theory of evolution is the strongest and most elegant explanation for the creation of the universe and humankind. Featured teacher of the radio ministry *Grace to You* and president of The Master's College in Santa Clarita, California, John MacArthur argues for divine creation. MacArthur believes that faithful Christians are being deceived by the naturalistic philosophy of evolution, and he provides conservative, scriptural arguments supporting a God-directed creation.

Psychiatrist and president of the International Center for the Integration of Health and Spirituality in Rockville, Maryland, David B. Larson argues that religious affiliation, belief, and practice are positively related to mental health. Psychologist and founder of rational-emotive therapy and president of the Institute for Rational-Emotive Therapy, located in New York City, Albert Ellis counters that religion is a contributor to emotional disturbance.

The editors of an interreligious, nonpartisan publication entitled *First Things* provide an argument defending military action, using both historical and theological backgrounds in support of just war theory. Walter Wink, professor of biblical interpretation at Auburn Theological Seminary in New York City, argues that victims of evil should not respond to evil on its own terms but choose a form of nonviolent resistance.

Richard Davis, professor of political science at Brigham Young University in Provo, Utah, argues for a strict interpretation of the Constitution concerning church and state issues. He states that history has demonstrated that when there is not a strict separation, the civil government, religion, and especially the people suffer. Mathew D. Staver, a Christian attorney specializing in religious liberty law and founder of Liberty Counsel, contends that a strict separation between church and state is not what the founding fathers had in mind when they established the Constitution. He presents evidence supporting the assertion that strict separation should exist on the federal but not the state level of government.

John B. Judis, senior editor of *The New Republic*, argues against the Religious Right using the political process to force its morally conservative political agenda on the American public. He maintains that government should be allowed to operate independently of the Religious Right's influence. Fred Barnes, cofounder of the weekly magazine *The Standard*, argues in support of the Religious Right keeping traditional moral issues alive in the public debate. He asserts that morality plays a vital role in the success of America, and without the influence of religious conservatism, the nation's freedom may be in jeopardy.

PART 6   DENOMINATIONAL ISSUES   333

Daniel K. Judd, professor of ancient Scripture at Brigham Young University in Provo, Utah, reasons why The Church of Jesus Christ of Latter-day Saints (LDS) should be considered a Christian religion. He states that because the LDS Church bases its theology and practice on Jesus Christ (particularly his atonement and resurrection), it should be considered a Christian Church even though its members do not accept many of the creeds of traditional Christendom. Craig L. Blomberg, New Testament professor at the Denver Seminary in Denver, Colorado, states that Mormons are not Christian either as a church or as individuals. He bases his statement on what he interprets as inconsistencies between The Church of Jesus Christ of Latter-day Saints and the Christian Church as represented in the Bible and in early Christian creeds.

Introduction

The Influence of Religious Belief and Practice

Daniel K. Judd

Religion, arguably, has had a more profound influence on the history of the world than has any other facet of human existence. From the debate over the creation of the world to the events noted on the nightly news, religion—for good and evil—is often a central factor in understanding the world in which we live. Religious belief and practice have found expression in almost every aspect of who we are as individuals, families, communities, and nations. The influence of religion is also found in nearly every aspect of our culture—anthropology, architecture, art, ethics, economics, education, family, gender role definition, geography, health, history, language, music, poetry, politics, and psychology—to name only a few.

The origin of the word *religion* is thought to be a combination of the words *re* (again) and *ligare* (connect), meaning to "reconnect" or to "tie back."[1] The etymology of the word implies a reconciliation between God and humankind. While the words *religion* and *theology* are often used synonymously, *The Oxford English Dictionary* defines theology as "the study or science which treats . . . God, His nature and attributes, and His relations with man and the universe."[2] Hence, *theology* pertains more to doctrine and belief, while *religion* primarily addresses the way in which one practices such beliefs. This volume of *Taking Sides*, while containing the word *religion* in its title, addresses both theological belief *and* religious practice.

Because *Taking Sides* is a series that tackles controversial issues and presents them in the format of two opposing opinions, some may wonder how and why a topic as sensitive as religion would be included in such a series. Shouldn't publications dealing with religious issues attempt to reconcile rather than divide? From the writings of the apostle Paul in the Christian New Testament, we find an important text that answers this question and contains a guiding principle that has been key to the completion of this project:

> For first of all, when ye come together in the church, I hear that there be divisions among you; and I partly believe it. *For there must be also heresies among you, that they which are approved may be made manifest among you.*

> — King James Version, Cor. 11:18–19; italics added

Though Paul wanted the members of the church at Corinth to be united, he also recognized the reality and necessity of opposition for them to understand the truth. Sometimes truth can be identified and understood only when placed in contrast with untruth. Some have described this method of learning as *dialectics*, which is "the theory and practice of weighing and reconciling juxtaposed or contradictory arguments for the purpose of arriving at truth especially through discussion and debate."[3] In addition to Paul's example of dialectical reasoning, other examples can also be found in ancient Hebrew, Greek, and Chinese traditions. From the dialectical perspective, joy can only be known in relationship to sorrow, good in contrast to evil, and the meaning of life in the context of death. Professor Brent D. Slife writes about the dialectical tradition:

> In this tradition, there can be no meaning (and thus no knowledge) without opposition. For example, there is no way to understand what "beauty" or "upness" means without implicitly understanding what "ugliness" or "downness" is, respectively. To judge the beauty of a work of art, one must have some notion of the contrast to beauty. In other words, opposing notions only make sense when considered at the same time, one complementing the other and together forming a complete concept. In this... conception of the dialectic, there are no quick and easy answers to difficult questions, and there are few incontestable facts to present. Instead there are at least two sides to every issue.[4]

From my own religious experience, it was an atheist grandfather (one of two grandfathers to whom this book is dedicated) who provided me with the philosophical opposition that helped me as a young man to clarify my beliefs about God and religion.

As the editor of this volume, I encourage you to carefully consider both sides of the various issues presented as a means of discovering truth. Do not be surprised if you find you cannot accept either of the two views presented on a given topic. This volume contains only a sampling of the many differing views on the various topics discussed. Perhaps the dialectical debates contained in this publication will play a part in helping you to articulate your own unique positions on these important issues.

Faith, Reason, and the Dialectical Method

There is much debate, inside as well as outside the religious world, concerning whether individuals such as Adam and Eve literally existed as historical characters or whether their existence is simply figurative. This same debate includes other biblical characters such as Noah, Abraham, Isaac, Jacob, Moses, and even Jesus. While there are some archeological and nonbiblical historical data that support the literal existence of biblical personalities and events, much of our belief or unbelief in such things comes as a matter of faith. Many agree that faith need *not* be separated from reason, which is another guiding assumption for this edition of *Taking Sides*. Faith and reason may serve as separate but companion witnesses, both necessary in assisting the reader to discern truth from error. British theologian N. T. Wright, one of the authors represented in this volume, states that his belief in Jesus as the Christ has been enhanced by the dialectical relationship of faith and historical reason:

> My view, that we come to know Jesus by both history and faith, is itself a product of a lifelong attempt to do just this.... When, during this attempt, I have found from time to time that the Jesus I knew by faith seemed less and less like the Jesus I was discovering by history, I have found that by living with the problem, turning it this way and that in the complex and often hidden world of personal and communal consciousness and reflection, faith has been able to discover not just that the new, and initially surprising, historical evidence was capable of being accommodated, but that it could actually be turned to advantage. Alternatively, there were times when faith stood its ground and, by looking at the challenge from all angles, was able to show that the historical evidence was as well if not better interpreted within a different framework.[5]

I tell my own students that *faith without reason* can become a mindless mysticism and that *reason without faith* can lead to a rational arrogance that will stifle our growth—intellectual as well as spiritual. Why would anyone want to close their eyes just because their sense of hearing was finely tuned? In this volume, I have attempted to include selections that address the various issues from the perspectives of both faith *and* reason.

A Brief Overview of the World's Religions

One estimate establishes that there are over "4,200 religions, churches, denominations, religious bodies, faith groups, tribes, cultures, movements, ultimate concerns, etc." in the world today.[6] Whether this ever-changing number is accurate or not, we may still conclude that the world has many different belief systems, which can be grouped in general categories. I will list each religious category by its estimated world population:

- Christianity: 2 billion
- Islam: 1.3 billion
- Hinduism: 900 million
- Buddhism: 360 million
- Taoism/Confucianism: 225 million
- Sikhism: 23 million
- Judaism: 14 million
- Baha'i: 6 million
- Jainism: 4 million
- Shinto: 4 million
- Zoroastrianism: 150 thousand

Table 1 lists the world's major religions, the approximate dates they were established, many of the major leaders, and some of the momentous events associated with their development.

Though the many variations among these different groups may at first appear staggering, there is actually more unity among them than first meets

Table 1

A Chronology of Momentous Religious Events[7]

Dates*	Events**	Dates*	Events**
B.C.E.***		C.E.***	
ca. 1750	Abraham journeyed to Canaan (Precursor to Judaism)	ca. 0-30	Christianity, **Jesus Christ**, and the New Testament
ca. 1500	Indo-Aryans entered India	ca. 45-65	Apostle Paul spread Christianity
ca. 1250	Judaism, **Moses**, and the Pentateuch (Torah)	ca. 90	Jewish canon, the Old Testament, fixed
ca. 1000	Zoroastrianism, **Zarathustra**, and the Avesta	ca. 100	Buddhism spread into China
ca. 850-400	Period of the Hebrew prophets	ca. 382	New Testament canon fixed
ca. 800-300	Period of the Hindu sages	ca. 500	Jewish Talmud completed
ca. 604-500	Taoism, **Lao Tzu** (604-?), and the Tao Te Ching	ca. 610	Islam, **Muhammad** (570-632), and the Qur'an
	Janism, **Vardhamana Mahavira** (599-527), and the Angas	ca. 625	Buddhism spread into Tibet
	Buddhism, **Siddhartha Gautama** (563-483), and the Tripitaka	ca. 651	First compilation of Qur'an
	Confucianism, **Confucius** (551-479), and the Chinese canon	ca. 747	Tantric Buddhism reached Tibet
587-586	Jews exiled to Babylon	1054	Christianity split into Eastern Orthodox and Roman Catholic
538	Cyrus permitted Jews to return to Jerusalem	ca. 1500	Sikhism, **Guru Nanak** (1469-1539), and beginning of the Adi Granth
ca. 246	King Asoka spread Buddhism	1517	**Martin Luther** (1483-1546) and the beginnings of Protestantism
		1530s	Church of England
		1530s	Presbyterianism, **John Calvin** (1509-1564)
		1609	The Baptist Church, **John Smyth** (1554-1612)
		1611	King James version of the Bible published
		1739	Methodism, **John Wesley** (1703-1791)
		1830	The Church of Jesus Christ of Latter-day Saints (Mormon), **Joseph Smith** (1805-1844), and the Book of Mormon
		1863	Seventh-day Adventists, **Ellen White** (1827-1915)
		1884	Jehovah's Witnesses, **Charles Russell** (1852-1916)

This table provides a sense of *when* each religion came on the scene:
*Many dates are approximate.
Religious Movement, **Religious Leader, scripture
***B.C.E. (before common era) and C.E. (common era) have been used in compliance with the standard terminology of the literature and discourse of comparative world religions.

the eye. Judaism, Christianity, and Islam all have a person in common—the Hebrew patriarch Abraham. The Hebrew Bible, Christian New Testament, and the Qur'an each describe Abraham as its common ancestor. Sadly, the common link between Judaism and Islam, which binds them to a common past, is also one of their greatest points of contention at present. The origins of the present conflict in Israel (and much of the Middle East) can be traced to the birthright controversy between Abraham's two sons, Isaac and Ishmael. Those of Jewish descent trace their ancestry through the Hebrew scriptures to Isaac, who was the son of Abraham and his first wife, Sarah. Muslims trace their lineage to Abraham as well—not to Sarah, but to his second wife, Hagar. Traditionally, followers of Islam (Muslims) believe that the birthright blessings of Abraham (land inheritance, authority, etc.) should go to Abraham's firstborn son, Ishmael. Jewish tradition argues that the birthright blessings should go to Isaac, the son of Abraham's first wife, Sarah. This battle over birthright is the same battle that some believe will eventually evolve into the final battle that will end the world as we know it—the battle of Armageddon (see the New Testament, Rev. 16:16).

The scriptures of all three religions—the Hebrew Bible (which is also the Christian Old Testament), the New Testament, and the Qur'an—accept Adam, Noah, Abraham, and Moses as prophets of God. Both Christians and Muslims accept Jesus as a prophet, although Christians also believe Jesus to be the Son of God and the promised Savior—the Messiah whose coming religious Jews continue to anticipate. While Islamic theologians and laypeople alike embrace the idea that each of the mentioned prophets were men of God, they believe that it was the prophet Muhammad who was the greatest of all prophets and the one chosen by God to prepare humankind for Final Judgment.

Swiss psychologist Carl G. Jung referred to the monotheistic religions—Judaism, Christianity, and Islam—as "Western" religions. In contrast, Jung referred to the religions originating in Asia as the "Eastern" religions—Hinduism, Jainism, and Buddhism. While there are a host of differences between Western and Eastern religions, the primary distinction focuses on the nature of God. Professor Spencer J. Palmer identifies the major difference between Eastern and Western religions:

> It is a clash between *theism*—that is, a belief in one God who is personal, worthy of adoration, and separate from the world but continually active in it—and *monism*—a belief that god, mind, and matter are not different. Jews, Christians, Zoroastrians, and Muslims hold that God is the creator and Lord of the universe. To them the world is a real, tangible place with an identifiable beginning and an expected historical end. They believe the God they worship is not "out there somewhere" but one who actually involves himself in history.... On the other hand, the religions of Hinduism, Jainism, and Buddhism hold that humanity's goal is some form of unity with an impersonal divine principle. For them the world is not concrete but illusory and thus has no identifiable beginning or end.[8]

Not only are there major differences between religions East and West, there are also significant differences within each religion as well. When we speak of Buddhism, are we referring to Theravada, Mahayana, or Lamaism? Like

Buddhism, Judaism, Christianity, and Islam all have like divisions, all providing ample material for "clashing views on controversial issues in religion."

Does the World Need Religion?

One of the leaders of my own personal religion often asks his colleagues the question, Therefore what? when discussing various theological and policy matters. In other words, does what we are doing or discussing really matter, and if so, where do we go from here?[9] This simple question has often helped me to remember the importance of trying to make whatever I do useful and meaningful to others. It is my intention that those who read this book will not only find it useful but will be able to answer a more important question that lies before us, Just how *meaningful* is religion in our own lives? Does religion really matter as we look for solutions to our personal problems and to the problems of the world?

The dialectical debate between those favoring the influence of religion and those in opposition has been an important part of my life personally, professionally, and ecclesiastically. I have learned from the advocates of both sides of the debate, as each side has assisted me in coming to a richer understanding of the issue. For example, Issue 13, "Does Religious Commitment Improve Mental Health?" addresses a question that I have spent much of my academic career answering. I have always believed the answer to be yes. As you will see in the selection written by Albert Ellis, however, not everyone agrees with my conclusion. Ellis states:

> Religiosity is in many respects equivalent to irrational thinking and emotional disturbance.... The elegant therapeutic solution to emotional problems is to be quite irreligious.... The less religious they are, the more emotionally healthy they will be.[10]

Many years ago, when I first read these words by Ellis, I was surprised and challenged by his boldness and found, based on my own personal experience, that I could not disagree with him more. I wrote a master's thesis, several journal articles, and edited a book examining Ellis's conclusions. Throughout this process I discovered that there was some truth to what he was saying (see D. K. Judd, *Religion, Mental Health, and The Latter-day Saints*, [Religious Studies Center/Bookcraft, 1999]).

Some years ago, Guenter Lewy, emeritus professor of political science at the University of Massachusetts at Amherst, set about the task of writing a book refuting the idea that unbelief was the major cause of most of the problems we face in the world today. Lewy, an atheist, believed morality to be important but that religion was unnecessary for morality to exist. See Issue 4, "Can Morality Exist Without Religion?" for an in-depth analysis of this discussion. While Lewy began to work on his project, his attitude toward religion began to change:

> A funny thing, if one can call it that, happened on the way to the completion of this book, which I envisaged as a defense of secular humanism and ethical relativism. Positions that I had always supported and taken for

granted turned out to be, on new reflection, far less convincing than I had assumed. This change in my outlook began with the realization that with regard to certain crucial moral issues concerning the meaning of life and death, I had more in common with religious moralists... than with most secular humanists.[11]

The title of Lewy's book, *Why America Needs Religion* (Eerdmans, 1996) reflects his change of heart as well as a change of mind concerning the necessity of religion. Even though he refers to himself as a "religious agnostic," Lewy asserts that religion is essential to the stability of our existence.

In an article appearing in the *Wall Street Journal* in 1993, William J. Bennett, former United States secretary of education, quantifies the moral decline America has undergone in the past several decades:

Since 1960, the U.S. population has increased 41%; the gross domestic product has nearly tripled; and total social spending by all levels of government [has experienced] more than a fivefold increase... But during the same... period there has been a 560% increase in violent crime; a 419% increase in illegitimate births; a quadrupling in divorce rates; a tripling of the percentage of children living in single-parent homes; more than a 200% increase in the teenage suicide rate.[12]

Bennett's article concludes by recommending that we address the moral decay of our culture by returning to the religious values espoused and transmitted by families, churches, schools, and civic associations. Inasmuch as religious values are viewed with suspicion by many educational and civic groups (see Issue 15, "Should There Be a Strict Separation Between Church and State?"), it may be up to the families and religions to provide the moral guidance and social support necessary to effectively address the problems that we face.

A similar description of the problems mentioned by Bennett and Lewy was given many years before by the apostle Paul:

This know also, that in the last days perilous times shall come. For men shall be lovers of their own selves, covetous, boasters, proud, blasphemers, disobedient to parents, unthankful, unholy, Without natural affection, trucebreakers, false accusers, incontinent, fierce, despisers of those that are good, Traitors, heady, highminded, lovers of pleasures more than lovers of God; Having a form of godliness, but denying the power thereof: from such turn away.... Ever learning, and never able to come to the knowledge of the truth.

— KJV, Tim. 3:2-5, 7

After describing what some theologians believe to be the time in which we are now living, the apostle Paul also provided a solution to these vexing problems:

But continue thou in the things which thou hast learned and hast been assured of, knowing of whom thou hast learned *them*; And that from a child thou hast known the holy scriptures, which are able to make thee wise unto salvation through faith which is in Christ Jesus. All scripture *is* given by inspiration of God, and *is* profitable for doctrine, for reproof, for correction, for instruction in righteousness: That the man of God may be perfect, throughly furnished unto all good works.

— KJV, 2 Tim. 3:14–17

Is religion—the reconnecting with God—the solution to the problems faced by humankind? Many who read this text will hold the opinion that there is a God and that religion is important, but many other questions will remain. If God does exist, why is there so much evil in the world today? Can we trust God to know what the future will bring and what is best for us? Isn't just being a good person enough? Do we really need religion to be moral? Does it matter to which religion we belong? Isn't the assertion that one must accept Jesus Christ to be saved closed-minded and prejudicial? Which is more important, our family or our faith? Is God really against abortion and same-sex relationships? Is God literally our creator? Did God use the principles of evolution to create humankind? Did he create us out of nothing less than 6,000 years ago, or are we simply the product of a random sequence of events in a primordial swamp?

The questions posed earlier, and many others as well, are addressed in this volume. Read and study carefully, be respectful of those whose opinions are different from your own, and be open to what they may have to teach you about what could be the most important subject of all—religion.

References

1. *The Compact Edition of the Oxford English Dictionary* (Oxford University Press, 1988), p. 2481.
2. Ibid., p. 3283.
3. *Merriam-Webster's Collegiate Dictionary,* 10th ed. (Merriam-Webster, 1999), p. 319.
4. B. D. Slife and S. C. Yancher, "Introduction: Unresolved Issues in Psychology," in B. D. Slife, ed., *Taking Sides: Clashing Views on Controversial Psychological Issues,* 9th ed. (Dushkin, 1996), p. xv.
5. N. T. Wright, "Knowing Jesus: Faith and History," in N. T. Wright and M. Borg, eds., *The Meaning of Jesus: Two Visions* (HarperSanFrancisco, 1999), p. 17.
6. http://www.adherents.com/.
7. S. J. Palmer, R. R. Keller, D. S. Choi, and J. A. Toronto, *Religions of the World: A Latter-day Saint View* (Brigham Young University Press, 1997), p. xv.
8. Ibid., p. 7. Palmer acknowledges E. L. Allen's *Christianity Among the Religions* as a general source for his statement.
9. See Elder Dallin H. Oaks, *Ensign* (November 1997), p. 72. See also http://www.lds.org/.
10. A. E. Ellis, "Psychotherapy and Atheistic Values: A Response to A. E. Bergin's 'Psychotherapy and Religious Values,'" *Journal of Consulting and Clinical Psychology* (vol. 48), p. 635.
11. G. Lewy, *Why America Needs Religion* (Eerdmans, 1996), p. x.
12. William J. Bennett, "Quantifying America's Decline," *The Wall Street Journal* (15 March 1993), p. A12.

On the Internet ...

Virtual Religion Index

The Virtual Religion Index Web site is maintained by Rutgers University and contains a massive database with references to various scholarly works on religious issues in philosophy.

http://religion.rutgers.edu/vri/phil.html

The Secular Web

The Secular Web is a site that offers a comprehensive view that includes agnosticism, atheism, and humanism. Explore the events, forum, and news links for more information.

http://www.infidels.org

Open Theism Information Site

The Open Theism Information Site provides a general introduction to open theism, which questions the idea of divine foreknowledge. This site also includes links to opposing viewpoints.

http://www.opentheism.org

Philosophy of Religion

Part of the Philosophy Online Web site, the Philosophy of Religion page provides a basic introduction to religious issues related to philosophical study through various links.

http://www.philosophyonline.co.uk/pages/about.htm

PART 1

Philosophical Issues

*A*cademics and laypersons alike recognize the profound importance that religion plays across cultures and throughout the world. This first part explores some of the most controversial issues in religion. These issues have been debated since the beginning of study on religion, and they continue to compel modern thinkers. We will explore the nature of God and existence in an effort to understand better the reasons why people have different belief systems. These issues affect humans in every condition, for their answers have everything to do with the nature of reality and the significance of religion in the world.

- Does God Exist?

- Can Evil Exist and There Still Be a God?

- Does God Have Absolute Knowledge of the Future?

- Can Morality Exist Without Religion?

ISSUE 1

Does God Exist?

YES: William Paley, from *Natural Theology; or, Evidences of the Existence and Attributes of the Deity, Collected From the Appearances of Nature*, 14th ed. (London, 1813)

NO: Sally Morem, from "Does God Exist?" *Religious Humanism* (vol. 32, 1998)

ISSUE SUMMARY

YES: William Paley (1743–1805), Christian philosopher and archdeacon of the Anglican Church, concludes that just as an intelligent watchmaker is the only explanation for the existence of an intricate watch, only an intelligent creator could be responsible for the even more complex creation of humankind.

NO: Sally Morem, author and current president of Humanists of Minnesota, provides contemporary arguments against both "intelligent design" (like Paley's position) and the moral arguments for the existence of God. Morem asks, If an omniscient, omnipotent God is the creator, why is there so much of creation that is poorly constructed?

The cover of the April 8, 1966, edition of *Time* magazine posed the question, "Is God Dead?" At least for the populace of the United States of America, the answer appears to be nearly unanimous. George Gallup of the Gallup poll reports that data for the past 60 years have shown that over 95 percent of Americans believes in God. It is interesting to note, however, that a smaller percentage (80 percent) believes in a God who watches over people and answers their prayers, and a still smaller number of people (60 percent) expresses complete trust in God. In spite of these differences, Americans' belief in God appears to have remained stable for at least as long as statistical data have been available on the subject.

Academic arguments for and against the existence of God can be divided into four general categories: *cosmological, teleological, ontological*, and *moral*.

Cosmological arguments attempt to trace the source, origin, and "first cause" of the world (cosmos) in order to prove or disprove God's existence. The theistic version of the "big bang" theory is an example of how some theologians have argued that God was the force behind the creation of the universe.

Teleological arguments are based on the idea that God had purpose in designing the world in the way it was created. William Paley's writings are an example of the teleological or "design" argument. Though Paley's writings are among the oldest available, the ideas embodied in his watchmaker analogy continue to influence academics and laypeople alike.

The *ontological* argument, an intellectual position, is for many the most difficult to understand; yet for others it is the most intriguing of the four general arguments for the existence of God. This argument, which was first formulated by Anselm of Canterbury (A.D. 1033–1109) in his *Proslogium*, is a reasoned "intellectual proof" of God's existence. Anselm argued that "God must exist inasmuch as the attribute of existence . . . is part of his nature."

The *moral* argument for God's existence is grounded in humankind's "moral nature." Many theologians and religionists from a wide variety of religious traditions believe that the mere fact that most people have a sense of right and wrong is evidence that God exists—for if humans possess a sense of moral law, there must also be a "Lawgiver."

Each of these four classifications is an example of *natural theology*, wherein the arguments are based on natural (not supernatural) proof. There is another general classification known as *revealed theology*, which indicates that the reality of God can be revealed to humankind through *special revelation*, such as the Holy Spirit. Because we are dealing with the question of the existence of God from an academic perspective, we will only concern ourselves with arguments grounded in natural theology.

In the first selection, Paley employs one of the most famous theological metaphors in the philosophy of science—the "watchmaker" metaphor. Paley, who was one of Charles Darwin's professors at Cambridge University, intimated that just as an intelligent watchmaker is the only viable explanation of the existence of something so intricate as a watch, only an intelligent creator could be responsible for the even more complex phenomenon of humankind.

In the second selection, Morem provides a refutation of both the teleological and moral arguments for the existence of God. She argues that if people base their beliefs on intelligent design, they must also be willing to acknowledge examples of "shoddy workmanship" throughout this world and the universe. Morem challenges the intelligent design argument by presenting evidence of colliding galaxies, black holes, and various physical and mental handicaps passed from one generation to the next. She reasons that if there is a God, why would such things as disorder, pain, and evil be allowed to exist? Morem also debates against the moral argument for God's existence by asking several questions, including, If God is the source of "morality," why does moral law differ from culture to culture? Why does one culture condone war and violence when another culture condemns the practice—while both profess to be directed by God?

Natural Theology

State of the Argument

In crossing a heath, suppose I pitched my foot against a *stone,* and were asked how the stone came to be there; I might possibly answer, that, for any thing I knew to the contrary, it had lain there for ever: nor would it perhaps be very easy to show the absurdity of this answer. But suppose I had found a *watch* upon the ground, and it should be inquired how the watch happened to be in that place; I should hardly think of the answer which I had before given, that, for any thing I knew, the watch might have always been there. Yet why should not this answer serve for the watch as well as for the stone? Why is it not as admissible in the second case, as in the first? For this reason, and for no other, viz, that, when we come to inspect the watch, we perceive (what we could not discover in the stone) that its several parts are framed and put together for a purpose, *e.g.* that they are so formed and adjusted as to produce motion, and that motion so regulated as to point out the hour of the day; that, if the different parts had been differently shaped from what they are, of a different size from what they are, or placed after any other manner, or in any other order, than that in which they are placed, either no motion at all would have been carried on in the machine, or none which would have answered the use that is now served by it. To reckon up a few of the plainest of these parts, and of their offices, all tending to one result:—We see a cylindrical box containing a coiled elastic spring, which, by its endeavour to relax itself, turns round the box. We next observe a flexible chain (artificially wrought for the sake of flexure), communicating the action of the spring from the box to the fusee. We then find a series of wheels, the teeth of which catch in, and apply to, each other, conducting the motion from the fusee to the balance, and from the balance to the pointer: and at the same time by the size and shape of those wheels, so regulating that motion, as to terminate in causing an index, by an equable and measured progression, to pass over a given space in a given time. We take notice that the wheels are made of brass in order to keep them from rust; the springs of steel, no other metal being so elastic; that over the face of the watch there is placed a glass, a material employed in no other part of the work, but in the room of which, if there had been any other than a transparent substance, the hour could not be seen without opening the

From William Paley, *Natural Theology; or, Evidences of the Existence and Attributes of the Deity, Collected From the Appearances of Nature,* 14th ed. (London, 1813).

case. This mechanism being observed (it requires indeed an examination of the instrument, and perhaps some previous knowledge of the subject, to perceive and understand it; but being once, as we have said, observed and understood), the inference, we think, is inevitable, that the watch must have had a maker: that there must have existed, at some time, and at some place or other, an artificer or artificers who formed it for the purpose which we find it actually to answer: who comprehended its construction, and designed its use.

I.   Nor would it, I apprehend, weaken the conclusion, that we had never seen a watch made; that we had never known an artist capable of making one; that we were altogether incapable of executing such a piece of workmanship ourselves, or of understanding in what manner it was performed; all this being no more than what is true of some exquisite remains of ancient art, of some lost arts, and, to the generality of mankind, of the more curious productions of modern manufacture. Does one man in a million know how oval frames are turned? Ignorance of this kind exalts our opinion of the unseen and unknown artist's skill, if he be unseen and unknown, but raises no doubt in our minds of the existence and agency of such an artist, at some former time, and in some place or other. Nor can I perceive that it varies at all the inference, whether the question arise concerning a human agent, or concerning an agent of a different species, or an agent possessing, in some respects, a different nature.

II.   Neither, secondly, would it invalidate our conclusion, that the watch sometimes went wrong, or that it seldom went exactly right. The purpose of the machinery, the design, and the designer, might be evident, and in the case supposed would be evident, in whatever way we accounted for the irregularity of the movement, or whether we could account for it or not. It is not necessary that a machine be perfect, in order to show with what design it was made: still less necessary, where the only question is, whether it were made with any design at all.

III.   Nor, thirdly, would it bring any uncertainty into the argument, if there were a few parts of the watch, concerning which we could not discover, or had not yet discovered, in what manner they conduced to the general effect; or even some parts, concerning which we could not ascertain, whether they conduced to that effect in any manner whatever. For, as to the first branch of the case; if by the loss, or disorder, or decay of the parts in question, the movement of the watch were found in fact to be stopped, or disturbed, or retarded, no doubt would remain in our minds as to the utility or intention of these parts, although we should be unable to investigate the manner according to which, or the connexion by which, the ultimate effect depended upon their action or assistance: and the more complex is the machine, the more likely is this obscurity to arise. Then, as to the second thing supposed, namely, that there were parts which might be spared, without prejudice to the movement of the watch, and that we had proved this by experiment,—these superfluous parts, even if we were completely assured that they were such, would not vacate the reasoning which we had instituted concerning other parts. The indication of contrivance remained, with respect to them, nearly as it was before.

IV.   Nor, fourthly, would any man in his senses think the existence of the watch, with its various machinery, accounted for, by being told that it was one out of possible combinations of material forms; that whatever he had found in the place where he found the watch, must have contained some internal configuration or other; and that this configuration might be the structure now exhibited, viz. of the works of a watch, as well as a different structure.

V.   Nor, fifthly, would it yield his inquiry more satisfaction to be answered, that there existed in things a principle of order, which had disposed the parts of the watch into their present form and situation. He never knew a watch made by the principle of order; nor can be even form to himself an idea of what is meant by a principle of order, distinct from the intelligence of the watch-maker.

VI.   Sixthly, he would be surprised to hear that the mechanism of the watch was no proof of contrivance, only a motive to induce the mind to think so.

VII.   And not less surprised to be informed, that the watch in his hand was nothing more than the result of the laws of *metallic* nature. It is a perversion of language to assign any law, as the efficient, operative cause of any thing. A law presupposes an agent; for it is only the mode, according to which an agent proceeds: it implies a power; for it is the order, according to which that power acts. Without this agent, without this power, which are both distinct from itself, the *law* does nothing; is nothing. The expression, "the law of metallic nature," may sound strange and harsh to a philosophic ear; but it seems quite as justifiable as some others which are more familiar to him, such as "the law of vegetable nature," "the law of animal nature," or indeed as "the law of nature" in general, when assigned as the cause of phaenomena, in exclusion of agency and power; or when it is substituted into the place of these.

VIII.   Neither, lastly, would our observer be driven out of his conclusion, or from his confidence in its truth, by being told that he knew nothing at all about the matter. He knows enough for his argument: he knows the utility of the end: he knows the subserviency and adaptation of the means to the end. These points being known, his ignorance of other points, his doubts concerning other points, affect not the certainty of his reasoning. The consciousness of knowing little, need not beget a distrust of that which he does know.

State of the Argument Continued

Suppose, in the next place, that the person who found the watch, should, after some time, discover, that, in addition to all the properties which he had hitherto observed in it, it possessed the unexpected property of producing, in the course of its movement, another watch like itself (the thing is conceivable); that it contained within it a mechanism, a system of parts, a mould for instance, or a complex adjustment of lathes, files, and other tools, evidently and separately calculated for this purpose; let us inquire, what effect ought such a discovery to have upon his former conclusion.

I.   The first effect would be to increase his admiration of the contrivance, and his conviction of the consummate skill of the contriver. Whether he regarded the object of the contrivance, the distinct apparatus, the intricate, yet in many parts intelligible mechanism, by which it was carried on, he would perceive, in this new observation, nothing but an additional reason for doing what he had already done,—for referring the construction of the watch to design, and to supreme art. If that construction *without* this property, or which is the same thing, before this property had been noticed, proved intention and art to have been employed about it; still more strong would the proof appear, when he came to the knowledge of this farther property, the crown and perfection of all the rest.

II.   He would reflect, that though the watch before him were, *in some sense,* the maker of the watch, which was fabricated in the course of its movements, yet it was in a very different sense from that, in which a carpenter, for instance, is the maker of a chair; the author of its contrivance, the cause of the relation of its parts to their use. With respect to these, the first watch was no cause at all to the second; in no such sense as this was it the author of the constitution and order, either of the parts which the new watch contained, or of the parts by the aid and instrumentality of which it was produced. We might possibly say, but with great latitude of expression, that a stream of water ground corn: but no latitude of expression would allow us to say, no stretch of conjecture could lead us to think, that the stream of water built the mill, though it were too ancient for us to know who the builder was. What the stream of water does in the affair, is neither more nor less than this; by the application of an unintelligent impulse to a mechanism previously arranged, arranged independently of it, and arranged by intelligence, an effect is produced, viz. the corn is ground. But the effect results from the arrangement. The force of the stream cannot be said to be the cause or author of the effect, still less of the arrangement. Understanding and plan in the formation of the mill were not the less necessary, for any share which the water has in grinding the corn: yet is this share the same, as that which the watch would have contributed to the production of the new watch, upon the supposition assumed in the last section. Therefore,

III.   Though it be now no longer probable, that the individual watch, which our observer had found, was made immediately by the hand of an artificer, yet doth not this alteration in anywise affect the inference, that an artificer had been originally employed and concerned in the production. The argument from design remains as it was. Marks of design and contrivance are no more accounted for now, than they were before. In the same thing, we may ask for the cause of different properties. We may ask for the cause of the colour of a body, of its hardness, of its heat; and these causes may be all different. We are now asking for the cause of that subserviency to a use, that relation to an end, which we have remarked in the watch before us. No answer is given to this question, by telling us that a preceding watch produced it. There cannot be design without a designer; contrivance, without a contriver; order, without choice; arrangement, without any thing capable of arranging; subserviency and relation to a purpose, without that which could intend a purpose; means suitable to an end, and executing their office in accomplishing that end, without the end ever having been contemplated, or the means accommodated to it. Arrangement, disposition of parts, subserviency of means to an end, relation of instruments to a use, imply the presence of intelligence and mind. No one, therefore, can rationally believe, that the insensible, inanimate watch, from which the watch before us issued, was the proper cause of the mechanism we so much admire in it;—could be truly said to have constructed the instrument, disposed its parts, assigned their office, determined their order, action, and mutual dependency, combined their several motions into one result, and that also a result connected with the utilities of other beings. All these properties, therefore, are as much unaccounted for, as they were before.

IV.   Nor is any thing gained by running the difficulty farther back, *i. e.* by supposing the watch before us to have been produced from another watch, that from a former, and so on indefinitely. Our going back ever so far, brings us no nearer to the least degree of satisfaction upon the subject. Contrivance is still unaccounted for. We still want a contriver. A designing mind is neither supplied by this supposition, nor dispensed with. If the difficulty were diminished the farther we went back, by going back indefinitely we might exhaust it. And this is the only case to which this sort of reasoning applies. Where there is a tendency, or, as we increase the number of terms, a continual approach towards a limit, *there,* by supposing the number of terms to be what is called infinite, we may conceive the limit to be attained: but where there is no such tendency, or approach, nothing is effected by lengthening the series. There is no difference as to the point in question (whatever there may be as to many points), between one series and another; between a series which is finite, and a series which is infinite. A chain, composed of an infinite number of links, can no more support itself, than a chain composed of a finite number of links. And of this we are assured (though we never *can* have tried the experiment), because, by increasing the number of links, from ten for instance to a hundred, from a hundred to a thousand, & c. we make not the smallest approach, we observe not the smallest tendency, towards self-support. There is no difference in this respect (yet there may be a great difference in several respects) between a chain of a greater or less length, between one chain and another, between one that is finite and one that is infinite. This very much resembles the case before us. The machine which we are inspecting, demonstrates, by its construction, contrivance and design. Contrivance must have had a contriver; design, a designer; whether the machine immediately proceeded from another machine or not. That circumstance alters not the case. That other machine may, in like manner, have proceeded from a former machine: nor does that alter the case; contrivance must have had a contriver. That former one from one preceding it: no alteration still; a contriver is still necessary. No tendency is perceived, no approach towards a diminution of this necessity. It is the same with any and every succession of these machines; a succession of ten, of a hundred, of a thousand; with one series, as with another; a series which is finite, as with a series which is infinite. In whatever other respects they may differ, in this they do not. In all equally, contrivance and design are unaccounted for.

The question is not simply, How came the first watch into existence? which question, it may be pretended, is done away by supposing the series of watches thus produced from one another to have been infinite, and consequently to have had no such *first,* for which it was necessary to provide a cause. This, perhaps, would have been nearly the state of the question, if nothing had been before us but an unorganised, unmechanised substance, without mark or indication of contrivance. It might be difficult to show that such substance could not have existed from eternity, either in succession (if it were possible, which I think it is not, for unorganised bodies to spring from one another), or by individual perpetuity. But that is not the question now. To suppose it to be so, is to suppose that it made no difference whether he had found a watch or a stone. As it is, the metaphysics of that question have no place; for, in the watch which we are examining, are seen contrivance, design; an end, a purpose; means for the end, adaptation to the purpose. And the question which irresistibly presses upon our thoughts, is, whence this contrivance and design? The thing required is the intending mind, the adapting hand, the intelligence by which that hand was directed. This question, this demand, is not shaken off, by increasing a number of succession of substances, destitute of these properties; nor the more, by increasing that number to infinity. If it be said, that, upon the supposition of one watch being produced from another in the course of that other's movements, and by means of the mechanism within it, we have a cause for the watch in my hand, viz. the watch from which it proceeded; I deny, that for the design, the contrivance, the suitableness of means to an end, the adaptation of instruments to a use (all which we discover in the watch), we have any cause whatever. It is in vain, therefore, to assign a series of such causes, or to allege that a series may be carried back to infinity; for I do not admit that we have yet any cause at all of the phaenomena, still less any series of causes either finite or infinite. Here is contrivance, but no contriver; proofs of design, but no designer.

V.   Our observer would farther also reflect, that the maker of the watch before him, was, in truth and reality, the maker of every watch produced from it; there being no difference (except that the latter manifests a more exquisite skill) between the making of another watch with his own hands, by the mediation of files, lathes, chisels, & c. and the disposing, fixing, and inserting of these instruments, or of others equivalent to them, in the body of the watch already made in such a manner, as to form a new watch in the course of the movements which he had given to the old one. It is only working by one set of tools, instead of another.

The conclusion which the *first* examination of the watch, of its works, construction, and movement, suggested, was, that it must have had, for the cause and author of that construction, an artificer, who understood its mechanism, and designed its use. This conclusion is invincible. A *second* examination presents us with a new discovery. The watch is found, in the course of its movement, to produce another watch, similar to itself; and not only so, but we perceive in it a system or organisation, separately calculated for that purpose. What effect would this discovery have, or ought it to have, upon our former inference? What, as hath already been said but to increase, beyond measure, our admiration of the skill, which had been employed in the formation of such a machine? Or shall it, instead of this, all at once turn us round to an opposite conclusion, viz. that no art or skill whatever has been concerned in the business, although all other evidences of art and skill remain as they were, and this last and supreme piece of art be now added to the rest? Can this be maintained without absurdity? Yet this is atheism.

NO ↵

Sally Morem

Does God Exist?

Does God exist? Whole libraries of books have addressed this complex question. How can I simplify the discussion to make my answer short enough to fit in this essay, yet coherent enough to satisfy philosophical rigor?

For the sake of brevity, I will be referring mainly to the Judeo-Christian God, although most of this discussion is applicable to other theological constructs. I will not get into the messy business of trying to assert and analyze in-depth definitions of the world *God,* leaving that work to theologians and philosophers. Instead, *God* will refer to the anthropomorphic concept of a supreme being who created the universe and all that is in it, a concept very familiar to most Americans.

I will concentrate on the two aspects of the question which seem to exercise the most power over the imagination of those theologians and philosophers who believe God must exist: the *Argument From Design* and the *Argument From Morality,* with a necessary detour through the *Problem of Evil.* Then, I will pose an alternative to the traditional concepts of theistic creation and command, namely—a self-organizing universe of growing complexity.

⁂

The *Argument From Design* runs roughly like this: the universe and everything within it seem to exhibit far too many elements of apparently deliberate and thoughtful design to have come into being without a Designer.

But does it? What is good design? The most appropriate definition for the noun *design* that I could find is the fifth sub-definition listed in *Webster's Seventh New Collegiate Dictionary*—" . . .an underlying scheme that governs functioning, developing, or unfolding: pattern, motif." We also observe that good design has elements of precision and craftsmanship: the careful selection of materials, the detailed pattern, the exact placement of elements. Does this definition fit our universe?

Good design presumes the existence of a Designer, one who planned, fabricated, and deployed it precisely as desired. But, I ask again, does the universe have good design? Could we ever tell? Perhaps not, but we do manage to see pattern in the cosmos and nature. We see a buildup of many levels of organization

From Sally Morem, "Does God Exist?" *Religious Humanism*, vol. 32, nos. 3 & 4 (1998). Copyright © 1998 by Sally Morem. Reprinted by permission of the author.

over time—subatomic particles making up atoms, atoms uniting in molecules, molecules bonding into larger, much more elaborate molecules known as amino acids, amino acids clumping together into proteins and nucleic acids, cells, multicellular life of lush variety and every changing form, brains of increasing complexity flashing neural patterns known better as human minds, humans shaping themselves and their ideas, first in the most intimate of societies known as families, then tribes, villages, cities, nations, empires, and superpowers which span continents. Surely such fecundity of nested patterns indicates the presence of a master Patternmaker.

But, we also see examples of what we might call shoddy workmanship: galaxies running into one another, black holes sucking in material from companion stars, misshapen disease-ridden, dying lifeforms. We also see examples of what for a lack of a better term might be called fuzziness or goopiness. Molecules jostle and bump into one another until some of them "stick," forming a larger molecule. Cells are not the orderly protein factories depicted in biology books. Bits of RNA, ribosomes and amino acids wander about the cell endlessly, occasionally running into one another. Then, and only then, do they build proteins for the body. When we study them up close, the processes producing nested patterns which earlier looked so marvelously precise take on a much more random character.

Scientists suspect that whatever order we do observe around us actually grows out of a kind of spontaneous ordering, a universe lifting itself up by its own bootstraps, if you will, Instead of the Creator God ordering everything just so—*Let There Be Light*—space itself actually expanded out of a microscopic quantum vacuum, carrying matter and energy with it. One wag called this version of the Big Bang theory "the ultimate free lunch." The universe in this scenario continued to grow into the vastness we know today. And still it grows and freely orders itself. Each level of organization builds upon whatever ordering pattern was already in existence in a thoroughly naturalistic way.

Ponder these questions. They bear directly on the question of God's reputed existence: Is the world a made thing or did it just happen? Is our perception of Design in the world accurate or is it merely a reflection of our deepest hopes and fears? Could we ever perceive the true nature of reality or must we be content with approximations? Does the Designer live outside or within ourselves?

❦

Now for the *Argument From Morality*. What is morality and how do we humans build it into vast, intricate systems of belief and governance of behavior? The same Webster's dictionary defines morality as " . . . a doctrine or system of morals" and "conformity to ideals of right human conduct." To theists, morality is God's shadow on the human soul. C. S. Lewis has written of this belief plainly and simply, yet most eloquently. " . . . I find that I do not exist on my own, that I am under a law, that somebody or something wants me to behave in a certain way."

Lewis believed that the somebody or something existed Before and Outside our reality and implanted messages within us. Such beliefs invite further questions. For instance, if you believe God exists and that He has something to do with the existence of morality, does God establish morality or enforce it? This question is a little trickier than it looks.

If God establishes morality, then morality is anything He wants it to be. You, a loyal Believer, could and should rob, rape and murder, *if* these are God's moral commands. A universe in which morality is ordained by God is a universe with a fundamentally arbitrary moral code. Lewis's messages would merely be a further reminder of God's own desires. They would have little to do with us.

But, if you believe that God merely enforces an inherent moral order, then that morality would exist pretty much as is whether commanded or not. At that point, your concept of God changes. God ceases to be the omnipotent Being you were postulating earlier. Lewis's messages in this situation would either be a plaintive cry for help from a deficient deity or merely an echo of a remembrance of moral laws laid down by ancient ancestors.

As far as moral systems are concerned, we must now face the fact that infinite goodness, knowledge, and power are mutually exclusive characteristics for a creative and sustentacular God. It is simply not possible for a supremely good and powerful deity to create a universe He must know will have evil in it. Here it is, then, the *Problem of Evil:* If God is so good, why does he permit evil to exist in His creation?

We grant that any being with great power can cause much that is good and much that is evil to take place. We humans observe much that is good and much that is evil in us and around us. In this question of God's existence (as in any other questions), our observations work as evidence for and against our conjectures. In light of these statements, let's consider the main possibilities as structured by the history of Western religious thought: 1. There is good and evil, therefore a God (or gods) who wished to create good and evil did so. 2. There is good and evil, therefore a God who wished to create only good failed to achieve His goals. 3. There is good and evil, but humans alone make the call, therefore God becomes redundant.

The first defines many religions. Ancient people believed in their gods, but didn't believe they were particularly good or kind. They feared their gods, certain that they were as willful and capricious as any human, but with far more power at their disposal. We acknowledge the history of these beliefs and call them mythologies, but they hold no power over the modern human imagination, save that of a few pagans and Druids. The thought of Zeus, Athena, Aphrodite or Thor commanding the elements and directing human lives has been rendered laughable by the sheer weight of the last 2,000 years of human cultural experience. We can dismiss this possibility out of hand.

The second defines the great monotheistic religions. Somehow, an All-Knowing, Omnipotent God, who wished to create a world with beings in it who would worship and obey Him, actually wound up creating stubborn, disobedient, immoral human beings. How could such a thing happen? There are various explanations given in various sacred books—a heavenly battle, a fallen angel, free will, the Garden of Eden, a serpent, an apple, and the wiles of woman

(Eve). But these are all merely parts of a mad existential scramble to attempt to bridge a paradox of astounding proportions—the Perfect Creator versus a Creation that should be recalled to the factory.

If we know nothing whatsoever of how we humans perceive the world and ourselves, if we know nothing whatsoever of physical and biological science, we would still have to opt for the third possibility simply because it involves no horrendously tangled logic or unbridgeable contradictions.

There is good and evil. These are judgments made only by humans with respect to many aspects of reality. Morality grew out of countless decisions made and stories told through hundreds of generations of human struggle and joy. That which we like we call *good;* that which we hate we call *evil.* It's as simple as that. If the question of God's existence rests on the acknowledged existence of good and evil, even though we humans are the ones who develop and employ moral systems, God need not exist. We humans can do it all by ourselves, thank you very much.

∾◑∾

Let's consider another possibility. Let's consider *self-organizing* systems of growing complexity. This alternative to the created, commanded, scripted universe of religion is a multi-level, self-ordering, evolutionary process in which humans can and do play a major role. In such a universe the *Problem of Evil* disappears. Evil doesn't exist because some deity inflicts it on us deliberately or because the deity in question was rather incompetent. Evil exists because we humans have named something we don't like, and we haven't figured out what to do about the existence of that thing—yet.

Evolution proceeds by aggregation. Simple systems build themselves into more and more complex systems, layer upon layer of self-organizing processes. Indeed it does proceed from less order to more as matter feeds on energy flow. As an alternative scenario to Creation, let's see where this three-step evolutionary paradigm takes us—physical, biological, and cultural.

Our story begins with the Big Bang, which is not an explosion at all. No primordial shrapnel flies off into empty space. Instead, a multi-dimensional "bubble" of space-time forms out of a quantum fluctuation and builds on itself. Titanic energy forces are unleashed. As the bubble spreads, the infant universe cools. Matter crystallizes energy. Matter spreads out smoothly in space-time— almost. Great galactic clusters gravitate around the slight imperfections. Giant stars form, burn their nuclear fuel, build up stores of heavy elements and then explode in spectacular supernovae, spewing their treasure trove into deep space. Much later, new star systems are born as the nuclear furnaces of a new generation of stars ignite within nebular stellar nurseries. Planets clump together out of planetesimals formed in orbit from the nebular remains of the ancient supernovae. Some stars are small, like our Sun, and begin a long, slow career of nuclear fusion, giving any planet orbiting it at the right distance the chance to bear liquid water for at least most of the year in the "water zone," and hence, having a good shot at bearing life.

We do know of at least one planet in which this took place—Earth. At some point, small molecules came together and formed amino acids, the building blocks of life. Research chemist Stanley Fox discovered that by copolymerizing a simple mixture of the twenty amino acids which make up all life on Earth and aspartic acid over low heat, the amino acids would *form themselves* into what Fox called "proteinoids." One would think that these proteinoids would be very disorderly, but they turned out to be orderly, closely resembling proteins produced by biological systems. Like biological proteins, some can act as enzymes, others are hormones. "The only logical explanation [Fox could come up with] was that the reactant amino acids themselves carried the instructions for their own order."

Fox continued to push his analysis of how life may have emerged from non-life in a naturalistic, emergent fashion. He dissolved proteinoids into warm salt water and then allowed them to cool. They aggregated into spherical, fine, cell-like structures which strongly resembled primitive spherical cells found in very early fossils. These *protocells* emerged from the proteinoid mixture as part of large protocell groups. They tended to form as "couples." Opposite-charged protocells attracted one another, just as real biological cells do. From this, Fox deduced that there was no one single "ancestral cell." Protocells gained lifelike attributes in groups.

Biological evolution continues this tendency. It can be described as a bundle of trends operating on large, genetically diverse populations of organisms over an extended period of time. Those organisms which interact with their environment most effectively live long enough to pass on their characteristics to their offspring. Those which don't, don't.

As the environment changes, desirable characteristics change. The environment plays a crucial role in determining the size, shape, hunting and feeding instincts, and mating habits of organisms at any given time. Genetic mutations deepen the gene pool, ensuring the emergence of further diversity from which selective pressures may choose.

The point at which biological evolution and cultural evolution meet is in the human brain. Our brains are powerful pattern hunters. They are primed to seek out and find. They search for every meaningful pattern in the world as if our lives depend on it—because they do!

Our brains enable us to hunt for food and keep a wary eye out for predators, to seek friends who may protect us and guard against enemies who may harm us. During our long history, friends and enemies were not limited to other humans, but were titles bestowed on anything appearing to be sufficiently humanlike to gain our fear and respect. We gave the sun, moon, and stars, thunderstorms, volcanoes and earthquakes the names of spirits and gods and we worshipped them with fear and hope. And thus, religion.

How can three pounds of gray matter perform such magical feats? Our visual cortex, for example, receives the most basic forms of stimuli from the eyes —lines, color, direction. Then, groups of neurons take the resulting information about the outside world and analyze it, giving more weight to some bits of it, while ignoring most perceptions in a manner directed by internal models of the world previously devised by the brain. Larger portions of the brain then push the analysis of what was perceived to greater and greater levels of abstraction. We "see" whatever we are looking at only after this process is done.

We never experience the world directly, only through these cerebral filters which protect us from the onslaught of sensation of the fuzziness of reality. We perceive reality through lenses of pattern perception which cull and code the vast assemblage of impressions and deductions to make them usable to us.

As a result, we humans become makers. Ever since the first Paleolithic flintknapper chipped his first handaxe, we have imparted design in the world. We naturally see design all around us, and where there is design we believe there must be a Designer, a greater Maker. We project humanlike qualities onto our surroundings, imagining intentionality where none exists.

Evolution is a long, slow, convoluted, impersonal process of development. But, on Earth at least, it led to the development of beings with minds powerful enough to categorize, classify, and model reality, and envision something better. And these beings, our first human ancestors, are the ones who set off an explosion of ideas whose reverberation we feel yet today. If we would further this process of cultural evolution, it behooves us to learn how such systems of self-organization work, so that we may participate in the human part of it knowledgeably and effectively. Evolution may be blind. It is we who see.

Evolution does not make good and evil, right and wrong disappear. These concepts grew naturally in the minds of humans out of hundreds and thousands of generation[s] of hard-earned knowledge. These are cumulative judgments on which things, events and behaviors are helpful and which are hurtful to humans. Every scrap of knowledge that turned out to be crucial in this ancient search for certainties is preserved in our oldest learning tool—human language. If you don't believe language is the keeper of moral system—consult your English thesaurus. Watch the streams of words sculpt the intricate landscape of human aspiration.

Here are just a few synonyms of the adjective 'good' that I have managed to find: virtuous, moral, righteous, honorable, honest, high-minded, noble, lofty, wholesome, pure, chaste, virginal, innocent, unsullied, untainted, pious, saintly, angelic, devout, right, correct, proper, decorous, seemly, permissible, allowable, fit, fitting, suitable, appropriate, timely, well-behaved, obedient, well-mannered, courteous, beneficent, altruistic, benevolent, kind, kindhearted, benign, sympathetic, *humane* [my emphasis].

Words are the keepers of ideas. Ideas are the core of cultural evolution. As you can see by my list, we humans are drenched in moral sentiment, even in this age of apparent moral relativism.

Biological evolution does not command people to be good or bad or anything else. Perhaps this is why many people find the concept of evolution distasteful. It leaves us to our own devices, guided only by our personal and aggregate knowledge and experience, and whatever instinctual attraction or revulsion our biological makeup bequeathed us. Evolution can't condemn anything, not even Hitler or Stalin. But *we* do. Morality is our slow-growing, cultural invention of dire necessity, as necessary to thinking, feeling beings as food and water are. It is not the universe's job to pick up after us. If we judge something or someone evil, it is up to us to stop them and to make sure they don't do it again. Hitler and Stalin were horribly wrong, not because they fell under the judgment of God or the universe, but because by our lights they and their devoted followers inflicted horrors untold.

The assertion that evolution removes decision-making power from us is just plain false. The opposite, as we've seen, is true. Instead, evolutionary processes explain how spontaneous order occurs in human societies, as well as in physical and biological systems. Self-organization is especially powerful in democratic societies, where large numbers of people wield a large amount of decision-making power and interact with one another freely in enormously complex and creative ways. The traditional religious creation story in which God commands and matter obeys more closely resembles the top-down command system of the traditional medieval monarchy or a dictatorship of the modern era.

In the end, the *Arguments from Design* and *Morality* fail for the same reason. Such arguments seriously underestimate the fecundity of self-organizing systems, and especially the profound creativity of the human mind.

Reality exists. The outside world is demonstrably there and has its own pattern, its own organization. But any indication of intelligent design or command that we may sense within us or see manifested around us lies only within our minds. God does not exist. It is *we* who string beads of light together, crafting the design of the world.

Notes

1. C. S. Lewis, *Mere Christianity,* originally published in 1943 as a compilation of transcripts of radio addresses (New York: Macmillan, 1960), p. 34.

2. Stanley Fox, *The Emergence of Life: Darwinian Evolution from the Inside,* (New York, Basic Books, 1988), p. 64.

POSTSCRIPT

Does God Exist?

For many, the title of Christian theologian C. S. Lewis's essay "God in the Dock" might seem obscure. It is helpful to look up the appropriate definition of the word "dock" to understand what Lewis meant by his title. According to the *Oxford English Dictionary*, "dock" in this context refers to "the enclosure in a criminal court in which the prisoner is placed at his trial."

> The ancient man approached God (or even the gods) as the accused person approaches his judge. For the modern man the roles are reversed. He is the judge: God is in the dock. He [man] is quite a kindly judge: if God should have a reasonable defense for being the god who permits war, poverty and disease, [man] is ready to listen to it. The trial may even end in God's acquittal. But the important thing is that Man is on the Bench and God in the Dock.

> — *God in the Dock* (Eerdmans, 1994), p. 244

In this passage, Lewis maintains that for modern man, God is on trial and humankind is his judge. Placing God in the role of defendant may seem like a negative metaphor to some, but Lewis is emphasizing that at least court is in session and humankind is taking the question of the existence of God seriously.

The two selections present an overview of some of the evidence pertaining to the existence of God. In a way, readers may view these arguments as a personal invitation to put God "in the dock" and to arrive at their own conclusion. This debate is central to most, if not all, religious and theological issues, as many of the arguments presuppose the existence or nonexistence of God. An early Catholic theologian, St. Thomas Aquinas (1225/27–1274), stated that if one is not able to accept the existence of God, further discussion of most religious questions will most likely be meaningless.

> Now, among the inquiries that we must undertake concerning God in Himself, we must set down in the beginning that whereby His Existence is demonstrated, as the necessary foundation of the whole work. For, if we do not demonstrate that God exists, all consideration of divine things is necessarily suppressed.

> — *Summa Contra Gentiles* I. 9, 5

What difference does it make whether one believes in God or not? Can't people be good, honest, caring, moral, healthy, happy, prosperous, and generous without believing in God? Hasn't history demonstrated that we should give up the study of God (theology) and follow the divine path (religion) in favor of the more reliable truths of science? In 1965, Harvard professor and theologian Harvey Cox published a book entitled *The Secular City* (MacMillan), in which he argued yes to these questions. He reasoned that we should give up all notions of God and spirituality in favor of a more enlightened lifestyle based on social science research. Cox believed, along with many others, that religion was in an inescapable tailspin that would end in the beginning of a post-Christian or postreligious era. However, the last 35 years (perhaps illustrated by the events of September 11, 2001) have clearly demonstrated that discussions surrounding the existence of God and the implications of our belief or unbelief have not ended, rather, they continue to be an important part of the world in which we live.

Suggested Readings

R. Dawkins, *The Blind Watchmaker: Why the Evidence of Evolution Reveals a Universe Without Design* (W. W. Norton, 1996).

W. A. Dembski, *Intelligent Design: The Bridge Between Science and Theology* (InterVarsity Press, 1999).

B. C. Johnson, *The Atheist Debater's Handbook* (Prometheus Books, 1981).

H. Küng, *Does God Exist?* (Doubleday, 1980).

C. S. Lewis, *Mere Christianity* (Macmillan, 1952).

G. H. Smith, *The Case Against God* (Prometheus Books, 1980).

ISSUE 2

Can Evil Exist and There Still Be a God?

YES: John Hick, from *Evil and the God of Love,* rev. ed. (Harper & Row, 1978)

NO: B. C. Johnson, from *The Atheist Debater's Handbook* (Prometheus Books, 1983)

ISSUE SUMMARY

YES: John Hick, theologian and philosopher at the University of Birmingham in the United Kingdom, asserts that God allows evil to exist as a means of enabling humankind to struggle in the process of gaining spiritual maturity. He argues that opposition, pain, and sorrow are all a necessary part of what he describes as "soul making."

NO: Author B. C. Johnson counters that the existence of evil proves the nonexistence of God—for if God exists and God is good, he would not allow evil to possess such a powerful influence.

If God exists and God is good, then why hasn't he prevented the terrible evils and tragedies so apparent in the world today and in times past? This question, sometimes called "the problem of evil," has challenged philosophers, theologians, and laypeople alike from the beginning. The problem of evil extends beyond the question of the existence of God to include a discussion concerning God's nature. If God is all-powerful (omnipotent), all-knowing (omniscient), and all-loving (omniloving), why, then, is evil allowed? Couldn't God prevent all of the evil and tragic events that touch most people's lives? The existence of evil is the central tenet of many, if not most, atheists' arguments against the existence of God.

Epicurus, a Stoic philosopher who lived during the third century B.C., was one of the first to describe the problem of evil when he wrote: "If he [God] is willing to prevent evil, but not able? Then he is impotent. Is he able, but not willing? Then he is malevolent. Is he both able and willing? Whence then is evil?"

Responding to the Epicurean argument, Catholic bishop and theologian St. Augustine (A.D. 354–430), who was considered by some to be the father of Western theology, argued that God *is* capable *and* willing to prevent evil, but he does not always choose to intervene. St. Augustine believed that it was God's purpose to draw good from evil rather than not allow evil to exist at all. From St. Augustine of the past to John Hick of the present, many have advocated what has come to be known as *theodicy*—a justification for why God allows the existence of evil.

Protestant theologian Gottfried Leibniz (1646–1716) is thought to have first coined the term *theodicy*. Leibniz believed that Adam and Eve's transgression in the Garden of Eden was a "fortunate fall" (*felix culpa*) because it necessitated the atonement of Jesus Christ, thus elevating humans to a higher place than they would have attained had their parents not partaken of the fruit of the tree of knowledge of good and evil.

While most theologians agree on the basic premise of God allowing evil so that a greater good may follow, there are some important differences between their perspectives. One example of these differences is found in the conflicting views of two early leaders of the Christian Church, St. Augustine and St. Irenaeus (125–202 A.D.). St. Augustine believed that because of Adam and Eve's partaking of the fruit of the tree of knowledge of good and evil, humankind became "naturally evil" and was condemned to hell with the exception of those who would accept the grace of Christ. In contrast, St. Irenaeus believed that Adam and Eve were not fully capable of making a freewill choice while in the Garden of Eden, but they were like children and not guilty of an act of rebellion. Theologians who have followed in the Irenaean tradition view the fall of Adam and Eve as a "fortunate fall," which allows humankind to continually progress, while those following the Augustinian tradition see the fall of Adam and Eve as a reprehensible act.

In addition to these theories (atheism and theodicy), the problem of evil has been addressed in various ways by a wide range of theologians. Those espousing the teachings of Mary Baker Eddy (*Christian Science*) have attempted to address the problem by describing suffering and evil as illusory, existing only in the mind. Others, including Rabbi Harold Kushner, author of *When Bad Things Happen to Good People* (Avon, 1983), assert that God's power is limited. Kushner believes that God would not allow bad things to happen if he could stop it, but because bad things do happen, God must not have all power.

The first selection is written by Hick, who is considered one of the most widely read theologians now living. The second selection is taken from the writings of an atheistic author who uses the pseudonym "B. C. Johnson."

Hick asserts that God allows evil to exist as a means of enabling humankind to struggle with the challenges of mortality. He believes that opposition, pain, and sorrow are all necessary parts of what he defines as "soul making." Johnson argues that the existence of evil proves the nonexistence of God—for if God does exist and is good, he would not allow evil to exist and to possess such a powerful influence. Johnson does not accept the assertion by Hick and other theists that evil and pain are necessary in order to comprehend good. He contends in *The Atheist Debater's Handbook* (Prometheus Books, 1981) that "a very small amount of evil, such as a toothache, would allow that. It is not necessary to destroy innocent human beings."

 **YES**

The "Vale of Soul-Making" Theodicy

Quotations from the Bible are taken from the American Revised Standard Version.

Instead of regarding man as having been created by God in a finished state, as a finitely perfect being fulfilling the divine intention for our human level of existence, and then falling disastrously away from this, the minority report sees man as still in process of creation. Irenaeus himself expressed the point in terms of the (exegetically dubious) distinction between the 'image' and the 'likeness' of God referred to in Genesis i. 26: 'Then God said, Let us make man in our image, after our likeness.' His view was that man as a personal and moral being already exists in the image, but has not yet been formed into the finite likeness of God. By this 'likeness' Irenaeus means something more than personal existence as such; he means a certain valuable quality of personal life which reflects finitely the divine life. This represents the perfecting of man, the fulfilment of God's purpose for humanity, the 'bringing of many sons to glory,'[1] the creating of 'children of God' who are 'fellow heirs with Christ' of his glory.[2]

And so man, created as a personal being in the image of God, is only the raw material for a further and more difficult stage of God's creative work. This is the leading of men as relatively free and autonomous persons, through their own dealings with life in the world in which He has placed them, towards that quality of personal existence that is the finite likeness of God. The features of this likeness are revealed in the person of Christ, and the process of man's creation into it is the work of the Holy Spirit. In St. Paul's words, 'And we all, with unveiled faces, beholding the glory of the Lord, are being changed into his likeness (*el'kẃv*) from one degree of glory to another; for this comes from the Lord who is the Spirit';[3] or again, 'For God knew his own before ever they were, and also ordained that they should be shaped to the likeness (*el'kẃv*) of his Son.'[4] In Johannine terms, the movement from the image to the likeness is a transition from one level of existence, that of animal life (*Bios*), to another and higher level, that of eternal life (*Zoe*), which includes but transcends the first. And the fall of man was seen by Irenaeus as a failure within the second phase of this creative process, a failure that has multiplied the perils and complicated the route of the journey in which God is seeking to lead mankind.

In the light of modern anthropological knowledge some form of two-stage conception of the creation of man has become an almost unavoidable Christian tenet. At the very least we must acknowledge as two distinguishable stages the fashioning of *homo sapiens* as a product of the long evolutionary process, and his sudden or gradual spiritualization as a child of God. But we may well extend the first stage to include the development of man as a rational and responsible person capable of personal relationship with the personal Infinite who has created him. This first stage of the creative process was, to our anthropomorphic imaginations, easy for divine omnipotence. By an exercise of creative power God caused the physical universe to exist, and in the course of countless ages to bring forth within it organic life, and finally to produce out of organic life personal life; and when man had thus emerged out of the evolution of the forms of organic life, a creature had been made who has the possibility of existing in conscious fellowship with God. But the second stage of the creative process is of a different kind altogether. It cannot be performed by omnipotent power as such. For personal life is essentially free and self-directing. It cannot be perfected by divine fiat, but only through the uncompelled responses and willing co-operation of human individuals in their actions and reactions in the world in which God has placed them. Men may eventually become the perfected persons whom the New Testament calls 'children of God', but they cannot be created ready-made as this.

The value-judgement that is implicitly being invoked here is that one who has attained to goodness by meeting and eventually mastering temptations, and thus by rightly making responsible choices in concrete situations, is good in a richer and more valuable sense than would be one created *ab initio* in a state either of innocence or of virtue. In the former case, which is that of the actual moral achievements of mankind, the individual's goodness has within it the strength of temptations overcome, a stability based upon an accumulation of right choices, and a positive and responsible character that comes from the investment of costly personal effort. I suggest, then, that it is an ethically reasonable judgement, even though in the nature of the case not one that is capable of demonstrative proof, that human goodness slowly built up through personal histories of moral effort has a value in the eyes of the Creator which justifies even the long travail of the soul-making process.

The picture with which we are working is thus developmental and teleological. Man is in process of becoming the perfected being whom God is seeking to create. However, this is not taking place—it is important to add—by a natural and inevitable evolution, but through a hazardous adventure in individual freedom. Because this is a pilgrimage within the life of each individual, rather than a racial evolution, the progressive fulfilment of God's purpose does not entail any corresponding progressive improvement in the moral state of the world. There is no doubt a development in man's ethical situation from generation to generation through the building of individual choices into public institutions, but this involves an accumulation of evil as well as of good. It is thus probable that human life was lived on much the same moral plane two thousand years ago or four thousand years ago as it is today. But nevertheless during this period uncounted millions of souls have been through the experience of earthly life, and God's purpose has gradually moved towards its fulfilment within each one of them, rather than within a human aggregate composed of different units in different generations.

If, then, God's aim in making the world is 'the bringing of many sons to glory',[5] that aim will naturally determine the kind of world that He has created. Antitheistic writers almost invariably assume a conception of the divine purpose which is contrary to the Christian conception. They assume that the purpose of a loving God must be to create a hedonistic paradise; and therefore to the extent that the world is other than this, it proves to them that God is either not loving enough or not powerful enough to create such a world. They think of God's relation to the earth on the model of a human being building a cage for a pet animal to dwell in. If he is humane he will naturally make his pet's quarters as pleasant and healthful as he can. Any respect in which the cage falls short of the veterinarian's ideal, and contains possibilities of accident or disease, is evidence of either limited benevolence or limited means, or both. Those who use the problem of evil as an argument against belief in God almost invariably think of the world in this kind of way. David Hume, for example, speaks of an architect who is trying to plan a house that is to be as comfortable and convenient as possible. If we find that 'the windows, doors, fires, passages, stairs, and the whole economy of the building were the source of noise, confusion, fatigue, darkness, and the extremes of heat and cold' we should have no hesitation in blaming the architect. It would be in vain for him to prove that if this or that defect were corrected greater ills would result: 'still you would assert in general, that, if the architect had had skill and good intentions, he might have formed such a plan of the whole, and might have adjusted the parts in such a manner, as would have remedied all or most of these inconveniences'.

But if we are right in supposing that God's purpose for man is to lead him from human *Bios,* or the biological life of man, to that quality of *Zoe,* or the personal life of eternal worth, which we see in Christ, then the question that we have to ask is not, Is this the kind of world that an all-powerful and infinitely loving being would create as an environment for his human pets? or, Is the architecture of the world the most pleasant and convenient possible? The question that we have to ask is rather, Is this the kind of world that God might make as an environment in which moral beings may be fashioned, through their own free insights and responses, into 'children of God'?

Such critics as Hume are confusing what heaven ought to be, as an environment for perfected finite beings, with what this world ought to be, as an environment for beings who are in process of becoming perfected. For if our general conception of God's purpose is correct the world is not intended to be a paradise, but rather the scene of a history in which human personality may be formed towards the pattern of Christ. Men are not to be thought of on the analogy of animal pets, whose life is to be made as agreeable as possible, but rather on the analogy of human children, who are to grow to adulthood in an environment whose primary and overriding purpose is not immediate pleasure but the realizing of the most valuable potentialities of human personality.

Needless to say, this characterization of God as the heavenly Father is not a merely random illustration but an analogy that lies at the heart of the Christian faith. Jesus treated the likeness between the attitude of God to man, and the attitude of human parents at their best towards their children, as providing the most adequate way for us to think about God. And so it is altogether relevant to a Christian understanding of this world to ask, How does the best parental love express itself in its influence upon the environment in which children are to grow up? I think it is clear that a parent who loves his children, and wants them to become the best human beings that they are capable of becoming, does not treat pleasure as the sole and supreme value. Certainly we seek pleasure for our children, and take great delight in obtaining it for them; but we do not desire for them unalloyed pleasure at the expense of their growth in such even greater values as moral integrity, unselfishness, compassion, courage, humour, reverence for the truth, and perhaps above all the capacity for love. We do not act on the premise that pleasure is the supreme end of life; and if the development of these other values sometimes clashes with the provision of pleasure, then we are willing to have our children miss a certain amount of this, rather than fail to come to possess and to be possessed by the finer and more precious qualities that are possible to the human personality. A child brought up on the principle that the only or the supreme value is pleasure would not be likely to become an ethically mature adult or an attractive or happy personality. And to most parents it seems more important to try to foster quality and strength of character in their children than to fill their lives at all times with the utmost possible degree of pleasure. If, then, there is any true analogy between God's purpose for his human creatures, and the purpose of loving and wise parents for their children, we have to recognize that the presence of pleasure and the absence of pain cannot be the supreme and overriding end for which the world exists. Rather, this world must be a place of soul-making. And its value is to be judged, not primarily by the quantity of pleasure and pain occurring in it at any particular moment, but by its fitness for its primary purpose, the purpose of soul-making.[6]

In all this we have been speaking about the nature of the world considered simply as the God-given environment of man's life. For it is mainly in this connection that the world has been regarded in Irenaean and in Protestant thought. But such a way of thinking involves a danger of anthropocentrism from which the Augustinian and Catholic tradition has generally been protected by its sense of the relative insignificance of man within the totality of the created universe. Man was dwarfed within the medieval world-view by the innumerable hosts of angels and archangels above him—unfallen rational natures which rejoice in the immediate presence of God, reflecting His glory in the untarnished mirror of their worship. However, this higher creation has in our modern world lost its hold upon the imagination. Its place has been taken, as the minimizer of men, by the immensities of outer space and by the material universe's unlimited complexity transcending our present knowledge. As the spiritual environment envisaged by Western man has shrunk, his physical horizons have correspondingly expanded. Where the human creature was formerly seen as an insignificant appendage to the angelic world, he is now seen as an equally insignificant organic excrescence, enjoying a fleeting moment of consciousness on the surface of one of the planets of a minor star. Thus the truth that was symbolized for former ages by the existence of the angelic hosts is today impressed upon us by the vastness of the physical universe, countering the egoism of our species by making us feel that this immense prodigality of existence can hardly all exist for the sake of man—though, on the other hand, the very realization that it is not all for the sake of man may itself be salutary and beneficial to man!

However, instead of opposing man and nature as rival objects of God's interest, we should perhaps rather stress man's solidarity as an embodied being with the whole natural order in which he is embedded. For man is organic to the world; all his acts and thoughts and imaginations are conditioned by space and time; and in abstraction from nature he would cease to be human. We may, then, say that the beauties and sublimities and powers, the microscopic intricacies and macroscopic vastnesses, the wonders and the terrors of the natural world and of the life that pulses through it, are willed and valued by their Maker in a creative act that embraces man together with nature. By means of matter and living flesh God both builds a path and weaves a veil between Himself and the creature made in His image. Nature thus has permanent significance; for God has set man in a creaturely environment, and the final fulfilment of our nature in relation to God will accordingly take the form of an embodied life within 'a new heaven and a new earth'.[7] And as in the present age man moves slowly towards that fulfilment through the pilgrimage of his earthly life, so also 'the whole creation' is 'groaning in travail', waiting for the time when it will be 'set free from its bondage to decay'.[8]

And yet however fully we thus acknowledge the permanent significance and value of the natural order, we must still insist upon man's special character as a personal creature made in the image of God; and our theodicy must still centre upon the soul-making process that we believe to be taking place within human life.

This, then, is the starting-point from which we propose to try to relate the realities of sin and suffering to the perfect love of an omnipotent Creator. And as will become increasingly apparent, a theodicy that starts in this way must be eschatological in its ultimate bearings. That is to say, instead of looking to the past for its clue to the mystery of evil, it looks to the future, and indeed to that ultimate future to which only faith can look. Given the conception of a divine intention working in and through human time towards a fulfilment that lies in its completeness beyond human time, our theodicy must find the meaning of evil in the part that it is made to play in the eventual outworking of that purpose; and must find the justification of the whole process in the magnitude of the good to which it leads. The good that outshines all ill is not a paradise long since lost but a kingdom which is yet to come in its full glory and permanence.

From this point of view we must speak about moral evil; about pain, including that of the lower animals; about the higher and more distinctively human forms of suffering; and about the relation between all this and the will of God as it has been revealed in Jesus Christ.

Notes

1. Hebrews ii. 10.
2. Romans viii. 17.
3. II Corinthians iii. 18.
4. Romans viii. 29. [See also:] Ephesians ii. 21; iii. 16; Colossians ii. 19; I John iii. 2; II Corinthians iv. 16.
5. Hebrews ii. 10.
6. The phrase 'the vale of Soul-making' was coined by the poet John Keats in a letter written to his brother and sister in April 1819. . . .
7. Revelation xxi. 1.
8. Romans viii. 21–22.

God and the Problem of Evil

Here is a common situation: a house catches on fire and a six-month-old baby is painfully burned to death. Could we possibly describe as "good" any person who had the power to save this child and yet refused to do so? God undoubtedly has this power and yet in many cases of this sort he has refused to help. Can we call God "good"? Are there adequate excuses for his behavior?

First, it will not do to claim that the baby will go to heaven. It was either necessary for the baby to suffer or it was not. If it was not, then it was wrong to allow it. The child's ascent to heaven does not change this fact. If it was necessary, the fact that the baby will go to heaven does not explain why it was necessary, and we are still left without an excuse for God's inaction.

It is not enough to say that the baby's painful death would in the long run have good results and therefore should have happened, otherwise God would not have permitted it. For if we know this to be true, then we know—just as God knows—that every action successfully performed must in the end be good and therefore the right thing to do, otherwise God would not have allowed it to happen. We could deliberately set houses ablaze to kill innocent people and if successful we would then know we had a duty to do it. A defense of God's goodness which takes as its foundation duties known only after the fact would result in a morality unworthy of the name. Furthermore, this argument does not explain why God allowed the child to burn to death. It merely claims that there is some reason discoverable in the long run. But the belief that such a reason is within our grasp must rest upon the additional belief that God is good. This is just to counter evidence against such a belief by assuming the belief to be true. It is not unlike a lawyer defending his client by claiming that the client is innocent and therefore the evidence against him must be misleading—that proof vindicating the defendant will be found in the long run. No jury of reasonable men and women would accept such a defense and the theist cannot expect a more favorable outcome.

The theist often claims that man has been given free will so that if he accidentally or purposefully causes fires, killing small children, it is his fault alone. Consider a bystander who had nothing to do with starting the fire but who refused to help even though he could have saved the child with no harm to himself. Could such a bystander be called good? Certainly not. If we would not consider a mortal human being good under these circumstances, what grounds could we possibly have for continuing to assert the goodness of an all-powerful God?

The suggestion is sometimes made that it is best for us to face disasters without assistance, otherwise we would become dependent on an outside power for aid. Should we then abolish modern medical care or do away with efficient fire departments? Are we not dependent on their help? Is it not the case that their presence transforms us into soft, dependent creatures? The vast majority are not physicians or firemen. These people help in their capacity as professional outside sources of aid in much the same way that we would expect God to be helpful. Theists refer to aid from firemen and physicians as cases of man helping himself. In reality, it is a tiny minority of men helping a great many. We can become just as dependent on them as we can on God. Now the existence of this kind of outside help is either wrong or right. If it is right, then God should assist those areas of the world which do not have this kind of help. In fact, throughout history, such help has not been available. If aid ought to have been provided, then God should have provided it. On the other hand, if it is wrong to provide this kind of assistance, then we should abolish the aid altogether. But we obviously do not believe it is wrong.

Similar considerations apply to the claim that if God interferes in disasters, he would destroy a considerable amount of moral urgency to make things right. Once again, note that such institutions as modern medicine and fire departments are relatively recent. They function irrespective of whether we as individuals feel any more urgency to support them. To the extent that they help others, opportunities to feel moral urgency are destroyed because they reduce the number of cases which appeal to us for help. Since we have not always had such institutions, there must have been a time when there was greater moral urgency than there is now. If such a situation is morally desirable, then we should abolish modern medical care and fire departments. If the situation is not morally desirable, then God should have remedied it.

Besides this point, we should note that God is represented as one who tolerates disasters, such as infants burning to death, in order to create moral urgency. It follows that God approves of these disasters as a means to encourage the creation of moral urgency. Furthermore, if there were no such disasters occurring, God would have to see to it that they occur. If it so happened that we lived in a world in which babies never perished in burning houses, God would be morally obliged to take an active hand in setting fire to houses with infants in them. In fact, if the frequency of infant mortality due to fire should happen to fall below a level necessary for the creation of maximum moral urgency in our real world, God would be justified in setting a few fires of his own. This may well be happening right now, for there is no guarantee that the maximum number of infant deaths necessary for moral urgency are occurring.

All of this is of course absurd. If I see an opportunity to create otherwise nonexistent opportunities for moral urgency by burning an infant or two, then I should *not* do so. But if it is good to maximize moral urgency, then I *should* do so. Therefore, it is not good to maximize moral urgency. Plainly we do not in general believe that it is a good thing to maximize moral urgency. The fact that we approve of modern medical care and applaud medical advances is proof enough of this.

The theist may point out that in a world without suffering there would be no occasion for the production of such virtues as courage, sympathy, and the like. This may be true, but the atheist need not demand a world without suffering. He need only claim that there is suffering which is in excess of that needed for the production of various virtues. For example, God's active attempts to save six-month-old infants from fires would not in itself create a world without suffering. But no one could sincerely doubt that it would improve the world.

The two arguments against the previous theistic excuse apply here also. "Moral urgency" and "building virtue" are susceptible to the same criticisms. It is worthwhile to emphasize, however, that we encourage efforts to eliminate evils; we approve of efforts to promote peace, prevent famine, and wipe out disease. In other words, we do value a world with fewer or (if possible) no opportunities for the development of virtue (when "virtue" is understood to mean the reduction of suffering). If we produce such a world for succeeding generations, how will they develop virtues? Without war, disease, and famine, they will not be virtuous. Should we then cease our attempts to wipe out war, disease, and famine? If we do not believe that it is right to cease attempts at improving the world, then by implication we admit that virtue-building is not an excuse for God to permit disasters. For we admit that the development of virtue is no excuse for permitting disasters.

It might be said that God allows innocent people to suffer in order to deflate man's ego so that the latter will not be proud of his apparently deserved good fortune. But this excuse succumbs to the arguments used against the preceding excuses and we need discuss them no further.

Theists may claim that evil is a necessary by-product of the laws of nature and therefore it is irrational for God to interfere every time a disaster happens. Such a state of affairs would alter the whole causal order and we would then find it impossible to predict anything. But the death of a child caused by an electrical fire could have been prevented by a miracle and no one would ever have known. Only a minor alteration in electrical equipment would have been necessary. A very large disaster could have been avoided simply by producing in Hitler a miraculous heart attack—and no one would have known it was a miracle. To argue that continued miraculous intervention by God would be wrong is like insisting that one should never use salt because ingesting five pounds of it would be fatal. No one is requesting that God interfere all of the time. He should, however, intervene to prevent especially horrible disasters. Of course, the question arises: where does one draw the line? Well, certainly the line should be drawn somewhere this side of infants burning to death. To argue that we do not know where the line should be drawn is no excuse for failing to interfere in those instances that would be called clear cases of evil.

It will not do to claim that evil exists as a necessary contrast to good so that we might know what good is. A very small amount of evil, such as a toothache, would allow that. It is not necessary to destroy innocent human beings.

The claim could be made that God has a "higher morality" by which his actions are to be judged. But it is a strange "higher morality" which claims that what we call "bad" is good and what we call "good" is bad. Such a morality can have no meaning to us. It would be like calling black "white" and white "black." In reply the theist may say that God is the wise Father and we are ignorant children. How can we judge God any more than a child is able to judge his parent? It is true that a child may be puzzled by his parents' conduct, but his basis for deciding that their conduct is nevertheless good would be the many instances of good behavior he has observed. Even so, this could be misleading. Hitler, by all accounts, loved animals and children of the proper race; but if Hitler had had a child, this offspring would hardly have been justified in arguing that his father was a good man. At any rate, God's "higher morality," being the opposite of ours, cannot offer any grounds for deciding that he is somehow good.

Perhaps the main problem with the solutions to the problem of evil we have thus far considered is that no matter how convincing they may be in the abstract, they are implausible in certain particular cases. Picture an infant dying in a burning house and then imagine God simply observing from afar. Perhaps God is reciting excuses in his own behalf. As the child succumbs to the smoke and flames, God may be pictured as saying: "Sorry, but if I helped you I would have considerable trouble deflating the ego of your parents. And don't forget I have to keep those laws of nature consistent. And anyway if you weren't dying in that fire, a lot of moral urgency would just go down the drain. Besides, I didn't start this fire, so you can't blame *me*."

It does no good to assert that God may not be all-powerful and thus not able to prevent evil. He can create a universe and yet is conveniently unable to do what the fire department can do—rescue a baby from a burning building. God should at least be as powerful as a man. A man, if he had been at the right place and time, could have killed Hitler. Was this beyond God's abilities? If God knew in 1910 how to produce polio vaccine and if he was able to communicate with somebody, he should have communicated this knowledge. He must be incredibly limited if he could not have managed this modest accomplishment. Such a God if not dead, is the next thing to it. And a person who believes in such a ghost of a God is practically an atheist. To call such a thing a god would be to strain the meaning of the word.

The theist, as usual, may retreat to faith. He may say that he has faith in God's goodness and therefore the Christian Deity's existence has not been disproved. "Faith" is here understood as being much like confidence in a friend's innocence despite the evidence against him. Now in order to have confidence in a friend one must know him well enough to justify faith in his goodness. We cannot have justifiable faith in the supreme goodness of strangers. Moreover, such confidence must come not just from a speaking acquaintance. The friend may continually assure us with his words that he is good but if he does not act like a good person, we would have no reason to trust him. A person who says he has faith in God's goodness is speaking as if he had known God for a long time and during that time had never seen Him do any serious evil. But we know that throughout history God has allowed numerous atrocities to occur. No one can have justifiable faith in the goodness of such a God. This faith would have to be based on a close friendship wherein God was never found to do anything wrong. But a person would have to be blind and deaf to have had such a relationship with God. Suppose a friend of yours had always claimed to be good yet refused to help people when he was in a position to render aid. Could you have justifiable faith in his goodness?

You can of course say that you trust God anyway—that no arguments can undermine your faith. But this is just a statement describing how stubborn you are; it has no bearing whatsoever on the question of God's goodness.

The various excuses theists offer for why God has allowed evil to exist have been demonstrated to be inadequate. However, the conclusive objection to these excuses does not depend on their inadequacy.

First, we should note that every possible excuse making the actual world consistent with the existence of a good God could be used in reverse to make that same world consistent with an evil God. For example, we could say that God is evil and that he allows free will so that we can freely do evil things, which would make us more truly evil than we would be if forced to perform evil acts. Or we could say that natural disasters occur in order to make people more selfish and bitter, for most people tend to have a "me-first" attitude in a disaster (note, for example, stampedes to leave burning buildings). Even though some people achieve virtue from disasters, this outcome is necessary if persons are to react freely to disaster—necessary if the development of moral degeneracy is to continue freely. But, enough; the point is made. Every excuse we could provide to make the world consistent with a good God can be paralleled by an excuse to make the world consistent with an evil God. This is so because the world is a mixture of both good and bad.

Now there are only three possibilities concerning God's moral character. Considering the world as it actually is, we may believe: (*a*) that God is more likely to be all evil than he is to be all good; (*b*) that God is less likely to be all evil than he is to be all good; or (*c*) that God is equally as likely to be all evil as he is to be all good. In case (*a*) it would be admitted that God is unlikely to be all good. Case (*b*) cannot be true at all, since—as we have seen—the belief that God is all evil can be justified to precisely the same extent as the belief that God is all good. Case (*c*) leaves us with no reasonable excuses for a good God to permit evil. The reason is as follows: if an excuse is to be a reasonable excuse, the circumstances it identifies as excusing conditions must be actual. For example, if I run over a pedestrian and my excuse is that the brakes failed because someone tampered with them, then the facts had better bear this out. Otherwise the excuse will not hold. Now if case (*c*) is correct and, given the facts of the actual world, God is as likely to be all evil as he is to be all good, then these facts do not support the excuses which could be made for a good God permitting evil. Consider an analogous example. If my excuse for running over the pedestrian is that my brakes were tampered with, and if the actual facts lead us to believe that it is no more likely that they were tampered with than that they were not, the excuse is no longer reasonable. To make good my excuse, I must show that it is a fact or at least highly probable that my brakes were tampered with—not that it is just a possibility. The same point holds for God. His excuse must not be a possible excuse, but an actual one. But case (*c*), in maintaining that it is just as likely that God is all evil as that he is all good, rules this out. For if case (*c*) is true, then the facts of the actual world do not make it any more likely that God is all good than that he is all evil. Therefore, they do not make it any more likely that his excuses are good than they are not. But, as we have seen, good excuses have a higher probability of being true.

Cases (*a*) and (*c*) conclude that it is unlikely that God is all good, and case (*b*) cannot be true. Since these are the only possible cases, there is no escape from the conclusion that it is unlikely that God is all good. Thus the problem of evil triumphs over traditional theism.

POSTSCRIPT

Can Evil Exist and There Still Be a God?

As the selections illustrate, there are several ways to address the problem of evil. While the selections address a Judeo-Christian view of the world, there are at least two other philosophical/religious perspectives that contain detailed views on the problem of evil that should be considered as well—*pantheism* and *dualism*.

Pantheistic religions, such as Hinduism and Buddhism, regard evil as ultimately unreal; suffering is the result of spiritual ignorance from previous lives and is experienced in this world through the dictates of karma ("what goes around comes around"). In contrast, dualistic religions, like Zoroastrianism and Gnosticism, teach that good and evil are two eternal and competing principles that have always existed and will continue to be in opposition throughout this world and beyond. Monotheistic religions, such as Christianity and Judaism, generally regard evil as originating with a personal being (the devil) and/or as humankind's free will to act in opposition to the will of God.

One of the challenges faced by monotheistic religions in their attempts to explain the problem of evil is understanding evil's origin. If God is the creator of all things and evil is one of his creations, then God appears to be responsible for evil and all of the trouble that results. If God is the ultimate creator of evil, then is he not directly or indirectly responsible for all of the murder, rape, abuse, violence, and immorality that have plagued this world since its creation?

One argument is that evil is not created by God but is the product of man's own choice. As Peter Kreeft writes:

> Evil is not a *thing*, an entity, a being. All beings are either the Creator or creatures created by the Creator. But everything God created is good.... Evil is not a thing but a choice, or the damage done by a wrong choice.

> — *Fundamentals of the Faith*, (Ignatius, 1988), p. 55

Some religionists take this view to mean that there is no devil and that evil is simply a freewill choice made by man to rebel against God. In other words, while some want to hold the devil accountable for all sin and suffering, others believe Satan to simply be a mythical representation of the evil humankind brings upon itself through sin. But there is yet another alternative, as Origen, an early Christian leader and theologian living in the second and third centuries A.D., recorded:

> He who is the devil is a created being. Since there is no other Creator but our God, he is a work of God. It is as if we should say that a murderer is not a work of God. However, we would also say that as to his being a man, God

34

made him. He received his existence as a *man* from God. However, we do not say that he received his existence as a murderer from God.

— The Ante-Nicene Fathers, 9:331

It is clear from Origen's writings that he believed Satan to be a real, personal being but one who rebelled against God and whose existence is at least a part of the explanation of the problem of evil.

Many wonder, perhaps God does not exist, and evil and suffering are simply a part of the mortal condition brought about by human choice and/or chance. Maybe suffering and evil were not created by God but are used by him as a means of blessing his children. Perhaps evil is simply an illusion that is best dealt with by changing our perspective. If the past is a reliable guide to the future, there is one thing that is certain concerning "the problem of evil"—it will continue to be a part of the human dilemma.

Suggested Readings

V. Frankl, *Man's Search for Meaning* (Washington Square Press, 1985).

M. Larrimore, ed., *The Problem of Evil: A Reader* (Blackwell, 2001).

C. S. Lewis, *The Problem of Pain* (Touchstone, 1996).

E. Wiesel, *Night* (Bantam Books, 1982).

P. Yancey, *Where Is God When It Hurts?* (Zondervan, 1990).

ISSUE 3

Does God Have Absolute Knowledge of the Future?

YES: Stephen N. Williams, from "What God Doesn't Know: Were the Biblical Prophecies Mere Probabilities?" *Books & Culture* (November/December 1999)

NO: John Sanders, from "Theological Lawbreaker? A Response to Stephen Williams," *Books & Culture* (January/February 2000)

ISSUE SUMMARY

YES: Stephen N. Williams, professor of systematic theology at Union Theological College in Belfast, Northern Ireland, provides a defense *against* the theory of open theism, which proposes that God's knowledge of the future is limited. Williams defends the classical view of God's omniscience, stating that God's knowledge of the past, present, and future is absolute.

NO: John Sanders, associate professor of philosophy and religion at Huntington College in Huntington, Indiana, defends the "openness of God" theory, stating that God's knowledge is not omniscient in the traditional sense. Sanders asserts that while God does have complete knowledge of the past and present, his knowledge of the future is not complete because it is subject to humankind's exercise of free will.

Many traditional theologians and laypeople alike believe that God has all knowledge (omniscience) and all power (omnipotence). From this classical perspective, God not only has absolute knowledge of the past, present, and future, but absolute power to bring about his purposes. In theological circles, this traditional understanding of deity is also referred to as belief in the complete sovereignty of God. Furthermore, this tradition generally supports the idea that whatever happens to humankind is either a manifestation of God's will or has been or will be imposed for the good of creation. Those who hold this view believe that even if humankind never comes to understand the divine purpose behind the existence of both the good and the evil in life, people can be confident that God has good reason for them to experience both good and evil.

This traditional view of God's sovereignty has several variations, most of which agree on God's omniscience but differ on what influence this has on the degree to which humankind is free to exercise free will. One perspective, first articulated by Protestant Reformer John Calvin, proposes that God knows the future because he has predestined it to come to pass. This view has come to be known as the *doctrine of predestination*. Today, many refer to this view as "Calvinism" or "reformed" theology.

Theologians and other followers of the theory of open theism, sometimes called "free-will theism," believe the arguments proposed by traditional theists concerning God's sovereignty to be unsatisfactory. Supporters of open theism propose that God's sovereignty is *general*, not specific. John Sanders, a major proponent of open theism, explains:

> This model does not claim that God has a specific purpose for each and every event which happens. Instead, God has general purposes in connection with the achievement of the divine project. Within these general structures God permits things to happen both good and bad, that he does not specifically intend. Yet God may act to bring about a specific event in order to bring the divine project to fruition.... But general sovereignty denies that each and every event has a divine intention.

> — *The God Who Risks* (InterVarsity Press, 1998), p. 214

Openness theologians agree that while there is personal comfort in believing God is behind every event in our lives, there are difficult questions that classical theism does not adequately answer. Gregory A. Boyd, professor of theology at Bethel College at St. Paul, Minnesota, writes:

> If God foreknew that Adolf Hitler would send six million Jews to their death, why did he go ahead and create a man like that? If I unleash a mad dog I am certain will bite you, am I not responsible for my dog's behavior? If so, how is God not responsible for the behavior of evil people he "unleashes" on the world—if, in fact, he is absolutely certain of what they will do once "unleashed"?

> Moreover, if God is eternally certain that various individuals will end up being eternally damned, why does he go ahead and create them? If hell is worse than never being born, as Jesus suggests (Matt. 26:24), wouldn't an all-loving God refrain from creating people he is certain will end up there?

> — *God of the Possible* (Baker, 2000), pp. 9–10

In the following selection, Stephen N. Williams argues for the traditional view of the sovereignty of God and against open theism. He asserts that God has a perfect knowledge of the future as well as the past and present. In the second selection, Sanders defends open theism by countering that God's knowledge of the future cannot be complete because much of the future is conditional upon the individual exercise of agency.

Stephen N. Williams  **YES**

What God Doesn't Know: Were the Biblical Prophecies Mere Probabilities?

Currently, the classical doctrine of God is being challenged by one wing of the broad evangelical theological constituency. A major contribution from John Sanders, one of its representatives, has now appeared under the title *The God Who Risks: A Theology of Providence*. If Sanders is right, the first chapter of the Gospel According to Luke (vv. 26–38) should be read as follows:

> In the sixth month, God sent the angel Gabriel to Nazareth, a town in Galilee, to a virgin pledged to be married to a man named Joseph, a descendant of David. The virgin's name was Mary. The angel went to her and said, "Greetings, you who are highly favoured! The Lord is with you." Mary was greatly troubled at his words and wondered what kind of greeting this might be. But the angel said to her, "Do not be afraid, Mary, you have found favor with God. You will be with child and give birth to a son, and you are to give him the name of Jesus." [Thinks: "That's the way I'll put it to encourage her. Actually, if she does not cooperate, she will not be with child and her high favor will turn into crushing personal failure. Still, if she does cooperate, it is surely most unlikely after this announcement that she will give him any other name except the name of Jesus.] He will be great and will be called the Son of the Most High [though there is no guaranteeing what he will do, and I suppose he could veer way off course]. The Lord God will give him the throne of his father David, and he will reign over the house of Jacob for ever; his kingdom will never end [at least that is the scenario we have every reason to expect, since God is incredibly resourceful at bringing these things about. Nor will you tax his resourcefulness too much, Mary, if you won't bear the child. Of course, if you refuse, we'll have to find someone else who will have some reason for going to Bethlehem for Jesus to be born, because that fits best with the prophecy of Micah. Alternatively, we could leave Bethlehem out of it and find some other way to make Micah's words prophetically meaningful. Still—it can be done]."
>
> "How will this be," Mary asked the angel, "since I am a virgin?"
>
> The angel answered, "[Well, strictly I can tell you only how it *would* be, if you were to consent, but not precisely how it *will* be, since that depends on you]. The Holy Spirit will come upon you, and the power of the Most High will overshadow you. So the holy one that will [in such an event]

be born will be called the Son of God. [As it turns out] Elizabeth your relative is going to have a child in her old age, and she who was said to be barren is in her sixth month. [Now the ideal role of that is that he should become the Baptist, the prophetic forerunner to his cousin, Jesus, and God is very much hoping that you will not disappoint him and force a change of plans.] Nothing is impossible with God."

"I am the Lord's servant," Mary answered. "May it be to me as you have said." Then the angel left her [relieved].

If any think that this is a caricature, let them read the whole volume by Sanders, including the treatment of Mary (pp. 92-94). And if any think it exceptional and unrepresentative of the author's theology, let them reread it and dwell instead on the treatment of Judas, Gethsemane, and Cross (pp. 98-106). The Cross was a contingent event—it might not have happened and is not definitely predicted in the Old Testament. The options for Jesus and God, as regards executing the project of salvation, narrow as Jesus' ministry progresses until in Gethsemane, "Father and Son, in seeking to accomplish the project, both come to understand that there is no other way." But before then, if not right then, the options were not foreclosed. In that case, Jesus' predictions of his death were a fallible, though justifiable, prognosis; he strongly *suspected* his imminent death when he was in the upper room and *presumed* that a new covenant would be instituted through his blood. But the divine establishment of a sacrificial system in the Old Testament did not guarantee it, and at the time of its institution, God could not have been justifiably as confident that the death was prefigured as the writer of Hebrews apparently was.

It is important to appreciate what is at stake here. On the face of it, the thesis that one ought to examine is the claim that God takes risks. On the traditional view, which Sanders wants to revise radically, God is immutable, perfectly knows the future, and, on some standard accounts, foreordains it exhaustively. The questions of God's power and love, eternity and impassibility are all implicated. Sanders wishes to argue that God takes risks. He does not perfectly control the future. He could if he wanted to, but voluntarily enters into a free, loving, reciprocal relationship with his creatures. They, like him, are genuinely free. God has intentions and desires, but he risks their nonrealization. He is genuinely surprised and disappointed, as we learn from the very earliest chapters of Scripture (Genesis 6) and Jeremiah 3:7, for example. But he is infinitely resourceful, guarantees the occurrence of at least some things, and can be entirely trusted to bring the whole story of salvation to a resounding conclusion through the cooperation—or despite the noncooperation—of his creatures.

This is our God, and Sanders's reading of Bethlehem and Calvary follows from this. Despite the subsequent philosophical discussions, the basis for theology is putatively biblical, so Scripture is the first and important port of call. Its language about God repenting, being disappointed, changing his mind and not knowing, must be taken as it stands. We have no right to make it mean something else in light of some other principle for reading the texts. Scripture itself nowhere gives us permission to do so. The project of deterministic theology, to which Sanders opposes his divine risk theology, is driven by a philosophical tradition that has excessively influenced our reading.

On the face of it, we have the issue laid out before us here. And this is no maverick idiosyncrasy within current evangelicalism. While pointing out that differences exist among the theologians concerned, Sanders is participating in a project associated with others, such as Clark Pinnock, which presses for a truly relational theism, a nondeterministic outlook on the relation of God to humans, a relation that must be truly reciprocal and that cannot be so if God controls everything. Those who take different sides in the debate agree on its importance: the way we see God decisively shapes the ethos of our lives, our words, and our worship. We must try to get things right.

If this is what it is all about, then the natural response is a direct theological assessment of the claims. Back we go to those things that occupied Augustine and Pelagius, Calvin and Arminius, Wesley and Barth. True, some of us will also conclude that most of what can be usefully theologically said probably has been said; that renewed exegesis per se will not settle the question; that analytic philosophy will not solve it. Still, we'll join the fray.

⁂

Despite all appearances, however, these are not the things primarily at stake. Challenging classical beliefs in divine impassibility and immutability or arguing for libertarian freedom and divine nondetermination of all that occurs is one thing. Portraying God as Sanders does in his book is quite another. For the beliefs reported at the beginning of this article are expounded in statements that will cut across the religious sensibilities of many sympathetic to some of the project. There is much more going on here than the stark theological challenge of a theology of risk. Let us give examples of such statements.

1. God expected humanity not to fall into sin: while the expectation was mistaken, it was reasonable and justified (p. 45).
2. Human sin, as recorded in chapter 6 of Genesis, causes God regret and disappointment, shock and grief, such that, as Philip Yancey says: "God learns how to be a parent," and, as Sanders himself puts it: "Whatever God decides, he will never be the same again. God now knows what it is to experience grief" (p. 49).
3. After the flood, "the sign of the rainbow that God gives is a reminder to himself that he will never again tread this path. It may be the case that although human evil caused God great pain, the destruction of what he had made caused him even greater suffering. Although his judgment was righteous, God decides to try different courses of action in the future" (p. 50).
4. When God says, "I thought Israel would return to me but she has not" (Jeremiah 3), not only is he "explicitly depicted as not knowing the specific future," but also "God himself says that he was mistaken about what was going to happen" (p. 74).

Why will some of us feel in the marrow of our bones that all this must be wrong and that one does not need to adjudicate all the substantive issues surrounding risk in order to conclude that? According to Sanders, if we find these statements doing violence to our concept of God and to our religious and theological sensibilities, it is because we have read our Bibles informed by a misguided tradition. After all, is he not just following the scriptural text?

Now one certainly appreciates the force of this general point. Doubtless, we read the Bible through lenses that ought to be corrected; there is no telling how far back in the tradition deeply ingrained habits, that ought to be corrected, go; *sola Scriptura* commits us to a radical and often painful principle of regular scrutiny and preparedness to give up cherished ideas.

But having said that, one must also allow that a cumulative reading of the Bible may intuitively disallow Sanders' description. Such intuitions can be profoundly objective prior to the provision of a positive considered alternative, just as in the case where readers feel that, whatever else he was saying, Jesus was never enjoining emotional hatred toward parents and relatives (Luke 14:26), and proceed to guide their exegesis by that light. The point is not to institute comparison between the relative clarity of Scripture on that particular question and the questions that concern Sanders, but to remark on the propriety of referring to intuitions.

However, let's try to produce something with flesh on it. Behind the foregoing response is the conviction that the cumulative force of Scripture goes against Sanders's reading of the texts. The issue is hermeneutical, and one of the most surprising features in Sanders's account is the failure to tackle hermeneutical issues seriously while accusing his opponents (sometimes justly, no doubt) of hermeneutical prejudice. But take his claim that God is open-minded or changes his mind in response to petitionary prayer. My wife has just left the house in a tearing hurry, having executed the physically near-impossible task of answering around five different queries from two children, executing necessary duties both initiatively and responsively, and finally interrupting her husband as he penned this article with a request that he found it hard to get his mind to attend to instantly because of his deep concentration on this noble assignment. All this has happened in about two minutes and 45 seconds. If God had no one in the world to attend to except Abraham and Sarah, Ishmael and Lot, while he harkened to and responded to one of Abraham's prayers, perhaps he might have kept one of the dialogues going in exactly the way narrated by Scripture. But if, while Abraham prays and God ponders and answers, he is also engaged in running the entire world, all within our time frame, the risk to his health and well-being is infinitely severer than any risk courted on Sanders's account.

Now the riposte is obvious: of course, God cannot possibly be operating within our time frame. That is true, but its hermeneutical implications are completely ignored by Sanders. For it quite simply means that the narrative cannot be taken as it stands. This does not at all mean that we ignore what the narrative says. One is free to produce a scheme that reminds us that one day is as a thousand years for God, so that what for Abraham took two minutes for God to think about, from God's standpoint took several weeks, during which he was able to get other things done as well. The point is not to deny directly (nor to affirm) that God leaves his options open in relation to our petitions.

The point is that the temporal scene for God must be radically different from the temporal scene for us. This immediately requires that we read the texts in terms of some hermeneutical principle of accommodation.

We are not remotely alerted to this by Sanders. Indeed, he challenges his opponents as to the provenance of their doctrine of accommodation when they interpret language of divine "repenting" or "changing his mind" in the traditional way. However, he himself must derive from somewhere the notion that God does not possess physical characteristics despite being portrayed as such. Of course, one might contend that this simply means that Sanders requires an appropriately refined hermeneutic in relation to the temporal and spatial characterization of God and that the fault is simply one of omission. But it is more than that: the ramifications are significant. For the whole morphology of surprise and disappointment, ignorance and risk takes on a different countenance once we dwell on the fact that in half an hour of Abraham's time or Jeremiah's time, God has spent an all but infinite number of half-hours with countless other individuals—let alone in all the uninhabited spaces of his world, all at the same time.

This response to Sanders admittedly ignores an important strand in his account. This has to do with metaphor, but his exposition is very unclear on this point. One reads his work for the most part as though he were referring literally to divine risk, repentance, or change of mind, and the logic of his discussion seems to vindicate such a reading. But actually he tells us that the terms are metaphorical. He even maintains that he is not committed to the temporality of God. In another context, we should inquire about the coherence on its own terms of an account that consistently seems to treat metaphors literally. However, I suspend judgment on that here, so as not to be deflected from pursuing what I have suggested is really at stake in this work. To get at this, let us move on to a second hermeneutical question.

Sanders's method is to take us through the Scriptures selectively according to the flow of the story of Israel and Christ. The result is that the narratives in Genesis and Exodus are hermeneutically central. But how can this be justified methodologically? It is rather as though Proverbs 8 were given hermeneutical control in Christology prior to the study of the New Testament data.[1] Sanders refers to passages such as we find in Job, in Psalm 139, and in Isaiah 40ff. that appear to announce a different concept of deity, one whose knowledge, foreknowledge, or control extends significantly beyond the one Sanders has limned. But why does the Wisdom literature at these points not distill our experience of God far better than the literal account of divine ignorance and surprise, particularly when we move on from it to prophets and apostles? Is not the impact of a canonically sequential reading to create in us a sense that the prophets, especially the major ones, present to us informed reflection on and understanding of the nature, ways, and purposes of God, Israel, and the peoples as they have been narrated to us in the preceding historical books?

These prophecies are hermeneutically significant. "Declare to us the things to come, tell us what the future holds, so that we may know that you are gods," says the Lord (Isa. 41:23), challenging his petty rivals to demonstrate their divinity by their foreknowledge. The divine announcement, where by "he foretold the former things long ago" (48:3) is not remotely like a "forecast" of what God "thinks might happen" (p. 131). Isaiah would not have recognized the Holy One of Israel in Sanders's depiction any more than Job would have taken him on as a replacement for the failed counselors. Whatever Sanders might make of the general matter of reading Scripture backward as well as forward (and he might either defend starting with Genesis or point out that he is not as dependent on the early accounts as I am suggesting), he agrees that Christology in particular must be hermeneutically pivotal, which is why we started the article there. Yet this is just where his account is hopelessly strained.

Other funny things happen in his hermeneutics. In attempting to defuse the argument that the narrative of Joseph shows how God controls everything, Sanders points out that God is absent from large stretches of the text. This is extremely curious; one wonders how he would resist the argument that the Book of Esther entails atheism. Still, one wonders whether hermeneutical shortcomings explain the religious sensibility evidenced in Sanders's work. Let the challenge to Augustinian-Calvinist "determinism" remain, for better or for worse. Let an account of divine self-representation in Old Testament narratives be offered, for richer or for poorer.[2] And let engagement with the philosophical issues at stake continue, unto increasing wisdom or confusion. When all is said, the real worry about Sanders's volume is the lack of any embarrassment at the emergent portrayal of the ways of God.

❦

Perhaps this article will seem to be driven by a massive subjective reaction that bypasses the hard arguments. I do not for a moment believe they should be bypassed: in their place, the detailed biblical, theological, and philosophical discussions are important, and the point is not at all to come down for or against much that is argued or concluded by Sanders. But the business of delimiting boundaries for what is acceptable is equally as important as trying to answer theological questions directly. The latter has to do with the relative merits of theological moves. The former has to do with the validity of fundamental theological rules. Whether or not they are transgressed by Sanders's opponents, this article is meant to express the worry that they are transgressed here. It is to be hoped that this work will alert us to the need of staking out boundaries of permissible biblical interpretation in the context of discussion of this particular theme, as well as stimulate us to reach our own conclusions.[3]

Notes

1. This point is exaggerated, but it would be fruitful in this connection to revisit the hermeneutical principles of Athanasius in his Christological discussion with the Arians—Proverbs 8 was an important text in the controversy: see Jaroslav Pelikan, *The Emergence of the Catholic Tradition* (100–600) (Univ. of Chicago Press, 1971), pp. 191–200.

2. My point is not that "didactic" portions of Scripture take precedence over the "narrative" ones; it has more to do with reading Scripture according to the analogy

of faith. Of course, knotty problems arise in relation to the early narratives, and failure to address them here is not a sign that they should be suppressed.

3. To use language such as "permissible" here seems arrogant: Who, pray, is seated in such a place of authority as to dispense permission? However, everyone involved in theological work has implicit convictions about what is credible and incredible, plausible and implausible, permissible and impermissible in biblical interpretation. And, of course, one must be sensitive to the distinction between what one regards as linguistically infelicitous and what is doctrinally controverted. I suspect that many who will reject the language of risk on the lips of Sanders will mind it less on the lips of C. S. Lewis, *Pilgrim's Regress* (London: Fount, 1998) p. 228. Finally, in the present climate, it ought to be said that we are no more concerned in this article with casting aspersions on people's Christianity than is Sanders himself when he deals with his theological opponents.

NO ◀

John Sanders

Theological Lawbreaker?
A Response to Stephen Williams

Stephen Williams' review of my book, *The God Who Risks* [Books & Culture, November/December 1999], raises some issues he believes I should address and others which he thinks I sophomorically ignored. Let me see if I can shed some light on three important issues he raises, and so make the book seem less naïve than the reader of his review might conclude.

Williams opens with a satire on what he believes would be my paraphrase of the Annunciation. Here the issue is predictive prophecy and whether things will happen precisely the way God says they will. It is true that there are many predictions in the Bible that come to pass exactly as God said. However, there are also a number of predictions where what God said would happen did not, in fact, occur. King Hezekiah, for example, falls ill and is informed by Isaiah, "Thus says the Lord . . . you shall die and not live" (2 Kings 20:1). God explicitly says that the king will not recover from this illness. However, Hezekiah prays, and God sends Isaiah back to the king to announce that God has rescinded his decision. Now, even though God spoke unconditionally, it turns out that this was a conditional prophecy (this will happen unless something changes), but we know it was conditional only because it did not occur as God first said.

One of the differences between Williams and myself is the number of conditional predictions we believe are in Scripture. Our habit is to classify the unfulfilled predictions as "conditional" and the fulfilled ones as "unconditional." In my view, many of those typically classed as unconditional were actually conditional prophecies which came about because God's unspoken conditions were met. The subtitle to Williams's review asks, "Were the biblical prophecies mere probabilities?" No. But were some (even many) of the biblical prophecies conditional utterances? The answer to that is, Yes.

Thus far, Williams has gotten me mostly correct. But am I committed to all he accuses me of in his satire? No, because he plays down the other two explanations of prophecy from the openness view. First, some predictions express God's intention to do something in the future irrespective of human decision. These predictions do not depend upon a "crystal ball" by which God sees the future; rather, they depend upon the power of God to carry them out (the issue is omnipotence, not omniscience). Second, some predictions are based on God's exhaustive knowledge of the past and present (our character, physical circumstances, and so on). God knew Mary's heart so thoroughly that God could be quite certain she would comply even though she retained the freedom to refuse God.[1]

Next, Williams claims that the passages I discuss regarding God changing his mind, regretting things, grieving over sin, and responding to prayer are not "hermeneutically significant" while the passages he cites are. He bases this claim on two grounds. First, by his deep feelings, intuitions, and "religious sensibilities" he just knows I'm wrong, so there is no need to "adjudicate all the substantive issues." This is like some present-day naturalists who say, "Because of our scientific sensibilities we just know intelligent design is wrong, so there is no need to consider any evidence which might call our sensibilities into question." What is there to argue with? Second, Williams claims that the view of God seen in the latter prophets should rule out the passages in earlier writings, such as Exodus and Samuel, where God changes his mind, grieves and responds to prayer. He asserts that I completely ignore this issue.

In fact, however, in *The God Who Risks* I cite several studies regarding the prophets, including some later than Isaiah, demonstrating that the belief that God changes his mind was a key doctrine throughout the Old Testament and not merely in the early writings. Jeremiah 18 has a lengthy discussion of divine repentance, and both Joel (2:13) and Jonah (4:2) have creedal formulations saying that God is a "gracious and compassionate God, slow to anger and abundant in loving kindness, and one who changes his mind." I take such creedal affirmations to disclose the unchanging nature of God, and it is hermeneutically significant that divine changing of mind is included in describing that nature. Williams asserts that Isaiah would not recognize the view of God portrayed in *The God Who Risks*. If so, then Isaiah would not recognize the God of Jeremiah, Joel, or Jonah either.

If these texts are not hermeneutically significant, then what do they mean? Williams never says what "God changed his mind" means. I claimed such texts were "reality-depicting" metaphors. Williams asks why I don't then take the metaphors of divine body parts literally as well. Well, the "arm of the Lord" is a metaphor for God's ability to deliver. God as the "husband of Israel" is a metaphor of the type of relationship Yahweh has with Israel. God "repenting" is a metaphor for God taking a different course of action from the one previously declared. Metaphors have meaning. What does Williams think grieving, repenting, and responding mean when applied to God? In 1 Samuel 13:13 God declares there would have been no "line of David" had King Saul followed the Lord. Read straightforwardly, this seems clearly to imply an open future, dependent to some degree on human choices in the sphere of freedom that God has granted to his creatures.

Because Williams understands Isaiah to teach exhaustive foreknowledge of future contingent events, he believes that it is impossible for God to grieve, repent, or respond.[2] Now I agree that if Isaiah taught exhaustive foreknowledge it would render such actions impossible, but I believe that Isaiah is saying

God declares the future and brings it about—unlike the other gods—because of Yahweh's power over creation, not because of some timeless knowledge. In my view, there are two kinds of scriptural texts of importance here. First, numerous texts portray God as declaring and/or predetermining certain future events. Second, numerous texts portray God as changing his mind, grieving, and not knowing certain details of the future. Williams believes the former cancel out the latter. That is, the repenting, grieving texts do not reveal God as God truly is but only as he appears to us. The approach of the openness of God view is to develop an understanding of God that does justice to both sets of texts, forming a coherent theological model.[3]

The third issue raised by Williams is God's relationship to time. His statements about this, however, are extremely difficult to decipher. What are we to make, for example, of the talk about God's spending an "infinite number of half-hours" in any given half-hour of time? And what conclusions are we supposed to draw from all this, other than that we are free to dismiss any biblical statements about God we don't like as "accommodation"? Most likely, this sort of talk is Williams's way of getting at the traditional doctrine of divine timelessness—at least, so I shall assume. In *The God Who Risks* I cited several classical studies of God and time by biblical scholars who conclude that the biblical writers did not understand God to be timeless. Moreover, I cited numerous theological and philosophical studies by esteemed Christian scholars such as Nicholas Wolterstorff, Richard Swinburne, and William Hasker who reject divine timelessness. Indeed, the past 40 years of scholarship has witnessed a huge debate on timelessness, so I am puzzled why Williams thinks I'm saying something new. Williams expresses his "worry" over my "lack of any embarrassment" regarding this understanding of God. I wonder if Nicholas Wolterstorff feels embarrassed? It seems not, since he has recently said, "If God really responds, then God is not metaphysically immutable; and if not metaphysically immutable, then not [timeless]."[4] Williams is within his rights to believe God never responds to our actions and prayers, but I see no compelling reason why those of us who do should be embarrassed to affirm what we believe the Bible teaches.

Incidentally, Williams might have been less shocked at my approach to divine foreknowledge if he had been familiar with the work of eminent British philosophers such as Peter Geach, J. R. Lucas, and Richard Swinburne—all of them devout orthodox Christians whose views on the subject are essentially the same as mine.

Williams thinks I should be embarrassed because I've transgressed "fundamental theological rules" such as divine timelessness and the content of omniscience. Yet, he also says, "Sola Scriptura commits us to a radical and often painful principle of regular scrutiny and preparedness to give up cherished ideas." With this I concur, and I acknowledge that I'm asking him to give up some cherished beliefs. However, I do not believe the issues raised in *The God Who Risks* are outside the boundaries of permitted theological discourse. Williams himself affirms that it is legitimate to debate divine impassibility and immutability. But for most of Christian history those doctrines functioned as "fundamental theological rules" not to be transgressed. It went against the "religious sensibilities" of philosophically minded Christians to believe God had emotions. This played an important role in discussions of Christology, where the Arians and the orthodox both "intuitively" knew that God could not suffer. It was not until the nineteenth century that serious debate about these "obvious" doctrines began. Other key beliefs, such as geocentrism or the damnation of children who die unbaptized, functioned as "obvious" theological rules for well over a millennium in Christian theology. They certainly do not function that way any longer. Furthermore, think of John Eck's assertion that Luther had broken fundamental theological rules and should be silenced for the well-being of the Roman church. Luther was a theological lawbreaker, but both Williams and I are glad of it.

Now, I believe there are fundamental rules for Christian theology, but they center in God's redemption in the death and resurrection of Christ Jesus, not divine timelessness. Williams and I are both committed to placing Scripture above the tradition of interpretation. We both want to be convinced by Scripture and sound reasoning. Thus, simply claiming that I've transgressed the religious sensibilities of proponents of timelessness and foreknowledge will not dissuade me. Perhaps I am wrong about the model of God developed in *The God Who Risks*. If so, I pray the Holy Spirit will correct me. This will likely come through the "detailed biblical, theological and philosophical discussions" which, unfortunately, Williams claims are unnecessary in regard to my views. Let us seriously engage the issues, not simply dismiss supposed theological lawbreakers.

Notes

1. Of course, as I acknowledge repeatedly in *The God Who Risks*, other proponents of the openness view are not committed to agreeing with all of my interpretations of particular texts.

2. Proponents of divine timeless knowledge agree that it is incoherent to claim such a deity grieves, and I cited studies by such scholars, while observing that although statements such as God "declares the end from the beginning" are certainly compatible with exhaustive foreknowledge, they do not require that theory.

3. See Gregory Boyd's *The God of the Possible,* forthcoming from Baker this spring.

4. "Does God Suffer?" Interview in *Modern Reformation* (September/October, 1999), p. 47.

POSTSCRIPT

Does God Have Absolute Knowledge of the Future?

Many readers may discover that they do not agree with either of the views on the sovereignty of God represented by the selections. Setting aside both extremes, what follows is a description of another alternative, termed the "simple foreknowledge" perspective.

Those who espouse simple foreknowledge theology believe God's knowledge of the past, present, and future to be absolute, but they do not believe that God's omniscience is the determining factor in the choices made by humankind, as in Calvinist/reformed theology. Neither do these theologians accept the idea that God's knowledge of the future is limited and determined by humankind's decisions.

From this perspective, God is simply aware of how mortals will exercise their free will and interacts with them to bring to pass all that is right and good. Yet at the same time, he fully acknowledges, sorrows, and rejoices at the good and evil that inevitably follow the exercise of agency.

One of the most common questions asked by people who are studying the nature of God is, How can I be free to make choices if God already knows what choice I am going to make? Those who support the simple foreknowledge position believe the strength of their view is that it fully accepts the sovereignty of God but also allows for the agency of humankind.

British writer and philosopher C. S. Lewis, who could be considered an advocate of the simple foreknowledge perspective, acknowledged in *Mere Christianity* (Scribner, 1952) the difficulties accompanying this debate but believed that a person "can be a perfectly good Christian without accepting it [God's omniscience], or indeed without thinking of the matter at all."

Suggested Readings

J. K. Beilby and P. R. Eddy, eds., *Divine Foreknowledge: Four Views* (InterVarsity Press, 2001).

J. M. Frame, *No Other God: A Response to Open Theism* (P & R Publishing, 2001).

C. Pinnock, R. Rice, J. Sanders, W. Hasker, and D. Basinger, *The Openness of God: A Biblical Challenge to the Traditional Understanding of God* (InterVarsity Press, 1994).

B. Ware, *God's Lesser Glory: The Diminished God of Open Theism* (Crossway Books, 2000).

ISSUE 4

Can Morality Exist Without Religion?

YES: John Arthur, from "Religion, Morality, and Conscience," in John Arthur, ed., *Morality and Moral Controversies,* 4th ed. (Prentice Hall, 1996)

NO: Leo Tolstóy, from *On Life and Essays on Religion,* trans. Aylmer Maude (Oxford University Press, 1959)

ISSUE SUMMARY

YES: John Arthur, professor of philosophy at the State University of New York at Binghamton asserts that religion is not necessary for a people to be moral. In addition to providing arguments against religion as a necessary "moral motivation" and as *the* source of truth, Arthur also asserts that morality is inherently social and is learned from interacting with others.

NO: Leo Tolstóy (1828–1910), moral philosopher and author of the classics *War and Peace* and *Anna Karenina*, argues for the necessity of God and religion in the existence of morality. Tolstóy contends that truth originates with God and that humankind must look to God (through religion) for continued guidance.

How important are God and religion to an individual, family, community, or culture? Can morality exist and thrive without belief in God and the exercise of religion? Leo Tolstóy proposes that:

> the attempts to found a morality apart from religion are "like the attempts of children who, wishing to transplant a flower that pleases them, pluck it from the roots that seem to them unpleasing and superfluous, and stick it rootless into the ground." He goes on to say, "Without religion there can be no real, sincere morality, just as without roots there can be no real flower."

Tolstóy's perspective is representative of those who believe genuine morality can only exist in relationship to God through religion. From his perspective, morality based merely on individual judgment or what society agrees upon may exist temporarily, but in the end it cannot be trusted and will not endure. This traditional argument for the necessity of morality *with* religion can be observed in the words of Jesus Christ: "I am the vine, ye *are* the branches: He that abideth in me, and I in him, the same bringeth forth much fruit: for without me ye can do nothing" (King James Version, John 15:5).

The alternative to placing God and religion as the source and means of morality is the increasingly popular philosophy of *humanism* and the practice of *moral relativism*. The philosophy of humanism is based on the idea that all ethics, morals, and codes of conduct originate from human beings. Moral relativism is defined by John Ladd:

> [Moral] relativism is the doctrine that the moral rightness and wrongness of actions varies from society to society and that there are no absolute universal moral standards binding on all men at all times. Accordingly, it holds that whether or not it is right for an individual to act in a certain way depends on or is relative to the society to which he belongs.

— *Ethics: Discovering Right and Wrong* (Wadsworth, 2001), p. 24

The modern debate over the relationship of religion and morality began in the nineteenth century, just a few years after evolutionist Charles Darwin's publication of *On the Origin of Species* in 1859. Englishman Sir Edward Tylor published an anthropological study that mirrored Darwin's theory of evolution, proposing that similar to biological evolution, humankind had evolved socially and religiously as well. Tylor believed that religion evolved from animism (the belief in spirits), to polytheism (many gods), and then to monotheism (one god). His views contribute to the arguments for cultural relativism in that he states that each culture arrives at its own unique and sometimes conflicting standards of morality.

In the following selection, John Arthur argues that religion is not necessary to morality. Arthur, echoing American philosopher and educator John Dewey's suggestion, asserts that standards of morality can be created and practiced through social discourse without the need for an appeal to God or through the practice of religion.

Tolstóy, on the other hand, argues for the centrality and the necessity of God and religion. His arguments were written in opposition to the social Darwinism of the day, particularly in refuting the writings of Thomas Henry Huxley, one of Darwin's most loyal colleagues. Tolstóy's basic argument is that truth originates with God, and though humankind can do much with God's truth, mortal wisdom is not the source of that truth.

Religion, Morality, and Conscience

$\mathbf{M}$y first and prime concern in this paper is to explore the connections, if any, between morality and religion. I will argue that in fact religion is not necessary for morality. Yet despite the lack of any logical or other necessary connection, I will claim, there remain important respects in which the two are related. In the concluding section I will discuss the notion of moral conscience, and then look briefly at the various respects in which morality is "social" and the implications of that idea for moral education. First, however, I want to say something about the subjects: just what are we referring to when we speak of morality and of religion?

Morality and Religion

A useful way to approach the first question—the nature of morality—is to ask what it would mean for a society to exist without a social moral code. How would such people think and behave? What would that society look like? First, it seems clear that such people would never feel guilt or resentment. For example, the notions that I ought to remember my parent's anniversary, that he has a moral responsibility to help care for his children after the divorce, that she has a right to equal pay for equal work, and that discrimination on the basis of race is unfair would be absent in such a society. Notions of duty, rights, and obligations would not be present, except perhaps in the legal sense; concepts of justice and fairness would also be foreign to these people. In short, people would have no tendency to evaluate or criticize the behavior of others, nor to feel remorse about their own behavior. Children would not be taught to be ashamed when they steal or hurt others, nor would they be allowed to complain when others treat them badly. (People might, however, feel regret at a decision that didn't turn out as they had hoped; but that would only be because their expectations were frustrated, not because they feel guilty.)

Such a society lacks a moral code. What, then, of religion? Is it possible that a people lacking a morality would nonetheless have religious beliefs? It seems clear that it is possible. Suppose every day these same people file into their place of worship to pay homage to God (they may believe in many gods or in one all-powerful creator of heaven and earth). Often they can be heard praying to God for help in dealing with their problems and thanking Him for their good fortune. Frequently they give sacrifices to God, sometimes in the form of money spent to build beautiful temples and churches, other times by performing actions they believe God would approve such as helping those in need. These practices might also be institutionalized, in the sense that certain people are assigned important leadership roles. Specific texts might also be taken as authoritative, indicating the ways God has acted in history and His role in their lives or the lives of their ancestors.

To have a moral code, then, is to tend to evaluate (perhaps without even expressing it) the behavior of others and to feel guilt at certain actions when we perform them. Religion, on the other hand, involves beliefs in supernatural power(s) that created and perhaps also control nature, the tendency to worship and pray to those supernatural forces or beings, and the presence of organizational structures and authoritative texts. The practices of morality and religion are thus importantly different. One involves our attitudes toward various forms of behavior (lying and killing, for example), typically expressed using the notions of rules, rights, and obligations. The other, religion, typically involves prayer, worship, beliefs about the supernatural, institutional forms and authoritative texts.

We come, then, to the central question: What is the connection, if any, between a society's moral code and its religious practices and beliefs? Many people have felt that morality is in some way dependent on religion or religious truths. But what sort of "dependence" might there be? In what follows I distinguish various ways in which one might claim that religion is necessary for morality, arguing against those who claim morality depends in some way on religion. I will also suggest, however, some other important ways in which the two are related, concluding with a brief discussion of conscience and moral education.

Religious Motivation and Guidance

One possible role that religion might play in morality relates to motives people have. Religion, it is often said, is necessary so that people will DO right. Typically, the argument begins with the important point that doing what is right often has costs: refusing to shoplift or cheat can mean people go without some good or fail a test; returning a billfold means they don't get the contents. Religion is therefore said to be necessary in that it provides motivation to do the right thing. God rewards those who follow His commands by providing for them a place in heaven or by insuring that they prosper and are happy on earth. He also punishes those who violate the moral law. Others emphasize less self-interested ways in which religious motives may encourage people to act rightly. Since God is the creator of the universe and has ordained that His plan should be followed, they point out, it is important to live one's life in accord with this divinely ordained plan. Only by living a moral life, it is said, can people live in harmony with the larger, divinely created order.

The first claim, then, is that religion is necessary to provide moral motivation. The problem with that argument, however, is that religious motives are far from the only ones people have. For most of us, a decision to do the right thing (if that is our decision) is made for a variety of reasons: "What if I get caught? What if somebody sees me—what will he or she think? How will I feel afterwards? Will I regret it?" Or maybe the thought of cheating just doesn't arise. We were raised to be a decent person, and that's what we are—period. Behaving fairly and treating others well is more important than whatever we might gain from stealing or cheating, let alone seriously harming another person. So it seems clear that many motives for doing the right thing have nothing whatsoever to do with religion. Most of us, in fact, do worry about getting caught, being blamed, and being looked down on by others. We also may do what is right just because it's right, or because we don't want to hurt others or embarrass family and friends. To say that we need religion to act morally is mistaken; indeed it seems to me that many of us, when it really gets down to it, don't give much of a thought to religion when making moral decisions. All those other reasons are the ones which we tend to consider, or else we just don't consider cheating and stealing at all. So far, then, there seems to be no reason to suppose that people can't be moral yet irreligious at the same time.

A second argument that is available for those who think religion is necessary to morality, however, focuses on moral guidance and knowledge rather than on people's motives. However much people may want to do the right thing, according to this view, we cannot ever know for certain what is right without the guidance of religious teaching. Human understanding is simply inadequate to this difficult and controversial task; morality involves immensely complex problems, and so we must consult religious revelation for help.

Again, however, this argument fails. First, consider how much we would need to know about religion and revelation in order for religion to provide moral guidance. Besides being sure that there is a God, we'd also have to think about which of the many religions is true. How can anybody be sure his or her religion is the right one? But even if we assume the Judeo-Christian God is the real one, we still need to find out just what it is He wants us to do, which means we must think about revelation.

Revelation comes in at least two forms, and not even all Christians agree on which is the best way to understand revelation. Some hold that revelation occurs when God tells us what he wants by providing us with His words: The Ten Commandments are an example. Many even believe, as evangelist Billy Graham once said, that the entire *Bible* was written by God using 39 secretaries. Others, however, doubt that the "word of God" refers literally to the words God has spoken, but believe instead that the *Bible* is an historical document, written by human beings, of the events or occasions in which God revealed Himself. It is an especially important document, of course, but nothing more than that. So on this second view revelation is not understood as *statements* made by God but rather as His *acts* such as leading His people from Egypt, testing Job, and sending His son as an example of the ideal life. The *Bible* is not itself revelation, it's the historical account of revelatory actions.

If we are to use revelation as a moral guide, then, we must first know what is to count as revelation—words given us by God, historical events, or both? But even supposing that we could somehow answer those questions, the problems of relying on revelation are still not over since we still must interpret that revelation. Some feel, for example, that the *Bible* justifies various forms of killing, including war and capital punishment, on the basis of such statements as "An eye for an eye." Others, emphasizing such sayings as "Judge not lest ye be judged" and "Thou shalt not kill," believe the *Bible* demands absolute pacifism. How are we to know which interpretation is correct? It is likely, of course, that the answer people give to such religious questions will be influenced in part at least by their own moral beliefs: if capital punishment is thought to be unjust, for example, then an interpreter will seek to read the *Bible* in a way that is consistent with that moral truth. That is not, however, a happy conclusion for those wishing to rest morality on revelation, for it means that their understanding of what God has revealed is itself dependent on their prior moral views. Rather than revelation serving as a guide for morality, morality is serving as a guide for how we interpret revelation.

So my general conclusion is that far from providing a short-cut to moral understanding, looking to revelation for guidance often creates more questions and problems. It seems wiser under the circumstances to address complex moral problems like abortion, capital punishment, and affirmative action directly, considering the pros and cons of each side, rather than to seek answers through the much more controversial and difficult route of revelation.

The Divine Command Theory

It may seem, however, that we have still not really gotten to the heart of the matter. Even if religion is not necessary for moral motivation or guidance, it is often claimed, religion is necessary in another more fundamental sense. According to this view, religion is necessary for morality because without God there could BE no right or wrong. God, in other words, provides the foundation or bedrock on which morality is grounded. This idea was expressed by Bishop R. C. Mortimer:

> "God made us and all the world. Because of that He has an absolute claim on our obedience.... From [this] it follows that a thing is not right simply because we think it is. It is right because God commands it."[1]

What Bishop Mortimer has in mind can be seen by comparing moral rules with legal ones. Legal statutes, we know, are created by legislatures; if the state assembly of New York had not passed a law limiting speed people can travel, then there would be no such legal obligation. Without the statutory enactments, such a law simply would not exist. Mortimer's view, the *divine command theory*, would mean that God has the same sort of relation to moral law as legislature has to statutes it enacts: without God's commands there would be no moral rules, just as without a legislature there would be no statutes.

Defenders of the divine command theory often add to this a further claim, that only by assuming God sits at the foundation of morality can we explain the objective difference between right and wrong. This point was forcefully argued by F. C. Copleston in a 1948 British Broadcasting Corporation radio debate with Bertrand Russell.

Copleston: ... The validity of such an interpretation of man's conduct depends on the recognition of God's existence, obviously.... Let's take a look at the Commandant of the [Nazi] concentration camp at Belsen. That appears to you as undesirable and evil and to me too. To Adolf Hitler we suppose it appeared as something good and desirable. I suppose you'd have to admit that for Hitler it was good and for you it is evil.

Russell: No, I shouldn't go so far as that. I mean, I think people can make mistakes in that as they can in other things. If you have jaundice you see things yellow that are not yellow. You're making a mistake.

Copleston: Yes, one can make mistakes, but can you make a mistake if it's simply a question of reference to a feeling or emotion? Surely Hitler would be the only possible judge of what appealed to his emotions.

Russell: ... You can say various things about that; among others, that if that sort of thing makes that sort of appeal to Hitler's emotions, then Hitler makes quite a different appeal to my emotions.

Copleston: Granted. But there's no objective criterion outside feeling then for condemning the conduct of the Commandant of Belsen, in your view.... The human being's idea of the content of the moral law depends certainly to a large extent on education and environment, and a man has to use his reason in assessing the validity of the actual moral ideas of his social group. But the possibility of criticizing the accepted moral code presupposes that there is an objective standard, that there is an ideal moral order, which imposes itself.... It implies the existence of a real foundation of God.[2]

Against those who, like Bertrand Russell, seek to ground morality in feelings and attitudes, Copleston argues that there must be a more solid foundation if we are to be able to claim truly that the Nazis were evil. God, according to Copleston, is able to provide the objective basis for the distinction, which we all know to exist, between right and wrong. Without divine commands at the root of human obligations, we would have no real reason for condemning the behavior of anybody, even Nazis. Morality, Copleston thinks, would then be nothing more than an expression of personal feeling.

To begin assessing the divine command theory, let's first consider this last point. Is it really true that only the commands of God can provide an objective basis for moral judgments? Certainly many philosophers have felt that morality rests on its own perfectly sound footing, be it reason, human nature, or natural sentiments. It seems wrong to conclude, automatically, that morality cannot rest on anything but religion. And it is also possible that morality doesn't have any foundation or basis at all, so that its claims should be ignored in favor of whatever serves our own self-interest.

In addition to these problems with Copleston's argument, the divine command theory faces other problems as well. First, we would need to say much more about the relationship between morality and divine commands. Certainly the expressions "is commanded by God" and "is morally required" do not *mean* the same thing. People and even whole societies can use moral concepts without understanding them to make any reference to God. And while it is true that God (or any other moral being for that matter) would tend to want others to do the right thing, this hardly shows that being right and being commanded by God are the same thing. Parents want their children to do the right thing, too, but that doesn't mean parents, or anybody else, can make a thing right just by commanding it!

I think that, in fact, theists should reject the divine command theory. One reason is what it implies. Suppose we were to grant (just for the sake of argument) that the divine command theory is correct, so that actions are right just because they are commanded by God. The same, of course, can be said about those deeds that we believe are wrong. If God hadn't commanded us not to do them, they would not be wrong.

But now notice this consequence of the divine command theory. Since God is all-powerful, and since right is determined solely by His commands, is it not possible that He might change the rules and make what we now think of as wrong into right? It would seem that according to the divine command theory the answer is "yes": it is theoretically possible that tomorrow God would decree that virtues such as kindness and courage have become vices while actions that show cruelty and cowardice will henceforth be the right actions. (Recall the analogy with a legislature and the power it has to change law.) So now rather than it being right for people to help each other out and prevent innocent people from suffering unnecessarily, it would be right (God having changed His mind) to create as much pain among innocent children as we possibly can! To adopt the divine command theory therefore commits its advocate to the seemingly absurd position that even the greatest atrocities might be not only acceptable but morally required if God were to command them.

Plato made a similar point in the dialogue *Euthyphro*. Socrates is asking Euthyphro what it is that makes the virtue of holiness a virtue, just as we have been asking what makes kindness and courage virtues. Euthyphro has suggested that holiness is just whatever all the gods love.

Socrates: Well, then, Euthyphro, what do we say about holiness? Is it not loved by all the gods, according to your definition?

Euthyphro: Yes.

Socrates: Because it is holy, or for some other reason?

Euthyphro: No, because it is holy.

Socrates: Then it is loved by the gods because it is holy: it is not holy because it is loved by them?

Euthyphro: It seems so.

Socrates: ... Then holiness is not what is pleasing to the gods, and what is pleasing to the gods is not holy as you say, Euthyphro. They are different things.

Euthyphro: And why, Socrates?

Socrates: Because we are agreed that the gods love holiness because it is holy: and that it is not holy because they love it.[3]

This raises an interesting question: Why, having claimed at first that virtues are merely what is loved (or commanded) by the gods, would Euthyphro so quickly contradict this and agree that the gods love holiness *because* it's holy, rather than the reverse? One likely possibility is that Euthyphro believes that whenever the gods love something they do so with good reason, not without justification and arbitrarily. To deny this, and say that it is merely the gods' love that makes holiness a virtue, would mean that the gods have no basis for their attitudes, that they are arbitrary in what they love. Yet—and this is the crucial point—it's far from clear that a religious person would want to say that God is arbitrary in that way. If we say that it is simply God's loving something that makes it right, then what sense would it make to say God wants us to do right? All that could mean, it seems, is that God wants us to do what He wants us to do; He would have no reason for wanting it. Similarly "God is good" would mean little more than "God does what He pleases." The divine command theory therefore leads us to the results that God is morally arbitrary, and that His wishing us to do good or even God's being just mean nothing more than that God does what He does and wants whatever He wants. Religious people who reject that consequence would also, I am suggesting, have reason to reject the divine command theory itself, seeking a different understanding of morality.

This now raises another problem, however. If God approves kindness because it is a virtue and hates the Nazis because they were evil, then it seems that God discovers morality rather than inventing it. So haven't we then identified a limitation on God's power, since He now, being a good God, must love kindness and command us not to be cruel? Without the divine command theory, in other words, what is left of God's omnipotence?

But why, we may ask, is such a limitation on God unacceptable? It is not at all clear that God really can do anything at all. Can God, for example, destroy Himself? Or make a rock so heavy that He cannot lift it? Or create a universe which was never created by Him? Many have thought that God cannot do these things, but also that His inability to do them does not constitute a serious limitation on His power since these are things that cannot be done at all: to do them would violate the laws of logic. Christianity's most influential theologian, Thomas Aquinas, wrote in this regard that "whatever implies contradiction does not come within the scope of divine omnipotence, because it cannot have the aspect of possibility. Hence it is more appropriate to say that such things cannot be done than that God cannot do them."[4]

How, then, ought we to understand God's relationship to morality if we reject the divine command theory? Can religious people consistently maintain their faith in God the Creator and yet deny that what is right is right because

He commands it? I think the answer to this is "yes." Making cruelty good is not like making a universe that wasn't made, of course. It's a moral limit on God rather than a logical one. But why suppose that God's limits are only logical?

One final point about this. Even if we agree that God loves justice or kindness because of their nature, not arbitrarily, there still remains a sense in which God could change morality even having rejected the divine command theory. That's because if we assume, plausibly I think, that morality depends in part on how we reason, what we desire and need, and the circumstances in which we find ourselves, then morality will still be under God's control since God could have constructed us or our environment very differently. Suppose, for instance, that he created us so that we couldn't be hurt by others or didn't care about freedom. Or perhaps our natural environment were created differently, so that all we have to do is ask and anything we want is given to us. If God had created either nature or us that way, then it seems likely our morality might also be different in important ways from the one we now think correct. In that sense, then, morality depends on God whether or not one supports the divine command theory.

"Morality Is Social"

I have argued here that religion is not necessary in providing moral motivation or guidance, and against the divine command theory's claim that God is necessary for there to be morality at all. In this last section, I want first to look briefly at how religion and morality sometimes *do* influence each other. Then I will consider the development of moral conscience and the important ways in which morality might correctly be thought to be "social."

Nothing I have said so far means that morality and religion are independent of each other. But in what ways are they related, assuming I am correct in claiming morality does not *depend* on religion? First, of course, we should note the historical influence religions have had on the development of morality as well as on politics and law. Many of the important leaders of the abolitionist and civil rights movements were religious leaders, as are many current members of the pro-life movement. The relationship is not, however, one sided: morality has also influenced religion, as the current debate within the Catholic church over the role of women, abortion, and other social issues shows. In reality, then, it seems clear that the practices of morality and religion have historically each exerted an influence on the other.

But just as the two have shaped each other historically, so, too, do they interact at the personal level. I have already suggested how people's understanding of revelation, for instance, is often shaped by morality as they seek the best interpretations of revealed texts. Whether trying to understand a work of art, a legal statute, or a religious text, interpreters regularly seek to understand them in the best light—to make them as good as they can be, which requires that they bring moral judgment to the task of religious interpretation and understanding.

The relationship can go the other direction as well, however, as people's moral views are shaped by their religious training and beliefs. These relationships between morality and religion are often complex, hidden even from ourselves, but it does seem clear that our views on important moral issues, from sexual morality and war to welfare and capital punishment, are often influenced by our religious outlook. So not only are religious and moral practices and understandings historically linked, but for many religious people the relationship extends to the personal level—to their understanding of moral obligations as well as their sense of who they are and their vision of who they wish to be.

Morality, then, is influenced by religion (as is religion by morality), but morality's social character extends deeper even than that, I want to argue. First, of course, we possess a socially acquired language within which we think about our various choices and the alternatives we ought to follow, including whether a possible course of action is the right thing to do. Second, morality is social in that it governs relationships among people, defining our responsibilities to others and theirs to us. Morality provides the standards we rely on in gauging our interactions with family, lovers, friends, fellow citizens, and even strangers. Third, morality is social in the sense that we are, in fact, subject to criticism by others for our actions. We discuss with others what we should do, and often hear from them concerning whether our decisions were acceptable. Blame and praise are a central feature of morality.

While not disputing any of this, John Dewey has stressed another, less obvious aspect of morality's social character. Consider then the following comments regarding the origins of morality and conscience in an article he titled "Morality Is Social":

> In language and imagination we rehearse the responses of others just as we dramatically enact other consequences. We foreknow how others will act, and the foreknowledge is the beginning of judgment passed on action. We know *with* them; there is conscience. An assembly is formed within our breast which discusses and appraises proposed and performed acts. The community without becomes a forum and tribunal within, a judgment-seat of charges, assessments and exculpations. Our thoughts of our own actions are saturated with the ideas that others entertain about them.... Explicit recognition of this fact is a prerequisite of improvement in moral education.... Reflection is morally indispensable.[5]

To appreciate fully the role of society in shaping morality and influencing people's sense of responsibility, Dewey is arguing, requires appreciating the fact that to think from the moral point of view, as opposed to the selfish one, for instance, means rejecting our private, subjective perspective in favor of the view of others, envisioning how they might respond to various choices we might make. Far from being private and unrelated to others, moral conscience is in that sense "public." To consider a decision from the moral perspective, says Dewey, requires that we envision an "assembly of others" that is "formed within our breast." In that way, our moral conscience cannot be sharply distinguished from our nature as social beings since conscience invariably brings with it, or constitutes, the perspective of the other. "Is this right?" and "What would this look like were I to have to defend it to others?" are not entirely separable questions.[6]

It is important not to confuse Dewey's point here, however. He is *not* saying that what is right is finally to be determined by the reactions of actually existing other people, or even by the reaction of society as a whole. What is right or fair can never be finally decided by a vote, and might not meet the approval of any specific others. But what then might Dewey mean in speaking of such an "assembly of others" as the basis of morality? The answer is that rather than actual people or groups, the assembly Dewey envisions is hypothetical or "ideal." The "community without" is thus transformed into a "forum and tribunal within, a judgment seat of charges, assessments and exculpations." So it is through the powers of our imagination that we can meet our moral responsibilities and exercise moral judgment, using these powers to determine what morality requires by imagining the reaction of Dewey's "assembly of others."

Morality is therefore *inherently* social, in a variety of ways. It depends on socially learned language, is learned from interactions with others, and governs our interactions with others in society. But it also demands, as Dewey put it, that we know "with" others, envisioning for ourselves what their points of view would require along with our own. Conscience demands we occupy the positions of others.

Viewed in this light, God would play a role in a religious person's moral reflection and conscience since it is unlikely a religious person would wish to exclude God from the "forum and tribunal" that constitutes conscience. Rather, for the religious person conscience would almost certainly include the imagined reaction of God along with the reactions of others who might be affected by the action. Other people are also important, however, since it is often an open question just what God's reaction would be; revelation's meaning, as I have argued, is subject to interpretation. So it seems that for a religious person morality and God's will cannot be separated, though the connection between them is not the one envisioned by defenders of the divine command theory.

Which leads to my final point, about moral education. If Dewey is correct, then it seems clear there is an important sense in which morality not only can be taught but must be. Besides early moral training, moral thinking depends on our ability to imagine others' reactions and to imaginatively put ourselves into their shoes. "What would somebody (including, perhaps, God) think if this got out?" expresses more than a concern with being embarrassed or punished; it is also the voice of conscience and indeed of morality itself. But that would mean, thinking of education, that listening to others, reading about what others think and do, and reflecting within ourselves about our actions and whether we could defend them to others are part of the practice of morality itself. Morality cannot exist without the broader, social perspective introduced by others, and this social nature ties it, in that way, with education and with public discussion, both actual and imagined. "Private" moral reflection taking place independent of the social world would be no moral reflection at all; and moral education is not only possible, but essential.

Notes

1. R. C. Mortimer, *Christian Ethics* (London: Hutchinson's University Library, 1950), pp. 7–8.
2. This debate was broadcast on the "Third Program" of the British Broadcasting Corporation in 1948.
3. Plato, *Euthyphro,* tr. H. N. Fowler (Cambridge MA: Harvard University Press, 1947).
4. Thomas Aquinas, *Summa Theologica,* Part I, Q. 25, Art. 3.
5. John Dewey, "Morality Is Social" in *The Moral Writings of John Dewey,* revised edition, ed. James Gouinlock (Amherst, NY: Prometheus Books, 1994), pp. 182–4.
6. Obligations to animals raise an interesting problem for this conception of morality. Is it wrong to torture animals only because other *people* could be expected to disapprove? Or is it that the animal itself would disapprove? Or, perhaps, duties to animals rest on sympathy and compassion while human moral relations are more like Dewey describes, resting on morality's inherently social nature and on the dictates of conscience viewed as an assembly of others?

NO ↰

Leo Tolstóy

Religion and Morality

Y ou ask me: (1) What I understand by the word *religion,* and, (2) Is it possible to have a morality independent of *religion* in the sense in which I understand that word?

I will do my best to answer these most important and excellently-put questions.

Three different meanings are commonly given to the word *religion.*

The first is, that religion is a special and true revelation given by God to man, and is a worship of God in accord with that revelation. This meaning is given to religion by people who believe in one or other of the existing religions and who consequently consider *that* particular religion to be the only true one.

The second meaning is, that religion is a collection of certain superstitious beliefs, as well as a superstitious form of worship accordant with such beliefs. This is the meaning given to religion by unbelievers in general, or by men who do not accept the particular religion they are defining.

The third meaning is, that religion is a collection of propositions and laws devised by wise men and needed to console the common people, to restrain their passions, and to make the masses manageable. This meaning is given to religion by those who are indifferent to religion as religion but consider it a useful instrument for Governments....

So to your first question, 'What do I understand by the word *religion,*' I reply: *Religion is a relation man sets up between himself and the endless and infinite universe, or its source and first cause.*

From this answer to the first question the answer to the second follows naturally.

If religion is a relation man establishes towards the universe—a relation which determines the meaning of life—then *morality* is the indication and explanation of such human activity as naturally results from men holding this or that relation towards the universe. And as only two such fundamental relations are known to us, if we consider the pagan, social relation as an enlargement of the personal, or three if we count the social, pagan relation separately—it follows that only three moral teachings exist: the primitive, savage, personal; the pagan, family, State, or social; and the Christian or divine teaching of service to man or to God.

From the first of these relations of man to the universe flows the teaching of morality common to all pagan religions that have at their base the striving after welfare for the separate individual, and that therefore define all the conditions yielding most welfare to the individual and indicate means to obtain such welfare. From this relation to the world flow the pagan teachings: the Epicurean in its lowest form; the Mohammedan teaching of morality which promises coarse personal welfare in this and the next world; the Church-Christian teaching of morality aiming at salvation—that is, at the welfare of one's personality, especially in the other world; and also the worldly utilitarian morality aiming at the welfare of the individual only in this world.

From the same teaching, which places the aim of life in personal welfare and therefore in freedom from personal suffering, flow the moral teaching of Buddhism in its crude form and the worldly doctrine of the pessimist.

From the second, pagan relation of man to the universe, which sees the aim of life in securing welfare for a group of individuals, flow the moral teachings which demand that man should serve the group whose welfare is regarded as the aim of life. According to that teaching personal welfare is only allowable to the extent to which it can be obtained for the whole group of people who form the religious basis of life. From that relation to the universe flow the well-known Roman and Greek moral teachings in which personality always sacrifices itself for society, and also the Chinese morality. From this relation flows also the Jewish morality—the subordination of one's own welfare to that of the chosen people—and also the Church and State morality of our own times, which demands the sacrifice of the individual for the good of the State. From this relation to the universe flows also the morality of most women, who sacrifice their whole personality for the benefit of their family and especially for their children.

All ancient history, and to some extent medieval and modern history, teems with descriptions of deeds of just this family, social, or State morality. And the majority of people to-day—though they think their morality is Christian because they profess Christianity—really hold this family, State, pagan morality, and hold it up as an ideal when educating the young generation.

From the third, the Christian, relation to the universe—which consists in man's considering himself to be an instrument of the Supreme Will for the accomplishment of its ends—flow the moral teachings which correspond to that understanding of life, elucidating man's dependence on the Supreme Will and defining its demands. From that relation of man to the universe flow all the highest moral teachings known to man: the Pythagorean, the Stoic, the Buddhist, the Brahminical, and the Taoist, in their highest manifestations, and the Christian teaching in its real meaning, demanding renunciation of one's personal will—and not only of one's own welfare, but even of that of one's family, society, and country—for the sake of fulfilling the will of him who sent us into life: a will revealed by our conscience. From the first, the second, or the third of these relations to the infinite universe or to its source, flows each man's real, unfeigned morality, no matter what he may profess or preach as morality or in what light he may wish to appear.

So that a man who considers the reality of his relation to the universe to lie in obtaining the greatest welfare for himself—however much he may say he considers it moral to live for his family, for society, for the State, for humanity, or for the performance of God's will—and however artfully he may pretend and may deceive men, will still always have as his real motive of action simply his individual welfare; so that when a choice has to be made he will not sacrifice his own personality for his family or State, nor to do the will of God, but will sacrifice them all for his own sake. Since he sees the meaning of life only in personal welfare he cannot do otherwise until such time as he alters his relation to the universe.

And similarly one whose relation to life consists in the service of his own family (as is the case with most women), or of his clan or nation (as among members of the oppressed nationalities and among men politically active in times of strife)—no matter how much he may declare himself to be a Christian, his morality will always be family or national and not Christian, and when any conflict arises between family or social welfare on one side, and that of his personality or the fulfilment of the will of God on the other, he will inevitably choose the service of the group for whom, in his view of life, he exists: for only in such service does he see the meaning of his life. And in the same way a man who regards his relation to the world as consisting in fulfilling the will of Him who sent him hither—however much you may impress upon him that he should (in accord with the demands of his personality, or of his family, his nation, empire, or all humanity) commit acts contrary to the Supreme Will of which the operation of the reason and love wherewith he is endowed makes him aware—will always sacrifice all human ties rather than fail to comply with the Will that has sent him here: for only in such compliance does he discern a meaning for his life.

Morality cannot be independent of religion, for not only is it a consequence of religion—that is, a consequence of the relation in which a man feels that he stands towards the universe—but it is implicit (*impliquée*, as the French say) in religion. Every religion is an answer to the question: 'What is the meaning of my life?' And the religious answer involves a certain moral demand, which may follow or may precede the explanation of the meaning of life. To the question, 'What is the meaning of life?' the reply may be: 'The meaning of life lies in the welfare of the individual, therefore make use of all the advantages within your reach'; or, 'The meaning of life lies in the welfare of a certain group of people, therefore serve that group with all your strength'; or, 'The meaning of life lies in fulfilling the will of Him that sent you, therefore try with all your strength to know that will and to fulfil it.' Or the same question may be answered in this way: 'The meaning of your life lies in your personal enjoyment, for that is the object of man's existence'; or, 'The meaning of your life lies in serving the group of which you consider yourself a member, for that is your destiny'; or, 'The meaning of your life lies in the service of God, for that is your destiny.'

Morality is included in the explanation of the meaning of life that religion gives, and can therefore in no way be separated from religion. This truth is particularly evident in the attempts of non-Christian philosophers to deduce a doctrine of the highest morality from their philosophy. Such philosophers see that Christian morality is indispensable, that we cannot live without it; they even see that it is an already existing fact, and they want to find some way to attach it to their non-Christian philosophy and even to put things in such a way that Christian morality may seem to result from their pagan social philosophy. That is what they attempt, but their very efforts show more clearly than anything else that Christian morality is not merely independent of pagan philosophy, but that it stands in complete contradiction to that philosophy of individual welfare, or of liberation from individual suffering, or of social welfare.

The Christian ethics, which in accord with our religious conception of life we acknowledge, demand not only the sacrifice of one's personality for the group, but the renunciation alike of one's personality and of one's group for the service of God; but pagan philosophy only investigates means of obtaining the greatest welfare for the individual or for the group of individuals, and therefore a contrast is inevitable. And there is only one way of hiding this contrast —namely, by piling up abstract conditional conceptions one on another, and keeping to the misty domain of metaphysics.

That is what most of the post-Renaissance philosophers have done, and to this circumstance—the impossibility of making the demands of Christian morality (which have been admitted in advance) accord with a philosophy built on pagan foundations—must be attributed the terrible unreality, obscurity, unintelligibility, and estrangement from life, that characterizes modern philosophy. With the exception of Spinoza (whose philosophy develops from truly Christian roots in spite of the fact that he did not consider himself a Christian) and Kant (a man of genius, who admittedly treated his system of ethics as not dependent on his metaphysics), all the philosophers, even the brilliant Schopenhauer, evidently devised artificial connexions between their ethics and their metaphysics.

It is felt that Christian ethics are something that must be accepted in advance, standing quite firmly, not dependent on philosophy and in no need of the fictitious props put to support them; and it is felt that Philosophy merely devises certain propositions in order that ethics may not contradict her but may rather be bound to her and appear to flow from her. All such propositions, however, only appear to justify Christian ethics while they are considered in the abstract. As soon as they are applied to questions of practical life, the non-correspondence, and more, the evident contradiction between the philosophic basis and what we consider to be morality, appears in full strength.

The unfortunate Nietzsche, who has latterly become so celebrated, rendered a valuable service by his exposure of this contradiction. He is incontrovertible when he says that all rules of morality, from the point of view of the current non-Christian philosophy, are mere lies and hypocrisy and that it is much more profitable, pleasant and reasonable, for a man to devise his own Supermen (Uebermenschen) and be one of them, than to be one of the mass which has to serve as the scaffold for these Supermen. No philosophical constructions founded on the pagan-religious view of life can prove to anyone that it is more profitable or wiser for him to live, not for a welfare he desires, comprehends, and sees to be possible for himself or for his family or his society, but for another's welfare—undesired, not understood, and unattainable by his puny human power. Philosophy founded on an understanding of life limited to the welfare of man will never be able to prove to a rational man, who knows that he may die at any moment, that he ought, and that it is good for him to forgo his own desired, understood, and undoubted welfare—not even for any certain welfare to others (for he can never know what will result from his sacrifices), but merely because it is right or good to do so: that it is a categorical imperative.

To prove this from the point of view of pagan philosophy is impossible. To prove that people are all equal—that it is better for a man to sacrifice his life in the service of others than to trample on the lives of others, making them serve him—one must redefine one's relation to the universe: one must prove that man's position is such that he has no option, since the meaning of his life lies only in the execution of the will of Him that sent him, and the will of Him that sent him is that he should give his life to the service of men. And such a change in man's relation to the universe comes only from religion.

Thus it is with the attempts to deduce Christian morality from, and to reconcile it with, the fundamental positions of pagan science. No sophistries or subtleties of thought can destroy this simple and clear position, that the law of evolution, which lies at the base of all the science of to-day, is founded on a general, eternal, and unalterable law—the law of the struggle for existence and the survival of the fittest; and that therefore each man, to attain his own and his group's welfare, should try to be that 'fittest' and to make his group such, in order that he and his group should not perish, but some other man or group that is less fit.

However much some naturalists, frightened by the logical consequences of this law and by their application to human life, may try to perplex the matter with words and to exorcise this law—their efforts only make still more evident the irresistibility of that law, which rules the life of the whole organic world, and therefore that of man regarded as an animal.

Since I began writing this article, a Russian translation has appeared of an article by Mr. Huxley, composed of a speech on Evolution and Ethics[1] delivered by him to some English Society. In this article the learned Professor—like our well-known Professor Bekétov and many others who have written on the same subject, and with as little success as his predecessors—tries to prove that the struggle for existence does not infringe morality, and that side by side with the acknowledgement of the struggle for existence as a fundamental law of life, morality may not merely exist but even progress. Mr. Huxley's article is full of all kinds of jokes, verses, and general views on ancient religion and philosophy, and is consequently so florid and complicated that it is only with great effort that one is able to reach its fundamental thought. That thought however is as follows: The law of evolution runs counter to the moral law; this was known to the ancient Greeks and Hindus. The philosophy and religion of both those peoples brought them to the doctrine of self-renunciation. That doctrine, the author thinks, is not correct; the correct one is this: A law exists, which the author calls the cosmic law, in accord with which all beings struggle against one another and only the fittest survive. Man also is subject to this law; and thanks only to it has man become what he now is. But this law runs counter to morality. How then can it be reconciled with morality? That can be accomplished in this way: A law of social progress exists which seeks to check the cosmic process and to replace it by another, an ethical, process, the object of which is the survival, not of the fittest but of the best in an ethical sense. Where this ethical process sprang from, Mr. Huxley does not explain, but in his twentieth footnote he says that the basis of this process is, on the one hand that people, like animals, prefer to be in company and therefore suppress in themselves qualities harmful to society; and on the other hand that the members of a society forcibly suppress actions contrary to social welfare. It seems to Mr. Huxley that this process, obliging men to curb their passions for the sake of preserving the group of which they are members, and for fear of being punished if they disturb the order of their group, supplies that ethical law the existence of which he wishes to demonstrate. It seems to Mr. Huxley in the naïveté of his soul, that in English society as it exists to-day—with its Irish problem, the poverty of its lowest classes, the insensate luxury of the rich, its trade in opium and spirits, its executions, its slaughter or extermination of tribes for the sake of trade and politics, its secret vice and its hypocrisy—the man who does not infringe the police regulations is a moral man guided by the ethical law. He forgets that the qualities needful to maintain the society in which a man lives may be useful for that society—as the members of a band of robbers may be useful to that band, and as in our own society we find a use for the qualities of executioners, jailers, judges, soldiers, and hypocrite-priests, & c.—but that these qualities have nothing in common with morality.

Morality is something continually developing and growing, and therefore conformity to the existing rules of a certain society and their preservation by means of the axe or the scaffold (to which Mr. Huxley alludes as to instruments of morality), will not only not tend to the maintenance, but will be an infringement, of morality. And on the contrary every infringement of the existing order—such as were not only the infringements committed by Jesus and his disciples of the regulations of a Roman province, but the infringements of present-day regulations by one who refuses to take part in legal proceedings, military service, or the payment of taxes levied for warlike preparations—will not only not be an infringement of morality, but will be an inevitable condition of its manifestation.

Every cannibal who perceives that he should not eat his fellow men and who acts accordingly, infringes the order of his society. And therefore though action infringing the order of any society *may* be immoral, every truly moral action which pushes forward the limits of morality is always *sure* to be an infringement of the order of society. If therefore a law has appeared in society in accord with which people sacrifice their personal advantages for the preservation of the integrity of their group, that law is not the ethical law, but on the contrary will generally be a law contrary to all ethics—that same law of the struggle for existence, but in a hidden latent form. It is the same struggle for existence, but carried over from the individual to a group of individuals. It is not the cessation of the fight, but only a backward swinging of the arm to strike a harder blow.

If the law of the struggle for existence and the survival of the fittest is the eternal law of all life (and it cannot but be admitted to be so when we regard man as an animal)—then no tangled discussions about social progress and an ethical law supposed to flow from it, or to spring up from no one knows where just when we happen to need it (like a *deus ex machina*), can disturb that law.

If social progress, as Mr. Huxley assures us, collects people into groups, then the struggle and the survival will continue among those families, clans, and nations, and the struggle will not only not be more moral, but it will be even more cruel and more immoral than that between individuals, as we see in actual life. Even if we admit the impossible, and suppose that in another thousand years all humanity will, by social progress alone, be united into one whole and form a single nation and a single State—even then (not to mention that the struggle abolished between nations and States will continue between man and the animal world, and will always remain a struggle—that is, will remain an activity quite excluding the possibility of the Christian morality we confess) —even then the struggle between individuals forming this union and between the groups of families, clans, and nationalities, will not be diminished but will continue in a new form, as we see in all aggregations of individuals, families, races, and States. The members of a family quarrel and fight with one another as well as with outsiders, and often to a greater degree and with more venom. It is just the same thing in the State; among people living in one State a struggle continues just as with people outside the State, only it is carried on under other forms. In the one case the slaughter is done with arrows and knives, in the other it is done by hunger. And if both in the family and in the State the weak are saved, that is not done by social union, but occurs because love and self-sacrifice exist among the people united in families and in States. If, outside the family, only the fittest of two children survives, while in a good mother's family both remain alive, this does not result from union into families, but from the fact that the mother possesses love and self-sacrifice. And neither self-sacrifice nor love can result from a social process.

To assert that a social process produces morality is like asserting that the construction of stoves produces heat.

Heat comes from the sun, and stoves produce heat only when fuel (the result of the sun's work) is put into them. Just so morality comes from religion. Special forms of social life produce morality only when the results of religious influence—which is morality—are put into them.

Stoves may be heated and give warmth, or may not be heated and may remain cold; just as social forms may contain morality and thus have a moral influence on society, or may not contain morality and so remain without influence on society.

Christian morality cannot be based on a pagan or social conception of life and cannot be deduced either from philosophy or from non-Christian science; and not only can it not be deduced from them, but it cannot even be reconciled with them.

That is how the matter has always been understood by every serious and strictly consistent philosophy and science, which said, quite reasonably: 'If our propositions do not tally with morality, so much the worse for morality', and continued their investigations.

Ethical treatises not founded on religion, and even secular catechisms, are written and taught, and people may suppose that humanity is guided by them; but that only seems to be the case, because people are really guided not by those treatises and catechisms but by the religions which they have always possessed and still possess, whereas these treatises and catechisms only counterfeit what flows naturally from religion.

The dictates of secular morality not based on a religious teaching are just like the action of a man who, though ignorant of music, should take the conductor's seat and begin to wave his arms before the experienced musicians who were performing. The music would continue for awhile by its own momentum and because of what the musicians had learned from former conductors; but the waving of a stick by a man ignorant of music would obviously not merely be useless, but would in course of time certainly confuse the musicians and disorganize the orchestra. A similar confusion begins to take place in people's minds at the present time in consequence of attempts made by leading men to teach people a morality not founded on that highest religion which begins to be assimilated, and has already been partly assimilated, by Christian humanity.

It is indeed desirable to have moral teaching unmixed with superstition, but the fact is that moral teaching is a result of a certain relation man holds towards the universe or towards God. If that relation is expressed in forms which seem to us superstitious, we should, to put the matter right, try to express that relation more reasonably, clearly, and exactly, or even to destroy the former relation (now become inadequate) of man to the universe and substitute for it one that is higher, clearer, and more reasonable; but we should in no case devise a so-called secular, non-religious morality founded on sophistry or simply founded on nothing at all.

The attempts to found a morality apart from religion, are like the attempts of children who, wishing to transplant a flower that pleases them, pluck it from the roots that seem to them unpleasing and superfluous, and stick it rootless into the ground. Without religion there can be no real, sincere morality, just as without roots there can be no real flower.

So in answer to your two questions, I say: *'Religion is a certain relation established by man between his separate personality and the infinite universe or its Source. And morality is the ever-present guide to life, which results from that relation.'*

Note

1. Thomas Huxley's Romanes Lecture, delivered in 1894, and contained in *Evolution and Ethics,* issued by Macmillan & Co.

POSTSCRIPT

Can Morality Exist Without Religion?

C*an We Be Good Without God?* Within the last few years, two books by this same title have been published by two different authors with two very different perspectives. Paul Chamberlain, associate professor of ethics and political philosophy at Trinity Western University in British Columbia, wrote his book as an argument in favor of the necessity of God and the importance of religion. Chamberlain believes that with the many difficult questions faced by society today, there is a critical need to rely on the absolute truth given by an omniscient and omnipotent God. Chamberlain's book has been criticized for the lack of coverage he gives to historical evidence of religious belief and practice used for evil as well as for good.

Robert Buckman, physician, atheist, and president of the Humanist Association of Canada, argues that much of the conflict and evil the world has witnessed was perpetated in the name of God. He illustrates this by referring to such historical incidents as the Crusades; the Spanish Inquisition; the ongoing struggles between Catholics and Protestants; as well as current conflicts between Jews, Christians, and Muslims. Buckman believes that religion is a great part of the *problem* faced by humankind rather than the *solution*.

Buckman's contention that religion is a part of the problem is acceptable to many, but he has been criticized for failing to address historical evidence that some of the greatest evil has also been perpetuated by individuals and governments who have attempted to create their own civilizations without God.

British philosopher C. S. Lewis spoke and wrote often of what he called "natural law." Lewis believed that God had provided and continues to provide a basic sense of right and wrong to all nations, kindreds, tongues, and peoples. Lewis believed that there is an objective moral code, one that transcends time and culture. He believed that the existence of Natural Law is a witness of the reality of God and humankind's dependence upon Him for the existence of morality.

Suggested Readings

H. Cox, *Religion in the Secular City: Toward a Postmodern Theology* (Touchstone, 1984).

W. S. Green and J. Neusner, eds., *The Religion Factor: An Introduction to How Religion Matters* (Westminster John Knox, 1996).

L. Guenter, *Why America Needs Religion: Secular Modernity and Its Discontents* (Eerdmans, 1996).

B. F. Skinner, *Walden Two* (MacMillan, 1982).

On the Internet ...

Apologetics Index

Apologetics Index is a massive Web site that includes information and links on both Christian and non-Christian perspectives. This site provides research resources on religious cults, sects, new religious movements, alternative religions, and more.

> http://www.gospelcom.net/apologeticsindex/

ChristianAnswers.net

ChristianAnswers.net is a broad site that deals with many facets of contemporary Christian life. This site also addresses a number of doctrinal issues from a biblical perspective.

> http://www.christiananswers.net

PART 2

Doctrinal Issues

*T*his part highlights more specific issues that touch most of the world's major religions. How are we to respond to ideas such as exclusive salvation or the divinity of Jesus Christ? These concerns influence the way people live and profoundly affect the dialogue between religious groups.

- Is There Only One Way to Receive Salvation?

- Is Acceptance of Christ Alone Sufficient for Salvation?

- Was Jesus Christ the Son of God?

- Is the Family Primary in God's Plan?

ISSUE 5

Is There Only One Way to Receive Salvation?

YES: Keith E. Johnson, from "Do All Paths Lead to the Same Destination?" Leadership University, http://www.leaderu.com/wri/articles/paths.html (November 19, 1998)

NO: John Hick, from "Whatever Path Men Choose Is Mine," in Richard J. Plantinga, ed., *Christianity and Plurality: Classic and Contemporary Readings* (Blackwell Publishers, 1999)

ISSUE SUMMARY

YES: Keith E. Johnson, regional coordinator for *Ongoing Theological Education* with the Campus Ministry of City Colleges of Chicago, Illinois, asserts that while other religious traditions provide a supportive community and important ethical and moral teachings, salvation can only be found through faith in Jesus Christ.

NO: John Hick, theologian and philosopher of religion, is the author of what has come to be known as the pluralistic hypothesis. He argues that all religions are simply differing manifestations of the same ultimate reality. Hick maintains that salvation can be found through following God in whatever form we find him (or her).

For many of us, our theological beliefs and religious practices are an integral part of our individual and cultural identities. Our religious beliefs not only influence many of the decisions we make but are at the very heart of who we are as human beings. Describing ourselves as Jewish, Muslim, Hindu, Buddhist, Christian, or agnostic also communicates to others something about us. While there is a great deal of theological and religious diversity between the various denominations and philosophical perspectives, most share a common bond—a belief in the divine. Even those who identify themselves as agnostic or atheistic have been influenced by the intellectual or cultural construct of the divine, though they may doubt or deny the literal existence of deity.

One of the theistic challenges many people face at some time in their personal, professional, or academic lives has to do with religious and theological diversity. In what ways do we think, feel, and respond to those of different faiths? A related question, the theme of this issue, concerns salvation—what must a person know and do to receive salvation? There are three basic perspectives concerning how salvation is achieved—pluralism, exclusivism, and inclusivism. All have compelling arguments, but each also has doctrinal and philosophical weaknesses.

A number of theologians, philosophers, and laypeople alike embrace the theological perspective known as *pluralism*. Generally, those coming from a pluralistic perspective believe that "all religions are equally effective in bringing salvation about." From the Bhagavad Gita, the sacred text of the Hindu people, comes a statement representative of pluralism: "Whatever path men choose is mine." This same pluralistic theology is also found in Buddhism. After sharing the well-known parable of the six blind men and the elephant, the Buddha is reported to have said, "How can you be so sure of what you cannot see? We are all like blind people in this world. We cannot see God. Each of you may be partly right, yet none completely so." In the following selection, John Hick represents this perspective.

Other theologians, sometimes called *exclusivists*, believe that salvation is possible only by following a specific path, which usually includes the worship of a specific God in a specific way. From the Book of Acts in the New Testament we read the words of the apostle Peter, "Neither is there salvation in any other: for there is none other name under heaven given among men, whereby we must be saved" (King James Version, Acts 4:12).

Historically, Muslims as well as Christians have rejected pluralism and are considered exclusivistic, but both religions generally espouse religious tolerance. Keith E. Johnson's selection represents the exclusivist position. While Johnson is respectful of the pluralist position and recognizes its views, he argues that salvation can only be found in the teachings of Jesus Christ.

A third philosophical perspective, *inclusivism*, includes the necessity of worshiping a particular God but recognizes that there is much good that is of God in other religious traditions. Christian inclusivist John Sanders writes in *What About Those Who Have Never Heard* (InterVarsity, 1995), "In this model God saves people only because of the work of Christ, but people may be saved even if they do not know about Christ. God grants them salvation if they exercise faith in God as revealed to them through creation and providence." In other words, God will not condemn someone who has not had the opportunity of accepting Christ. God will judge them by what light and knowledge they have been given while in mortality, or they will be given an opportunity after death. The perspective outlining that those who have never heard the gospel in mortality will have the opportunity after death has been termed "postmortem evangelism" or "divine perseverance."

While this issue deals with the writings of two Christian theologians, the principles of pluralism and particularism are applicable to non-Christian religious traditions as well.

Johnson asserts that while other religious traditions provide much that is beneficial to humankind, salvation can be found *only* through faith in Jesus Christ. Hick argues that Christianity is not the only way to obtain salvation but simply one of many paths God has created to bless humankind.

Keith E. Johnson

 **YES**

Do All Paths Lead to the Same Destination?

The Irish playwright George Bernard Shaw once said, "There is only one religion, though there are a hundred versions of it." In our pluralistic society an increasing number of people find Shaw's interpretation of religion appealing. Is it possible that Buddhism, Christianity, Hinduism, Islam, Judaism, etc. represent differing, yet valid, paths to the same destination? Were this the case, there would be no need to argue about which religion is the "true" religion. Such disputes would be pointless. Perhaps viewing religion in this way would eventually lead to less religious bigotry and greater cooperation among people of differing faiths.

On the other hand, what if all paths do not lead to the same destination? Religious traditions such as Islam and Buddhism differ significantly from one another. How does one account for these differences and maintain that all paths lead to the same destination? If all paths do not lead to the same destination then each of us must make an informed choice which may have significant consequences. In this article I will briefly examine arguments for and against the claim that all (religious) paths lead to the same destination.

Option One: All Paths Lead to the Same Destination

Some claim that all religions represent differing, yet equally valid, routes to the same destination. Though each religion may choose its own path, all paths converge at the top of the same mountain. Advocates of this position are aware of the diversity in belief and practice that differentiate Buddhists from Christians, Hindus from Jews, and Muslims from Shintos. Nevertheless, they typically offer the following points in support of their thesis:

1. It is intolerant and ethnocentric to assert that one religion is the true religion and others, which disagree, are false. This type of intolerance, it is pointed out, has caused much bloodshed.

2. The contrasting claims of different religions do not prove that one religion is true and others are false. Instead it suggests that no religion possesses the entire truth, but only bits and pieces of it. Imagine, for example, that three blind men are touching an elephant. The first blind man is holding on to the elephant's leg. He explains, "I think an elephant is like the trunk of a great tree." The second blind man disagrees. "No, I believe an elephant is like a snake," he says while holding the elephant's trunk. The third blind man responds, "No, you both are wrong, an elephant is like a wall." (He is touching the elephant's side.) Each blind man thinks he is right and that the others are wrong even though all three of them are all touching the same elephant. In a similar way, is it not possible that all religions are in contact with the same ultimate reality and merely describe it in different ways?

3. There is an ethical core which all religions share in common. Some formulation of the Golden Rule, for example, is found in Judaism, Hinduism, Jainism, Christianity, Taoism, Islam, and Buddhism. In addition, each of these traditions produces a similar ethical/moral transformation in the lives of its followers. Certainly it would be difficult to prove that one religious tradition is more effective than others in transforming the lives of its followers.

These three arguments are typically offered in support of the claim that all paths are valid means to the same destination. Perhaps the most sophisticated formulation of this position is the "pluralistic hypothesis" proposed by philosopher John Hick.[1] Hick's pluralistic hypothesis attempts to explain four phenomena: the fact that people are inherently religious, the diversity of religious belief, the assumption that religious belief is not an illusion, and reality that almost every religious tradition positively changes its followers' lives. Hick claims that there is one ultimate reality (which he calls the "Real"); that each religious tradition, suffering from a Kantian blindness, does not have direct perception of this ultimate reality; and that each religious tradition represents an authentic way in which this reality is conceived and experienced.

Hick is fully aware that different religious traditions hold conflicting beliefs on a number of key points. Nevertheless, he claims that almost every religion brings positive moral change (what he calls "salvation/liberation") in the lives of its followers. In light of this, he believes that it does not make sense to conceive of one religion as true and others as false. Instead, Hick claims that all religions are equally valid means to salvation/liberation.

Pluralistic interpretations of religion like Hick's possess a strong appeal. Nevertheless, I find that they possess two deficiencies which, in the final analysis, render them unacceptable. First, they are unable to properly account for the conflicting truth-claims of different religions. Second, they radically reinterpret the beliefs of specific traditions in order to avoid the first problem.

The Achilles' heel of the claim that all paths lead to the same destination is the problem of internal consistency. Each religious tradition makes truth-claims which contradict the truth-claims of other religious traditions. We will briefly examine three areas of disagreement.

1. The first area of contradiction regards the nature of the ultimate reality (such as God). One discovers there is a vast chasm between monotheistic religions (such as Judaism, Christianity and Islam), and pantheistic religions (such as Hinduism, Buddhism). Muslims claim that there is only one God, *Allah*, who created the universe from nothing. Some Hindus, on the other hand, believe not in a personal creator, but in *Brahman*, an impersonal absolute reality which permeates all things. Other Hindus believe that there are millions of deities (such as *Brahma, Vishnu, Shiva, and Krishna*) which are manifestations of *Brahman.*
2. A second area of contradiction relates to the fate of individuals at death. According to Islam, each of us will die once and then face judgement by *Allah*. Depending on *Allah*'s judgement we will spend eternity in heaven or hell. In contrast, many Hindus claim that we will live (and have already lived) many lives on earth. Hindus believe that the conditions of our past and future existence are determined by the cosmic laws of *karma*. Following death each of us is reincarnated into a different form (human, animal, etc.).
3. Each religious tradition also identifies a universal problem that afflicts humanity. This brings us to a third area of disagreement. Hindus, for example, claim that the universal problem is *samsara. Samsara* is an endless cycle of birth, death and rebirth (reincarnation) in which every person is trapped. Only through knowledge of one's relationship to *Brahman* and religious devotion can this cycle be broken and *moksha* (release) experienced. Christianity, on the other hand, maintains that the universal problem facing every person is separation from God. According to Christianity, each person has rebelled against God by violating his commands (what the Bible calls sin). Christianity insists that there is no human solution to this problem. Only through a relationship with Jesus Christ can this problem of separation from God be overcome. Christians believe that Jesus Christ paid our sin-penalty through his death on the cross in order that our relationship with God might be restored.

These conflicting claims about the nature of the Ultimate, the fate of individuals at death, as well as the universal problem facing humanity are only a few of the conflicting assertions made by different religious traditions. These conflicts render implausible the claim that "all paths lead to the same destination." Perhaps the following will help illustrate why this is the case. Consider the following two statements:

- Northwestern University won the Big Ten championship in football in 1995.
- Northwestern University did not win the Big Ten championship in football in 1995.

It is obvious that both of the these statements cannot be correct at the same time. This self-evident truth is often referred to as the principle of "non-contradiction." This principle has a significant implication for our investigation. Two contradictory assertions cannot both be correct. Thus, if two religions make truth-claims which contradict each other, they cannot both be right. For example, when Hindus claim that there are many Gods and Jews claim that there in only one God, one of them must be wrong. In addition, when Muslims claim that each person lives only once and then faces judgement and Hindus claim that each person lives many lives determined by the law of Karma, one of them must be wrong.

One might agree, in principle, that religious traditions make conflicting claims yet still disagree with my conclusion regarding the significance of these conflicts. Instead, it might be argued that all this talk about conflicting "truth-claims" misunderstands the true nature of religious language. After all, religious language is highly symbolic. The Bible, for example, uses many anthropomorphisms to describe God (like King David's description of God as a shepherd who cares for his sheep). Thus, would it not be better to speak of differing metaphors rather than conflicting truth-claims?

Interpreting all religious language symbolically does avoid the problem of conflicting truth-claims, however, only at a very high price. Claiming that all religious language is symbolic in order to eliminate all conflict is like sawing off one's arm to stop a finger from bleeding. It stops the bleeding, but only by creating a bigger problem. In order to demonstrate why this is the case I will comment briefly on the nature of religious language.

Just as an orchestral composition utilizes a wide array of musical instruments, so religious language utilizes a rich variety of literary genres including poetry, myth, history, and straightforward prose. Yet the reality that some religious language is highly symbolic does not negate the fact that religions make truth-claims. Instead, it suggests that religious truths come packaged in a variety of forms and that proper interpretation of religious language requires careful attention to the particular literary genre one is reading.

The critical question is this: Does religious language intend to describe realities which exist independent of our perception, or are statements such as "God exists" merely statements of a person's subjective emotional state? If religious statements—regardless of their particular genre—intend to describe realities which objectively exist, then they are subject to contradiction. If, on the other hand, all religious language is symbolic in such a way that religious statements cannot contradict one another, then it would seem religious language *does not* refer to anything which exists independent of us. This makes religious language little more than a commentary on our subjective psychological states.[2] Interestingly, this position is very similar to Sigmund Freud's view of religious language. In *Future of an Illusion* Freud wrote,

> These [religious ideas], which are given out as teachings, are not precipitates of experience or end-results of thinking: they are illusions, fulfillments of the oldest, strongest and most urgent wishes of mankind.... Thus the benevolent rule of a divine Providence allays our fear of the dangers of life....[3]

Freud believed that religious language was completely metaphorical. He claimed that statements—such as "God exists"—merely express certain psychological needs. The point is that one cannot consistently invoke the category of metaphor/symbolism to resolve the conflicting claims of different religions and maintain that Freud was wrong.

It will be helpful at this point to return to the parable of the three blind men and the elephant. Earlier we examined the possibility that religious traditions are like the three blind men who were attempting to describe the same elephant. Each of them described the same elephant differently. Are the religions of the world like the three blind men?

As appealing as this story is, it leaves one important question unanswered: How do we *know* the blind men were all describing the same elephant? What if the first blind man, while holding an oak tree, said, "I think an elephant is like the trunk of a great tree." Imagine the second blind man, while holding a fire hose, exclaimed, "No, you're wrong; an elephant is like a snake." What if the third blind man, while touching the side of the Sears Tower, asserted, "I think you are both wrong; an elephant is like a great wall." The critical problem with this story is that it assumes the very thing it allegedly proves—that all the blind men are touching an elephant. Yet how do we know the blind men are touching an elephant? Only because the story assumes it.

To take it a step further, what if each of the blind men made assertions about an (alleged) elephant which were not merely different, but contradictory? Would it still be plausible to believe they are all describing the same elephant? How much contradiction would be required in their accounts before it would become obvious that they were not describing the same elephant? A similar question can be asked of the claim that all paths lead to the same destination. How do we know all paths lead to the same destination? In light of the conflicting truth-claims of various religions it does not seem rational to believe that all paths lead to the same destination.

Option Two: All Paths Do Not Lead to the Same Destination

This bring us to our second alternative—all paths do not lead to the same destination. At first glance, this position may seem unreasonable. Isn't this type of claim incredibly intolerant? Second, isn't the real issue the sincerity of one's belief? Finally, even if only one path is "valid," how could it ever be identified? Before discussing these questions it will be helpful to examine the arguments offered in support of this position.

One strength of this position is that it takes the truth-claims of religious traditions seriously. It attempts to understand the beliefs of Buddhists, Hindus, Jews, Muslims and Christians in their proper context. This is a critical point. Option one—the claim that all paths lead to the same destination—can be rendered plausible only by radically reinterpreting the teachings of the various religious traditions so they no longer conflict.

Yet, the founders of many religious traditions made claims which they *knew* contradicted the claims of other religions. The Buddha, for example, rejected Hindu belief regarding the cause of *samsara* (the endless cycle of birth, death and rebirth). Moses, a key figure in Judaism, rejected the polytheism of the Canaanite nations that surrounded the nation of Israel and claimed that only one God, *Yahweh*, created the world and should be worshiped. In fact, certain portions of Moses' teaching in the *Pentateuch* are probably best understood as a polemic against the religious beliefs of the surrounding Canaanite nations. Muhammad, the founder of Islam, rejected the polytheism to which he was exposed in sixth century Arabia. Jesus Christ, the founder of Christianity, claimed, "I am the way the truth and the life. No one comes to the father but through me." (John 14:6) In other words, these religious founders knew that certain claims they made contradicted the claims of other religions.

Our second option begins with the observation that every religion makes truth-claims about the nature of an ultimate reality (whether God, Brahman, Nirvana), the origin of humanity, the fate of humanity at death, and the path to salvation or liberation. The fact that religions make such claims has a significant entailment. As we have already seen, when two religions make claims which contradict each other, they cannot both be correct. The laws of logic necessitate this.

Not everyone, however, is persuaded that religions make truth-claims.[4] To clarify this issue it will be helpful to examine a distinction philosopher Mortimer Adler makes in his book *Truth in Religion*. Adler distinguishes what he calls "matters of truth" and "matters of taste."[5] It will be easiest to illustrate Adler's distinction through the following statements:

- Carmen's has the best stuffed pizza in the city of Chicago.
- *Star Trek* is my favorite television show.
- The Cubs are my favorite baseball team.

Adler would categorize these statements as matters of taste. Consider, however, the following statements:

- The University of Michigan is a member of the Big Ten conference.
- [George W. Bush] is currently president of the United States.
- John F. Kennedy was assassinated in Dallas, Texas.

Adler would describe these statements as matters of truth. Adler claims that matters of truth require us to make a decision anytime the "mass of evidence or weight of reasons point in one direction rather than another . . ."[6] Adler's helpful distinction raises the following question: What kinds of claims do religious traditions make? Are the claims of religion merely matters of taste, or, are they *also* matters of truth? Consider the following claims of Christianity:

- Jesus Christ was a Jew who lived in Palestine during the early part of the first century.
- Jesus was executed by Roman soldiers on a cross about 30 A.D.

- Jesus rose from the dead, three days after his death, and appeared to over five-hundred witnesses.

While one might argue over truthfulness of these assertions, one cannot deny the fact that these claims fall in the category of matters of truth.

Several objections are typically raised against the claim that all paths do not lead to the same destination. First, it is argued that such a position is narrow and intolerant. Second, it is frequently suggested that truth is really not that important and that what really matters is the sincerity of one's belief. Third, even if one path is valid and others are not, it is argued that there is no way to know which path is "true," that is there are no neutral criteria which can be used to evaluate religious traditions. I will examine each of these objections.

1. Tolerance is a buzz-word of the nineties. We are frequently reminded that we should be tolerant of those with whom we disagree. Who can argue with this? It is certainly preferable to the other alternatives. World history is replete with the consequences of religious bigotry—holy wars, religious crusades, inquisitions, etc. Activities like these, carried out under the banner of religion, are morally reprehensible. Hence, it is important that we continue to work to create a world where there is greater religious freedom.

   Nevertheless, it is important that tolerance not be confused with truthfulness. My alma mater, the University of Michigan, won the NCAA championship in basketball in 1989. Imagine a Duke fan, who heard me claim that Michigan won the championship in 1989, replied, "Well that is an incredibly intolerant thing to say!" This response is, at best, confusing and blurs an important distinction. Does this statement mean that my communication style is kindness impaired or that my assertion is false? Being a zealous Michigan fan it is possible I was obnoxious, however, the way in which I communicate a statement must be carefully distinguished from its truthfulness.

   Similarly, when examining the claims of religious traditions we must be careful not to confuse tolerance and truthfulness. Claiming that it is intolerant to say that "all paths do not lead to the same destination" misses the point. The important issue is the truth or falsity of this assertion.

2. A second objection relates to the matter of sincerity. Someone may say, "What a person believes really is not that important. What really matters is the sincerity of their belief." Certainly sincerity is important. However, the sincerity with which one holds a particular belief must be carefully distinguished from its truthfulness. To illustrate this distinction, imagine that you are in a chemistry lab. Your professor announces that your first experiment will involve studying the properties of acids. She places a 500ml Pyrex beaker containing clear liquid on the lab table and says, "This is sulfuric acid." In response to her explanation, imagine that your lab partner, Jim, blurts out, "I don't believe that is sulfuric acid. It looks like water to me." Jim, you discover, is so sincere

about his belief that the Pyrex beaker contains water that he decides to drink it.

What will happen to Jim? Obviously, he will be lucky if he lives long enough to participate in next week's lab once the sulfuric acid finishes off his digestive tract. Despite his sincerity, Jim's belief that the beaker contained water did not change the nature of its contents. He may believe with all of his heart that the beaker only contains water but the acid will still kill him. One's belief about an object (or state of affairs) must be carefully distinguished from the actual object or state of affairs. One may be sincere and yet sincerely wrong.

3. A third objection relates to the problem of objectivity. Even if one re-ligion is true, and others are false, it is suggested there are no neutral criteria by which one can evaluate religious traditions. If, for example, you ask a Muslim why he rejects Hinduism he will say that it does not agree with the teachings of the Koran. Similarly, if a Buddhist is asked why he rejects Christianity, he will say that it does not square with the teachings of the Buddha.

While it is true that adherents of one tradition may reject the teachings of other religions because they fail to cohere with their own teachings, it does not follow from this that there are no criteria which can be used to evaluate religious traditions. I believe that there are at least five "tradition-independent" criteria.[7] These include (1) logical consistency, (2) adequate factual support, (3) experiential relevance, (4) consistency with other fields of knowledge, and (5) moral factors.[8] These criteria are relevant to the evaluation of any theory— whether it be historical, scientific or religious.

At the beginning of this essay I raised the question, "Do all paths lead to same destination?" Our brief examination of the truth-claims of religious traditions such as Buddhism, Hinduism, Christianity, Islam and Judaism has produced no evidence to suggest that all paths lead to the same destination. On the contrary, the mutually exclusive truth-claims [of] different religions suggest precisely the opposite. Hence, if I am to be intellectually honest, I believe the answer to the question I raised at the beginning of the essay is no—all paths do not lead to the same destination. Consequently it is our responsibility to examine the paths before us and make an informed choice.

A Postscript . . .

Some will find my conclusion unsettling. Faced with a myriad of religions, where does one begin? Perhaps I can offer my own experience. From my study of the Christian faith I am persuaded of the truthfulness of its claims. Although I grew up in a Christian family, my personal study began as a freshman at the University of Michigan. I found myself asking a lot of questions such as "How do I know God exists?" "Can I trust the Bible?" Over the course of that year I carefully read much of the New Testament. I was surprised to discover that Christianity provides criteria by which its truth-claims can be evaluated. Permit me to explain.

The central claim of Christianity is that God entered human history 2000 years ago through a man named Jesus Christ who died on a cross between two thieves and rose from the dead three days later. The truthfulness of Christianity depends upon a critical historical event—the resurrection of Jesus Christ from the dead. In a first-century letter to a group of Christians the apostle Paul wrote the following about the significance of Christ's resurrection: "If Christ has not been raised, our preaching is useless and so is your faith." (I Cor. 15:14) In other words, if Christ did not rise from the dead, then Christianity is false.

Thus, to disprove Christianity one would only need to show Christ was never raised from the dead. Some years ago a skeptic of Christianity named Josh McDowell set out to do precisely this. He wanted to write a book that would refute Christianity. In his book *Evidence that Demands a Verdict* he writes,

> After more than 700 hrs of studying this subject, and thoroughly investigating its foundation, I have come to the conclusion that the resurrection of Jesus Christ is one the most wicked, vicious, heartless hoaxes ever foisted upon the minds of men, or it is the most fantastic fact of history.[9]

As a skeptic of Christianity Josh McDowell not only found the evidence for Christ's resurrection from the dead compelling, but himself became a follower of Jesus Christ. Because Christianity offers criteria by which its truth-claims can be evaluated, this makes it a great place to start one's investigation. Perhaps the best way to begin examining Christianity is to carefully study the four biographical accounts of Christ's life found in the New Testament (Matthew, Mark, Luke, and John).

Notes

1. See John Hick, *An Interpretation of Religion: Human Responses to the Transcendent* (New Haven: Yale, 1989). Space considerations do not permit me to interact with Hick's pluralistic hypothesis. For an evaluation of Hick's hypothesis see Harold A. Netland, *Dissonant Voices: Religious Pluralism and the Question of Truth* (Grand Rapids: Eerdmanns, 1991), 196–233.

2. It is also worth noting that viewing religious language in this way involves a radical reinterpretation of religious language that the adherents of most religious traditions would find unacceptable. Even if some adherents hold that religious beliefs express, in a metaphorical way, their subjective emotional states, certainly not all adherents do. Many, I suspect, believe that their religious doctrines intend to describe objective realities.

3. Sigmund Freud. *The Future of an Illusion*, trans. W. D. Robson-Scott, rev. James Strachey (New York: Doubleday, 1964), 47–48.

4. Oxford scholar Don Cupitt, for example, claims that the truth of religion is like the truth of art. See Don Cupitt, "The Death of Truth," *New Statesman*, April 5, 1991, 23–24.

5. Mortimer J. Adler, *Truth in Religion: The Plurality of Religions and the Unity of Truth* (New York: MacMillan, 1990), 2–5.

6. Ibid., 3.

7. This is not to suggest the evaluation of religious truth-claims is an easy task. Many complicated epistemological issues arise when one attempts to demonstrate the truthfulness of religious beliefs. Nevertheless, I do believe it is possible to provide warrant for religious truth-claims. For a helpful discussion of issues related to providing warrant for truth-claims in religion see Basil Mitchell, *The Justification of Religious Belief.* New York: Seabury, 1973.

8. A discussion of these criteria is outside the scope of this article, however, others have discussed them in detail as they relate to the evaluation of religious traditions. See Harold A. Netland, Dissonant Voices: Religious Pluralism and the Question of Truth (Grand Rapids: Eerdmanns, 1991), 151–95.

9. Josh McDowell, *Evidence That Demands a Verdict: Historical Evidences for the Christian Faith,* rev. ed. (San Bernardino: Here's Life, 1979), 179.

Whatever Path Men Choose Is Mine

For many of us in the West the relation between Christianity and the other world religions has until recently been a rather theoretical issue to which rather theoretical responses have seemed sufficient. We have lived within the cultural borders of Christendom and—many of us—within the ecclesiastical borders of the Church. From this centre we—that is, our forebears, and still the church today—have been sending out missionaries into all the continents of the earth, and have enjoyed a vague sense that the world is, however tardily, in process of becoming Christianized. And so we have in the past generally thought of the non-Christian world in negative terms, as the unfortunate not-yet-Christianized portion of humanity and as potential recipients of the divine grace which is coming through the evangelists whom we send out to them.

However, several things have happened to shatter this attitude of religious imperialism.

One has been the growing awareness, produced by the news media and by travel, of the sheer size and religious variety of mankind outside our own Anglo-Saxon tribe. The estimated Christian population of the world is 983.6 million, constituting just under a quarter of the world's total population of 4123.9 million (*Encyclopedia Britannica 1978 Book of the Year*, p. 616). But whilst the total number of Christians is slowly rising, the proportion of Christians is slowly declining, because the explosion in the human population (the number of which will have roughly doubled between 1970 and about 2005) is taking place more rapidly outside Christendom than within it. Thus the Christian faith is held today, as in the past, only by a minority of the human race; and it looks as though this minority may well be smaller rather than larger in the future. This thought casts a massive shadow over any assumption that it is God's will that all mankind shall be converted to the Christian faith.

Again, it is a fact evident to ordinary people (even though not always taken into account by theologians) that in the great majority of cases—say, 98 or 99 per cent—the religion in which a person believes and to which he adheres depends upon where he was born. That is to say, if someone is born to Muslim parents in Egypt or Pakistan, that person is very likely to be a Muslim; if to Buddhist parents in Sri Lanka or Burma, that person is very likely to be a Buddhist; if to Hindu parents in India, that person is very likely to be a Hindu; if to Christian

From John Hick, "Whatever Path Men Choose Is Mine," in Richard J. Plantinga, ed., *Christianity and Plurality: Classic and Contemporary Readings* (Blackwell Publishers Ltd., 1999). Originally published in J. Hick and B. Hebblethwaite, eds., *Christianity and Other Religions: Selected Readings* (HarperCollinsPublishers, 1980). Copyright © 1980 by John Hick. Reprinted by permission of the author.

parents in Europe or the Americas, that person is very likely to be a Christian. Of course in each case he may be a fully committed or a merely nominal adherent of his religion. But whether one is a Christian, a Jew, a Muslim, a Buddhist, a Sikh, a Hindu—or for that matter a Marxist or a Maoist—depends nearly always on the part of the world in which one happens to have been born. Any credible religious faith must be able to make sense of this circumstance. And a credible Christian faith must make sense of it by relating it to the universal sovereignty and fatherhood of God. This is rather conspicuously not done by the older theology which held that God's saving activity is confined within a single narrow thread of human life, namely that recorded in our own scriptures.

Another factor making for change is that the old unflattering caricatures of other religions are now being replaced by knowledge based on serious objective study. Our bookshops now carry shelves of good popular as well as technical works on the history of religion, the phenomenology of religion, and the comparative study of religions; and only one who prefers to be ignorant can any longer complacently congratulate himself upon knowing nothing about other faiths. It is no longer acceptable to plead ignorance concerning the wide religious life of mankind as an excuse for parochial theological prejudices. Times have changed and today no one wishes to present the eighteenth-century image of Fielding's Parson Thwackum who said, "When I mention religion, I mean the Christian religion; and not only the Christian religion, but the Protestant religion; and not only the Protestant religion, but the Church of England."

And, perhaps most importantly of all, since the 1950s Asian immigration from India, Pakistan and (as it now is) Bangladesh has brought sizeable Muslim, Hindu and Sikh communities to many of our cities, adding three more non-Christian groups to the Jews who had already been there for more than two centuries. By their very existence these non-Christian communities presented the Church with a number of new questions, which it has generally chosen to see as difficult problems. Should we try to help the Muslims, Sikhs and Hindus to find suitable premises in which to worship? Should we be willing to sell them redundant church buildings? Should local religious broadcasting include or exclude them? Should we try to insist that all children in the state schools shall receive Christian religious instruction, regardless of the religion which they or their parents profess? And so on. These questions all have theological implications, and have helped to turn the attention of Christians to the problem of the relation of Christianity to the other world religions.

When you visit the various non-Christian places of worship in one of our big cities you discover—possibly with a shock of surprise—that phenomenologically (or in other words, to human observation) the same kind of thing is taking place in them as in a Christian church. That is to say, human beings are coming together to open their minds to a higher reality, which is thought of as the personal creator and Lord of the universe, and as making vital moral demands upon the lives of men and women. Of course the trappings are very different —in a church men wear shoes and no hat; in mosque, gurdwara and temple, a hat and no shoes; in a synagogue, both. In some you sit on a pew, in others on the floor. In some there is singing, in others there is not. Different musical instruments or none are used. More importantly, the supreme being is referred to as God in a Christian church, as Adonai in a Jewish synagogue, as Allah in a Muslim mosque, as Param Atma in a Sikh gurdwara, as Rama or as Krishna in a Hindu temple. And yet there is an important sense in which what is being done in the several forms of worship is essentially the same.

In the Jewish synagogue God is worshipped as maker of heaven and earth and the God of Abraham and Isaac and Jacob, who led the children of Israel out of Egypt into the promised land and who has called them to live as a light to lighten the world. Worship is very close in form and ethos to Christian worship in the Protestant traditions. Here is a passage of typical Jewish prayer:

> With a great love have You loved us, O Lord our God, and with exceeding compassion have You pitied us. Our Father and King, our fathers trusted in You, and You taught them the laws of life: be gracious also to us, and teach us. Have compassion upon us, and guide us, our Merciful Father, that we may grasp and understand, learn and teach, observe and uphold with love all the words of Your law.

In Muslim mosques God is worshipped as the maker of heaven and earth, and as the sovereign Lord of the Universe, omnipotent, holy and merciful, before whom men bow in absolute submission. Here is a typical passage of Muslim prayer:

> Praise be to God, Lord of creation,
> Source of all livelihood, who orders the morning.
> Lord of majesty and honour, of grace and beneficence.
> He who is so far that he may not be seen and so near that he
>   witnesses the secret things.
> Blessed be He and for ever exalted.

. . . In the light of the phenomenological similarity of worship in these different traditions we have to ask whether people in church, synagogue, mosque, gurdwara and temple are worshipping different Gods or are worshipping the same God? Are Adonai and God, Allah and Param Atma, Rama and Krishna different Gods, or are these different names for the same ultimate Being?

There would seem to be three possibilities. One is that there exist, ontologically, many gods. But this conflicts with the belief concerning each that he is the creator or the source of the world. A second possibility is that one faith-community, let us say our own, worships God whilst the others vainly worship images which exist only in their imaginations. But even within Christianity itself, is there not a variety of overlapping mental images of God—for example, as stern judge and predestinating power, and as gracious and loving heavenly Father—so that different Christian groups, and even different Christian individuals, are worshipping the divine Being through their different images of him? And do not the glimpses which I have just offered of worship within the various religious traditions suggest that our Christian images overlap with many non-Christian images of God? If so, a third possibility must seem the most probable, namely that there is but one God, who is maker and lord of all; that in his infinite fullness and richness of being he exceeds all our human attempts to grasp him in thought; and that the devout in the various great world religions are in fact worshipping that one God, but through different, overlapping concepts or mental images of him.

If this is so, the older Christian view of other faiths as areas of spiritual darkness within which there is no salvation, no knowledge of God, and no acceptable worship must be mistaken. This older view, which few still entertain in practice today, was enshrined in the traditional Roman Catholic dogma, *extra ecclesiam nulla salus* (outside the Church no salvation). To quote a classic utterance from this point of view, the Council of Florence in 1438–45 declared that "no one remaining outside the Catholic Church, not just pagans, but also Jews or heretics or schismatics, can become partakers of eternal life; but they will go to the everlasting fire which was prepared for the devil and his angels, unless before the end of life they are joined to the church". The Protestant missionary equivalent, which likewise is entertained by few today, is the doctrine that outside Christianity there is no salvation. As a fairly recent expression of this, the Congress on World Mission at Chicago in 1960 declared, "In the years since the war, more than one billion souls have passed into eternity and more than half of these went to the torment of hell fire without even hearing of Jesus Christ, who He was, or why He died on the cross of Calvary."

This older view has come to seem increasingly implausible and unrealistic in the light of growing knowledge of other faiths and as a result of better contacts with their adherents. Consequently Christian theologians, perhaps most notably within the Roman communion, have been making strenuous efforts to escape from the unacceptable implications of the older view, though usually without feeling entitled explicitly to renounce it. . . .

Or again there is Karl Rahner's notion of the anonymous Christian. The devout Muslim, or Hindu, or Sikh, or Jew can be regarded as an anonymous Christian, this being an honorary status granted unilaterally to people who have not expressed any desire for it. Or again there is the claim that Christianity, properly understood, is not a religion but is a revelation which judges and supersedes all religions. Or finally there is Hans Küng's distinction between the ordinary way of salvation in the world religions and the extraordinary way in the Church. Küng says, "A man is to be saved within the religion that is made available to him in his historical situation. Hence it is his right and duty to seek God within that religion in which the hidden God has already found him." Thus the world religions are, he says, "the way of salvation in universal salvation history; the general way of salvation, we can even say, for the people of the world religions: the more common, the 'ordinary' way of salvation, as against which the way of salvation in the Church appears as something very special and extraordinary". This sounds at first extremely promising. However, Küng goes on to take away with one hand what he has given with the other. The ordinary way of salvation for the majority of mankind in the world religions turns out to be only an interim way until, sooner or later, they come to an explicit Christian faith. The people of the world religions are, he says, "pre-Christian, directed towards Christ. . . . The men of the world religions are not professing Christians but, by the grace of God, they are called and marked out to be Christians." One is reminded of the British amnesty for illegal immigrants. Although they are unauthorized entrants into the Kingdom of Heaven, the Indian and Pakistani and other foreign worshippers of God will be accepted if sooner or later they come forward to be legally registered by Christian baptism!

Thus all of these thinkers, who are trying so hard to find room for their non-Christian brethren in the sphere of salvation, are still working within the presuppositions of the old dogma. Only Christians can be saved; so we have to say that devout and godly non-Christians are really, in some metaphysical sense, Christians or Christians-to-be without knowing it. Although to the ordinary non-ecclesiastical mind this borders upon double-talk, yet in intention it is a charitable extension of the sphere of grace to people who had formerly been regarded as beyond the pale. As such it can function as a psychological bridge between the no longer acceptable older view and the new view which is emerging. But sooner or later we have to get off the bridge on to the other side. We have to make what might be called a Copernican revolution in our theology of religions. You will remember that the old Ptolemaic astronomy held that the earth is the centre of the solar system and that all the other heavenly bodies revolve around it. And when it was realized that this theory did not fit the observed facts, particularly the wandering movements of the planets, epicycles were added, circles revolving on circles to complicate the theory and bring it nearer to the facts. By analogy the "no salvation outside Christianity" doctrine is theologically Ptolemaic. Christianity is seen as the centre of the universe of faiths, and all the other religions are regarded as revolving round it and as being graded in value according to their distance from it. And the theories of implicit faith, baptism by desire, anonymous Christianity, the latent Church, the "ordinary" and "extraordinary" ways of salvation, and the claim that the Christian religion is not a religion whereas all the others are, are so many epicycles added to this Ptolemaic theology to try to accommodate our growing knowledge of other faiths and our awareness of the true piety and devotion which they sustain.

It is worth noting that just as a Ptolemaic astronomy could be developed, not only from the standpoint of this earth, but from any of the other planets, so also a Ptolemaic theology can be developed not only from a Christian standpoint but equally from the standpoint of any other faith. From, let us say, a Hindu centre one could say that devout Christians are implicit Hindus in virtue of their sincere desire for the truth even though they do not yet know what the truth is; that other faiths provide the "ordinary way" of salvation whilst Hinduism is the "extraordinary" way, in which the truth is manifest which in the others is latent; that Hinduism is not a religion but the eternal truth judging and superseding all religions. The Ptolemaic stance can be taken by anyone. But it can only serve as an interim position whilst we prepare our minds for a Copernican revolution. Copernicus realized that it is the sun, and not the earth, that is at the centre, and that all the heavenly bodies, including our own earth, revolve around it. And we have to realize that the universe of faiths centres upon *God,* and not upon Christianity or upon any other religion. He is the sun, the originative source of light and life, whom all the religions reflect in their own different ways.

This must mean that the different world religions have each served as God's means of revelation to and point of contact with a different stream of human life. Such a conclusion makes sense of the history of religions. The first period was one in which the innate religiousness of the human mind expressed itself in the different forms of what we can call natural religion—the worship of spirits, ancestors, nature gods, and often bloodthirsty national deities. But about 900 or 800 B.C. there began what Karl Jaspers has called the axial period in which seminal moments of religious experience occurred in each of the four principal centres of civilization—Greece, the Near East, India, and China—out of which the higher religions have come. In this immensely rich and important band of time the great Hebrew prophets lived; in Persia, Zoroaster; in China, Confucius and the author (or authors) of the Taoist Scriptures; in India, the Buddha, and Mahavira, and the writers of the Upanishads and of the Bhagavad Gita; in Greece, Pythagoras, Socrates and Plato. And then later, out of the stream of prophetic religion established by the Hebrew prophets there came Jesus and the rise of Christianity, and Mohammad and the rise of Islam.

Now in this axial period, some two and a half thousand years ago, communication between the continents and civilizations of the earth was so slow that for all practical purposes men lived in different cultural worlds. There could not be a divine revelation, through any human means, to mankind as a whole, but only separate revelations within the different streams of human history. And so it is a natural and indeed an inevitable hypothesis that God, the ultimate divine reality, was in this axial period revealing his presence and his will to mankind through a number of specially sensitive and responsive spirits. In each case the revelatory experiences, and the religious traditions to which they gave rise, were conditioned by the history, culture, language, climate, and indeed all the concrete circumstances of human life at that particular time and place. Thus the cultural and philosophical form of the revelation of the divine is characteristically different in each case, although we may believe that everywhere the one divine Spirit has been at work, pressing in upon the human spirit.

I shall return presently to this historical view of the different religious traditions to ask what difference it makes that the world has now become a communicational unity. But let me first ask the question that is so important to us as Christians, namely, what does all this imply concerning the person of our Lord? What about the uniqueness of Christ, the belief that Jesus was God Incarnate, the second Person of the Holy Trinity become man, the eternal Logos made flesh? Did he not say, "I and the Father are one", and "No one comes to the Father, but by me"? Here, unfortunately, we have to enter the realm of New Testament criticism: and I say "unfortunately" because of the notorious uncertainties of this realm. There are powerful schools of thought, following fashions which tend to change from generation to generation, but no consensus either across the years or across the schools. But this at least can be said: that whereas until some three or four generations ago it was generally accepted among biblical scholars that Jesus claimed to be the Son of God, with a unique consciousness of oneness with the Heavenly Father, so that the doctrine of the Incarnation was believed to be firmly based in the consciousness and teaching of Jesus himself, today this is no longer generally held and is indeed very widely thought not to be the case. I am not going to enter into a detailed discussion of the New Testament evidence: I am neither competent to do this, nor is there time. I will only quote some summarizing words of Wolfhart Pannenberg in his massive work, *Jesus: God and Man* (SCM Press, London, 1968), where he says that "After D. F. Strauss and F. C. Bauer, John's Gospel could no longer be claimed uncritically as a historical source of authentic words of Jesus. Consequently, other concepts and titles that were more indirectly connected with Jesus's relation to God came into the foreground of the question of Jesus's 'Messianic self-consciousness'. However, the transfer of these titles to Jesus ... has been demonstrated with growing certainty by critical study of the Gospels to be the work of the post-Easter community. Today it must be taken as all but certain that the pre-Easter Jesus neither designated himself as Messiah (or Son of God) nor accepted such a confession to him from others" (p. 327). Not all New Testament scholars would endorse Pannenberg's words. But certainly one can no longer regard it as a fact proved out of the New Testament that Jesus thought of himself as God Incarnate. On the contrary, this now seems to be very unlikely. And certainly we cannot rest anything on the assumption that the great Christological sayings of the Fourth Gospel (such as "I and my Father are one") were ever spoken, in sober historical fact, by the Jesus who walked the hills and villages of Galilee. It seems altogether more probable that they reflect the developing theology of the Church at about the end of the first century.

Now if Jesus himself did not think of himself as God Incarnate, one might well ask whether his disciples ought to do so....

When we see the Incarnation as a mythological idea applied to Jesus to express the experienced fact that he is our sufficient, effective and saving point of contact with God, we no longer have to draw the negative conclusion that he is man's one and only effective point of contact with God. We can revere Christ as the one through whom we have found salvation, without having to deny other points of reported saving contact between God and man. We can commend the way of Christian faith without having to discommend other ways of faith. We can say that there is salvation in Christ without having to say that there is no salvation other than in Christ.

Let us return, finally, to the historical situation. We have seen that the great world religions arose within different streams of human life and have in the past flowed down the centuries within different cultural channels. They have until recently interacted with one another only spasmodically, and nearly always in hostile clashes rather than in mutual dialogue and friendly interpenetration. But latterly this situation has been changing radically. Since the late nineteenth century there has been a positive influence of Christianity upon Hinduism, bearing fruit in a new social concern in India; and an influence of both Hinduism and Buddhism upon Christianity, bearing fruit in the new Western appreciation of meditation and the arts of spiritual self-development. And today the world religions are increasingly in contact with one another in conscious dialogue and in deliberate attempts to learn about and to learn from one another. These mutual influences can only increase in the future. It is I think very important to notice that each of the world religions is in practice an on-going history of change. Each likes to think of itself as immutable, the same yesterday, today and for ever. But the historian can see that this is not so. Each of the major world faiths has gone through immense historical developments, revolutions and transformations. Each has experienced both times of rapid change, in sudden expansions, schisms, reformations and renaissances, and also periods of relative stability. Islam has perhaps changed less than the others; but even within Islam there have been immense evolutionary developments and also the growth of important divisions. Hinduism has always been able to change, and to absorb new influences into its own life. Christianity and Buddhism have both developed through the centuries almost out of recognition. And in each case there is in principle no limit to the further developments that may take place in the future. In the next period these will occur in a context of interaction. The future of Christianity will be formed partly by influences stemming from Hinduism, Buddhism, and Islam; and so also, in a mutually interactive system, with the other world faiths. And all partly also by influences stemming from the secular civilization within which they will all exist.

Can we peer into the future and anticipate the pattern of development? Obviously, in trying to do so we are guessing. However, such guessing is today dignified by the name of Futurology and large books are written about the state of the planet in, say, the year 2000. These speculations are not random guesses, but are based on the projection of present trends, together with the foreseeable emergence of new trends. If secular seers can speculate in these ways about the future of man, why should we not try to consider the forms which the religious life of mankind will take in, say, a hundred years' time if the present basic trends continue? I am making the very major assumption, which there is no time here to defend, that man's religiousness is innate and that religion will continue in some form so long as human nature remains essentially the same. But what forms will it take? The broad trend of the present century is ecumenical. Old divisions are being transcended. The deeper essentials in which people agree are tending to seem more important than the matters on which they differ. Projecting this trend into the future we may suppose that the ecumenical spirit which has already so largely transformed Christianity will increasingly affect the relations between the world faiths. There may well be a growing world ecumenism, in which the common commitment of faith in a higher spiritual reality which demands brotherhood on earth will seem more and more significant, whilst the differences between the religious traditions will seem proportionately less significant. The relation between them may thus become somewhat like that between the Christian denominations in Britain—that is to say, they are on increasingly friendly speaking terms; they freely visit one another's worship and are beginning to be able to share places of worship; they co-operate in all sorts of service to the community; their clergy are accustomed to meet together for discussion, and there is even a degree of interchange of ministries; and so on.

What we are picturing here as a future possibility is not a single world religion, but a situation in which the different traditions no longer see themselves and each other as rival ideological communities. A single world religion is, I would think, never likely, and not a consummation to be desired. For so long as there is a variety of human types there will be a variety of kinds of worship and a variety of theological emphases and approaches. There will always be the more mystical and the more prophetic types of faith, with their corresponding awareness of the ultimate Reality as non-personal and as personal. There will always be the more spontaneous, warm and Spirit-filled forms of devotion, and the more liturgical, orderly and rationally controlled forms. There will always be the more vivid consciousness of the divine as gracious love, and as infinite demand and judgement, and so on. But it is not necessary, and it may in a more ecumenical age not be felt to be necessary, to assume that if God is being truly worshipped by Christians he cannot also be being truly worshipped by Jews and Muslims and Sikhs and by theistic Hindus and Amida Buddhists; or even that if the Ultimate Divine Reality is being validly experienced within the theistic streams of religious life as a personal presence, that Reality may not also be validly experienced within other streams of religious life as the infinite Being-Consciousness-bliss (*Satchitananda*) of some forms of Hinduism, or as the ineffable cosmic Buddha-nature (the *Dharmakaya*) of some forms of Buddhism.

Let me then end with a quotation from one of the great revelatory scriptures of the world: "Howsoever man may approach me, even so do I accept them; for, on all sides, whatever path they may choose is mine."

POSTSCRIPT

Is There Only One Way to Receive Salvation?

Two Iranian scholars were discussing religion. One of them asked the other, "In the last analysis, who goes to paradise?" The other, a poet well known for his sense of humor, answered, "Well, it is really very simple. First, all religions other than Islam are obviously false, so we do not have to consider them. That leaves Islam. But among Muslims, some are Shi'ites and some Sunnis, and we all know that the Sunnis have strayed from the right path and will be thrown into hell. That leaves the Shi'ites. But among Shi'ites, there are the common people and the ulama. Everyone knows that the common people don't care about God and religion, so they will burn in the Fire. That leaves the ulama. But the ulama have become ulama in order to lord it over the common people. That leaves you and me. And I am not so sure about you."

— S. Murata and W. C. Chittick, *The Vision of Islam*
(Paragon House, 1994), p. 175

This humorous Shi'ite anecdote represents the view of salvation held by many people for whom religion is an important part of their lives. As we are confronted with the theological beliefs and religious practices of others, we can dogmatically dismiss them, be politically patronizing, or we can be sincere in our desire to allow all people to believe and worship "how, where, or what they may." Whether we are Shi'ites or Sikhs, Baptists or Buddhists, we walk a careful line when we consider salvation and its context. These two selections are just a beginning in the quest to answer a most important question.

Suggested Readings

E. L. Allen, *Christianity Among the Religions* (Beacon Press, 1960).

P. J. Griffiths, *Problems of Religious Diversity* (Blackwell, 2001).

J. Hick, *God Has Many Names* (Westminister John Knox, 1986).

D. L. Okholm and T. R. Phillips, eds., *Four Views on Salvation in a Pluralistic World* (Zondervan, 1996).

ISSUE 6

Is Acceptance of Christ Alone Sufficient for Salvation?

YES: Charles C. Ryrie, from *So Great Salvation: What It Means to Believe in Jesus Christ* (Moody Press, 1997)

NO: John F. MacArthur, Jr., from *Faith Works: The Gospel According to the Apostles* (Word Publishing, 1993)

ISSUE SUMMARY

YES: Charles C. Ryrie, former president and current professor at Philadelphia Biblical University, argues that "good works" are not in any way a part of salvation—salvation is obtained exclusively through the grace of Christ. While Ryrie believes that most people who accept Christ will manifest their acceptance of Him through good works, others will not.

NO: John F. MacArthur, Jr., president of The Master's College in Santa Clarita, California, and host of the *Grace to You* radio ministry, asserts that verbally accepting Christ is not sufficient for salvation. He believes that genuine acceptance of Christ is manifest through repentance and a sincere desire to live a moral life. MacArthur contends that those who have truly accepted Christ will manifest their commitment through their good works.

Christian tradition maintains that on the evening of October 31, 1517 (All Saints' Day Eve), Martin Luther nailed a document with 95 theses of protest to the front door of the Castle Church in Wittenberg, Germany. Luther, a Catholic monk, wrote his theses in Latin, hoping to spark a debate among Catholic theologians, but the document was quickly translated into German and distributed throughout the country. Chief among Luther's concerns was the Catholic practice of selling *indulgences*, which had been introduced during the Crusades. In theory, the selling of indulgences allowed people to avoid punishment for sin if they paid a certain amount of money or performed a righteous deed. Luther's *protest* (the origin of the word *Protestant*) against the practice of indulgences was based primarily on the idea that man's own actions, and not the grace of

Christ, were becoming understood as the means to mankind's salvation. Ironically, Luther believed that the practice of indulgences was for "lazy Christians who did not want to do good works."

Luther was excommunicated from the Catholic Church in 1521 primarily because he continued to emphasize the grace of Christ and not the works of man as a central tenet of salvation. What began as one man's attempt to reform the Catholic Church sparked what has now come to be known as the Protestant Reformation.

The controversy between works and grace has long been a debate among Christian churches. Those who side with the argument for grace often cite this Scripture from the writings of the apostle Paul:

> For by grace are ye saved through faith; and that not of yourselves: *it is* the gift of God: Not of works, lest any man should boast.

> — King James Version, Eph. 2:8–9

Those arguing for the importance of good works quote the following from the Epistle of James:

> Even so faith, if it hath not works, is dead, being alone. Yea, a man may say, Thou hast faith, and I have works: shew me thy faith without thy works, and I will shew thee my faith by my works.

> — KJV, James 2:17–18

It is interesting to note that Luther did not accept the Epistle of James as legitimate. He called it a "strawy epistle without any evangelical sense" as quoted in *Martin Luther: The Christian Between God and Death* (Harvard University Press, 1999).

The history of this debate between the importance of grace and the inclusion of works has continued from New Testament times to the present. What began with the writings of Paul and James continued with debates between Augustine and Pelagius, as well as Luther and the Catholic Church. With the following selections, the age-old controversy continues in a discussion that has come to be known as the debate over "Lordship salvation." Contemporary scholars Charles C. Ryrie and John F. MacArthur, Jr., take the pro and con positions.

Ryrie and those who are opposed to the "Lordship Salvation" perspective contend that even though many who accept Christ will show evidence of their faith by their works, others will not. Good works, from this perspective, are not a necessary part or manifestation of salvation.

MacArthur and other advocates of Lordship salvation assert that for people to receive salvation, they must not only accept Jesus Christ as their Savior but also as their Lord. By sincerely accepting Jesus Christ as Lord, he believes, their lives will genuinely reflect this relationship through their good works.

So Great Salvation

All Scripture quotations, unless indicated, are taken from the *New American Standard Bible*.

Scripture quotations marked NKJV are taken from the New King James Version.

Grace at Camp

Grace is a difficult, perhaps impossible, concept to understand.

In seminary days I had a job working with underprivileged junior-high and high-school kids at the downtown YMCA. On what was then the outskirts of Dallas was a camp we used every Friday night when weather permitted. We would load a bus with forty to fifty kids, head for the camp, and enjoy an evening cookout and games. On special occasions we would sleep there overnight and return Saturday afternoon. Overnight camping trips were usually rewards given to those who had successfully passed certain requirements in our weekly Bible clubs. So the kids who stayed overnight after the others went home were rather special.

One Friday night—or, more accurately, early one Saturday morning—I awoke, startled by some unexplained noise. Soon I discovered that a few of my leaders had sneaked out of the dorm, gone down to the lake, launched one of the boats, and were having a great time far from shore. Not only was this against every rule in the book, but it was dangerous. When the kids knew I knew where they were, they came immediately into shore. Like dogs with tails between their legs, they meekly went back to bed, wondering what punishment awaited them in the morning.

For me, sleep was now impossible. The night before, I had talked to these Christian young people about forgiving one another. So as I paced the grounds in those early-morning hours deliberating their fate, my own words from the night before kept coming back to me, and back to me, and back to me.

If I don't give them some punishment, I argued with myself, *they will never be impressed with the seriousness of what they did. I have a responsibility to the Y to enforce their rules and punish the violators.*

But the more I debated with myself, talked to the Lord, thought about a number of relevant Bible verses (I discovered again that night that you can prove almost anything with a Bible verse), the more Ephesians 4:32 grew larger and larger in my thinking: "Be kind to one another, tender-hearted, forgiving each other, just as God in Christ also has forgiven you."

But, Lord, I can't forgive them; they don't deserve it.

Neither did I.

But, Lord, I have to enforce the rules.

I'm glad, Lord, You didn't.

But, Lord, if I'm too kind, the kids will think I'm weak.

I never thought You were weak, only loving.

But, Lord, first I'll make them promise never to do something like this again, and then I'll forgive them.

It's a good thing You didn't require that of me, or I never would have been forgiven.

. . . just as God forgave me.

How was that? No conditions or promises ahead of time. No works at the time. No remembrance afterward.

But, Lord, You're God—You can do anything.

"You're My child," He said. "Imitate Me."

So with great reluctance and with very little faith, I told the Lord I would.

And then, in the morning, I told the kids.

"You did a terrible thing. It could have had disastrous consequences for yourselves, your families, the Y, and me. But I forgive you unconditionally and completely."

"You're kidding," they said. "There's got to be a catch somewhere."

"No," I insisted, "you are fully forgiven." And then I told them what the Lord had been saying to me that night about His grace, and how I wanted them to have another taste of that grace.

I didn't even make them do the cleaning up that day. I did it myself because I didn't want them to think they could earn even a little bit of that forgiveness.

The rest of the story? As long as those particular kids were in my clubs they were the epitome (as much as kids that age can be) of goodness, helpfulness, and usefulness. They never presumed on that grace.

Grace is indeed a difficult, perhaps impossible, concept to understand.

If it was difficult for those kids to understand an act of grace that forgave one sin on one night, how much more difficult for us to comprehend God's grace that forgives all our sins every day and night, without preconditions, without works, and without remembrance.

We can learn some important matters about grace from this experience.

First, grace is unmerited favor. As a concise definition of grace, this serves well. More elaborate definitions have their place; but simply stated, grace is unmerited favor. It is undeserved on the part of the recipient. It is unearned and unearnable. Those kids had no claim on my grace. They were in a state of total demerit. Anything I might do could not be in response to any merit they had (for they had none at that point) nor as a reward for anything they had done (they only deserved to be punished). My grace that night was pure unmerited favor.

Second, grace is not cheap. Grace is expensive. It is free to the recipient but costly to the donor. The only way one may say that grace is not very costly is if the particular benefit costs the donor very little. My forgiveness that night cost those kids nothing. It cost me a lot of agonizing and soul-searching, which is nothing in comparison with what grace cost our Lord. But to use the word *cheap* in the same breath with the grace of God in salvation seems almost blasphemous. It cost our Lord Jesus His life. Some may insult grace, reject it, trample on it, or disgrace it, but that does not lower its infinite value.

Third, it is not easy to believe someone who offers grace. Those kids were dumbfounded when I announced the verdict of grace. They could not believe what they were hearing. And why should they? From day one they had been reared (and so are we all) in a merit system, in which acceptance is based on performance. "Do this and you will be rewarded. Fail to do this and you will be punished." This kind of merit system permeates all of life and most religions. It is not easy to believe someone who says that he or she will do something good for us that we do not deserve.

Human works are like termites in God's structure of grace. They start small, but, if unchecked, they can bring down the entire structure. And what are such works? Anything I can do to gain any amount of merit, little or much. Water baptism could be one such work if I view it not as an important or even necessary result of being saved, but as a requisite to be saved. It is work even if I insist that it is God who gives me the desire to want to be baptized that I might be saved.

The same is true for surrender. If surrender is something I must do as a part of believing, then it is a work, and grace has been diluted to the extent to which I actually do surrender.

Fourth, grace that is received changes one's life and behavior. Those kids, though really not bad before that night, showed a number of changes in their lives. Their bond to me personally was much stronger. They followed me around like puppy dogs anxious to do whatever they could to please me. And they had new insight into the love of their Savior for them.

The Gospel is the good news of the grace of God to give forgiveness and eternal life. Let's keep that Gospel so full of grace that there is no room for anything else to be added to dilute or pollute the true grace of God....

Straw Men

Differences of opinion often create straw men. The reason is simple: Straw men are easy to demolish.

According to the dictionary, a straw man is "a weak or imaginary opposition (as an argument or adversary) set up only to be easily confuted."

In the contemporary discussion over the meaning of the Gospel and areas related to it, a number of straw men have been created. In reality these are spurious arguments often raised by proponents of a lordship salvation. Such arguments against those straw men seem more devastating. Realize that a straw man usually is not a total fabrication; it usually contains some truth, but truth that is exaggerated or distorted or incomplete. The truth element in a straw man makes it more difficult to argue against, while the distortion or incompleteness makes it easier to huff and puff and blow the man down.

[A]t this point in the discussion it may help to examine some of [the straw men] in order to clear the air and keep the discussion on realities, not figments.

Straw Man #1

The first straw man deals with the role of the intellect and knowledge in salvation. Simply stated, it is: *The Gospel is a sterile set of facts to which we need only give intellectual assent in order to be saved.*

This is the accusation leveled against those who do not hold to so-called lordship/discipleship/mastery salvation. They are accused of teaching that intellectual assent to a set of facts is sufficient for salvation. Sometimes this is labeled "decisional" salvation, for all one needs to do is make an intellectual decision confirmed perhaps by a formula prayer. No one can be saved, says the lordship position, "by a casual acceptance of the facts regarding Jesus Christ."[1]

What makes this a straw man are words like *sterile, intellectual assent,* and *casual.*

Facts are essential. In describing the Gospel he preached, Paul said it was "that Christ died for our sins according to the Scriptures, and that He was buried, and that He was raised on the third day according to the Scriptures" (1 Corinthians 15: 3–4). These historical and doctrinal facts are "of first importance" (v. 3), for without them there is no Gospel.

Do these basic facts about the Gospel require only a casual, academic, or intellectual acceptance in order for one to be saved? Not if one defines *faith* as the Greek dictionary does: to "be convinced of something" or to "give credence to." Specifically, to believe in the Gospel is "to put one's trust in" the Gospel.[2] Being convinced of something or putting one's trust in the Gospel could hardly be said to be a casual acceptance of something. When a person gives credence to the historical facts that Christ died and rose from the dead and the doctrinal fact that this was for his sins, he is trusting his eternal destiny to the reliability of those truths.

And that is as far from casual as anything could be.

So you see, the argument erected about the non-lordship view is nothing more than a straw man. With such telling words as *sterile* and *only intellectual assent,* opponents can more easily destroy this straw man. Make no mistake, non-lordship people do not say what straw man #1 alleges they say.

Straw Man #2

The second straw man deals with carnality in a believer's life. It is: *A carnal Christian is someone who is saved but who shows nothing of the outworking of his salvation. Or, a true believer can be carnal all of his Christian life and never produce fruit.*

What makes this a straw man are phrases like "shows nothing" or "all of his Christian life." That a Christian can be characterized as carnal cannot be denied, simply because the texts of 1 Corinthians 3: 1–3 says there were carnal believers at Corinth. Paul addresses these people as "brethren" and "babes in Christ" in verse 1 [NKJV], then he describes them as "men of flesh" and "fleshly" in verses 1 and 3. So there were carnal or fleshly Christians in Paul's day.

What characterizes such Christians? Paul says they walk as mere men (verse 3), that is, like unsaved people. That does not mean that they were in fact not believers; Paul addresses them as believers. But it does indicate that believers may live like unsaved people. To be sure, Christians are not supposed to live like unsaved people, but the reality is that some do.

For how long? More than a moment or a day or a month or a year? When Paul wrote 1 Corinthians, those believers were four to five years old in the faith, and obviously some of them were still carnal or fleshly. Yet Paul expected that by that time they should have matured to the point where he could address them as spiritual.

At this point, one of those "what if" questions will inevitably be asked. What if a true believer seems to live like an unsaved person all of his life? Is he really a believer? Can a believer be carnal all of his life? Or, to phrase it another way, can a believer remain a babe in Christ all his Christian life? If the answer is no, then two options follow. Either such a person was not in fact a believer, or he was and lost that salvation because he did not grow out of spiritual babyhood.

But as long as we are asking "what if" questions, let's ask another. What if one or more of those babes in Christ in Corinth died between the time of conversion and the time Paul wrote 1 Corinthians? In other words, what if a babe in Christ at Corinth died before growing out of that baby state? Did he or she go to heaven? Assuming that such an individual *did* live all his (or her) Christian life in a baby state, if he *is* "in Christ," whether baby or mature, he will certainly be in heaven.

But let's be clear. Even if a believer could be characterized as carnal all of his life, that does not mean that he is carnal in all areas of life. Nor does that mean he will not bear some spiritual fruit during his life. Every believer will bear some fruit. . . .

This straw man eliminates the work, if not the presence, of the Holy Spirit in the life of a believer. As long as the Spirit lives within, no believer can show nothing of the work of salvation and thus be totally carnal all of his life.

Straw Man #3

The third straw man concerns the antiquity or recency of a teaching. *If something was taught by the early church, then it must be true. If a teaching is more recent, then its truthfulness is at least suspect, if not untrue.*

Christians can be carnal, living by and for their fleshly desires. . . . This teaching, however, is said to be new in this century, allegedly making it suspect, if not unbiblical. On the other hand, lordship and lordship-like statements by those who lived earlier in the history of the church must surely indicate that the lordship view is true.

Sometimes this straw man has a mate. Not only does the antiquity of a view make it truthful but also the number of people who held or hold it makes it true. The more the better to substantiate its truthfulness.

Of course, the smoke screen this straw man and its mate throw up can be easily dispelled. The fact that something was taught in the first century does not make it right (unless taught in the canonical Scriptures), and the fact that something was not taught until the nineteenth or twentieth century does not make it wrong, unless, of course, such teaching is clearly unscriptural. Baptismal regeneration was taught in the early centuries, but it is wrong. The majority of the church doesn't practice immersion. Does that make a belief in immersion wrong? Today, the majority of the church is not premillennial (believing in Christ's return for His church before His earthly reign). Does that make that doctrine wrong? The ransom-to-Satan theory regarding Christ's atonement (i.e., that in His death Christ paid a ransom to Satan) was taught in the early church. Does that make it right?

The antiquity or recency of a teaching and the number of people who are for or against it make for interesting study, but neither factor proves or disproves the truth of that teaching.

The charge of newness was leveled against the teachings of the Reformers. With characteristic straightforwardness, John Calvin responded to it this way:

> First, by calling it "new" they do great wrong to God, whose Sacred Word does not deserve to be accused of novelty.... That it has lain long unknown and buried is the fault of man's impiety. Now when it is restored to us by God's goodness, its claims to antiquity ought to be admitted at least by right of recovery.[3]

Straw Man #4

The fourth straw man underscores the need to represent accurately opposing viewpoints. *Quoting from someone exactly (as indicated by quotation marks around the quote) guarantees an accurate representation of what the person believes.* That is what proponents of lordship salvation sometimes do when they lift from context quotes by those who hold a position contrary to their own.

It is not difficult to extract a quotation from its context and make it seem to say what you wanted it to say rather than what the author intended it to say and what in fact it *does* say. That kind of straw man is easily demolished, especially if you quote something that seems ridiculous out of context.

The misuse of exact quotations has always made me very wary when writing book reviews. A good book review should evaluate a book from several aspects—what is good about it, what may have been omitted, what the reviewer disagrees with. Relatively few books I have reviewed in my lifetime have been totally and completely bad. Therefore, I try to point out in what areas the book will be helpful. But what often happens is that when the second edition of the book appears, the publisher will redo the dust jacket to include excerpts from published reviews. It goes without saying that the publisher will not publicize any detrimental comments. But in quoting only positive remarks from reviews, the reviewer's evaluation will be misrepresented and sometimes grossly so.

I reviewed a book some years ago and said that it filled "an important gap in our literature," that it "should be studied," and that "The publication of this book will be welcomed by evangelicals." But I also pointed out some of the author's basic presuppositions with which I disagreed and some of his exegesis which I thought to be wrong. What do you think the publisher quoted on the jacket to the second edition?

So be on guard. If for any reason you suspect that a quotation does not fairly represent what you think you know of someone's teaching, then check into it. It goes without saying that to misrepresent intentionally, even if quoting exactly, is unworthy of a Christian author or publisher.

Notes

1. John MacArthur, *The Gospel According to Jesus* (Grand Rapids: Zondervan, 1988), 179.
2. Arndt and Gingrich, *A Greek-English Lexicon of the New Testament* (Chicago: Univ. of Chicago, 1957), 666.
3. John Calvin, "Prefatory Address to King Francis," *Institutes of the Christian Religion,* 3.

NO

John F. MacArthur, Jr.

A Primer on the "Lordship Salvation" Controversy

All Scripture quotations in this book, except those noted otherwise, are from the New American Standard Bible.

❦

Beloved, while I was making every effort to write you about our common salvation, I felt the necessity to write to you appealing that you contend earnestly for the faith which was once for all delivered to the saints.

— Jude 3

"Why do you want to do another book on 'lordship salvation'?" a friend recently asked. "Hasn't that issue been beaten to death?"

I admit that a part of me echoes that sentiment. Originally I had no intention of writing a sequel to *The Gospel According to Jesus.* That book was in preparation for several years, and when I finally completed it I was eager to move on to something different. Although I felt there was much more that *could* be said, I was satisfied that the book adequately covered the subject. I was not trying to place myself at the nucleus of an ongoing debate. Most of all, I did not want the "lordship salvation" controversy to become the single focus of my ministry.

That was five years ago. Today I sense something of what Jude must have felt when he penned the verse quoted above. An urgent prompting in the deepest part of my soul constrains me to say more.

Is This Really a Crucial Issue?

A major reason for my concern has to do with some popular misconceptions that cloud the whole controversy. "Lordship salvation" has become the most talked about and least understood theological topic in evangelical Christendom. Nearly everyone seems to know *about* the debate; few truly understand the issues. It is easy to find strong opinions on both sides. But ferreting out people with genuine understanding is another matter. Many suppose the whole thing is a superficial conflict and the church would be better off if everyone forgot about it. One very well known Christian leader told me he had purposely avoided reading any books on the matter; he didn't want to be forced to take sides. Another told me the issue is unnecessarily divisive.

Yet this is not theological trivia. How we proclaim the gospel has eternal ramifications for non-Christians and defines who we are as Christians. Nor is the lordship question a theoretical or hypothetical problem. It raises several fundamental questions that have repercussions at the most practical level of Christian living.

How should we proclaim the gospel? Do we present Jesus to unbelievers as Lord, or as Savior only? What are the essential truths of the gospel message? What does it mean to be *saved?* How can a person know his or her faith is real? Can we have absolute assurance of salvation? What kind of transformation is accomplished in the new birth? How do we explain sin in the Christian's life? How far in sinning can a Christian go? What relationship is there between faith and obedience? Every area of Christian living is affected by one or more of those questions.

Of course, that's not to say the lordship discussion is purely pragmatic. A number of crucial doctrines have surfaced in the debate: dispensationalism, election, the *ordo salutis* ("order of salvation"), the relationship of sanctification and justification, eternal security, perseverance of the saints, and so on.

Don't be put off. You may not immediately recognize some of those terms or be able to define them all, but if you're a Christian, every one of them is important to you. You ought to have a basic understanding of what they mean and how they relate to Scripture and the gospel message. Doctrine is not the exclusive domain of seminary professors. All true Christians must be concerned with understanding sound doctrine. Doctrine properly understood can never be a merely academic pursuit. It is the discipline of discerning and digesting what God is saying to us in His Word so we can live lives that glorify Him. Doctrine forms the belief system that controls and compels behavior. What could be more practical—or more important?

Let's keep that perspective in mind as we approach this controversial topic. Do we disagree on doctrinal matters? Let's look together at what *God's Word* says. Theological systems, polemics, elegant rhetoric, or bombast and bravado may persuade some people, but not those who seek to know the mind of God. God's truth is revealed in His Word, and it is there we must ultimately go to settle this or any other doctrinal issue.

What Is "Lordship Salvation" All About?

The gospel call to faith presupposes that sinners must repent of their sin and yield to Christ's authority. That, in a sentence, is what "lordship salvation" teaches.

I don't like the term *lordship salvation.* I reject the connotation intended by those who coined the phrase. It insinuates that a submissive heart is extraneous or supplementary to saving faith. Although I have reluctantly used the term to describe my views, it is a concession to popular usage. Surrender to Jesus' lordship is not an addendum to the biblical terms of salvation; the summons to submission is at the heart of the gospel invitation throughout Scripture.

Those who criticize lordship salvation like to level the charge that we teach a system of works-based righteousness. Nothing could be further from the truth. Although I labored to make this as plain as possible in *The Gospel According to Jesus,* some critics continue to hurl that allegation. Others have imagined that I am advocating a new or modified doctrine of salvation that challenges the Reformers' teaching or radically redefines faith in Christ. Of course, my purpose is just the opposite.

Therefore, let me attempt to state the crucial points of my position as plainly as possible. These articles of faith are fundamental to all evangelical teaching:

- Christ's death on the cross paid the full penalty for our sins and purchased eternal salvation. His atoning sacrifice enables God to justify sinners freely without compromising the perfection of divine righteousness (Rom. 3:24–26). His resurrection from the dead declares His victory over sin and death (1 Cor. 15:54–57).
- Salvation is by grace through faith in the Lord Jesus Christ alone—plus and minus nothing (Eph. 2:8–9).
- Sinners cannot earn salvation or favor with God (Rom. 8:8).
- God requires of those who are saved no preparatory works or prerequisite self-improvement (Rom. 10:13; 1 Tim. 1:15).
- Eternal life is a gift of God (Rom. 6:23).
- Believers are saved and fully justified before their faith ever produces a single righteous work (Eph. 2:10).
- Christians can and do sin (1 John 1:8, 10). Even the strongest Christians wage a constant and intense struggle against sin in the flesh (Rom. 7:15–24). Genuine believers sometimes commit heinous sins, as David did in 2 Samuel 11.

Alongside those truths, I believe Scripture teaches these:

- The gospel calls sinners to faith joined in oneness with repentance (Acts 2:38; 17:30; 20:21; 2 Pet. 3:9). Repentance is turning from sin (Acts 3:19; Luke 24:47). It is not a work but a divinely bestowed grace (Acts 11:18; 2 Tim. 2:25). Repentance is a change of heart, but genuine repentance will effect a change of behavior as well (Luke 3:8; Acts 26:18–20).
- Salvation is all God's work. Those who believe are saved utterly apart from any effort on their own (Titus 3:5). Even faith is a gift of God, not a work of man (Eph. 2:1–5, 8). Real faith therefore cannot be defective or short-lived but endures forever (Phil. 1:6, cf. Heb. 11).
- The object of faith is Christ Himself, not only a creed or a promise (John 3:16). Faith therefore involves personal commitment to Christ (2 Cor. 5:15). In other words, all true believers follow Jesus (John 10:27–28).

- Real faith inevitably produces a changed life (2 Cor. 5:17). Salvation includes a transformation of the inner person (Gal. 2:20). The nature of the Christian is different, new (Rom. 6:6). The unbroken pattern of sin and enmity with God will not continue when a person is born again (1 John 3:9–10).
- The "gift of God," eternal life (Rom. 6:23), includes all that pertains to life and godliness (2 Pet. 1:3; Rom. 8:32), not just a ticket to heaven.
- Jesus is Lord of all, and the faith He demands involves unconditional surrender (Rom. 6:17–18; 10:9–10). He does not bestow external life on those whose hearts remain set against Him (James 4:6).
- Those who truly believe will love Christ (1 Pet. 1:8–9; Rom. 8:28–30; 1 Cor. 16:22). They will therefore long to obey Him (John 14:15, 23).
- Behavior is an important test of faith. Obedience is evidence that one's faith is real (1 John 2:3). On the other hand, the person who remains utterly unwilling to obey Christ does not evidence true faith (1 John 2:4).
- Genuine believers may stumble and fall, but they *will* persevere in the faith (1 Cor. 1:8). Those who later turn completely away from the Lord show that they were never truly born again (1 John 2:19).

That is my position on "lordship salvation." Anyone who supposes I have some deeper agenda has misunderstood what I am saying.

Radical or Orthodox?

Most Christians will recognize that the points I've listed are not new or radical ideas. The preponderance of Bible-believing Christians over the centuries have held these to be basic tenets of orthodoxy. They are standard precepts of doctrine affirmed, for example, by all the great Reformed and Calvinist creeds. Though our Wesleyan brethren might disagree on a few of the particulars, most of them would quickly affirm that the lordship of Christ is at the heart of the gospel message.[1] No major orthodox movement in the history of Christianity has ever taught that sinners can spurn the lordship of Christ yet lay claim to Him as Savior.

The truth is, the no-lordship gospel is a fairly recent development. Although most advocates of the no-lordship view write and speak as if their teaching represented historic mainstream evangelical Christianity, it does not. Except for a circle of North American pastors, authors, and conference speakers, practically no church leader in the world defends no-lordship doctrine as orthodox. Until recently in Eastern Europe and the Soviet Union, for example, being a Christian could literally cost a person everything. There the notion of faith without commitment is unthinkable. In England and the rest of Europe, Christian leaders I have met condemn no-lordship teaching as an American aberration. The same is true in other parts of the world I'm familiar with.

This is not to say that no-lordship teaching poses no threat outside the United States. Over the past three or four decades gospel tracts, how-to books on witnessing, radio and television broadcasts, and other media have carried the no-lordship message to the uttermost parts of the earth. The so-called simple-faith gospel—no repentance, no surrender, no commitment, no changed life—has had a horrific influence on the vocabulary of evangelism. Because no-lordship terminology ("accept Jesus as Savior" now, "make Him Lord" later) has become familiar and comfortable, many Christians' thinking about the gospel is fuzzy. When so many of the purveyors of no-lordship salvation brashly level charges of heresy against those who oppose their teaching, is it any wonder sincere Christians are genuinely confused? Which system represents true orthodoxy?

What Does the No-Lordship Gospel Teach?

I have listed sixteen beliefs of lordship salvation. The first seven are tenets every major no-lordship advocate would also affirm:

- Christ's death purchased eternal salvation.
- The saved are justified through faith in Christ alone.
- Sinners cannot earn divine favor.
- God requires no preparatory works or pre-salvation reformation.
- Eternal life is a gift.
- Believers are saved before their faith produces any righteous works.
- Christians sin, sometimes horribly.

On that much we all agree. Those who espouse the no-lordship position, however, differ dramatically from lordship salvation on the remaining nine points, Instead they teach:

- Repentance is a change of mind about Christ (*SGS* 96, 99).[2] In the context of the gospel invitation, *repentance* is just a synonym for *faith* (*SGS* 97–99). No turning from sin is required for salvation (*SGS* 99).
- The whole of salvation, including faith, is a gift of God (*SGS* 96). But faith might not last. A true Christian can completely cease believing (*SGS* 141).
- Saving faith is simply being convinced or giving credence to the truth of the gospel (*SGS* 156). It is confidence that Christ can remove guilt and give eternal life, not a personal commitment to *Him* (*SGS* 119).
- *Some* spiritual fruit is inevitable in every Christian's experience. The fruit, however, might not be visible to others (*SGS* 45). Christians can even lapse into a state of permanent spiritual barrenness (*SGS* 53–54).
- Only the *judicial* aspects of salvation—such as justification, adoption, imputed righteousness, and positional sanctification—are guaranteed for believers in this life (*SGS* 150–52). *Practical* sanctification and growth in grace require a postconversion act of dedication.[3]

- Submission to Christ's supreme authority as Lord is not germane to the saving transaction (*SGS* 71–76). Neither dedication nor *willingness* to be dedicated to Christ are issues in salvation (*SGS* 74). The news that Christ died for our sins and rose from the dead is the *complete* gospel. Nothing else must be believed for salvation (*SGS* 40–41).
- Christians may fall into a state of lifelong carnality. A whole category of "carnal Christians"—born-again people who continuously live like the unsaved—exists in the church (*SGS* 31, 59–66).
- Disobedience and prolonged sin are no reason to doubt the reality of one's faith (*SGS* 48).
- A believer may utterly forsake Christ and come to the point of not believing. God has guaranteed that He will not disown those who thus abandon the faith (*SGS* 141). Those who have once believed are secure forever, even if they turn away (*SGS* 143).

Some of the more radical advocates of no-lordship doctrine do not stop there. They further stipulate:

- Repentance is not essential to the gospel message. In no sense is repentance related to saving faith (*AF* 144–46).[4]
- Faith is a human act, not a gift from God (*AF* 219). It occurs in a decisive moment but does not necessarily continue. (*AF* xiv, 107). True faith can be subverted, be overthrown, collapse, or even turn to unbelief (*AF* 111).
- To "believe" unto salvation is to believe the *facts* of the gospel (*AF* 37–39). "Trusting Jesus" means believing the "saving facts" about Him (*AF* 39), and to believe those facts is to appropriate the gift of eternal life (*AF* 40). Those who add any suggestion or commitment have departed from the New Testament idea of salvation (*AF* 27).
- Spiritual fruit is not guaranteed in the Christian life (*AF* 73–75, 199). Some Christians spend their lives in a barren wasteland of defeat, confusion, and every kind of evil (*AF* 119–25).
- Heaven is guaranteed to believers (*AF* 112) but Christian victory is not (*AF* 118–19). One could even say "the saved" still need salvation (*AF* 195–99). Christ offers a whole range of postconversion deliverance experiences to supply what Christians lack (*AF* 196). But these other "salvations" all require the addition of human works, such as obedience, submission, and confession of Jesus as Lord (*AF* 74, 119, 124–25, 196). Thus God is dependent to some degree on human effort in achieving deliverance from sin in this life (*AF* 220).
- Submission is not in any sense a condition for eternal life (*AF* 172). "Calling on the Lord" means *appealing* to Him, not *submitting* to Him (*AF* 193–95).
- Nothing guarantees that a true Christian will love God (*AF* 130–31). Salvation does not necessarily even place the sinner in a right relationship of harmonious fellowship with God (*AF* 145–60).

- If people are sure they believe, their faith *must* be genuine (*AF* 31). *All* who claim Christ by faith as Savior—even those involved in serious or prolonged sin—should be assured that they belong to God come what may (*AF* 32, 93–95). It is dangerous and destructive to question the salvation of professing Christians (*AF* 18–19, 91–99). The New Testament writers *never* questioned the reality of their readers' faith (*AF* 98).
- It is possible to experience a moment of faith that guarantees heaven for eternity (*AF* 107), then to turn away permanently and live a life that is utterly barren of any spiritual fruit (*AF* 118–19). Genuine believers might even cease to name the name of Christ or confess Christianity (*AF* 111). . . .

What Is Really at the Heart of the Lordship Debate?

It should be obvious that these are real doctrinal differences; the lordship controversy is not a semantic disagreement. The participants in this debate hold widely differing perspectives.

Nevertheless, the issues have often been obscured by semantic distractions, distorted interpretations of lordship teaching, mangled logic, and emotion-laden rhetoric. Often it is easier to misconstrue a point than answer it, and sadly that is the tack many have taken. All it has done is confuse the real issues.

Please allow me to address some of the most troublesome fallacies that have hampered understanding and resolution of the lordship question.

The lordship controversy is *not* a dispute about whether salvation is by faith only or by faith plus works   No true Christian would ever suggest that works need to be added to faith in order to secure salvation. No one who properly interprets Scripture would ever propose that human effort or fleshly works can be *meritorious*—worthy of honor or reward from God.[5]

The lordship controversy *is* a disagreement over the nature of true faith. Those who want to eliminate Christ's lordship from the gospel see faith as simple trust in a set of truths about Christ. Faith, as they describe it, is merely a personal appropriation of the promise of eternal life. Scripture describes faith as more than that—it is a wholehearted trust in Christ personally (e.g., Gal. 2:16; Phil. 3:9). Not merely faith *about* Him; faith *in* Him. Note the difference: If I say I believe some promise you have made, I am saying far less than if I say I trust *you*. Believing in a person necessarily involves some degree of commitment. Trusting Christ means placing oneself in His custody for both life and death. It means we rely on His counsel, trust in His goodness, and entrust ourselves for time and eternity to His guardianship. Real faith, saving faith, is all of me (mind, emotions, and will) embracing all of Him (Savior, Advocate, Provider, Sustainer, Counselor, and Lord God).

Those who have such faith will love Christ (Rom. 8:28; 1 Cor. 16:22; 1 John 4:19). They will therefore want to do His bidding. How could someone who truly believes in Christ continue to defy His authority and pursue what He hates? In this sense, then, the crucial issue for lordship salvation is not merely authority and submission, but the affections of the heart. Jesus as Lord is far more than just an authority figure; He's also our highest treasure and most precious companion. We obey Him out of sheer delight.

So the gospel demands surrender, not only for authority's sake, but also because surrender is the believer's highest joy. Such surrender is not an extraneous adjunct to faith; it is the very essence of believing.

Lordship salvation does *not* teach true Christians are perfect or sinless
Wholehearted commitment to Christ does not mean that we never disobey or that we live perfect lives. The vestiges of our sinful flesh make it inevitable that we will often do what we do not want to do (rom. 7:15). But commitment to Christ *does* mean that obedience rather than disobedience will be our distinguishing trait. God will deal with the sin in our lives and we will respond to His loving chastisement by becoming more holy (Heb. 12:5–11). I labored to make this clear in *The Gospel According to Jesus.* For example, I wrote, "Those with true faith will fail—and in some cases, frequently—but a genuine believer will, as a pattern of life, confess his sin and come to the Father for forgiveness (1 John 1:9)" (p. 192).

Nevertheless, a few critics have tried to portray lordship salvation as a thinly disguised form of perfectionism. One dear brother—a Christian radio personality—wrote me to suggest that qualifying comments in the book like the one I just quoted are actually inconsistent with my overall position. He assumed that these were "disclaimers" added by an editor trying to "tone down" my book. He evidently surmised that my real intent was to teach sinless perfection as the test of true salvation. He had missed the point entirely.

Of course Christians sin. They disobey. They fail, We *all* fall far short of perfection in this life (Phil. 3:12–5). "We all stumble in many ways" (James 3:2). Even the most mature and godly Christians "see in a mirror dimly" (1 Cor. 13:12). Our minds need constant renewing (Rom. 12:2). But that doesn't invalidate the truth that salvation in some real sense makes us practically righteous. The same epistle that describes the Christian's hatred of and battle with sin (Rom. 7:8–24) first says that believers are free from sin and slaves of righteousness (6:18). The same apostle who wrote, "If we say that we have no sin, we are deceiving ourselves" (1 John 1:8) later wrote, "No one who abides in Him sins" (3:6). In one place he says, "If we say that we have not sinned, we make Him a liar, and His word is not in us" (1:10), and in another, "No one who is born of God practices sin, because His seed abides in Him" (3:9).

There's a true paradox—not an inconsistency—in those truths. All Christians sin (1 John 1:8), but all Christians also obey: "By this we know that we have come to know Him, if we keep His commandments" (1 John 2:3). Sin and carnality are still present with all believers (Rom. 7:21), but they cannot be the hallmark of one's character (Rom. 6:22).

Scripture clearly and repeatedly confirms the lordship viewpoint on this matter: "Beloved, do not imitate what is evil, but what is good. The one who does good is of God; the one who does evil has not seen God" (3 John 11). That speaks of *direction,* not *perfection.* But it clearly makes behavior a test of faith's reality.

The sinner's role in salvation is *not* the main issue in the lordship controversy   The heart of the debate deals with how much *God* does in redeeming the elect.

What happens at regeneration? Is the believing sinner really born again (John 3:3, 7; 1 Peter 1:3, 23)? Is our old self really dead, "crucified... that we should no longer be slaves to sin" (Rom. 6:6)? Are believers really "partakers of the divine nature" (2 Pet. 1:4)? Is it true that "if any man is in Christ, he is a new creature; the old things passed away; behold, new things have come" (2 Cor. 5:17)? Can we really say, "Having been freed from sin, [we are] slaves of righteousness" (Rom. 6:18)?

Lordship salvation says yes.

This, after all, is the whole point of redemption: "Whom He foreknew, He also predestined to become conformed to the image of His Son" (Rom. 8:29). Does that conforming work of God—sanctification—begin in this lifetime? Again, lordship salvation says yes.

Scripture agrees. "We all, with unveiled face beholding as in a mirror the glory of the Lord, are being transformed into the same image from glory to glory" (2 Cor. 3:18). Though "it has not appeared as yet what we shall be," it is nevertheless certain that "when He appears, we shall be like Him.... And everyone who has this hope fixed on Him purifies himself, just as He is pure" (1 John 3:2–3).

There's more: "Whom He predestined, these He also called; and whom He called, these He also justified; and whom He justified, these He also glorified" (Rom. 8:30). Notice God's part in salvation begins with election and ends in glory. In between, every aspect of the redemptive process is God's work, not the sinner's. God will neither terminate the process nor omit any aspect of it.

Titus 3:5 is clear: Salvation—all of it—is "not on the basis of deeds which we have done." It is God's work, done "according to His mercy." It is not merely a declaratory transaction, legally securing a place in heaven but leaving the sinner captive to his sin. It involves a transformation of the disposition, the very nature, through "the washing of regeneration and renewing by the Holy Spirit" as well.

The question is *not* whether we're saved by grace, but *how* grace operates in salvation   No-lordship advocates love to portray themselves as champions of grace. But they characterize grace in an anemic way that misses the whole point. God's grace is a spiritual dynamic that works in the lives of the redeemed, "instructing us to deny ungodliness and worldly desires and to live sensibly, righteously and godly in the present age" (Titus 2:12). True grace is more than just a giant freebie, opening the door to heaven in the sweet by and by, but leaving us to wallow in sin in the bitter here and now. Grace is God presently at work in our lives. By grace "we are His workmanship, created in Christ Jesus for good works, which God prepared beforehand, that we should walk in them" (Eph. 2:10). By grace He "gave Himself for us, that He might redeem us from every lawless deed and purify for Himself a people for His own possession, zealous for good deeds" (Titus 2:14).

That ongoing work of grace in the Christian's life is as much a certainty as justification, glorification, or any other aspect of God's redeeming work. "I am confident of this very thing, that He who began a good work in you will perfect it until the day of Christ Jesus" (Phil. 1:6). Salvation is wholly God's work, and He finishes what He starts. His grace *is* sufficient. And potent. It cannot be defective in any regard. "Grace" that does not affect one's behavior is not the grace of God.

Repentance is *not* incidental to the gospel What is the gospel, after all, but a call to repentance (Acts 2:38; 3:19; 17:30)? In other words, it demands that sinners make a change—stop going one way and turn around to go the other (1 Thess. 1:9). Paul's evangelistic invitations always demanded repentance: "God is now declaring to men that all everywhere should repent" (Acts 17:30). Here's how Paul described His own ministry and message: "I did not prove disobedient to the heavenly vision, but kept declaring both to those of Damascus first, and also at Jerusalem and then throughout all the region of Judea, and even to the Gentiles, *that they should repent and turn to God, performing deeds appropriate to repentance*" (Acts 26:19–20, emphasis added). Repentance is what leads to life (Acts 11:18) and to the knowledge of the truth (2 Tim. 2:25). Thus salvation is impossible apart from repentance.

Advocates of the no-lordship position frequently suggest that preaching repentance adds something to the biblical doctrine of salvation by grace through faith alone.

But faith presupposes repentance. How can those who are mortal enemies of God (Rom. 5:10) sincerely believe in His Son *without* repenting? How can anyone truly comprehend the truth of salvation from sin and its consequences, unless that person also genuinely understands and hates what sin is? The whole sense of faith is that we trust Christ to liberate us from the power and penalty of sin. Therefore sinners cannot come to sincere faith apart from a complete change of heart, a turnaround of the mind and affections and will. That is repentance. It is not a supplement to the gospel invitation; it is precisely what the gospel demands. Our Lord Himself described His primary mission as that of calling sinners to repentance (Matt. 9:13).

We often speak of the salvation experience as "conversion." That is biblical terminology (Matt. 18:3; John 12:40; Acts 15:3). *Conversion* and *repentance* are closely related terms. Conversion occurs when a sinner turns to God in repentant faith. It is a complete turnaround, an absolute change of moral and volitional direction. Such a radical reversal is the response the gospel calls for, whether the plea to sinners is phrased as "believe," "repent," or "be converted." Each entails the others.

If someone is walking away from you and you say, "Come here," it is not necessary to say "*turn around* and come." The U-turn is implied in the direction "come." In like manner, when our Lord says, "Come to Me" (Matt. 11:28), the about-face of repentance is understood. Nowhere does Scripture issue an evangelistic appeal that does not at least imply the necessity of repentance. Our Lord offers nothing to impenitent sinners (Matt. 9:13; Mark 2:17; Luke 5:32).

Again, repentance is not a human work. Jesus said, "No one can come to Me, unless the Father who sent Me draws him" (John 6:44). It is God who grants repentance (Acts 11:18; 2 Tim. 2:5). Repentance is *not* pre-salvation self-improvement. It is *not* a question of atoning for sin or making restitution *before* turning to Christ in faith. It is an inward turning from sin to Christ. Though it is not itself a "work" the sinner performs, genuine repentance will certainly produce good works as its inevitable fruit (Matt. 3:8).

The lordship salvation controversy is *not* churchwide   Because of the publicity given to the lordship debate over the past five years, one might get the impression that the entire worldwide evangelical movement is split over these issues. But as I noted earlier, modern no-lordship theology is primarily a North American phenomenon. Certainly it has been exported to some parts of the world by missionaries and others trained in American schools, but I know of no prominent Christian leaders from outside North America who have undertaken to defend the no-lordship view on doctrinal grounds.

To be even more specific, the modern lordship controversy is primarily a dispute among dispensationalists.... Without getting into a technical discussion about theology at this point, let me simply note that one arm of the dispensationalist movement has developed and defended no-lordship doctrine. Their influence on the evangelical culture has been widespread. As the lordship controversy has been debated on radio talk shows and in other popular formats, it has begun to seem like a monumental conflict threatening to divide Protestant Christianity in a major way. The truth is, only one branch of dispensationalism has risen to defend the no-lordship view.

Who are the defenders of no-lordship dispensationalism? Nearly all of them stand in a tradition that has its roots in the teaching of Lewis Sperry Chafer.... Dr. Chafer is the father of modern no-lordship teaching. Every prominent figure on the no-lordship side descends from Dr. Chafer's spiritual lineage. Though Dr. Chafer did not invent or originate any of the key elements of no-lordship teaching, he codified the system of dispensationalism on which all contemporary no-lordship doctrine is founded. That system is the common link between those who attempt to defend no-lordship doctrine on theological grounds.

The New Testament epistles do *not* present a different gospel than Jesus Himself preached   One of the hallmarks of Dr. Chafer's brand of dispensationalism was the way he segmented the New Testament and particularly the teachings of Christ.... Chafer believed many of our Lord's sermons and evangelistic invitations were intended for people in another dispensation. He contrasted Jesus' "kingdom teachings" and His "grace teachings." Only the "grace teachings," according to Chafer, can be legitimately applied to this present age.

Many dispensationalists have abandoned that kind of thinking, but some still do not believe the gospel according to Jesus is even relevant to the discussion of lordship salvation. "Of course Jesus taught a lordship message," one old-line dispensationalist brother wrote me. "He was preaching to people under law. Under grace we must be careful to preach a grace message. We must preach the gospel according to the apostles." . . .

The gospel according to Jesus *is* the same as the gospel according to the apostles. The faith it calls for is not dormant, but dynamic; it is a repentant, submissive, trusting, enduring faith that works.

Notes

1. Wesleyans believe, for example, that genuine believers can fall away from the faith, but they generally teach that those who do fall away lose their salvation. Their system makes no room for "Christians" who live in continuous rebellion against Christ.

2. Throughout this book, I will use the abbreviation *SGS* in reference to Charles Ryrie, *So Great Salvation* (Wheaton, Ill.: Victor, 1989).

3. Charles C. Ryrie, *Balancing the Christian Life* (Chicago: Moody, 1969), 186.

4. *AF* refers to Zane Hodges, *Absolutely Free!* (Grand Rapids, Mich.: Zondervan, 1989).

5. Though, curiously, no-lordship doctrine is often married to a view that sees post-salvation works as meritorious. Zane Hodges, for one, holds this view. He teaches that eternal life may be obtained freely by faith, but the abundant life of John 10:10 is a reward that may be acquired only by works (*AF* 230).

POSTSCRIPT

Is Acceptance of Christ Alone Sufficient for Salvation?

As many of the Protestant Reformers left the Catholic Church, their cry was *Sola Fide!* or "Faith Alone!" This Protestant tradition has continued to the present and is found within many Christian churches. However, other Christian clergy and scholars have argued that while grace is central, good works are also a part of the good news of salvation.

This debate has centered on the Christian perspective of the relationship between grace and works. Other non-Christian religions, while not focusing on the doctrine of grace, espouse theologies based on good works.

Judaism and Islam are similar in their approach to the topic of salvation. The Qu'ran rejects the doctrine of redemption, believing salvation to be based on a person's actions and attitudes. Judaism, while awaiting a coming Messiah, also stresses obedience to law—613 laws, to be exact. One criticism of Christian salvation by Jewish scholars is Christianity's emphasis on *individual* salvation, while Judaism focuses more on family and community.

Buddhist philosophy describes the "Noble Eightfold Path" to which each person is directed to follow in order to achieve "nirvana." This path is composed of 1) right understanding, 2) right speech, 3) right thoughts, 4) right action, 5) right livelihood, 6) right effort, 7) right mindfulness, and 8) right concentration. This is evidently a very work-oriented belief system.

Salvation in Hinduism is to escape the cycle of birth, death, and rebirth. Followers of Hinduism believe in reincarnation as a means of learning new truth and moving to higher and still higher levels of understanding. Some sects of Hinduism believe a kind of divine power can assist them in moving along this path of growth.

Though not a part of many of the great world religions, the controversy of grace and works will certainly continue as part of the Christian tradition.

Suggested Readings

Z. C. Hodges, *Absolutely Free: A Biblical Reply to Lordship Salvation* (Academie Books, 1989).

M. Luther, *By Faith Alone* (Penguin, 1998).

J. MacArthur, Jr., *The Gospel According to Jesus* (Zondervan, 1994).

E. F. Winter, ed. and trans., *Erasmus-Luther: Discourse on Free Will* (Frederick Ungar, 1973).

P. Yancy, *What's So Amazing About Grace?* (Zondervan, 1997).

ISSUE 7

Was Jesus Christ the Son of God?

YES: N. T. Wright, from "The Divinity of Jesus," in Marcus J. Borg and N. T. Wright, *The Meaning of Jesus: Two Visions* (HarperSanFrancisco, 1999)

NO: Marcus J. Borg, from "Jesus and God," in Marcus J. Borg and N. T. Wright, *The Meaning of Jesus: Two Visions* (HarperSanFrancisco, 1999)

ISSUE SUMMARY

YES: N. T. Wright, canon theologian of Westminster Abbey and former dean of Lichfield Cathedral, argues for the divinity of Jesus. He maintains that faith and scholarship need not be mutually exclusive with respect to the debate over the divinity of Jesus Christ. Wright defends his position against the assertions of participants in the Jesus Seminar.

NO: Marcus J. Borg, professor of religion and culture at Oregon State University in Corvallis, Oregon, and a fellow of the Jesus Seminar, asserts that historical evidence does not support Jesus as being divine. A practicing Christian, Borg acknowledges Jesus as a great teacher and an embodiment of truth but not as the divine Son of God.

One of the critical issues debated among theologians today is the divinity of Jesus of Nazareth. Was Jesus the literal son of God or simply a gifted teacher of moral truth who was the biological son of mortal parents?

While most Jews, Muslims, Buddhists, Hindus, and other non-Christians do not accept Jesus as the son of God, many do believe he was an inspired teacher. Yet even among some Christians there is debate about the authenticity of the scriptural passages where Jesus refers to himself as the Son of God. Some believe these passages were later additions by over-zealous translators, and Jesus' only claim was that he was directed by God to teach moral truth. Christian theologian and moral philosopher C. S. Lewis concluded that one could not read of the New Testament and regard Jesus as simply a great teacher:

> I am trying here to prevent anyone saying the really foolish thing that people often say about Him: "I'm ready to accept Jesus as a great moral teacher, but I don't accept His claim to be God." That is the one thing we must not say. A man who was merely a man and said the sort of things Jesus said would not be a great moral teacher. He would either be a lunatic—on a level with the man who says he is a poached egg—or else he would be the Devil of Hell. You must make your choice. Either this man was, and is, the Son of God: or else a madman or something worse. You can shut Him up for a fool, you can spit at Him and kill Him as a demon; or you can fall at His feet and call Him Lord and God. But let us not come [UP?] with any patronising [sic] nonsense about His being a great human teacher. He has not left that open to us. He did not intend to.

— Mere Christianity (Scribner, 1952), pp. 40–41

Some Christians strongly contest Lewis's statement, asserting that Jesus did perhaps leave this debate open to us or that he did not even intend this issue to be debated in the first place. In 1985 a group of scholarly critics, called the Jesus Seminar, gathered together to evaluate evidence concerning the divinity of Jesus. The critics' general conclusion was that Jesus did not actually make the statements about his divinity that are found in the New Testament. Marcus Borg states, "I and most mainline scholars do not think Jesus said these things. He did not speak like this."

Borg is referring to statements such as "I am the light of the world" (King James Version, John 8:12); "I am the way, the truth, and the life" (KJV, John 14:6); "Before Abraham was, I am" (KJV John 8:58); and "I am the Son of God" (KJV, John 10:36). Borg and other participants in the Jesus Seminar assert that of the statements attributed to Jesus in the New Testament, only a small percentage (18 percent) can actually be accepted as uttered by him. Although Borg identifies himself as Christian, he does not accept Jesus as the Son of God or Christianity as the only way to salvation.

N. T. Wright counters with arguments for the divinity of Jesus Christ. He takes caution not to cross the line between scholar and evangelist and makes the assertion that Jesus did indeed teach and identify himself as the Messiah. In addition to describing the persona of the historical Jesus, Wright also writes of a Savior who "accomplished for us something that we desperately needed and could not have done ourselves."

Borg and Wright were students together at Oxford University and consider themselves friends despite their opposite views. Borg's arguments against and Wright's arguments in favor of the divinity of Jesus are both key to our understanding of this important topic. Perhaps in addition to understanding their scholarly arguments, the reader will also come to appreciate how these two scholars can disagree without being disagreeable.

The Divinity of Jesus

Bible quotations, unless otherwise noted, are from the New Revised Standard Version of the Bible.

When people ask "Was Jesus God?," they usually think they know what the word *God* means and are asking whether we can fit Jesus into that. I regard this as deeply misleading.

For seven years I was college chaplain at Worcester College, Oxford. Each year I used to see the first-year undergraduates individually for a few minutes, to welcome them to the college and make a first acquaintance. Most were happy to meet me, but many commented, often with slight embarrassment, "You won't be seeing much of me; you see, I don't believe in God."

I developed a stock response: "Oh, that's interesting. Which god is it you don't believe in?" This used to surprise them; they mostly regarded the word *God* as univocal, always meaning the same thing. So they would stumble out a few phrases about the god they didn't believe in: a being who lived up in the sky, looking down disapprovingly at the world, occasionally intervening to do miracles, sending bad people to hell while allowing good people to share his heaven. Again, I had a stock response for this very common "spy-in-the-sky" theology: "Well, I'm not surprised you don't believe in that god. I don't believe in that god either."

At this point the undergraduate would look startled. Then, perhaps, a faint look of recognition; it was sometimes rumored that half the college chaplains at Oxford were atheists. "No," I would say, "I believe in the god I see revealed in Jesus of Nazareth." What most people mean by *god* in late-modern Western culture simply isn't the mainstream Christian meaning.

The same is true for meanings of *god* within postmodernity. We are starting to be more aware that many people give allegiance to "gods" and "goddesses" which are personifications of forces of nature and life. An obvious example is the earth goddess, Gaia, revered by some within the new age movement. Following the long winter of secularism, in which most people gave up believing in anything religious or spiritual, the current revival of spiritualities of all sorts is an inevitable swing of the pendulum, a cultural shift in which people have been able once more to celebrate dimensions of human existence that the Enlightenment had marginalized. But one cannot assume that what people mean by *god* or *spirit, religion* or *spirituality* within these movements bears very much relation to Christianity. I even heard, not long ago, an Italian justifying the pornography that featured his high-profile wife on the grounds that its portrayal of sexuality was deeply "religious." The pope, he thought, should have welcomed it.

Eros has of course been well known to students of divinities time out of mind. But only when a culture has forgotten, through long disuse, how god language actually works can someone assume that the deeply "religious" feelings, evoking a sense of wonder and transcendence, that serious eroticism (and lots of other things) can produce can be straightforwardly identified with anything in the Judeo-Christian tradition. Did they never hear of paganism?

God in First-Century Judaism

What did first-century Jews, including Jesus and his first followers, mean by *god?* This is obviously the place to start. Their belief can be summed up in a single phrase: *creational and covenantal monotheism.* This needs spelling out.

Adherents of some theologies, for example ancient Epicureanism and modern Deism, believe in a god or gods but think they have nothing much to do with the world we live in. Others, as in Stoicism, believe that god, or "the divine" or "the sacred," is simply a dimension of the world we live in, so that god and the world end up being pretty much the same thing. Both of these can give birth to practical or theoretical atheism. The first can let its god get so far away that he disappears; this is what happened with Marx and Feuerbach in the nineteenth century, allowing the "absentee landlord" of eighteenth-century Deism to become simply an absentee. The second can get so used to various gods around the place that it ceases to care much about them; this is what happened with a good deal of ancient paganism in Greece and Rome, until, as Pliny wryly remarks, the arrival of Christianity stirred up pagans to a fresh devotion to their gods.

The Jews believed in a quite different god. This god, YHWH, "the One Who Is," the Sovereign One, was not simply the objectification of forces and drives within the world but was the maker of all that exists. Several biblical books, or parts thereof, are devoted to exploring the difference between YHWH and the pagan idols: Daniel, Isaiah 40–55, and a good many psalms spring obviously to mind. The theme is summed up in the Jewish daily prayer: "YHWH our God, YHWH is one!"

Classic Jewish monotheism, then, believed, first, that there was one God, who created heaven and earth and who remained in close and dynamic relation with his creation; and, second, that this God had called Israel to be his special people. This twin belief, tested to the limit and beyond through Israel's checkered career, was characteristically expressed through a particular narrative: the chosen people were also the *rescued* people, liberated from slavery in Egypt, marked out by the gift of Torah, established in their land, exiled because of disobedience, but promised a glorious return and final settlement. Jewish-style monotheism meant living in this story, trusting in this one true God, the God of creation and covenant, of exodus and return.

This God was utterly different from the pantheist's "one god." Utterly different, too, from the faraway ultratranscendent gods of the Epicureans. Always active within his world—did he not feed the young ravens when they called upon him?—he could be trusted to act more specifically on behalf of Israel. His eventual overthrow of pagan power at the political level would be the revelation of his overthrow of the false gods of the nations. His vindication of his people, liberating them finally from all their oppressors, would also be the vindication of his own name, his reputation.

This monotheism was never, in our period, an inner analysis of the being of the one God. It was always a way of saying, frequently at great risk: our God is the true God, and your gods are worthless idols. It was a way of holding onto hope.

Precisely because this God was both other than the world and continually active within it (the words *transcendent* and *immanent* are pointers to this belief but do not clarify it much), Jews of Jesus' day had developed several ways of speaking about the activity of this God in which they attempted to hold together what they dared not separate. Emboldened by deep-rooted traditions, they explored what appears to us a strange, swirling rhythm of mutual relations within the very being of the one God: a to-and-fro, a give-and-take, a command-and-obey, a sense of love poured out and love received. God's Spirit broods over the waters, God's Word goes forth to produce new life, God's Law guides his people, God's Presence or Glory dwells with them in fiery cloud, in tabernacle and temple. These four ways of speaking moved to-and-fro from metaphor to trembling reality claim and back again. They enabled Jews to speak simultaneously of God's sovereign supremacy and his intimate presence, of his unapproachable holiness and his self-giving compassionate love.

Best known of all is perhaps a fifth. God's Wisdom is his handmaid in creation, the firstborn of his words, his chief of staff, his delight. Through the Lady Wisdom of Proverbs 1–8, the creator has fashioned everything, especially the human race. To embrace Wisdom is therefore to discover the secret of being truly human, of reflecting God's image.

Monotheism and Early Christology

This rich seam of Jewish thought is where the early Christians went quarrying for language to deal with the phenomena before them. Some have suggested that it was only when the early church started to lose its grip on its Jewish roots and began to compromise with pagan philosophy that it could think of Jesus in the same breath as the one God. Jewish polemic has often suggested that the Trinity and the incarnation, those great pillars of patristic theology, are sheer paganization.

Whatever we say of later theology, this is certainly not true of the New Testament. Long before secular philosophy was invoked to describe the inner being of the one God (and the relation of his God to Jesus and to the Spirit), a vigorous and very Jewish tradition took the language and imagery of Spirit, Word, Law, Presence (and/or Glory), and Wisdom and developed them in relation to Jesus of Nazareth and the Spirit. One might think that a sixth was also explored, namely God's Love; except that, for them, God's Love was already no mere personification, a figure of speech for the loving God at work, but a person, the crucified and risen Jesus.

Several of these Jewish themes come together in the famous Johannine prologue. Jesus is here the Word of God; the passage as a whole is closely dependent on the Wisdom tradition and is thereby closely linked with the Law and the Presence, or Glory, of God. "The Word became flesh, and tabernacled in our midst; we saw his glory, glory as of God's only son." However much the spreading branches of Johannine theology might hang over the wall, offering fruit to the pagan world around, the roots of the tree are firmly embedded in Jewish soil.

John is usually regarded as late. What about the early material? Paul is our earliest Christian writer, and the earliest parts of his letters may be those that embody or reflect pre-Pauline Christian tradition.

Within that strand of material, three passages stand out. In 1 Corinthians 8.6, within a specifically Jewish-style monotheistic argument, he adapts the *Shema* itself, placing Jesus within it; "For us there is one God—the Father, from whom are all things and we to him; and one Lord, Jesus Christ, through whom are all things and we through him." In Philippians 2.5–11, he draws on the fiercely monotheistic theology of Isaiah 40–55 to celebrate Christ's universal lordship: "At the name of Jesus," he declares, "every knee shall bow." Isaiah has YHWH defeating the pagan idols and being enthroned over them; Paul has Jesus exalted to a position of equality with "the Father" because he has done what, in Jewish tradition, only the one God can do. Colossians 1.15–20, with its clear poetic structure, is a Wisdom poem, exploring the classic Jewish theme that the world's creator is also its redeemer, and vice versa. But at every point of creation and redemption we discover, not Wisdom, but Jesus.

So, too, in Galatians 4.1–11, Paul tells the story of the world as the story of God's freeing of slaves and his making them his children, his heirs. As in the Exodus, the true God reveals himself as who he is, putting the idols to shame. But the God who has now revealed himself in this way is the God who "sends the son" and then "sends the Spirit of the Son." In these passages we have, within thirty years of Jesus' death, what would later be called a very high Christology. It is very early and very Jewish.

Within these passages and others like them, Paul, like other New Testament writes, uses the phrase "son of God" to denote Jesus. Later theologians, forgetting their Jewish roots, would of course read this as straightforwardly Nicene Christology: Jesus was the second person of the Trinity. Paul's usage, though, is much subtler and offers further clues not only as to what the earliest Christians believed, but also why. "Son of God" in Jewish thought was used occasionally for angels, sometimes for Israel, and sometimes for the king. These latter uses were influential both in sectarian Judaism ("son of God" is found as a messianic title at Qumran) and in early Christianity. Since the early Christians all regarded Jesus as the messiah of Israel, the one in whom Israel's destiny had been summed up, it is not surprising, whatever language Jesus had or had not used of himself, that they exploited this phrase (to call it a "title" is perhaps too formal, and too redolent of the wrong way of doing New Testament Christology), which was available both in their Bible and in their surrounding culture, to denote Jesus and to connote his messiahship.

But already by Paul's day something more was in fact going on. "Son of God" came quickly to be used as a further way, in addition to the five Jewish ways already available and exploited by the early Christians, of saying that what had happened in Jesus was the unique and personal action of the one God of Israel. It became another way of speaking about the one God present, personal, active, saving, and rescuing, while still being able to speak of the one God sovereign, creating, sustaining, sending, remaining beyond. Another way, in fact, of doing what neither Stoicism nor Epicureanism needed to do and paganism in general could not do: holding together the majesty and compassion of God, the transcendence and immanence of God, creation and covenant, sovereignty and presence.

Similar exegetical points could be made, were there more space, from other New Testament writings, not least those very Jewish books, the letter to the Hebrews and the book of Revelation. But I have said enough to indicate, or at least point in the direction of, the remarkable phenomenon at the heart of earliest Christianity. Long before anyone talked about "nature" and "substance," "person" and "Trinity," the early Christians had quietly but definitely discovered that they could say what they felt obliged to say about Jesus (and the Spirit) by telling the Jewish story of God, Israel, and the world in the Jewish language of Spirit, Word, Torah, Presence/Glory, Wisdom, and now Messiah/Son. It is as though they discovered Jesus within the Jewish monotheistic categories they already had. The categories seemed to have been made for him. They fitted him like a glove.

The Origin of Christology

This, of course, raises in an acute form the question: why did they tell it like this?

At this point we need to ward off a frequent misunderstanding. It is often supposed that the resurrection (whatever we mean by that) somehow "proves" Jesus' "divinity."

This seems to me to short-circuit the reasoning that in fact took place. Suppose one of the two brigands crucified alongside Jesus had been raised from the dead. People would have said the world was a very odd place; they would not have said that the brigand was therefore divine. No: the basic meaning of Jesus' resurrection, as Paul says in Romans 1.4, was that Jesus was indeed the messiah. As we saw in chapter 6, this led quickly, within earliest Christianity, to the belief that his death was therefore not a defeat but a victory, the conquest of the powers of evil and the liberation, the Exodus, of God's people and, in principle, of the world. In Jesus, in other words, Israel's God, the world's creator, had accomplished at last the plan he had been forming ever since the covenant was forged in the first place. In Jesus God had rescued Israel from its suffering and exile. And then the final step: in Jesus God had done what, in the Bible, God had said he would do himself. He had heard the people's cry and had come to help them.

Ultimately, then, it is true that Jesus' resurrection led the early church to speak of him within the language of Jewish monotheism. But there was no easy equation. Resurrection pointed to messiahship; messiahship, to the task performed on the cross; that task, to the God who had promised to accomplish it himself. From there on it was a matter of rethinking, still very Jewishly, how these things could be.

Does any of this train of thought go back to Jesus himself? I have argued that it does. This is not the same as Jesus' messianic vocation. It cannot be read off from the usage of any "titles" such as "son of God" or "son of man." It grows out of Jesus' basic kingdom proclamation and from Jesus' conviction that it was his task and role, his vocation, not only to speak of this kingdom, but also to enact and embody it.

As I said in chapter 3, a central feature of Jewish expectation, and kingdom expectation at that, in Jesus' time was the hope that YHWH would return in person to Zion. Having abandoned Jerusalem at the time of the exile, his return was delayed, but he would come back at last. Within this context, someone who told cryptic stories about a king, or a master, who went away, left his servants tasks to perform, and then returned to see how they were getting on must—not "might," *must*—point to this controlling, overarching metanarrative. Of course, the later church, forgetting the first-century Jewish context, read such stories as though they were originally about Jesus himself going away and then returning in a "second coming." ... Of course, cautions scholars, noticing this, deny that Jesus would have said such things. I propose that here, at the heart of Jesus' work, and at the moment of its climax, Jesus not only told stories about the king who came back to Zion to judge and to save, he also acted as though he thought the stories were coming true in what he was himself accomplishing. This is the context, at last, in which I think it best to approach the question with which this chapter began.

It is of course a huge and difficult matter. Caricatures abound: the Jesus who wanders around with a faraway look, listening to the music of the angels, remembering the time when he was sitting up in heaven with the other members of the Trinity, having angels bring him bananas on golden dishes. (I do not wish to caricature the caricatures; but you would be surprised what devout people sometimes believe.) Equally, scholars sometimes throw up the Jesus who wandered around totally unreflectively, telling stories without perceiving how they would be heard, announcing God's kingdom, speaking of bringing it about, yet failing to ruminate on his own role within the drama. We must not lose our nerve and start asking the sort of questions (for example, "what sort of a person would think he was divine?") that depend for their rhetorical force on the implied assumption "within our culture." We must hold onto the question: how would a first-century Jew have approached this matter?

There is some evidence—cryptic, difficult to interpret, but evidence nonetheless—that some first-century Jews had already started to explore the meaning of certain texts, not least Daniel 7, that spoke of Israel's God sharing his throne with another (something expressly denied, of course, in Isaiah 42.8). These were not simply bits of speculative theology. They belonged, as more or less everything did at that period, to the whirling world of politics and pressure groups, of agendas and ambitions, all bent on discovering how Israel's God would bring in the kingdom and how best to speed the process on its way. To say that someone would share God's throne was to say that, through this one, Israel's God would win the great decisive victory. This is what, after all, the great Rabbi Akibas seems to have believed about Bar-Kochba.

And Jesus seems to have believed it about himself. The language was deeply coded, but the symbolic action was not. He was coming to Zion, doing what YHWH had promised to do. He explained his action with riddles all pointing in the same direction. Recognize this, and you start to see it all over the place, in parables and actions whose other layers have preoccupied us. Why, after all, does Jesus tell a story about a yearning father in order to account for his own behavior? This also accounts for his sovereign attitude to Torah; his speaking on behalf of Wisdom; his announcement of forgiveness of sins. By themselves, none of these would be conclusive. Even if they are allowed to stand as words and actions of Jesus, they remain cryptic. But predicate them of the same young man who is then on his way to Jerusalem to confront the powers that be with the message, and the action, of the kingdom of God, and who tells stories as he does so that are best interpreted as stories of YHWH returning to Zion; and you have reached, I believe, the deep heart of Jesus' own sense of vocation. He believed himself called to do and be what, in the scriptures, only Israel's God did and was.

His actions during the last week focused on the temple. Judaism had two great incarnational symbols, temple and Torah: Jesus seems to have believed it was his vocation to upstage the one and outflank the other. Judaism spoke of the presence of its God in its midst, in the pillar of cloud and fire, in the Presence ("Shekinah") in the temple. Jesus acted and spoke as if he thought he were a one-man countertemple movement. So, too, Judaism believed in a God who was not only high and mighty but also compassionate and caring, tending his flock like a shepherd, gathering the lambs in his arms. Jesus used just that God image, more than once, to explain his own actions. Judaism believed that its God would triumph over the powers of evil, within Israel as well as outside. Jesus spoke of his own coming vindication, after his meeting the Beast in mortal combat. Jesus, too, used the language of the Father sending the Son. The so-called parable of the Wicked Tenants could just as well be the parable of the Son Sent at Last. His awareness, in faith, of the one he called Abba, Father, sustained him in his messianic vocation to Israel, acting as his Father's personal agent to Israel. So we could go on. Approach the incarnation from this angle, and it is no category mistake but the appropriate climax of creation. Wisdom, God's blueprint for humans, at last herself becomes human.

I do not think Jesus "knew he was God" in the same sense that one knows one is tired or happy, male or female. He did not sit back and say to himself, "Well I never! I'm the second person of the Trinity!" Rather, "as part of his human vocation, grasped in faith, sustained in prayer, tested in confrontation, agonized over in further prayer and doubt, and implemented in action, he believed he had to do and be, for Israel and the world, that which according to scripture only YHWH himself could do and be." The question is often raised as to whether such a position compromises Jesus' modesty or his sanity. These objections gain their force from anachronistic assumptions about the way normal people behave; but in any case Jesus was frequently challenged on both grounds, and we have no reason to suppose the early church made this material up. The Jesus I have described is both thoroughly credible as a first-century Jew and thoroughly comprehensible as the one to whom early, high, Jewish Christology looked back.

Jesus and Christology Today

What are the implications of all this for how we approach questions of Christology today?

Thinking and speaking of God and Jesus in the same breath are not, as often has been suggested, a category mistake. Of course, if you start with the deist god and the reductionists' Jesus, they will never fit, but then they were designed not to. Likewise, if you start with the new age gods-from-below, or for that matter the gods of ancient paganism, and ask what would happen if such a god were to become human, you would end up with a figure very different from the one in the gospels. But if you start with the God of the Exodus, of Isaiah, of creation and covenant, and of the psalms, and ask what that God might look like were he to become human, you will find that he might look very much like Jesus of Nazareth, and perhaps never more so than when he dies on a Roman cross.

Anyone can, of course, declare that this picture was read back by the early church into Jesus' mind. The evidence for this is not good. The early church did not make much use of these themes; there is, of course, some overlap, but also quite substantial discontinuity. (This, ironically, may be why this latent Christology has often gone unnoticed; scholar and pietist alike have preferred the early church's christological formulations to Jesus' christological vocation, the pietist reading them back into Jesus' mind, the scholar declaring this impossible.) As with Jesus' messiahship and his vocation to suffer and die, the key sayings remain cryptic, coming into focus only when grouped around the central symbolic actions. Such riddles make sense, find a natural life setting, only within Jesus' own ministry. The early church was not reticent about saying that Jesus was messiah, that his death was God's saving act, and that he and his Father belonged together within the Jewish picture of the one God.

I see no reason why the contemporary church should be reticent about this, either. Using incarnational language about Jesus, and trinitarian language about God, is of course self-involving: it entails a commitment of faith, love, trust, and obedience. But there is a difference between self-involving language and self-referring language. I do not think that when I use language like this about Jesus and God I am merely talking about the state of my own devotion. I think I am talking, self-involvingly of course, about Jesus and God.

Jesus and God

As Christians, we live in a tradition that affirms the most extraordinary things about Jesus. In our worship services, we regularly speak of him as divine. In the words of the Nicene Creed, he is "very God of very God," "of one substance with the Father," as well as the second person of the Trinity. In our hymns, we praise him as "Lord" and "king." At Christmas we sing about him: "Veiled in flesh, the Godhead see; hail, incarnate deity"; and "Of the Father's love begotten, ere the worlds began to be; he is Alpha and Omega, he the source, the ending he." In our prayers, we pray to him as to God. Indeed, for many Christians, Jesus is one of the names of God.

It is therefore not surprising that most Christians think of Jesus as divine, and most non-Christians think this is what Christians believe. Some Christians see agreement with this claim as a primary test of orthodoxy. I am sometimes asked, usually by a hostile questioner, "Do you believe Jesus was God?" Typically the question includes a demand for "a simple yes-or-no answer." My response to this question is the same as my response to the question "Do you believe Jesus died for our sins?": no, and yes.

Though the response sounds evasive, what I mean is quite precise. Do I think Jesus thought of himself as divine? No. Do I think he had the mind of God—that is, did he know more than his contemporaries (and anybody who has ever lived) because, in addition to having a human mind, he had a divine mind? No. Do I think he had the power of God? That he could, for example, have called down twelve legions of angels to protect himself, as Matthew 26.53 reports he said? No. But if we make the distinction between the pre-Easter Jesus and the post-Easter Jesus, then my answer would be, "Yes, the post-Easter Jesus is a divine reality—is indeed one with God." And about the pre-Easter Jesus, I would say, "He is the embodiment or incarnation of God."

In this [selection], I will explain more fully what I mean by the above. I will describe how I see both the pre-Easter Jesus and post-Easter Jesus in relationship to God. Doing so will involve treating the emergence of christological images in the early Christian movement and their conceptual development in the Nicene Creed of the fourth century.

The Pre-Easter Jesus and God

As I argued [previously], I do not think that Jesus proclaimed himself with any of the exalted titles by which he is known in the Christian tradition. I grant that it is possible that Jesus thought of himself as the messiah, as Tom [N. T. Wright] argues, but I am not at all confident about such a claim. If by *messiah,* one means something as modest as believing oneself to have been anointed by God, I could accept that Jesus thought that, in which case *messiah* and *prophet* would be closely related terms (though I still don't think Jesus spoke of himself as messiah). But if by *messiah* one means much more than this, as Tom does, namely, one anointed by God to be the climactic figure in Israel's history who would lead the final and decisive battle against evil, then I have misgivings like those I have about Jesus seeing his own death as central to the God-Israel relationship.

Let me put the misgiving in extreme and provocative form: if you think you are the light of the world, you're not. That is, perceiving oneself in such grand terms is a fairly good indicator that you're off base. The parallel statement, of course, is: if you think you are the messiah, you're not. I am not proposing this as a law of the universe; perhaps you can think you are the messiah and really be the messiah.

But as the New Testament scholar John Knox argued a generation ago, thinking that Jesus thought of himself in such grand terms raises serious questions about the mental health of Jesus. And though saints and Spirit persons are a bit crazy, when judged by conventional standards, they typically do not think of themselves in grandiose terms. I don't think people like Jesus have an exalted perception of themselves.

What I am confident about is that Jesus as a Jewish mystic knew God. Moreover, as a Spirit person and healer, he would have experienced himself as one "anointed by the Spirit," whether he used this particular phrase or not. This claim is the starting point for how I think of the historical Jesus in relationship to God.

As Incarnation of God

Christians commonly speak of the relationship between Jesus and God using incarnational language: Jesus is the incarnation of God. *Incarnation* means "embodiment": in Jesus, God became embodied, the Word became flesh. But there are two quite different ways of understanding this, connected to the two different ways of thinking about God described earlier.

The first understanding of Jesus as the incarnation of God sees the meaning of this claim within the framework of supernatural theism. Common in popular-level Christianity throughout the centuries, it flows out of taking biblical and creedal language quite literally. Supernatural theism sees God as a being "out there" and not "here." Within this framework, God's relationship to the world is seen in interventionist terms. From "out there," God intervened by sending Jesus as the only Son of God into the world to live and die for us.

For thirty years or so, more or less, God was here, incarnate in Jesus. But normally God isn't here. This view sees Jesus as the unique incarnation of an absent interventionist God, an unparalleled divine insertion into the natural order.

A second way of understanding Jesus as the incarnation of God is to do so within the framework of pantheism or dialectical theism. Namely, God is not "out there" but "right here" as well as *more* than right here, both transcendent and immanent. God is the encompassing Spirit in whom we live and move and have our being. Within this view, Jesus as a Spirit person was open to the presence of God. Writers on spirituality sometimes speak of "emptiness" as a condition of the psyche that makes possible being filled by God. For whatever combination of reasons (genetic inheritance, socialization, spiritual practices, and so forth), we may imagine that Jesus was so "empty" in this sense that he could be filled with the Spirit. Thus I see Jesus as the embodiment and incarnation of the God who is everywhere present. But he is not a visitor from elsewhere, sent to the world by a god "out there." He is not different in kind from us but as completely human as we are. In the fully human life of this utterly remarkable Spirit person, we see the incarnation of God.

The Post-Easter Christological Images

In the decades after his death, a host of striking images for speaking about Jesus emerged within the early Christian community. All of them have their roots in the Jewish tradition, even though some later came to have additional nuances of meaning in the larger Mediterranean world. Many of them have become christological "titles" or designations within the Christian tradition.

The list is impressive: messiah, Son of God, Lord, Word of God, Wisdom (Sophia) of God, lamb of God, true light, Light of the World, bread of life, the way, great high priest and sacrifice, servant of God, good shepherd, true vine, and so forth. Jesus was spoken of in the most exalted language known in his tradition.

The Origin of the Images

Why did this happen? In my judgment, there were two primary factors. One was the Easter experience. As I said [previously], I do not mean a specific experience on a particular day or a set of such experiences over a period of forty days (to use Luke's time frame). Rather, I mean experiences (which continue to this day) of Jesus as a living reality with the qualities of God, a figure of the present and not of the past.

But it was not only the Easter experience that accounts for the application of exalted language to Jesus. The high estimate of him expressed by these metaphors also flows out of what his followers experienced in the pre-Easter Jesus. I think they sometimes experienced him as an epiphany of the Spirit, as one in whom the Spirit was present. I think they found his healing ability to be remarkable, even as I think they were struck by his wisdom teaching and awed by his courage and determination. I do not think they experienced him as ordinary. Thus, ultimately, the exalted language is grounded in what he was like as a historical person, even though I am skeptical that he or his followers used this language during his lifetime.

The Christological Images as the Voice of the Community

I began with a comment building on my claim that explicitly christological language is the voice of the community after Easter and not the voice of Jesus. I will do so by using the remarkable collection of "I am" sayings attributed to Jesus in the gospel of John:

> I am the light of the world.
> I am the bread of life.
> I am the way, truth, and life.
> I am the true vine.
> I am the resurrection and the life.
> I am the door.
> I am the good shepherd.
> Before Abraham was, I am.

Jesus also makes other grand statements about himself in John's gospel:

> I and the Father are one.
> Whoever has seen me has seen God.

As already mentioned, I and most mainline scholars do not think Jesus said these things. He did not speak like this.

To some Christians, this statement comes as a bit of a shock and seems to devalue the "I am" sayings and the other christological sayings in John. But I find these statements to be far more powerful as the voice of the community than if I were to think of them as claims of Jesus about himself.

To explain, what would we think of a person who solemnly said about himself, "I am the light of the world" or "Whoever has seen me has seen God"? Or, to expand one of the statements with more language from John: "I am the bread of life; unless you eat the flesh of the Son of Man and drink his blood, you have no life in you." As self-statements, these are highly problematic. Indeed, we have categories of psychological diagnosis for people who talk like this about themselves.

But if we think of these not as self-statements of Jesus but as the voice of the community, they become very powerful. If a community says about someone, "We have found in this person the light of the world who has shown us the way out of darkness," "We have found in this person the way that leads from death to life," "We have found in this person the spiritual food that feeds us in the midst of our journey even now," that is very impressive indeed. In short, I find the christological language of the New Testament much more compelling when I hear it as the testimony of the community rather than as the self-proclamation of a Galilean Jewish peasant. It is worth taking seriously.

Finally, though the exalted christological images are the post-Easter voice of the community, they are not simply statements about the community's experience. They are also affirmations about the pre-Easter Jesus. The community says, in effect, "This one who was among us as Jesus of Nazareth is also the Word of God, the Son of God, and the Wisdom of God." In him, we see what God is like.

The Christological Images as Metaphors

The christological affirmations of the New Testament are metaphors. When one thinks about it, this is quite obvious: Jesus was not literally a door, a vine, a light, or a loaf of bread. Moreover, the multiplicity of images points to their metaphoricity. Putting the images into a single sentence makes the point: Jesus is the Word of God, Wisdom of God, Son of God, lamb of God, light of the world, great high priest, and so forth. He was all of this. That is, it is not that one of these is literally true and the rest "only" metaphors. Rather, all are mataphors. Metaphors can, of course, be true, but their truth is not literal.

The essential meaning of metaphor is "to see as."

Thus, to say "Jesus is the true vine" is to *see him as* the true vine, and to say "Jesus is the Son of God" is to *see him as* the Son of God. The point is not to believe *that* Jesus is the true vine or the Son of God, as if these were facts about him. But to see him *as* the true vine implies taking him very seriously as the one upon whom we as the branches depend for life, and as one whose life flows through us.

I will further illustrate the meaning of metaphor as "to see as" with two of the most important christological images in the New Testament: Jesus as Son of God, and Jesus as Wisdom of God. The first uses male imagery to speak about Jesus, the second uses female imagery.

"Son of God" is perhaps the single most familiar christological title. Indeed, it is so familiar that many people think it is the "real" one, with the others perhaps being metaphorical. Tracing its development illuminates the meaning of the phrase. It has a history in the Hebrew Bible and the Jewish tradition.

"Son of God" could refer to Israel. In the story of the Exodus, Moses is told to say to Pharaoh: "Thus says the Lord: Israel is my first born son.... Let my son go that he may worship you." Hosea says in the name of God, "When Israel was a child, I loved him, and out of Egypt I called my son."

"Son of God" could also refer to the king of Israel. Speaking in the name of God, Nathan the prophet said about the king, "I will be a father to him, and he shall be a son to me." In a psalm probably used in a coronation liturgy in ancient Israel, the divine voice addresses the king and says, "You are my son; today I have begotten you."

In the book of Job, angels or perhaps members of the divine council are referred to as sons of God: "One day the sons of God came to present themselves before the Lord, and Satan also was among them."

One further use of the metaphor in the Jewish tradition is also worth nothing. Near the time of Jesus, other Jewish Spirit persons were sometimes called "son" of God.

What do Israel, the king, angels, and Jewish religious ecstatics have in common? All have a close relationship with God. That is, "Son of God" is a relational metaphor, pointing to an intimate relationship with God, like that of beloved child to parent.

This seems to be its initial meaning as applied to Jesus: an affirmation that Jesus stood in an intimate relationship with God. Moreover, in the world of Jesus, a son could also represent his father: he could speak for his father, and act on behalf of his father. Sonship has resonances of agency. Then it became a biological metaphor in the birth stories: Jesus as Son of God was conceived by the Spirit of God, not by a human father. Ultimately, it became a metaphysical or ontological claim: Jesus as the only begotten Son of God is of one substance with God. But initially, to see Jesus as the Son of God points to a relationship of special intimacy and agency.

A second important christological image is female: Jesus as the wisdom of God. Because the Greek word for *wisdom is sophia,* it is now common to speak of a Sophia Christology. Wisdom/Sophia in the Jewish tradition is often personified as a woman. Sophia was with God at creation, and the world was created with her aid. She is also spoken of as a Spirit that pervades everything and is everywhere present. She speaks through prophets and invites people to her banquet of bread and wine. And, of course, she invites people to follow her way, which is the way of wisdom rather than folly.

The use of Sophia imagery to speak of Jesus is early and widespread in the New Testament. In the synoptics, Paul, and John, Jesus is spoken of as the child, prophet, and incarnation of divine Sophia. Presumably the historical ground for this is Jesus' roles as a wisdom teacher and prophet who was also known for inviting all and sundry to banquet with him.

Thus to say Jesus is the Son of God is to see Jesus *as* the Son of God, just as to say Jesus is the Sophia of God is to see Jesus *as* the Sophia of God. What it means to see him *as* Son and Sophia is illuminated by the resonances the metaphors have in the tradition from which they came. But it is not the case that Jesus is literally the Son of God and only metaphorically the Sophia of God. Both are metaphors.

The Christological Images as Confessional Language

The christological metaphors are confessional. That is, they are confessions of faith, not statements of verifiable fact. To say "Jesus is the messiah" or "Jesus is the Wisdom of God" is not a fact about Jesus in the sense that "He was five feet three inches tall and weighed 125 pounds" (or whatever size he was) is a fact about Jesus. The latter statement was open to verification by anybody with a tape measure and a scale. The former statements involve conviction and commitment. To see Jesus as "the Wisdom of God" and "Son of God" and "messiah" means to take very seriously what we see in him as a disclosure of God.

As I end this section on the christological metaphors, I want to emphasize that as a Christian I think these affirmations about Jesus are true. But they are true as metaphors. The recognition that this is metaphorical language is crucial. When we do not see this, we take the language literally. Unfortunately, this has often happened within the Christian tradition. Very early on, we metaphorized our history, and since then we have often historicized our metaphors. When we literalize metaphors, we get nonsense. We also lose the metaphors, with their rich resonances of meaning.

The Creed and the Trinity

As early Christianity developed, the post-Easter Jesus increasingly functioned as a divine reality within the community. Even before the gospels were written, prayers were addressed to Jesus as if to God, and hymns praised Jesus as divine. By the early second century, Ignatius could speak of "our God, Jesus Christ."

This created a conundrum of sorts. How could early Christians reconcile their experience of and devotion to the post-Easter Jesus as a divine reality with their commitment to monotheism? The solution to the conundrum was ultimately the Trinity, expressed in the trinitarian pattern of the Nicene Creed.

To continue with a personal comment: I have no difficulty saying and affirming the Nicene Creed. I see it as both the crystallization and indigenization of early Christian theological development. It crystallizes the developing tradition at a particular point in time, even as it also indigenizes it in a particular culture by combining biblical language with categories drawn from Hellenistic philosophy.

By indigenization, I mean that the creed is the product of adapting the essentially biblical language of earliest Christianity into the cultural categories of the larger Mediterranean world of the fourth century. For example, the terms *substance* and *persons,* as they are used in the creed and the doctrine of the Trinity, are both derived from Hellenistic thought. They are culturally relative terms, as is the language of the Bible, for that matter.

The cultural relativity of biblical and creedal language struck me with considerable force when I was in South Africa on a lecture trip a few years ago, soon after the official end of apartheid. My schedule included lecturing at a black theological seminary, an interesting learning experience. On the drive back to Pretoria with my white host, I was told that the black church was being encouraged to develop its own creed. The reason? Because the status of "only son" was not a very high status in that particular black culture. One has no access to an "only son"; he is socially isolated. A much higher status was that of "oldest brother." Thus, if one were to speak of Jesus with the highest status known in that culture, one would speak of him as "our oldest brother" and not as an "only son." The cultural relativity of creedal and biblical language hit home. To say the obvious, if the creed had been formulated in a different culture, its language would have been very different.

This awareness relativizes the creed and the Trinity, even as it helps us to understand it. The meaning of its language is to be understood in the fourth-century context in which it was framed. As I have thus far been able to understand what the creed and the Trinity affirm about Jesus, I see it as having three functions.

First, it affirms what Christian experience and devotion already knew and still know; that the living risen Christ is a divine reality. Though the claim that

Jesus is "of one substance" with God uses metaphysical language, it is ultimately not simply the product of philosophical speculation but is grounded in early Christian experience of the risen Christ.

Second, it reconciles the above with monotheism by speaking of one God in three *personae*. This means something quite different from "persons" in modern English, where *person* commonly means a separate center of personality. Thus popular notions of the Trinity commonly imagine God as a committee of three somewhat separate divine beings. But in both Greek and Latin, the word translated "person" means a mask, such as that worn by an actor in the theater —not as a means of concealment, but as a way of playing different roles. Applying this to the notion of God, the one God is known in three primary ways: as the God of Israel, as the Word and Wisdom of God in Jesus, and as the abiding Spirit.

The risen living Christ is thus not a second God but is one with God. And though I am aware that some theologians emphasize that the Trinity means more than this, it seems to me to mean at least this much.

Third, like the christological metaphors of the New Testament, the creed also makes an affirmation about the historical Jesus. At first glance, it appears not to: the creed moves from Jesus' birth to death with nothing at all about his historical life. I once saw this as a defect, as if it implied no interest in the historical Jesus. I now see it as a clue to the function of the creed: namely, by framing the life of Jesus within conception by the Spirit and resurrection to God's right hand, it affirms that what happened in Jesus was "of God."

Aware of all of the above, I can say the creed without misgivings. I do not see it as a set of literally true doctrinal statements to which I am supposed to give my intellectual assent, but as a culturally relative product of the ancient church. Were we to try to write a creed today, we would not use their language, not because we have become unfaithful, but simply because it is not our language. But I do see it as affirming the reality of God, known to us in creation and in the abiding Spirit and preeminently in Jesus.

When I say the creed, I understand myself to be identifying with the community that says these words together. For those of us in creedal churches, doing so is part of our identity. Moreover, I identify not only with the community in the present, but also with generations of long-dead Christians who said these same ancient words as they stood in the presence of sacred mystery. I experience a momentary participation in the communion of saints. Given all of the above, I think we would understand the purpose of the creed better if we sang it or chanted it.

The Cumulative Christological Claim

As I move toward a concluding crystallization, I begin by emphasizing the riches of the multiple christological metaphors of the New Testament. Each metaphor has its own nuances, and it is important and illuminating to explore them individually. Jesus as "the light of the world" invites us to explore the multiple resonances of "light" and "darkness" as images of the human condition, just as Jesus as "the bread of life" invites us to tease out the resonances of "hunger" and "being filled" as metaphors of yearning and satisfaction. Thus I do not want my somewhat abstract crystallization to detract in any way from the richness of the individual metaphors.

The christological metaphors and the more conceptual language of the Nicene Creed make a cumulative claim about the significance of Jesus. Taken together, and put very compactly, they claim that Jesus is the decisive revelation of God. The word *revelation* has a number of synonyms: *disclosure, manifestation, epiphany.* Jesus discloses what God is like. Jesus is the epiphany of God, a word that means the manifestation on the surface of something from the depths. He is, to return to the metaphors, the Word of God, Wisdom of God, Son of God, and Light of the World.

To affirm that Jesus is the decisive revelation of God does not require affirming that he is the only, or only adequate, revelation of God. Christians have sometimes thought so. Indeed, a few passages in the New Testament suggest as much. The Jesus of John's gospel says, "I am the Way, the Truth and the Life; no one comes to God except through me." In the book of Acts, Peter is reported to have said about Jesus, "There is salvation in no one else, for there is no other name under heaven by which we must be saved."

However, whatever these passages may have meant in their first-century contexts, they need not be understood to mean that Jesus (or Christianity) is the only way of salvation. Instead, we might understand them (and similar Christian statements about Jesus being "the only way") as reflecting the joy of having found one's salvation through Jesus, and the intensity of Christian devotion to Jesus. They should be understood as exclamations, not doctrines, and as "the poetry of devotion and the hyperbole of the heart." So *decisive* need not mean "only."

But the claim does mean that for us, *as Christians,* Jesus is the decisive revelation of God, and of what a life full of God is like. Indeed, I see this as the defining characteristic that makes us Christian rather than something else. If we found the decisive revelation of God in the Torah or in the Koran, then we would be Jews or Muslims. But to be Christian is to affirm, "Here, in Jesus, I see more clearly than anywhere else what God is like." This affirmation can be made with one's whole heart while still affirming that God is also known in other traditions.

The New Testament itself contains an exceedingly compact christological crystallization: "Jesus is the image of the invisible God." Jesus is the image of God: in him, we see what God is like. The Greek word behind *image* is *icon,* which suggestively adds another nuance of meaning. An icon is a sacred image; further, its purpose is to mediate the sacred. Jesus as image and icon of God not only shows us what God is like but also mediates the sacred. The one who was and is Word of God, Wisdom of God, and Son of God is also the sacrament of God.

POSTSCRIPT

Was Jesus Christ the Son of God?

There are many names for the man called Jesus. Christians refer to Jesus as the "Christ" as well as the "Messiah." The words "Christ" and "Messiah" are English versions of the respective Greek and Hebrew words for "the Anointed One." In ancient Israel, high priests, kings, and prophets were set apart for their calling by the pouring of sacred oil upon their heads. This "anointing" was to symbolize that their appointment came from God. To refer to Jesus as the Christ is to acknowledge that he was indeed the one called and anointed of God to fulfill a divine role. Some scholars are careful not to refer to Jesus as the Christ for fear of crossing or confusing the line between objective scholar and subjective disciple. The name "Jesus" is the Greek form of the Hebrew name "Joshua," which by interpretation means "savior."

Christian tradition asserts that the majority of the Jewish population of the day did not accept Jesus as the Messiah because the spiritual freedom he offered was much different from the political and economic freedom they were anticipating. The Greeks judged the Christian message as "foolishness" because of their inability to reconcile Jesus' teachings with the Greek philosophical traditions of the day (see also KJV, Matt. 16:13–17 and KJV, Acts 26:28).

Was Jesus of Nazareth simply one of many great leaders who have walked the earth, or was he in addition the literal Son of God? Christian apologist Josh McDowell has framed the question of the divinity of Jesus into the trilemma of "Lord, liar, or lunatic?" However we choose to answer the question, the controversy over the divinity of Jesus has been and will continue to be one of the central topics of debate in Christian theology.

Suggested Readings

M. J. Borg, *Meeting Jesus Again for the First Time: The Historical Jesus and the Heart of Contemporary Faith* (HarperSanFrancisco, 1995).

J. S. Spong, *Liberating the Gospels: Reading the Bible With Jewish Eyes* (HarperCollins, 1997).

M. J. Wilkins and J. P. Moreland, eds., *Jesus Under Fire: Modern Scholarship Reinvents the Historical Jesus* (Zondervan, 1995).

N. T. Wright, *The Challenge of Jesus: Rediscovering Who Jesus Was and Is* (InterVarsity Press, 1999).

ISSUE 8

Is the Family Primary in God's Plan?

YES: Michael Gold, from "Family: A Spiritual Guide," Address Given at the World Congress on Families II, Geneva, Switzerland (November 14–17, 1999)

NO: Stanley Hauerwas, from "The Family as a School for Character," in Gabriel Palmer-Fernandez, comp., *Moral Issues: Philosophical and Religious Perspectives* (Prentice-Hall, 1996)

ISSUE SUMMARY

YES: Michael Gold, a Jewish rabbi who heads Temple Beth Torah in Tamarac, Florida, argues for the primacy of the traditional family in God's plan. Gold believes that the rescue of our decaying culture is dependent upon returning to the traditional family structure where moral values can be properly taught and modeled.

NO: Stanley Hauerwas, professor of theological ethics at Duke Divinity School in Durham, North Carolina, believes the family to be of great importance, but he states that it is not primary to God's plan. Hauerwas reasons from Scripture that it is the church that is primary and not the family. Putting the family first would be a form of idolatry, he concludes.

From the beginning, the family has been one of the central pillars of the religious world. From the Hebrew Bible we read that two of the first commandments given by God to Adam and Eve in the Garden of Eden were concerned with family issues: "Be fruitful, and multiply and replenish the earth" (King James Version, Gen. 1:28) and "Therefore shall a man leave his father and his mother, and shall cleave unto his wife: and they shall be one flesh" (KJV, Gen. 2:24). Other words and phrases such as "the *house* of Israel" (KJV, Exod. 16:31, italics added) and "the *families* of the earth" (KJV, Gen. 28:14, italics added), as well as God himself choosing to be called by the name "father" (KJV, Mat. 5:16) appear to suggest that family relationships are central to God's purposes.

There is great controversy over the definition of "family." The image of the traditional family composed of a married heterosexual couple with children is being challenged by those who are arguing for the legitimacy of alternate definitions. Even the religious world contains a wide variety of definitions. Leaders of The Church of Jesus Christ of Latter-day Saints, long known for their strong emphasis on the family, have formally stated:

> We, The First Presidency and the Council of the Twelve Apostles of The Church of Jesus Christ of Latter-day Saints, solemnly proclaim that marriage between a man and a woman is ordained of God and that the family is central to the Creator's plan for the eternal destiny of His children.

> — "The Family: A Proclamation to the World," *Ensign*
> (November, 1995), p. 102

Most conservative religious groups would support such a statement, but others would argue that it is too narrow and should be broadened to include alternative lifestyles, including gay and lesbian relationships. Michelle McCarty, in her book entitled *Loving—A Catholic Perspective on Vocational Lifestyle Choices* (Brown, 1993), writes:

> "Family" no longer means only a man and a woman who are married to each other and their children.... Catholic teaching has perhaps the best, most inclusive definition of the family in its ideal expression: a community of individual persons joined by human love and living a community life that provides for the greatest expression of individualism.

While not representative of the *traditional* Catholic perspective, McCarty's interpretation of Catholic teachings exemplifies the philosophy of those who want to liberalize the definition of family. Theologians who support (to a greater or lesser degree) this interpretation of what constitutes a family believe that Christian values such as "compassion, love, and inclusion not only prohibit the condemnation of other types of family but demand the acceptance of all families who have been the victims of social injustice" (Lisa Sowel Cahill, *Family: A Christian Social Perspective*, Fortress, 2000).

While acknowledging the important and sometimes bitter debate between conservative and liberal theologians with regard to family, this issue focuses on an aspect of the debate that challenges both sides: which is more important to put first, the church or the family? Most people of faith agree that without the sustaining influence of God, humankind has and will falter and fail. These same people will also acknowledge the necessity of community, whether it be expressed as familial relationships at home and/or the relationships afforded by the church. Michael Gold and Stanley Hauerwas address the question of the primacy of the family in God's plan. The selections are written by two men of faith—yet they come to different conclusions.

Gold argues for continued support of the traditional family as God's time-tested standard for healthy and happy individuals and for the stability of the general culture as well. He provides scriptural and linguistic support for the unique contributions that can only be made by a mother and father.

Hauerwas counters that if we place God as the means of achieving the end of family stability, we have made the family into an "idolatrous institution." He believes it is God, accessed through the church, that should be the primary object of our worship, thus making the family secondary.

Michael Gold  **YES**

Family: A Spiritual Guide

Rabbi Irving Lehrman tells a wonderful story from his own childhood. A little boy walks into an office building and sees a clock too high on the wall for anyone to reach. To adjust the time, workmen must climb a tall ladder. The boy asks his father, "Why is the clock set so high, where nobody can reach it?" "It's simple," answers the father. "The clock used to be lower, within reach of everybody. People would pass by, look at their watch, and adjust the clock to match their watch. When they moved the clock higher, people would look at it and adjust their watches accordingly."

The meaning of the metaphor is clear. We need an ideal, a vision, a clock high on the wall that we can refer to. Certainly not every individual nor every family will live their lives according to that ideal. But without some recognized standard, everybody will simply do "what is right in their own eyes." (Judges 21:25)

Family is a spiritual entity. The meaning of family goes beyond the biological and material to touch the spiritual dimension of life. This paper will view family as a spiritual ideal. This ideal includes a man and a woman committed to one another through the covenant of marriage, raising the children they sire or adopt, honoring their parents, being the keepers of their brothers and sisters, and expressing their love through their devotion and service to one another. It is an ideal that grew out of the Bible, and is central to the vision of family articulated by those religious traditions based on the Bible: Judaism, Christianity, and Islam.

One of the key messages of the creation story in Genesis is that we human beings are qualitatively different from animals. We are created in the image of God, with the ability to make moral choices. We are commanded to be holy (Leviticus 19:2), holiness being those actions which help raise us above animal behavior and towards the Godliness within us.

Let us begin our exploration by comparing the animal world and the human world. In the realm of family life, we clearly see the difference between animals and humans. We may use the same words—mother, father, sister, brother, son, daughter—but they take on an entirely different meaning in the animal kingdom and the world of humans.

From Michael Gold, "Family: A Spiritual Guide," Address Given at the World Congress on Families II, Geneva, Switzerland (November 14–17, 1999). Copyright © 1999 by Rabbi Michael Gold. Reprinted by permission of World Congress of Families and Rabbi Michael Gold. References omitted.

Animals have parents. They received half of their genetic material from a male who served as sperm donor, and half from a female who gave the egg. An animal grew inside its mother, and if it is a mammal, it nursed at her nipple. Within the animal kingdom, after a relatively brief period of time, the parents are finished with their tasks.

Humans also have a birth mother and father. But that is a biological fact which has little to do with parenting. After we are born and after we are weaned, our parents' tasks are just beginning.

Animals have siblings. They may share genetic material, or even grow in the same womb with other animals. But the relationship stops there. No animal would ever ask the question, "Am I my brother's keeper?"

Animals procreate children. Male animals join sexually with female animals to create a new generation. For animals, this is totally a biological act, with no larger moral or spiritual purpose. In fact, most animals have sexual encounters only when in heat, when there is a probability of procreation. A male leaves his sperm in a female and moves on to other conquests.

In the animal kingdom, following birth and a short period of nursing and nurturing, children are set loose to survive on their own. There is no expectation of any ongoing relationship between the biological parents and their offspring. In the real world, it is unlikely that adult animals even recognize their progenitors.

Perhaps the best way to demonstrate the difference between animals and humans is to speak of two metaphors, the cycle and the chain. Animals live in the world of the cycle. The human quest is to break out of the cycle, to see life as a chain.

To demonstrate the world of the cycle, let us look at the beautiful Disney movie *The Lion King*. The movie begins with Elton John singing the theme song of this movie, *The Circle of Life*. A baby lion is born and held high for all the animals to see. The song tells of a great cycle, with events repeated over and over as each new generation comes. At the end of the movie, a new generation of lions is born, and the same scene is repeated once again.

To the animal world, life is a cycle. Each generation repeats what was done before. The life of a lion or a kangaroo or a parakeet is almost precisely the same as the life of these animals one generation ago. If we went back ten thousand generations and looked at the way a lion lives, it would be more or less the same as today.

It was the power of this cycle that Disney caught so beautifully in the movie. Birth, weaning, adulthood, procreation, death, the cycle continues unchanging from generation to generation.

There is a book in the Bible which also speaks of life as an endless, unchanging circle. The book of Ecclesiastes, traditionally attributed to King Solomon and perhaps the most cynical book in the entire Bible, laments the vanity and meaninglessness of life.

> Vanity of vanities, all is vanity. What real value is there for man
> in all the gains he makes beneath the sun? One generation goes,
> another comes, but the earth remains the same forever....

> All streams flow into the sea, Yet the sea is never full; To the place from which they flow the streams flow back again.... Only that shall happen which has happened, Only that occur which has occurred; There is nothing new beneath the sun.

One senses Solomon's depression and futility. Is life but an endless cycle, with nothing new to show for it? Are we forced to relive the fate of our parents and grandparents over and over? If we are mere animals, forced to relive the same thing over and over, how can there be any ultimate purpose to life? The cycle as a metaphor may work for animals, but not for human beings.

Thomas Cahill, in his best selling book *The Gifts of the Jews: How a Tribe of Desert Nomads Changed the Way Everyone Thinks and Feels,* wrote that the ancient Israelites gave the world a new metaphor. To quote Cahill, "All evidence points to there having been, in the earliest religious thought, a vision of the cosmos that was profoundly cyclical. The Jews were the first people to break out of this circle, to find a new way of thinking and experiencing, a new way of understanding and feeling the world."

The ancient pagan world, like the animal world, saw life as an endless repetitive cycle. The gift of the Bible was the vision that we humans can rise above that cycle, that we are more than mere animals. The Bible introduces a new metaphor, one with a beginning and an end. It is best represented by a chain, with each generation a new link. That is why the Bible is so concerned with who begat whom.

Each generation builds and adds to the previous link. Previous generations contain a repository of wisdom and knowledge on which a new generation can build. Each new generation stands on the shoulders of their parents and grandparents. Each new generation sees itself as closer to the perfect Messianic age still to come.

Humans experience a link between generations, an appreciation of the past and a vision of the future, which animals can never know. To be part of a chain, part of some greater purpose, gives human life its spiritual quality. It is family that creates that chain.

Let us explore the family as a spiritual entity. To do so, we must travel back to the dawn of creation, to that mystical place called the Garden of Eden.

Family life began when God created man, placed him in the garden, and declared "it is not good for man to be alone. I will make him a fitting helper." (Genesis 2:18) God brought each animal to the man, but none was an appropriate helper nor a proper fit. The word family does not apply to the animal kingdom.

Only then did God cause a deep sleep to fall on the man and remove his rib. (Jewish mystics would say that the primordial man was originally androgynous, both male and female, and God split him/her in half.) God created the woman from the rib and declared one of the most important verses in the Torah, "Therefore a man shall leave his mother and father and cleave unto his wife and they shall be one flesh." (Genesis 2:24) No other male in the entire animal kingdom is given that responsibility.

We should note that the Torah does not say "a man should leave his mother and father for a series of sexual conquests and one night stands." Sexual discipline stands at the center of the Torah's vision of family life. A human male is not to scatter his seed wherever he wishes, although it would be in his genetic self-interest to do so.

Nor does the Torah say "a man shall leave his mother and father and cleave to his wives." Polygamy may have been permitted in Biblical times, but it is scarcely the ideal. In fact, one can argue that the Biblical stories of Abraham, Sarah, and Hagar, or Jacob, Rachel, and Leah, are polemics against polygamy. It is noteworthy that all of the great Biblical religions have long outlawed polygamy.

Nor does the Torah countenance serial monogamy, one wife after another. The book of Deuteronomy, recognizing the reality of human weakness, does permit divorce. (See Deuteronomy 24:1–4.) But it is considered a sad, last resort, far from the ideal. In fact, the Prophet Malachi wrote, "You cover the alter of God with tears, weeping and moaning. . . . Because the Lord is witness between you and the wife of your youth with whom you have broken faith, though she is your partner and covenanted spouse." (Malachi 2:13–14) Based on this verse, the rabbis taught that when a man divorces the wife of his youth, even the altar of God cries tears. (Gittin 90b)

Lifelong marriage between one man and one woman is the ideal articulated by the Garden of Eden story. Jewish tradition uses the term kiddushin, literally holiness, to describe such a marriage. It is marriage, the commitment of a man and a woman to a lifelong exclusive sexual relationship that helps us rise above the animal kingdom.

All of the legal traditions that grew out of the Bible—Jewish halakhah, Church canon law, Moslem Shari'ah—are concerned with the legal niceties of marriage: Who may marry whom? How is a marriage effected? What are the legal obligations of spouses towards one another? May a marriage be dissolved?

All agree that marriage is more than a mere legal contract. The Bible often compares the relationship of husband and wife to the relationship between God and Israel. Perhaps the best word is brit—covenant. The word covenant implies something eternal and unbroken. In fact, in Mormon theology the highest degree of salvation comes through eternal marriage or sealing, a dispensation that carried the marital state beyond this lifetime.

According to the Biblical ideal, marriage has two purposes. The first is companionship, for "it is not good for man to be alone." (Genesis 2:18) The second is in order to fulfill God's commandment to "Be fruitful and multiply." (Genesis 1:28)

Judaism understands the commandment of procreation as applying to men, although obviously a man needs a woman partner to fulfill his obligation. There is much speculation in Jewish sources why this commandment was given to men only. Perhaps women do not need an explicit commandment; they have a natural, maternal urge. Men on the other hand are too often happy to avoid the obligations of fatherhood, particularly when children demand a huge financial commitment. This is one reason that abortion is often a boon to men, who are happy to tell the woman to "take care of the problem."

Jewish law teaches that minimally, a man must have one boy and one girl to fulfill the commandment of procreation. However, the Talmud continues that these children must be capable of having their own children. In other words, in order to completely fulfill the commandment, a man must have grandchildren. As the Talmud teaches, "a man's love is towards his son, the son's love is towards his own son." (Sota 49a) The major concern is the chain of generations.

This ideal of marriage and procreation raises a deep question: Why are human males asked to do what no other animal must do, forsake sexual conquests to cleave onto one wife? To answer this question, we must delve even deeper into the creation of both humans and animals.

The Torah uses the Hebrew word yitzer—literally "formed," for the creation of both humans and animals. "The Lord God formed (yitzer) the man of the dust of the ground, and breathed into his nostrils the breath of life, and man became a living soul." (Genesis 2:7) "The Lord God formed (yitzer) out of the ground every beast of the field, and every fowl of the air." (Genesis 2:19)

There is a slight difference in the spelling of the word—the Hebrew letter yud is used only once for the creation of animals, twice for the creation of humans. In this one tiny letter is the key to the Torah's message about family. The term yetzer from the same root as yitzer has a double meaning in Hebrew. It means formed, but it also means inner drive.

Both animals and humans have a yetzer, an inner drive which underlies and defines their behavior. The rabbis noted that the slight difference in spelling is because animals have only one yetzer or inner drive, humans beings have two yetzers or inner drives. (Berachot 61a)

Animals survive through natural, instinctual behavior. They follow patterns of behavior that have been hard wired into their brains from birth. Certainly animals may be capable of some learning, but animals do not make moral choices. When a coyote attacks a farmer's sheep, he is simply doing what coyotes are hard-wired to do. One would not say that such a coyote is doing wrong.

Whether it is a salmon swimming upstream to its spawning ground, a dog in heat copulating with another dog, or a lion attacking its prey, animals are following instinct. Even the ox that continually gores in Exodus is simply following inbred behavior, the ox's owner is liable for damages. One would not call the ox a sinner. Or as I often say in my sermons, "Horses don't need Yom Kippur."

Humans are fundamentally different. We are born with a minimum number of instinctual behaviors, sucking, crying, and a few others necessary to survive our youngest years. Mostly we are a blank slate ready to be molded. (Avot 4:25) As the Bible hints, we humans have two yetzers, two inner drives, that struggle with one another and define us throughout our lives. The rabbis called these the yetzer hara, the evil inclination, and the yetzer hatov, the good inclination.

The yetzer hara consists of those primitive drives within us which seek immediate gratification. They are what Freud defined as the id. The yetzer hara is the sexual drive, the drive for violence, the drive for acquisition, the emotion of anger, all out of control. The evil inclination is that part of us which says, "I want what I want and I want it now!"

The rabbis recognized the importance of the yetzer hara. They said without it no man would build a house or marry a wife. According to a famous rabbinic legend, the rabbis once captured the yetzer hara and hid it in a barrel. (Yoma 69a) For three days nothing happened, no one went to work, even the chickens stopped laying eggs. The rabbis had to let it go. The key is not to destroy the yetzer hara, but control it and sublimate it for good. Ben Zoma taught, "Who is strong? Whoever controls their evil inclination." (Avot 4:1)

The yetzer hatov or good inclination is the drive to be altruistic. It is the part of us willing to delay gratification, practice self-control, share with others, sacrifice for a greater good, and do the right thing. For humans, life is a constant struggle between these two inclinations, between "I want what I want and I want it now" and "do the right thing." We see this struggle when we decide whether or not to indulge in a forbidden sexual encounter, whether to spend or save money, whether to act out on our anger, even whether or not to eat the ice cream when we are trying to diet.

The rabbis have another profound insight about this struggle between our two yetzers. The yetzer hara, or evil inclination, is present at full force from the moment of birth. Babies cry until their needs are met, and they do not care whom they disturb. Children seek immediate gratification. Children can be selfish and sometimes cruel. William Golding's novel The *Lord of the Flies* is a classic example of children out of control, untempered by adult authority.

The yetzer hatov, or good inclination, is only present in potential at birth. It needs to be carefully nurtured and developed, and only enters at full force at the moment of adulthood. (Ecclesiastes Rabbah 4:13) From this deep human insight, we begin to understand why the Torah asks a man to stay around, to commit to the woman he chooses and the children he sires through her. His presence is necessary for the key activity which a child needs, the activity that defines the very word parent, developing the yetzer hatov.

Here is where humans differ substantially from the animal kingdom. Someone must take primary responsibility for developing the good inclination and showing control over the evil inclination. The Bible places that obligation clearly upon fathers.

The Torah wants men around to assume an essential role in raising their young, developing the sense of right and wrong and the self-discipline to do the right thing. That is why, according to Jewish law, it is the father's duty to teach his children Torah (Kiddushin 29a), defining the word Torah in the broadest sense teaching.

Why is this a particular obligation for fathers? Certainly mothers also have a role in developing a conscience and self control in children. There are many single mothers who are forced by circumstances to bear the entire burden of teaching right from wrong, developing the yetzer hatov. They do so because the men who impregnated them have abandoned their parental responsibilities. Or some chose to do it alone, following the example set in Hollywood by the fictional television character Murphy Brown, or such real life celebrities as pop singer Madonna and actress Jodie Foster.

The Torah places the ultimate responsibility for developing the yetzer hatov on the man for reasons related to the essential nature of men and women. Scholars such as Deborah Tannen and Carol Gilligan are beginning to recognize that, in certain fundamental ways, men and women are different. Women by their very nature are primarily concerned with relationships. They are nurturers. Men by their very nature are primarily concerned with accomplishments. They are far more competitive. These different primary concerns manifest themselves in parenting roles.

To paraphrase a wonderful distinction made by columnist Don Feder, "Mothers are concerned with survival, fathers are concerned with success." The Torah recognizes that fathering is different from mothering. Children need two types of parenting if they are to grow up to be successful, competent adults. They need the self-esteem and confidence that a loving, nurturing mother can provide, one who will always accept her child unconditionally. And they need the survival skills, self-discipline, and moral values that a strong father can provide, one who makes demands and sometimes enacts punishment.

Rabbi Daniel Lapin, founder of "Towards Tradition," has a brilliant insight from the Hebrew which makes this same point. There is a Hebrew word for mother and for father, but no Hebrew for the generic parent. One cannot even say single parent in Hebrew. One can only say parents, horim, from the same root as to teach. This simple Hebrew insight seems to indicate that it takes two to parent, each with slightly different roles.

I do not want to oversimplify the role of mothers and fathers in nurturing and teaching right from wrong. As a male, I am involved in nurturing my children, and my wife is certainly involved in teaching and disciplining them. True parenting is a partnership. However, as with all good partnerships, there seem to be primary roles. The primary role of a father is to lay down the rules and teach the self-discipline necessary for a successful life.

It is important to note that one does not need to be a biological father to perform the key role of fatherhood. Adoptive fathers can do the job as well as birth fathers. Often step-fathers, grandfathers, and other key males in the life of the child assume this mentoring role. Other men from the community— teachers, coaches, religious youth leaders, scoutmasters—can become the mentors for children without fathers. The Torah wants a male presence in the life of a child.

Social critic Barbara Dafoe Whitehead has brilliantly demonstrated in her article "Dan Quayle Was Right" that when a father is absent or uninvolved, too many children grow up undisciplined and out of control. Their yetzer hara has never been brought under control. As many social scientists have pointed out, children growing up without fathers are the basis of many of our worst social problems, from gangs to crime to teenage pregnancy. All of this proves that the family is a uniquely human institution.

Animals manage without families; their genetic survival seems to work out fine. Humans need more than genetic survival, we need to learn to control our yetzer hara and develop our yetzer hatov. Fathers are essential for this to succeed. When fathers step back from this primary task, we humans seem to be acting more animal like.

Parents raise their children with the prayer that ultimately they will leave home, seek their own spouse, and have their own children. They will add a new link to the chain. In fact, it is important to note the language of the Bible, "a man shall leave his mother and father and cleave unto his wife." He must leave before he can cleave. However, even as they leave home and enter adulthood, humans must do something no other animal is obligated to do. They must honor the father and mother who raised them. (Note that the honor is to the parents who raised them, not necessarily the ones who gave birth to them. Again we are speaking of a value beyond biology.)

In Jewish tradition, this honor takes on two separate obligations. (Kiddushin 31b) First, a man or woman must be sure that parents are properly fed and cared for, particularly in old age. Humans have a value, even after they have completed the tasks of siring and raising children. Second, a man and woman must respect the dignity and standing of a parent, and do nothing to detract from that role. This commandment applies even if one's parents did a poor job. The contemporary notion that parents must earn their children's respect has no place in Biblical tradition.

An important aspect of honoring parents is the child's relationship with his or her siblings. The book of Proverbs teaches: "A friend is devoted at all times, but a brother is born for adversity." (Proverbs 17:17) With the help of the Ralbag, one of the classical Biblical commentators, we can understand what the passage really means. A friend is there for good times. He or she may go out socially with us, party with us; we may enjoy each other's company. But when difficult times hit, a person turns to his or her brother or sister. Because they are flesh and bone, they have a mutual obligation to one another.

When Cain asked the rhetorical question "Am I my brother's keeper?" the answer was yes. By caring for our siblings, we ultimately are honoring our parents. This idea can be expanded beyond our immediate family—by caring for all humanity, we ultimately honor the father of us all. "Have we not one father, did not one God create us all?" (Malachi 2:10)

Human beings live in a web of relationships. According to the Biblical ideal, a man and a woman must commit to one another in the holy covenant we call marriage. Together they must care for, provide for, and serve the needs of their spouse, ensuring that the marriage will succeed. They must nurture and mentor children, teaching them the values and self-discipline to succeed as adults. When the children grow up and leave home, they must honor parents and be the keeper of siblings. They must see themselves not as autonomous individuals but as links in the chain of generations. It is in this web of fundamental human relationships that we humans rise above the animal kingdom and ultimately find spiritual meaning.

Love begins with service to those in our own family. And in love do we ultimately see the face of God.

Stanley Hauerwas  **NO**

The Family as a School for Character

I

In my past work I have stressed the significance of character and marriage for understanding the nature of our moral existence, but I have not tried to make explicit how they may be related. I have relied on our intuitions that there is probably some very important relation between the development of character and the family, but I think it important now that I try to make candid what I understand that relation to be because I suspect that many of our assumptions about the relation between morality and the family may not only be descriptively mistaken, but theologically suspect as well.

For even though I am sure there is a relation between character and the family, I suspect it is not the one we think. The accepted account about the relation runs something like this: the family is where we learn to be moral or develop character, thus good families produce good children and adults, bad families produce bad children and adults. We know there are exceptions to these generalizations. We all know of people who have overcome extraordinarily bad families; we also know of tragedies where very good families are beset by extremely unpleasant children. But we persist in believing that the generalization on the whole is true.

Moreover the generalization underwrites a certain disquiet about our contemporary situation, for it seems that we live during a time of familial breakdown. If the family is destroyed, so is our morality; if our morality is destroyed, so it our society. So if we want to begin to do something about renewing our society, we should begin with the family. Therefore the concern with many about the family is really a concern about the very foundation of our civilization.

I think, however, that there is quite a number of things wrong with this set of assumptions about the relation of character and the family. First, it may be true that marriage and the family are, like suffering, a test of character, but I do not believe these are the setting where character should be formed. Or to put it more accurately, I do not think that the kind of character developed by the family is sufficient to sustain the moral demands made by being married or by learning to live, as we all must do, as part of a family.

From Stanley Hauerwas, "The Family as a School for Character," in Gabriel Palmer-Fernandez, comp., *Moral Issues: Philosophical and Religious Perspectives* (Prentice Hall, 1996). Originally published in *Religious Education,* vol. 80 (Spring 1985), pp. 272–285. Copyright © 1985 by The Religious Education Association. Reprinted by permission. Notes omitted.

Put simply, no one gets married or begins a family in order to develop character. It may be that being married or learning to raise a family becomes for many the decisive occasion for moral growth; but that is quite different from saying that the family, in and of itself, is the institution that should provide the context for our most decisive moral development. For example, I suspect it is true, as many attest, that they never realized how self-centered they were until they had children. Yet I do not think that our self-centeredness is necessarily cured by our relation with our children. Indeed, too often, our selfishness is only transmuted into more virulent forms as *my* children become a moral legitimation for me to ignore the claims of others in my life.

Though I will suggest that the character necessary for marriage may be enhanced through formation by the family, I do not believe that our character should be formed primarily by the family. Of course, part of the difficulty about such claims is that, as yet, we have little idea about what is meant by character. I have been using character as equivalent with morality; but as I hope to show, to use the language of character challenges many contemporary assumptions about how we should think about morality. But more of that later.

The second reason I think it a mistake to assume a direct correlation between the development of character with the family, and it is related to the first point, is that such an association can too easily turn the family into an idolatrous institution. Too often the church is supported because people care about the family. They assume the church is good because it produces a good family. This attitude is best exemplified by the horrendous claim that the "family that prays together stays together." That makes prayer valuable for some other reason than it being a crucial way of our making ourselves available to God. To give the family such significance is idolatrous as it means God is worshipped as a means to help sustain what we really care about—the family.

Ironically, when we turn the family into that kind of god the result is the destruction of the family. For when the family is asked to carry such moral significance, when the family is thought to be the one place in the moral wilderness in which we live that provides an anchor of moral stability, it is broken by being made to do more than it is able. When the family is invested with such significance, it cannot help but be morally tyrannical; and the tyranny is made all the more perverse by being clothed in the form of love and care. It is no wonder that children, seeking to be free from such care, rebel against everything their parents care about. In doing so, of course, the person they often end up hurting the worst is themselves, but sometimes even injury to self seems better than having no self at all.

Therefore, to spell out how the family should contribute to the development of character I need to say a good deal more about how Christians should understand the nature and status of the family. In the process I hope not only to illumine questions concerning the family, but also the nature and kind of character that should be associated with being a Christian.

II

In order to begin to understand the place of the family for Christians, we cannot begin with the family. Indeed, one of the interesting things about the New Testament is not what it has to say about the family, but that it has so little to say about the family. We have to look hard to find texts to analyze, and even then we often seem to end up with half a picture; or even worse, it seems that at least some of the texts have a positive anti-family ring. We often forget that the disciples, after hearing Jesus on marriage and divorce, suggested that it would be better not to marry; and Jesus' reply did nothing to dissuade them from that notion (Matthew 19:10–12). Moreover we tend, on Mother's Day, not to preach on texts that suggest that our only primary relations are to those who are members of the Kingdom of God—"who are my mother and brother but those that do the will of God" (Mark 3:31–35).

It is not my intention to try to develop an account of the family by referring to one text after another. While valuable, I do not think that such a procedure can give us the kind of overview that we need in order to appreciate the kind of revolution the early Christians perpetrated in relation to the status of the family. The account I develop, while trying to be true to the scripture, is an attempt to provide a more general account of the early church's understanding of the family.

Therefore when I say that, to understand the early church's views about the family, you cannot begin with the family, I mean exactly that. For the first way of being Christian for the early church was not in the family, but by being single. Protestants have tended to forget this inasmuch as part of our political power has depended on our renaturalizing the family as the essential institution for social order. We have therefore selectively interpreted the scripture, trying to show that we Christians, like most people, are on the side of the family. But that is just not so.

The most startling fact of the early church is that singleness was regarded as good as marriage, if not preferred to it, for those who joined this new community. I simply think the evidence for that is undeniable. The question is, how we are to understand it, as well as try to appreciate its significance for us? Many attempt to explain the emphasis on singleness by noting it was a pragmatic necessity. The early Christians were, after all, a minority under persecution and there was much to be done. Therefore, some remained single in order to devote all their time and energy to the work of the kingdom. When times got better, there was less need to stress singleness.

While such considerations no doubt played their part, they are clearly not sufficient to explain the early, as well as the later, emphasis in the church on the importance of singleness as a vocation. For pragmatic reasons are really only the result of profounder theological convictions which made, and continue to make, singleness so crucial to the nature of the church. For the church, we believe, is an eschatological community that lives through witness and conversion. That some, and perhaps many, remain single in the church, is therefore not accidental, but a crucial sign of the kind of people we have been called to be. For we believe that the church grows, not through a socialization process rooted in the family, but through God's constant call to the outsider to be part of his kingdom. Therefore singleness stands as a remarkable witness to the world that this is God's community, God's people, and not another human invention.

Indeed, from this perspective you can tell the church is in deep trouble just when it tries to make the family a substitute for its obligation to be a witness. No longer confident we have a message that can attract others, we rely on the family to bring new members into the church by making sure our children never seriously consider they have other alternatives. Of course, in the process we ironically begin to look more and more like our surrounding culture, as the familization of the church increasingly makes Christians end up looking just like everyone else.

Though the emphasis on singleness may appear odd in a Protestant context, I assume it is intrinsic to the free church tradition. For it is the free church that refuses legal support by the nation to make clear that the church has a loyalty that cannot be captured by the nation. We have little choice not to be an American, or a Canadian, or a Frenchman. Of course, nations in the liberal tradition try to give us the illusion that we freely choose to be American, but in fact we know that we are determined to be so. Just try not to pay your taxes. But the free church stands as the challenge to all such determinism by maintaining that one can only become a member of the church through being called and by responding through willing commitment. Essential to maintaining that freedom is the refusal to turn the family into an idol in the interest of becoming a cultural force.

It is only with this account of singleness in the background that we can understand the church's transformation of marriage. For no longer is marriage a "natural" institution for the preservation of the species or a paradigm for interpersonal relations. Rather, now marriage is a practice put in service to a wider community—and that community is not the "society" but the church. Marriage, in effect, like singleness, becomes a vocation to which some, perhaps the majority, of the church are called. In that sense, marriage is a reality prior to any couple's decision to be married. For marriage is a set of expectations carried by the community that offers an opportunity for some to be of service in the community.

The reason that singleness makes marriage possible is that, only when we realize that we do not have to marry, does marriage between Christians become a vocation rather than a necessity. Marriage is of service to the community by reminding the church that if we live by hope we do so as a patient people. As much as we long for the kingdom, for justice, we know it is not we who make the kingdom come. We cannot storm the walls of God's will to force the world to be ruled by love. God's kingdom will come when God wills it to come. In the meantime we can rest secure in the conviction that we have everything we need through the life, death, and resurrection of Jesus of Nazareth. As a result we can take the time, even in a world as unjust as ours, to be faithful to one another and to have and raise children.

III

For marriage between Christians is shaped by our commitment of lifelong fidelity to another and by our willingness to be open to new life. Christians believe that such fidelity is the hallmark of marriage. By pledging ourselves to another for a lifetime we believe we learn something of God's fidelity. Marriage thus stands as a fitting vocation in the church to remind us of the faithfulness of a God who has made it possible for us to be open to the call of another without qualification. Children are but result of that openness, as we do not believe the fidelity and love demanded of those who would be married can be true unless it is orientated to and expressed in new life. Christians have children not because they believe that God has willed the indefinite life of the human species, but because they are hopeful and patient people. Ironically, when marriage is justified in the name of the perpetuation of the human species, we lose exactly the kind of hope that makes it possible for the human species to continue to live. For in that process we deny that it is God, but the human species, who is our ultimate loyalty.

Putting this in a somewhat different way, the first family of every Christian is not what we call the "biological" family, but the church. In that sense we must not forget the kind of family appropriate to our Christian convictions cannot help but challenge the conventionally secular assumptions which sustain family habits outside the church.

Let met try to illustrate this by telling you what I do sometimes when I teach a course on marriage and the family. I read to the students a letter I have composed from parents to friends which describes a family tragedy. It says that their son was doing very well. He had been an outstanding student and athlete. After serving in the military he had gone to law school and seemed to have an unlimited future ahead of him. There was even talk of his having high political office. However, he had recently joined a religious sect from the east and he had turned his back on his former life and family. He said that he now wanted nothing to do with the world or with his family. Moreover, he claimed that his whole ambition was to be of service to his religious brothers and sisters and in fact he never intended to marry. The family says they are just heart-sick from all this and do not know what to do.

I ask my students who they think wrote this letter. They usually assume it is from a family whose son has become a Moonie or joined one of the many Hindu sects. I then point out to them it could have quite easily been written by a fourth-century Roman senatorial family about their son's conversion to Christianity. We forget that from the Roman point of view the church struck at the heart of the moral presuppositions that underlay the grand achievement of Rome. From Rome's perspective, the family was an absolute necessity for providing not only the numbers but the kinds of people necessary to run a vast empire. The church decisively challenged those assumptions by making the family a secondary loyalty next to loyalty to the church.

From the church's perspective, Rome no longer had first claim on their children; but then neither do, as is often claimed, the biological parents. Given the church's creation of marriage, parenting is now no longer understood biologically. Rather, just as marriage is a vocation, so is parenting. That means that parenting is an office of the whole community and not just of those who happen to have children. Both the single as well as the married exercise parental responsibility for the community; they just exercise different forms of that responsibility. Therefore those who teach, those who take care of the sick, those who stand as moral examples, all perform a parental role.

That such is the case is exactly why the church can expect those who marry to be open to the possibility and prospect of having children even under times of hardship. For it is assumed that the whole community is ready to support those who have children by relieving them of total and exclusive responsibility. It has been, and often still is, assumed that those who have biological children have primary, and even sole, responsibility for their care; but that assumption is not because of biological identity. Rather, Christians assume that they are called to care for those children because that is part and parcel of their vocation by entering the institution of marriage.

It is only against this background that we can understand the church's stand on abortion. Often the general Christian "no" to abortion is interpreted as a legalistic and heartless judgment that ignores the genuinely tragic circumstances associated with some births. But the church's "no" to abortion is in fact a "yes" about the kind of community we want and are intended to be. For we do not assume that the biological mother, unless she wishes, has to care [for] and raise the child. We, as a community, stand ready to provide such care exactly because we do not believe biology makes a parent in the first place.

Indeed, I sometimes think the deepest failure of the contemporary church derives from our willingness to underwrite the pagan assumptions about parenting. We thus train people to think that they have a special relation to biological children. That is why people who adopt are often asked, "now which are your 'real' children?" From the perspective of the church, all our children are our real children and we will abandon none of them to the kind of possessiveness based on biology. Precisely, that same possessiveness is the kind of demonic assumption that makes us assume, as Christians, that we can kill some other's children in the name of our responsibilities to "our children."

IV

But what does all this have to do with the relation of the family and morality; or more exactly, what does it have to do with how the family is or should be a school for character? So far all that I seem to have done is to make some rather bizarre claims about marriage that have almost nothing to do with the working assumption of most Christians in our society. However, I now hope to show that what I have said to this point is important if we are to understand why character is so crucial for sustaining the Christian understanding of marriage and the family.

For, in effect, what I have suggested is that *the character necessary to sustain the life of marriage or singleness is not formed by the family but by the church.* I do not deny the obvious power of the family for making us who we are; but note that the kind of character necessary to sustain the kind of family Christians care about involves more substantive convictions than the family itself can provide. Put simply, if we have not first learned what it means to be faithful to self and other in the church, then we have precious little chance of learning it through marriage and the family. Marriage and family may help reinforce, or even awaken us to, what we have learned in the church; but it cannot be the source of the fidelity necessary for either marriage or family.

Let me try to illustrate this by challenging one of the basic working assumptions that forms a great deal of pastoral practice. I suspect that most pastors, as they counsel people preparing to be married, primarily probe to determine if in fact they are "in love." The assumption is that what Christians primarily care about is whether the marriage will be constituted by a loving and caring relation between the couple, which will then extend to their family. We thus underwrite the general cultural assumption that the warrant necessary to justify two people deciding publicly to commit themselves to each other for a lifetime is the extent of their emotional attachment.

Nothing could be farther from the truth, nor could any practice betray more fundamentally what the church cares about in relation to marriage. What the church cares about is not love, but whether you are a person capable of sustaining the kind of fidelity that makes love, even in marriage, a possibility. Such fidelity, the kind of constancy that promises we will be present through good and evil times, through sickness and health, is not developed in marriage; it is first of all demanded by and developed by being part of a people who have the right to demand it of us. It is a fidelity that comes by being formed by a community whose life is sustained by a God who has proved faithful to us through the call of his people, Israel, and the establishment of the new age in Jesus Christ. Only a people so formed are capable of the kind of promise we make in marriage—that is, of lifelong fidelity.

Moreover, we believe that only when we have that kind of fidelity, that kind of character, are we capable of love. For love, in the first of it, is not some affection for another that contributes to my own sense of well-being. Love is rather the steady gaze on another that does not withdraw regard simply because they fail to please. The paradigm of such love is not learned in marriage and the family; it is first learned through being required to love our brothers and sisters who, like us, are pledged to be disciples of Christ. The love that we have toward our spouses and our children follows, rather than determines, the kind of love that we learn in the church through our being a people pledged to be faithful to God's call.

Without such training we lack the ability to have character in the first place. The problem with the claim that "I love you" is not that I am insincere in my avowal, but that I lack a self, I lack a character, sufficient to the claim. I may well love another, but I simply am not substantive enough to be capable to know what I have said. That is why fidelity necessarily precedes love: it is only through learning to be faithful in relation to God's faithfulness that I have a character capable of the declaration of love.

Character, and our growth in character, places the emphasis in ethics not on decisions about this or that, but rather on our having a history that makes a whole range of what many consider to be decisions no longer possibilities. Thus the Christian must enter marriage with the assumption that divorce is simply not a matter of decision. We do not become married with our fingers crossed or with the assumption that there is always an "out" somewhere down the line. Only be being so formed do we honestly face the reality of the "other" in a way that his/her differences can act to expand the limits of my life so that I might claim that I genuinely love another. And through such an expansion I discover that, rather than being less than who I am, I increasingly have a history that makes me more than I had ever dare hope.

I do not pretend that any of us ever have a character sufficient for marriage when we enter a marriage, but I am contending that at least some beginning has to have been made if we are to have the ability to grow into the kind of person capable of being called to undertake the church's understanding of the vocation of marriage. Indeed, that is why marriage is only possible if it is sustained by a community more significant than the marriage itself. We are sustained not only by convictions about what marriage is about, but by concrete human relations that give us the support we need to face the demands of sharing a history with another human being for a lifetime.

V

I am aware that all this may seem a bit abstract, ideal, or foreign to those who must advise people who are seemingly caught in impossible marriages; so let me call your attention to some examples that may help make the position I am trying to develop more concrete and practical. First, I ask you to consider the fact that for most of the church's life it has legitimated marriage of people who often did not know each other well before the wedding. Indeed, they often did not know each other at all. Though many may think that this is a practice we have well left behind, I think it unwise to overlook the profound moral presuppositions that made it possible for us to bless arranged marriages.

In the first place it is a doubtful empirical claim that, in fact, we have ceased blessing arranged marriage. For example, that is what Notre Dame-St. Mary's, Southern Methodist University, and many other colleges and universities, are about. Students are sent there to meet people of the opposite sex of approximately the same social background, economic potential, and religious affiliation. Such a situation has the advantage of being a form of "arranged marriage" that gives the illusion of choice. There is certainly nothing wrong with such a system except that, like all illusions, it tends to be the breeding ground of self-deception. For as soon as difficulties begin to appear in the marriage, one is invited to think that they simply chose wrongly—forgetting that they were only "choosing" in the first place under very narrow constraints.

More importantly, I think the reality of arranged marriages reminds us that the early church had no illusions about love creating or legitimating marriage. The assumption was that those called to marriage would, drawing on their convictions schooled by the church, have the character to be married faithfully and lovingly. Character preceded marriage; it was not created by marriage. Indeed, one can even push the matter further by noting that, not only has the church blessed arranged marriages, but it even arranged marriages between very young people who had had as yet little chance to develop character one way or the other. While I in no way wish to underwrite this as a good idea, it nonetheless reminds us that such practice rightly assumes that marriage is only possible if it assumes a prior community sufficient for sustaining an ethos for the growth of those who will someday come to maturity and discover they are married.

In this respect I suspect that the family is a crucial institution for the development of character required by the church. In this sense it is a "nature" that makes us prepared for the reception of God's grace. For the one unavoidable fact we all must face is that we do not choose our parents nor do we choose our brothers and sisters. We awaken to discover that we are simply stuck with certain people with no good reason or justification. One way or the other, most of us learn that we simply have to make the best of it. I have no doubt that such a learning is the beginning of growth in moral character for most of us. For it requires that we learn to be faithful to others, to love others, even though *we* did not choose *them* as particular objects worthy of our care or love.

The difficulty occurs when we have no way of explaining to ourselves or even knowing how to describe that formation. We often say that such commitments are simply "natural," but such a description fails to indicate adequately the powerful moral presuppositions that make us turn those "natural" affections into a way of life sponsored by a formative community. Indeed we are becoming increasingly aware, through the tragic evidence of child battering, that such "natural" affections can hardly be relied on to sustain our moral commitments. For what we require is a community that has the convictions as well as the habits that help us to integrate our "nature" into a wider set of expectations that will sustain and enhance our "natural" desires. We need to be taught the "natural affections" we feel are the gracious pull and source necessary for us to be on the road to being people capable of being faithful to ourselves and others—thus people of character.

VI

In a last attempt to suggest that all this may not be quite as crazy as it sounds, let me call your attention to one undeniable fact about marriage and the family that I think helps sustain my account—namely, no one knows what they are doing when they get married and/or begin a family. Do not misunderstand me. I am for marriage preparation. I am for people testing their emotional responses to one another. I am particularly for them working on the planning of the wedding, for as the impeccable authority Miss Manners reminds us, you really only find out about the other person when you have to decide whom you will or will not invite, what color the dresses should be, and so on.

Even more, I am for people being forced to have to consider how they will work out their financial future. For nothing determines our commitment more than our willingness to share our financial destiny. Indeed, I wish the church was more rigorous in suggesting to young people that they may well be in love, but they simply lack the financial resources to enter into the responsibility of marriage and family. Such a challenge would at least help remind us of the kind of commitment which you are making.

Yet I think what finally must be admitted is that no matter how much we may have been prepared to be married, no matter how much we may have considered every possible question, in fact no one can be prepared to be married or for being a family. For how can you prepare for lifetime commitment? How can you prepare for countless small annoyances that you could not know without the experience of marriage itself? How could you prepare yourself for the goods of marriage and the family without the actual experience itself to know? In fact, we must admit that we simply cannot know what we are doing, what we are promising, when we accept the call to be married.

And that is why we so desperately need character, and a community of character sufficient to sustain our growth in character, if we are to enter the extraordinary adventure we call marriage. But what is interesting about this aspect of our commitment is that it reminds us that our acceptance of a call whose implications we do not fully understand is not all that odd. That, in fact, is what almost any important moral commitment involves. It is a promissory note that we can be relied on, even when we do not fully understand the implications of the life we were taking up. Being courageous may well make our world more dangerous than we had anticipated, but that is no reason not to be courageous.

For, finally, marriage and character gain their significance from our recognition of the inherently temporal character of our existence. Morally we are pulled into the future by the commitments we have made, whose implications we hardly understood or anticipated. But that is the way it should be for a people who believe that we serve a God who forever calls us from a life of sin to a new life, free from our fears and our obsessions with safety and control. To serve such a God certainly does require that we be people of constancy, of steadfastness, in the face of the continual temptations to deny that we have a future. But exactly because we are Christians who have experienced God's future in the church, we can continue to accept the call to marriage and family knowing that God has given us all we need to face the challenges of marriage and family with joy, and perhaps even confidence.

POSTSCRIPT

Is the Family Primary in God's Plan?

On February 4, 2002, the *American Academy of Pediatrics* (AAP) issued a press release supporting the legal adoption of children by gay and lesbian parents: "Children who are born to or adopted by one member of a same-sex couple deserve the security of two legally recognized parents." That same day, the *Family Research Council* countered the AAP statement with a press release of its own:

> There is an abundance of research demonstrating that children do best when raised by a mother and a father who are committed to one another in marriage. Mothers and fathers alike make significant contributions to the physical, emotional and social development of their children. To support a policy that would intentionally deprive a child of such benefits is unconscionable.

> — Family Research Council press release (February 4, 2002)

The public debate over the definition of family was brought to the forefront in the infamous "Murphy Brown" squabble involving Vice President Dan Quayle. On his campaign trail in San Francisco, California, Quayle made the following comment:

> Right now the failure of our families is hurting America deeply. When families fall, society falls. The anarchy and lack of structure in our inner cities are testament to how quickly civilization falls apart when the family foundation cracks. . . . It doesn't help matters when primetime TV has Murphy Brown—a character who supposedly epitomizes today's intelligent, highly paid, professional woman—mocks the importance of a father, by bearing a child alone, and calling it just another "lifestyle choice."

> — Vice President Dan Quayle, addressing the Commonwealth Club of
> San Francisco (May 19, 1992)

Quayle's comments brought a firestorm of reaction from both liberal and conservative theologians as well as politicians. But perhaps the most thoughtful response came from Barbara Defoe Whitehead's article, "Dan Quayle Was Right," published in the *Atlantic Monthly* (April 1993). Her piece carefully reviewed the extensive research concerning the family and offered conclusions supportive of Quayle's comments.

It is important to point out that the controversy over what constitutes a family is not simply a debate between the traditionalists and those who advocate the inclusion of gay males, lesbians, and the "Murphy Browns" of the world. There are other groups who should be considered as well:

Single Parent Families: With the American divorce rate at approximately 50 percent, this group appears to be the fastest-growing family. Single-parent families are formed when one parent dies, abandons the family, or is out of the home for an extended period of time.

Step Families: These families are created by remarriage after a death or divorce of a parent.

Joint/Shared Custody Families: Children in these families are raised by both parents who are not married but have retained a legal relationship with their children.

Grandparent Families: With parents who are declared by the courts to be unfit or because of the death or work schedules of parents, this group is also growing rapidly.

Foster Families: These families are formed by legal authorities to assist children to be cared for while problems with parents are being resolved.

Family, no matter which way it is defined, is a part of the world we live in. People of all faiths have an opportunity and responsibility to continue their involvement in contributing to the debate with the intent of strengthening this vital unit of society.

Whether the debate concerns the definition of family or its level of importance to humankind, it appears that it will continue on multiple fronts. If the controversy over family continues to mirror other debates in social science, it will be difficult to rely on research alone to determine what is right or wrong, healthy or unhealthy for the family. Perhaps theologians and religious laypeople alike will continue to feel the responsibility to represent the religious perspectives on the argument as well.

Suggested Readings

D. S. Browning, B. J. Miller-McLemore, P. D. Couture, K. B. Lyon, and R. M. Franklin, eds., *From Culture Wars to Common Ground* (Westminster John Knox, 2000).

L. Hodgkinson, *Unholy Matrimony: The Case for Abolishing Marriage* (Columbus Books, 1988).

C. Lee, *Beyond Family Values: A Call to Christian Virtue* (InterVarsity Press, 1998).

J. Stacey, *In the Name of the Family: Rethinking Family Values in a Postmodern Age* (Beacon Press, 1996).

On the Internet ...

DUSHKIN ONLINE

Ethics Updates: Abortion and Ethics

Ethics Updates: Abortion and Ethics is a Web site that offers links to articles and information from both sides of the ongoing abortion debate.

http://ethics.acusd.edu/Applied/abortion/

Religion-online.org

Religion-online.org contains full-text links to articles and chapters that address a wide array of religious issues and their relationship to society. Topics include the Old and New Testaments, the history and sociology of religion, ethics, worship, religious education, and theologians.

http://www.religion-online.org

PART 3

Social Issues

*T*his part deals with the kinds of issues that constantly show up in the news. These are dilemmas that will likely affect every individual to some extent, and few people remain neutral for very long when confronted with them.

- Is Abortion Wrong?

- Is Capital Punishment Wrong?

- Does the Bible Forbid Same-Sex Relationships?

ISSUE 9

Is Abortion Wrong?

YES: The Vatican, from "1974 Declaration on Procured Abortion," in Lloyd Steffen, ed., *Abortion: A Reader* (The Pilgrim Press, 1996)

NO: Daniel C. Maguire, from "Abortion: A Question of Catholic Honesty," in Lloyd Steffen, ed., *Abortion: A Reader* (The Pilgrim Press, 1996)

ISSUE SUMMARY

YES: This official "1974 Declaration on Procured Abortion" was written by the Vatican and ratified by Pope Paul VI. The declaration is both a statement of faith and reason for the Catholic Church's long-standing position against abortion. It also addresses critics within the Catholic Church who assert that abortion should be a personal decision based on conscience and not obedience to authority.

NO: Daniel C. Maguire, Catholic professor of ethics at Marquette University in Milwaukee, Wisconsin, argues for more flexibility in the Catholic Church's stand on abortion. Maguire outlines the Catholic tradition of *probabilism*, which was originally designed to provide a legitimate rationale for going against Church authority concerning moral issues.

There are few topics in American culture more controversial than abortion. Pollster George Gallup, Jr., has concluded, "Abortion ranks as the top moral dilemma of the last three decades of the twentieth century." In general, public opinion concerning the morality of abortion has remained constant over the past 30 years, but the number of Americans who believe that abortion should be illegal under any circumstance has decreased significantly. Also, the number of those who believe that abortion should be legal under any circumstance has increased. The majority opinion among Americans is that abortion should be *legal* in *some* circumstances. Several analysts and pollsters believe the main factor contributing to this difference of opinion is religious faith.

Most religions have issued formal statements with regard to their positions on abortion, which can be categorized into three main alternatives: (1) complete opposition to abortion, (2) recognition of the sanctity of life but acceptance of abortion in specific circumstances, and (3) an acceptance of abortion because the fetus is not considered a human being. Cases involving rape or incest are examples of what some religious leaders have identified as just causes. Pregnancies where the life of the mother is in jeopardy or where the baby is severely deformed and will not survive birth are also considered legitimate reasons for performing an abortion.

Some consider the abortion debate among churchgoers to be largely a Catholic–Protestant debate, but research demonstrates that both Catholic and Protestant populations are similar in their acceptance of abortion under some circumstances. The Vatican's document, from which the following selection has been taken, reveals that the official position of the Catholic Church does not reflect the collective opinion of its membership. Nevertheless, the Catholic leadership unequivocally rejects abortion under any condition.

Both selections provide a window into the Catholic debate over abortion. While many within the Catholic tradition view the Church's position on abortion as inviolate, there are some scholars, clergy, and Church members who are unhappy with what they perceive as Vatican rigidity.

The 1974 "Official Declaration on Procured Abortion" articulates the Catholic position that "death was not God's doing, he takes no pleasure in the extinction of the living" (New English Bible, Wis. of Sol. 1:13). The Catholic Church's tradition has always upheld the sacredness of life, espousing that life must be protected from the time of conception forward.

The opposing view is taken by Daniel C. Maguire, who represents a growing body of Catholic scholars who are attempting to persuade the Church to modify its position on abortion. Maguire provides a logic for Catholics to justify abortion, which is based on the Catholic tradition of *probabilism*. Probabilism is a system whereby moral questions that are difficult to answer may be solved by appeal to principle and the support of recognized authority, even though the answer may contradict the views established by the hierarchy, as in this case, the Vatican.

The Vatican  **YES**

1974 Declaration on Procured Abortion

I. Introduction

1. The problem of procured abortion and of its possible legal liberalization has become almost everywhere the subject of impassioned discussion. These debates would be less grave were it not a question of human life, a primordial value, which must be protected and promoted. Everyone understands this, although many look for reasons, even against all evidence, to promote the use of abortion. One cannot but be astonished to see on the one hand an increase of unqualified protests against the death penalty and every form of war and on the other hand the vindication of the liberalization of abortion, either in its entirety or in ever broader indications. The Church is too conscious of the fact that it belongs to her vocation to defend man against everything that could disintegrate or lessen his dignity to remain silent on such a topic. Because the Son of God became man, there is no man who is not his brother in humanity and who is not called to become a Christian in order to receive salvation from him.

2. In many countries the public authorities which resist the liberalization of abortion laws are the object of powerful pressures aimed at leading them to this goal. This, it is said, would violate no one's conscience, for each individual would be left free to follow his own opinion, while being prevented from imposing it on others. Ethical pluralism is claimed to be a normal consequence of ideological plurlism. There is, however, a great difference between the one and the other, for action affects the interests of others more quickly than does mere opinion. Moreover, one can never claim freedom of opinion as a pretext for attacking the rights of others, most especially the right to life.

3. Numerous Christian lay people, especially doctors, but also parents' associations, statesmen, or leading figures in posts of responsibility have vigorously reacted against this propaganda campaign. Above all, many episcopal conferences and many bishops acting in their own name have judged it opportune to recall very strongly the traditional doctrine of the Church.[1] With a striking convergence these documents admirably emphasize an attitude of respect for life which is at the same time human and Christian. Nevertheless it

has happened that several of these documents here or there have encountered reservation or even opposition.

4. Charged with the promotion and the defense of faith and morals in the universal Church,[2] the Sacred Congregation for the Doctrine of the Faith proposes to recall this teaching in its essential aspects to all the faithful. Thus, in showing the unity of the Church, it will confirm by the authority proper to the Holy See what the bishops have opportunely undertaken. It hopes that all the faithful, including those who might have been unsettled by the controversies and new opinions, will understand that it is not a question of opposing one opinion to another, but of transmitting to the faithful a constant teaching of the supreme Magisterium, which teaches moral norms in the light of faith.[3] It is therefore clear that this Declaration necessarily entails a grave obligation for Christian consciences.[4] May God deign to enlighten also all men who strive with their whole heart to "act in truth" (Jn. 3:21).

II. In the Light of Faith

5. "Death was not God's doing, he takes no pleasure in the extinction of the living" (Wis. 1:13). Certainly God has created beings who have only one lifetime and physical death cannot be absent from the world of those with a bodily existence. But what is immediately willed is life, and in the visible universe everything has been made for man, who is the image of God and the world's crowning glory (cf. Gen. 1:26–28). On the human level, "it was the devil's envy that brought death into the world" (Wis. 2:24). Introduced by sin, death remains bound up with it: death is the sign and fruit of sin. But there is no final triumph for death. Confirming faith in the Resurrection, the Lord proclaims in the Gospel: "God is God, not of the dead, but of the living" (Matt. 22:32). And death like sin will be definitively defeated by resurrection in Christ (cf. 1 Cor. 15:20–27). Thus we understand that human life, even on this earth, is precious. Infused by the Creator,[5] life is again taken back by him (cf. Gen. 2:7; Wis. 15:11). It remains under his protection: man's blood cries out to him (cf. Gen. 4:10) and he will demand an account of it, "for in the image of God man was made" (Gen. 9:5–6). The commandment of God is formal: "You shall not kill" (Exod. 20:13). Life is at the same time a gift and a responsibility. It is received as a "talent" (cf. Matt. 25:14–30); it must be put to proper use. In order that life may bring forth fruit, many tasks are offered to man in this world and he must not shirk them. More important still, the Christian knows that eternal life depends on what, with the grace of God, he does with his life on earth.

6. The tradition of the Church has always held that human life must be protected and favored from the beginning, just as the various stages of its development. Opposing the morals of the Greco-Roman world, the Church of the first centuries insisted on the difference that exists on this point between those morals and Christian morals. In the Didache it is clearly said: "You shall not kill the fetus by abortion and you shall not murder the infant already born."[6] Athenagoras emphasizes that Christians consider as murderers those women who take medicines to procure an abortion; he condemns the killers of children, including those still living in their mother's womb, "where they

are already the object of the care of divine Providence."[7] Tertullian did not always perhaps use the same language; he nevertheless clearly affirms the essential principle: "To prevent birth is anticipated murder; it makes little difference whether one destroys a life already born or does away with it in its nascent stage. The one who will be a man is already one."[8]

7. In the course of history, the Fathers of the Church, her Pastors and her Doctors have taught the same doctrine—the various opinions on the infusion of the spiritual soul did not introduce any doubt about the illicitness of abortion. It is true that in the Middle Ages, when the opinion was generally held that the spiritual soul was not present until after the first few weeks, a distinction was made in the evaluation of the sin and the gravity of penal sanctions. Excellent authors allowed for this first period more lenient case solutions which they rejected for following periods. But it was never denied at that time that procured abortion, even during the first days, was objectively a grave fault. This condemnation was in fact unanimous. Among the many documents it is sufficient to recall certain ones. The first Council of Mainz in 847 reconsiders the penalties against abortion which had been established by preceding Councils. It decided that the most rigorous penance would be imposed "on women who procure the elimination of the fruit conceived in their womb."[9] The Decree of Gratian reports the following words of Pope Stephen V: "That person is a murderer who causes to perish by abortion what has been conceived."[10] Saint Thomas, the Common Doctor of the Church, teaches that abortion is a grave sin against the natural law.[11] At the time of the Renaissance Pope Sixtus V condemned abortion with the greatest severity.[12] A century later, Innocent XI rejected the propositions of certain lax canonists who sought to excuse an abortion procured before the moment accepted by some as the moment of the spiritual animation of the new being.[13] In our days the recent Roman Pontiffs have proclaimed the same doctrine with the greatest clarity. Pius XI explicitly answered the most serious objections.[14] Pius XII clearly excluded all direct abortion, that is, abortion which is either an end or a means.[15] John XXIII recalled the teaching of the Fathers on the sacred character of life "which from its beginning demands the action of God the Creator."[16] Most recently, the Second Vatican Council, presided over by Paul VI, has most severely condemned abortion: "Life must be safeguarded with extreme care from conception; abortion and infanticide are abominable crimes."[17] The same Paul VI, speaking on this subject on many occasions, has not been afraid to declare that this teaching of the Church "has not changed and is unchangeable."[18]

III. In the Additional Light of Reason

8. Respect for human life is not just a Christian obligation. Human reason is sufficient to impose it on the basis of the analysis of what a human person is and should be. Constituted by a rational nature, man is a personal subject, capable of reflecting on himself and of determining his acts and hence his own destiny: he is free. He is consequently master of himself, or rather, because this takes place in the course of time, he has the means of becoming so: this is his task. Created immediately by God, man's soul is spiritual and therefore

immortal. Hence man is open to God; he finds his fulfillment only in him. But man lives in the community of his equals; he is nourished by interpersonal communication with men in the indispensable social setting. In the fact of society and other men, each human person possesses himself, he possesses life and different goods; he has these as a right. It is this that strict justice demands from all in his regard.

9. Nevertheless, temporal life lived in this world is not identified with the person. The person possesses as his own a level of life that is more profound and that cannot end. Bodily life is a fundamental good; here below it is the condition for all other goods. But there are higher values for which it could be legitimate or even necessary to be willing to expose oneself to the risk of losing bodily life. In a society of persons the common good is for each individual an end which he must serve and to which he must subordinate his particular interest. But it is not his last end and, from this point of view, it is society which is at the service of the person, because the person will not fulfill his destiny except in God. The person can be definitively subordinated only to God. Man can never be treated simply as a means to be disposed of in order to obtain a higher end.

10. In regard to the mutual rights and duties of the person and of society, it belongs to moral teaching to enlighten consciences, it belongs to the law to specify and organize external behavior. In fact, there are a certain number of rights which society is not in a position to grant since these rights precede society; but society has the function to preserve and to enforce them. These are the greater part of those which are today called "human rights" and which our age boasts of having formulated.

11. The first right of the human person is the right to life. He has other goods of which some are more precious, but this one is fundamental—the condition of all the others. Hence it must be protected above all others. It does not belong to society, nor does it belong to public authority in any form to recognize this right for some and not for others: all discrimination is evil, whether it be founded on race, sex, color or religion. It is not recognition by another that constitutes this right. This right is antecedent to its recognition; it demands recognition and it is strictly unjust to refuse it.

12. Any discrimination based on the various stages of life is no more justified than any other discrimination. The right to life remains complete in an old person, even one greatly weakened, it is not lost by one who is incurably sick. The right to life is no less to be respected in the small infant just born than in the mature person. In reality, respect for human life is called for from the time that the process of generation begins. From the time that the ovum is fertilized, a life is begun which is neither that of the father nor of the mother; it is rather the life of a new human being with his or her own growth. It would never be made human if it were not human already.

13. To this perpetual evidence—perfectly independent of the discussions on the moment of animation[19]—modern genetic science brings valuable confirmation. It has demonstrated that, from the first instant there is established the programme of what this living being will be: a man, this individual man with his characteristic aspects already well determined. Right from fertilization

is begun the adventure of a human life, and each of its capacities requires time —a rather lengthy time—to find its place and to be in a position to act. The least that can be said is that present science, in its most evolved state, does not give any substantial support to those who defend abortion. Moreover, it is not up to biological sciences to make a definitive judgment on questions which are properly philosophical and moral, such as the moment when a human person is constituted or the legitimacy of abortion. From a moral point of view this is certain: even if a doubt existed concerning whether the fruit of conception is already a human person, it is objectively a grave sin to dare to risk murder. "The one who will be a man is already one."[20]

IV. Reply to Some Objections

14. Divine law and natural reason, therefore, exclude all right to the direct killing of an innocent man. However, if the reasons given to justify an abortion were always manifestly evil and valueless the problem would not be so dramatic. The gravity of the problem comes from the fact that in certain cases, perhaps in quite a considerable number of cases by denying abortion one endangers important values to which it is normal to attach great value, and which may sometimes even seem to have priority. We do not deny these very great difficulties. It may be a serious question of health, sometimes of life or death, for the mother; it may be the burden represented by an additional child, especially if there are good reasons to fear that the child will be abnormal or retarded; it may be the importance attributed in different classes of society to considerations of honor or dishonor, of loss of social standing, and so forth. We proclaim only that none of these reasons can ever objectively confer the right to dispose of another's life, even when that life is only beginning. With regard to the future unhappiness of the child, no one, not even the father or mother, can act as its substitute, even if it is still in the embryonic stage, to choose in the child's name, life or death. The child itself, when grown up, will never have the right to choose suicide; no more may his parents choose death for the child while it is not of an age to decide for itself. Life is too fundamental a value to be weighed against even very serious disadvantages.[21]

15. The movement for the emancipation of women, in so far as it seeks essentially to free them from all unjust discrimination, is on perfectly sound ground.[22] In the different forms of cultural background there is a great deal to be done in this regard. But one cannot change nature. Nor can one exempt women, any more than men, from what nature demands of them. Furthermore, all publicly recognized freedom is always limited by the certain rights of others.

16. The same must be said of the claim to sexual freedom. If by this expression one is to understand the mastery progressively acquired by reason and by authentic love over instinctive impulse, without diminishing pleasure but keeping it in its proper place—and in this sphere this is the only authentic freedom—then there is nothing to object to. But this kind of freedom will always be careful not to violate justice. If, on the contrary, one is to understand that men and women are "free" to seek sexual pleasures to the point of satiety, without taking into account any law or the essential orientation of sexual life to its fruits

of fertility,[23] then this idea has nothing Christian in it. It is even unworthy of man. In any case it does not confer any right to dispose of human life—even if embryonic—or to suppress it on the pretext that it is burdensome.

17. Scientific progress is opening to technology—and will open still more—the possibility of delicate interventions, the consequences of which can be very serious, for good as well as for evil. These are achievements of the human spirit which in themselves are admirable. But technology can never be independent of the criterion of morality, since technology exists for man and must respect his finality. Just as there is no right to use nuclear energy for every possible purpose, so there is no right to manipulate human life in every possible direction. Technology must be at the service of man, so as better to ensure the functioning of his normal abilities, to prevent or to cure his illnesses, to contribute to his better human development. It is true that the evolution of technology makes early abortion more and more easy, but the moral evaluation is in no way modified because of this.

18. We know what seriousness the problem of birth control can assume for some families and for some countries. That is why the last Council and subsequently the Encyclical *Humanae Vitae* of July 25, 1968, spoke of "responsible parenthood."[24] What we wish to say again with emphasis, as was pointed out in the conciliar Constitution *Gaudium et Spes,* in the Encyclical *Populorum Progressio* and in other papal documents, is that never, under any pretext, may abortion be resorted to, either by a family or by the political authority, as a legitimate means of regulating births.[25] The damage to moral values is always a greater evil for the common good than any disadvantage in the economic or demographic order.

V. Morality and Law

19. The moral discussion is being accompanied more or less everywhere by serious juridical debates. There is no country where legislation does not forbid and punish homicide. Furthermore, many countries had specifically applied this condemnation and these penalties to the particular case of procured abortion. In these days a vast body of opinion petitions the liberalization of this latter prohibition. There already exists a fairly general tendency which seeks to limit as far as possible all restrictive legislation, especially when it seems to touch upon private life. The argument of pluralism is also used. Although many citizens, in particular the Catholic faithful, condemn abortion, many others hold that it is licit, at least as a lesser evil. Why force them to follow an opinion which is not theirs, especially in a country where they are in the majority? In addition it is apparent that, where they still exist, the laws condemning abortion appear difficult to apply. The crime has become too common for it to be punished every time, and the public authorities often find that it is wiser to close their eyes to it. But the preservation of a law which is not applied is always to the detriment of authority and of all other laws. It must be added that clandestine abortion puts women who resign themselves to it and have recourse to it in the most serious dangers for future pregnancies and also in many cases for

their lives. Even if the legislator continues to regard abortion as an evil, may he not propose to restrict its damage?

20. These arguments and others in addition that are heard from varying quarters are not conclusive. It is true that civil law cannot expect to cover the whole field of morality or to punish all faults. No one expects it to do so. It must often tolerate what is in fact a lesser evil, in order to avoid a greater one. One must, however, be attentive to what a change in legislation can represent. Many will take as authorization what is perhaps only the abstention from punishment. Even more, in the present case, this very renunciation seems at the very least to admit that the legislator no longer considers abortion a crime against human life, since murder is still always severely punished. It is true that it is not the task of the law to choose between points of view or to impose one rather than another. But the life of the child takes precedence over all opinions. One cannot invoke freedom of thought to destroy this life.

21. The role of law is not to record what is done, but to help in promoting improvement. It is at all times the task of the State to preserve each person's rights and to protect the weakest. In order to do so the State will have to right many wrongs. The law is not obliged to sanction everything, but it cannot act contrary to a law which is deeper and more majestic than any human law: the natural law engraved in men's hearts by the Creator as a norm which reason clarifies and strives to formulate properly, and which one must always struggle to understand better, but which it is always wrong to contradict. Human law can abstain from punishment, but it cannot declare to be right what would be opposed to the natural law, for this opposition suffices to give the assurance that a law is not a law at all.

22. It must in any case be clearly understood that whatever may be laid down by civil law in this matter, man can never obey a law which is in itself immoral, and such is the case of a law which would admit in principle the liceity of abortion. Nor can he take part in a propaganda campaign in favour of such a law, or vote for it. Moreover, he may not collaborate in its application. It is, for instance, inadmissible that doctors or nurses should find themselves obliged to cooperate closely in abortions and have to choose between the law of God and their professional situation.

23. On the contrary it is the task of law to pursue a reform of society and of conditions of life in all milieux, starting with the most deprived, so that always and everywhere it may be possible to give every child coming into this world a welcome worthy of a person. Help for families and for unmarried mothers, assured grants for children, a statute for illegitimate children and reasonable arrangements for adoption—a whole positive policy must be put into force so that there will always be a concrete, honorable and possible alternative to abortion.

VI. Conclusion

24. Following one's conscience in obedience to the law of God is not always the easy way. One must not fail to recognize the weight of the sacrifices and the burdens which it can impose. Heroism is sometimes called for in order

to remain faithful to the requirements of the divine law. Therefore we must emphasize that the path of true progress of the human person passes through this constant fidelity to a conscience maintained in uprightness and truth; and we must exhort all those who are able to do so to lighten the burdens still crushing so many men and women, families and children, who are placed in situations to which in human terms there is no solution.

25. A Christian's outlook cannot be limited to the horizon of life in this world. He knows that during the present life another one is being prepared, one of such importance that it is in its light that judgments must be made.[26] From this viewpoint there is no absolute misfortune here below, not even the terrible sorrow of bringing up a handicapped child. This is the contradiction proclaimed by the Lord: "Happy those who mourn: they shall be comforted" (Matt. 5:5). To measure happiness by the absence of sorrow and misery in this world is to turn one's back on the Gospel.

26. But this does not mean that one can remain indifferent to these sorrows and miseries. Every man and woman with feeling, and certainly every Christian, must be ready to do what he can to remedy them. This is the law of charity, of which the first preoccupation must always be the establishment of justice. One can never approve of abortion; but it is above all necessary to combat its causes. This includes political action, which will be in particular the task of the law. But it is necessary at the same time to influence morality and to do everything possible to help families, mothers and children. Considerable progress in the service of life has been accomplished by medicine. One can hope that such progress will continue, in accordance with the vocation of doctors, which is not to suppress life but to care for it and favor it as much as possible. It is equally desirable that, in suitable institutions, or, in their absence, in the outpouring of Christian generosity and charity every form of assistance should be developed.

27. There will be no effective action on the level of morality unless at the same time an effort is made on the level of ideas. A point of view—or even more perhaps a way of thinking—which considers fertility as an evil cannot be allowed to spread without contradiction. It is true that not all forms of culture are equally in favor of large families. Such families come up against much greater difficulties in an industrial and urban civilization. Thus the Church has in recent times insisted on the idea of responsible parenthood, the exercise of true human and Christian prudence. Such prudence would not be authentic if it did not include generosity. It must preserve awareness of the grandeur of the task of cooperating with the Creator in the transmission of life, which gives new members to society and new children to the Church. Christ's Church has the fundamental solicitude of protecting and favoring life. She certainly thinks before all else of the life which Christ came to bring: "I have come so that they may have life and have it to the full" (Jn. 10:10). But life at all its levels comes from God, and bodily life is for man the indispensable beginning. In this life on earth sin has introduced, multiplied and made harder to bear suffering and death. But in taking their burden upon himself Jesus Christ has transformed them: for whoever believes in him, suffering and death itself become instruments of resurrection. Hence Saint Paul can say: "I think that what we suffer in

this life can never be compared to the glory, as yet unrevealed, which is waiting for us" (Rom. 8:18). And, if we make this comparison we shall add with him: "Yes, the troubles which are soon over, though they weigh little, train us for the carrying of a weight of eternal glory which is out of all proportion to them" (2 Cor. 4:17).

The Supreme Pontiff Pope Paul VI, in an audience granted to the undersigned Secretary of the Sacred Congregation for the Doctrine of the Faith on June 28, 1974 has ratified this Declaration on Procured Abortion and has confirmed it and ordered it to be promulgated.

Given in Rome, at the Sacred Congregation for the Doctrine of the Faith, on November 18, the Commemoration of the Dedication of the Basilicas of Saints Peter and Paul, in the year 1974.

Franciscus. Card. Seper
Prefect

Hieronymus Hamer
Titular Archbishop of Lorium
Secretary

Notes

1. A certain number of bishops' documents are to be found in Gr. Caprile, *Non Uccidere: Il magistero della Chiesa sull'aborto,* Part II (Rome, 1973), 47–300.

2. *Regimini Ecclesiae Universae,* III, 1, 29. Cf. Ibid., 31 (AAS 59, 1967): 897. On the Sacred Congregation for the Doctrine of the Faith depend all the questions which are related to faith and morals or which are bound up with the faith.

3. *Lumen Gentium* 12 (AAS 57, 1965): 16–17. The present Declaration does not envisage all the questions which can arise in connection with abortion: it is for theologians to examine and discuss them. Only certain basic principles are here recalled which must be for the theologians themselves a guide and a rule, and confirm certain fundamental truths of Catholic doctrine for all Christians.

4. *Lumen Gentium* 25 (AAS 57, 1965): 29–31.

5. The authors of Scripture do not make any philosophical observations on when life began but they speak of the period of life which precedes birth as being the object of God's attention: he creates and forms the human being, like that which is moulded by his hand (cf. Ps. 118:73). It would seem that this theme finds expression for the first time in Jr. 1:5. It appears later in many other texts. Cf. Isa. 49:1, 5; 46:3; Job 10:8–12; Ps. 22:10, 71:6, 139:13. In the Gospels we read in Luke 1:44: "For the moment your greeting reached my ears, the child in my womb leapt for joy."

6. *Didache Apostolorum,* edition Funk, *Patres Apostolici,* V, 2. *The Epistle of Barnabas,* XIX, 5 uses the same expressions (cf. Funk, l.c., 91–93).

7. Athenagoras, *A Plea on Behalf of Christians,* 35 (cf. PG 6,970: S.C. 3, pp. 166–67). One may also consult the *Epistle to Diognetus,* V, 6 Funk, o.c., I, 399: S.C. 33), where it says of Christians: "They procreate children, but they do not reject the foetus."

8. Tertullian, *Apologeticum,* IX, 8 PL 1, 371–72: *Corp. Christ.* I, 103, 1.31–36.

9. Canon 21 (Mansi, 14, p. 909). cf. Council of Elvira, canon 63 (Mansi, 2, p. 16) and the Council of Ancyra, canon 21 (ibid., 519). See also the decree of Gregory III regarding the penance to be imposed upon those who are culpable of this crime (Mansi 13, 292, c. 17).

10. Gratian, *Concordantia Discordantium Canonum,* c. 20, C. 2, q. 2. During the Middle Ages appeal was often made to the authority of Saint Augustine who wrote as follows in regard to this matter in *De Nuptiis et Concupiscentiis,* c. 15: "Sometimes this sexually indulgent cruelty or this cruel sexual indulgence goes so far as to procure potions which produce sterility. If the desired result is not achieved, the mother terminates the life and expels the foetus which was in her womb in such a way that the child dies before having lived or, if the baby was living already in its mother's womb, it is killed before being born" (PL 44, 423–424: CSEL 33, 619). Cf. the *Decree of Gratian* q. 2, C 32, c. 7.

11. *Commentary on the Sentences,* book IV, dist. 31, exposition of the text.

12. Constitutio *Effraenatum* in 1588 (*Bullarium Romanum,* V, 1, 25–27; *Fontes Iuris Canonici,* 1, no. 165, 308–11.

13. Dz-Sch 1184. Cf. also the Constitution *Apostolicae Sedis* of Pius IX (Acta Pii IX, V, 55–72; *ASS* 5 (1869), 305–31; *Fontes Iuris Canonici* III, no. 552, 24–31.

14. Encyclical *Casti Connubii,* (AAS 22, 1930), 562–65; Dz-Sch. 3719–21.

15. The statements of Pius XII are express, precise and numerous; they would require a whole study on their own. We quote only this one from the Discourse to the Saint Luke Union of Italian Doctors of November 12, 1944, because it formulates the principle in all its universality: "As long as a man is not guilty, his life is untouchable, and therefore any act directly tending to destroy it is illicit, whether such destruction is intended as an end in itself or only as a means to an end, whether it is a question of life in the embryonic stage or in a stage of full development or already in its final stages" (Discourses and Radio-messages, VI, 183 ff.).

16. Encyclical *Mater et Magistra* (AAS 53, 1961), 447.

17. *Gaudium et Spes* 51. Cf. 27 (AAS 58, 1966): 1072; cf. 1047.

18. The Speech: *Salutiamo con paterna effusione,* 9 December 1972, *AAS 64,* 777. Among the witnesses of this unchangeable doctrine one will recall the declaration of the Holy Office, condemning direct abortion (Denzinger 1890, *AAS* 17 (1884): 556; 22 (1888–1890), 748; Dz-Sch 3258).

19. This declaration expressly leaves aside the question of the moment when the spiritual soul is infused. There is not a unanimous tradition on this point and authors are as yet in disagreement. For some it dates from the first instant, for others it could not at least precede nidation. It is not within the competence of science to decide between these views, because the existence of an immortal soul is not a question in its field. It is a philosophical problem from which our moral affirmation remains independent for two reasons: (1) supposing a belated animation, there is still nothing less than a *human* life, preparing for and calling for a soul in which the nature received from parents is completed; (2) on the other hand it suffices that this presence of the soul be probable (and one can never prove the contrary) in order that the taking of life involve accepting the risk of killing a man, not only waiting for, but already in possession of his soul.

20. Tertullian, cited in note 8.

21. Cardinal Villot, Secretary of State, wrote on 10 October 1973 to Cardinal Döpfner, regarding the protection of human life: "(Die Kirche) kann jedoch sur Behebung solcher Notsituationen weder empfängnisverhütende Mittel noch erst recht nicht die Abtreibung als sittlich erlaubt erkennen" (*L'Osservatore Romano,* German edition, 26 October 1973), 3.

22. Encyclical *Pacem in Terris* (AAS 55, 1963), 267. Constitution *Gaudium et Spes* 29. Speech of Paul VI, *Salutiamo* (AAS 64, 1972), 779.

23. *Gaudium et Spes* 48: "Indole autem sua naturali, ipsum institutum matrimonii amorque coniugalis ad procreationem et educationem prolis ordinantur, iisque

veluti suo fastigio coronantur." Also paragraph 50: "Matrimonium et amor coniugalis indole sua ad prolem procreandam et educandam ordinantur."

24. *Gaudium et Spes* 50–51. Paul VI, Encyclical *Humanae Vitae* 10 (*AAS* 60, 1968): 487.

25. *Gaudium et Spes* 87. Paul VI, Encyclical *Populorum Progressio* 31: Address to the United Nations (*AAS* 57, 1965): 883. John XXIII, *Mater et Magistra* (*AAS* 53, 1961): 445–48. Responsible parenthood supposes the use of only morally licit methods of birth regulation. cf. *Humanae Vitae* 14 (ibid., 490).

26. Cardinal Villot, Secretary of State, wrote to the World Congress of Catholic Doctors held in Barcelona, 26 May 1974:

Por lo que a la vida humana se refiere, esta non es ciertamente univoca; más bien se podria decir que es un haz de vidas. No se puede reducir, sin mutilarlas gravemente, las zonas de su ser, que, en su estrecha dependencia e interacción están ordenadas las unas a las otras: zona corporal, zona afectiva, zona mental, y ese transfondo del alma donde la vida divina, recibida por la gracia, puede desplegarse mediante los dones del Espiritu Santo." (*L'Osservatore Romano*, 29 May 1974)

NO ↫

Daniel C. Maguire

Abortion: A Question of Catholic Honesty

In the 'already but not yet' of Christian existence, members of the church choose different paths to move toward the realization of the kingdom in history. Distinct moral options coexist as legitimate expressions of Christian choice." This "prochoice" statement recently made by the Catholic bishops of the United States has nothing to do with abortion. Rather, it addresses the possibility of ending life on earth through nuclear war. On that cataclysmic issue, the bishops' pastoral letter on peace warns against giving "a simple answer to complex questions." It calls for "dialogue." Hand-wringingly sensitive to divergent views, the bishops give all sides a hearing, even the winnable nuclear war hypothesis—a position they themselves find abhorrent. At times they merely raise questions when, given their own views, they might well have roundly condemned.

Change the topic to abortion, and nothing is the same. On this issue, the bishops move from the theological mainstream to the radical religious right. Here they have only a single word to offer us: No! No abortion ever—yesterday, today or tomorrow. No conceivable tragic complexity could ever make abortion moral. Here the eschaton is reached: there is no "already but not yet"; there is only "already." "Distinct moral options" do not exist; only unqualified opposition to all abortions moves toward "the realization of the kingdom in history." There is no need for dialogue with those who hold other views or with women who have faced abortion decisions. Indeed, as Marquette University theologian Dennis Doherty wrote some years ago, there seems to be no need even for prayer, since no further illumination, divine or otherwise, is anticipated.

Here we have no first, second, third and fourth drafts, no quibbles over "curbing" or "halting." Here we have only "a simple answer to complex questions." The fact that most Catholics, Protestants and Jews disagree with this unnuanced absolutism is irrelevant. The moral position of those who hold that not every abortion is murder is treated as worthless. Moreover, the bishops would outlaw all disagreement with their view if they could, whether by way of the Buckley-Hatfield amendment, the Helms-Hyde bill, or the Hatch amendment.

From Daniel C. Maguire, "Abortion: A Question of Catholic Honesty," in Lloyd Steffen, ed., *Abortion: A Reader* (The Pilgrim Press, 1996). Originally published in *The Christian Century* (September 14–21, 1983). Copyright © 1983 by Christian Century Foundation. Reprinted by permission. References omitted.

As a Catholic theologian, I find this situation abhorrent and unworthy of the richness of the Roman Catholic traditions that have nourished me. I indict not only the bishops, but also the "petulant silence" (Beverly Harrison's phrase) or indifference of many Catholic theologians who recognize the morality of certain abortions, but will not address the subject publicly. I indict also the male-dominated liberal Catholic press which does too little to dissipate the myth of a Catholic monolith on abortion. It is a theological fact of life that there is no *one* normative Catholic position on abortion. The truth is insufficiently known in the American polity because it is insufficiently acknowledged by American Catholic voices.

This misconception leads not only to injustice but to civil threat, since non-Catholic as well as Catholic citizens are affected by it. The erroneous belief that the Catholic quarter of the American citizenry unanimously opposes all abortions influences legislative and judicial decisions, including specific choices such as denying abortion funding for poor women. The general public is also affected in those communities where Catholic hospitals are the only health care facilities. The reproductive rights of people living in such communities are curtailed if (as in common) their hospital is administratively locked into the ultraconservative view on abortion, and even on such reproductive issues as tubal ligation and contraception. Physicians practicing at such hospitals are compromised. Academic freedom is frequently inhibited at Catholic universities and colleges—public agencies that often are federal contractors—with consequent injustice to the students and to the taxpayers. (In the face of all of this, non-Catholic citizens have been surprisingly and—I dare aver—uncourageously polite.)

Ten years ago, Catholic theologian Charles E. Curran stated in the *Jurist* (32:183 [1973]) that "there is a sizable and growing number of Catholic theologians who do disagree with some aspects of the officially proposed Catholic teaching that direct abortion from the time of conception is always wrong." That "sizable number" has been growing since then despite the inhibiting atmosphere. It is safe to say that only a minority of Catholic theologians would argue that all abortions are immoral, though many will not touch the subject for fear of losing their academic positions. (As one woman professor at a large eastern Catholic university said, "I could announce that I had become a communist without causing a stir, but if I defended *Roe v. Wade* [the 1973 Supreme Court decision legalizing abortion in the United States], I would not get tenure.")

To many, the expression "Catholic pluralism" sounds like a contradiction in terms. The Catholic system, however, does have a method for ensuring a liberal pluralism in moral matters: a system called "probabilism." While it is virtually unknown to most Catholics, probabilism became standard equipment in Catholic moral theology during the 17th century. It applies to situations where a rigorous consensus breaks down and people begin to ask when they may in good conscience act on the liberal dissenting view—precisely the situation with regard to abortion today.

Probabilism was based on the insight that a doubtful moral obligation may not be imposed as though it were certain. "Where there is doubt, there is freedom" (*Ubi dubium, ibi libertas*) was its cardinal principle. It gave Catholics the right to dissent from hierarchical church teaching on a moral matter, if they could achieve "solid probability," a technical term. Solid probability could come about in two ways: *intrinsically,* in a do-it-yourself fashion, when a person prayerfully discovered in his or her conscience "cogent," nonfrivolous reasons for dissenting from the hierarchically supported view; or *extrinsically,* when "five or six" theologians of stature held the liberal dissenting view, even though all other Catholic theologians, including the pope, disagreed. Church discipline required priest confessors who knew that a probable opinion existed to so advise persons in confession even if they themselves disagreed with it.

In a very traditional book, *Moral and Pastoral Theology,* written 50 years ago for the training of seminarians, Henry Davis, S.J., touched on the wisdom of probabilism by admitting that since "we cannot always get metaphysical certainty" in moral matters, we must settle for consenting "freely and reasonably, to sufficiently cogent reasons."

Three things are noteworthy about probabilism: (1) a probable opinion which allows dissent from the hierarchically maintained rigorous view is entirely based on *insight*—one's own or that of at least five or six experts. It is not based on permissions, and it cannot be forbidden. (2) No moral debate—and that includes the abortion debate—is beyond the scope of a probabilistic solution. To quote Father Davis again: "It is the merit of Probabilism that there are no exceptions whatever to its application: once given a really probable reason for the lawfulness of an action in a particular case, though contrary reasons may be stronger, there are no occasions on which I may not act in accordance with the good probable reason that I have found." (3) Probabilism is theologically deep, going back to John and Paul's scriptural teaching that Spirit-filled persons are "taught of God," and to Thomas Aquinas's doctrine that the primary law for the believer is the grace of the Holy Spirit poured into the heart, while all written law—including even Scripture, as well as the teachings of the popes and councils—is secondary. Probabilism allows one to dissent from the secondary through appeal to the primary teaching of the Spirit of God. It is dangerous, of course, but it is also biblical and thoroughly Catholic.

There are far more than five or six Catholic theologians today who approve abortions under a range of circumstances, and there are many spiritual and good people who find "cogent," nonfrivolous reasons to disagree with the hierarchy's absolutism on this issue. This makes their disagreement a "solidly probable" and thoroughly respectable Catholic viewpoint. Abortion is always tragic, but the tragedy of abortion is not always immoral.

Teilhard de Chardin, S.J., pointed out that nothing is intelligible outside of its history. I would add that no conclusion is intelligible unless one knows the history and method of thought that produced it, since moral opinions do not pop out of a void. Whence the moral taboo on all abortions?

The Bible does not forbid abortion. Rather, the prohibition came from theological and biological views that were seriously deficient in a number of ways and that have been largely abandoned. There are at least nine reasons why the old taboo has lost its footing in today's Catholic moral theology. In a 1970 article "A Protestant Ethical Approach," in *The Morality of Abortion* (with which few

Catholic theologians would quarrel), Protestant theologian James Gustafson pointed out five of the foundational defects in the traditional Catholic arguments against all abortions: (1) These arguments relied on "an external judge" who would paternalistically "claim the right to judge the past actions of others as morally right or wrong," with insufficient concern for the experience of and impact on mothers, physicians, families and society. (2) The old arguments were heavily "juridical," and, as such, marked by "a low tolerance for moral ambiguity." (3) The traditional arguments were excessively "physical" in focus, with insufficient attention to "other aspects of human life." (I would add that the tradition did not have the advantage of modern efforts to define personhood more relationally. The definition of person is obviously central to the abortion question.) (4) The arguments were "rationalistic," with necessary nuances "squeezed out" by "timeless abstractions" which took the traditional Catholic reasoning "far from life." (5) The arguments were naturalistic and did not put "the great themes of the Christian faith at a more central place in the discussion." It would be possible to parallel Gustafson's fair and careful criticisms with exhortations from the Second Vatican Council, which urged correctives in precisely these areas.

Other criticisms can be added to Gustafson's list: (6) The theology that produced the traditional ban on all abortions was not ecumenically sensitive. The witness of Protestant Christians was, to say the least, underesteemed. Vatican II condemned such an approach and insisted that Protestants are "joined with us in the Holy Spirit, for to them also He gives His gifts and graces, and is thereby operative among them with His sanctifying power." The bishops and others who condemn all abortion *tout court* should show some honest readiness to listen in the halls of conscience to Protestant views on abortion before they try to outlaw them in the halls of Congress.

(7) Furthermore, the old theology of abortion proceeded from a primitive knowledge of biology. The ovum was not discovered until the 19th century. Because modern embryology was unknown to the tradition, the traditional arguments were spawned in ignorance of such things as twinning and recombination in primitive fetal tissue and of the development of the cortex.

On the other hand, the teachings about abortion contained some remarkable scientific premonitions, including the insight that the early fetus could not have personal status. Said St. Augustine: "The law does not provide that the act [abortion] pertains to homicide. For there cannot yet be said to be a live soul in a body that lacks sensation when it is not formed in flesh and so is not endowed with sense." As Joseph Donceel, S.J., notes, up until the end of the 18th century "the law of the Roman Catholic Church forbade one to baptize an aborted fetus that showed no human shape or outline." If it were a personal human being, it would deserve baptism. On the question of a rational soul entering the fetus, Donceel notes that Thomas Aquinas "spoke of six weeks for the male embryo and three months for the female embryo." In Aquinas's hylomorphic theory, the *matter* had to be ready to receive the appropriate *form*. According to such principles, as Rosemary Ruether points out, "Thomas Aquinas might well have had to place the point of human ensoulment in the last trimester if he had been acquainted with modern embryology."

If the bishops and other negative absolutists would speak of tradition, let them speak of it in its full ambiguity and subtlety, instead of acting as though the tradition were a simplistic, Platonic negative floating through time untouched by contradiction, nuance or complexity.

(8) Vatican II urged priests and church officers to have "continuous dialogue with the laity." The arguments prohibiting all abortion did not grow out of such dialogue, nor are the bishops in dialogue today. If they were, they would find that few are dancing to the episcopal piping. A November 1982 Yankelovich poll of Catholic women shows that fewer than one-fifth would call abortion morally wrong if a woman has been raped, if her health is at risk, or if she is carrying a genetically damaged fetus. Only 27 per cent judge abortion as wrong when a physically handicapped woman becomes pregnant. A majority of Catholic women would allow a teen-ager, a welfare mother who can't work, or a married woman who already has a large family to have an abortion.

Since the tradition has been shaped by the inseminators of the species (all Catholic theologians, priests and bishops have been men), is the implication that there is no value in the witness of the bearers? Why has all authority on this issue been assumed by men, who have not been assigned by biology to bear children or by history to rear them? Are the Catholic women who disagree with the bishops all weak-minded or evil? Is it possible that not a single Catholic bishop can see any ambiguity in any abortion decision? The bishops are not unsubtle or unintelligent, and their pastoral letter on peace shows a surefooted approach to complexity. Their apparent 100 per cent unanimity against all abortion is neither admirable nor even plausible. It seems, rather, imposed.

(9) This leads to the question of sin and sexism. Beverly Harrison (professor of Christian ethics at Union Theological Seminary in New York) charges that "much discussion of abortion betrays the heavy hand of the hatred of women." Are the negative absolutists sinlessly immune to that criticism? Since the so-called "prolife" movement is not dominated by vegetarian pacifists who find even nonpersonal life sacred, is the "prolife" fetal fixation innocent? Does it not make the fertilized egg the legal and moral peer of a woman? Indeed, in the moral calculus of those who oppose all abortion, does not the *potential* person outweigh the *actual* person of the woman? Why is the intense concern over the 1.5 million abortions not matched by an equal concern over the male-related causes of those 1.5 million unwanted pregnancies? Has the abortion ban been miraculously immune to the sexism rife in Christian history?

Feminist scholars have documented the long record of men's efforts to control the sexuality and reproductivity of women. Laws showcase our biases. Is there no sexist bias in the new Catholic Code of Canon Law? Is the code *for* life or *against* women's control of their reproductivity? After all, canon law excommunicates a person for aborting a fertilized egg, but not for killing a baby after birth. One senses here an agenda other than the simple concern for life. What obsessions are operating? A person could push the nuclear button and blow the ozone lid off the earth or assassinate the president (but not the pope) without being excommunicated. But aborting a five-week-old precerebrate, prepersonal fetus would excommunicate him or her. May we uncritically allow such an embarrassing position to posture as "prolife"? Does it not assume that women cannot be trusted to make honorable decisions, and that only male-made laws and male-controlled funding can make women responsible and moral about their reproductivity?

The moral dilemma of choosing whether to have an abortion faces only some women between their teens and their 40s. The self-styled "prolife" movement is made up mainly of men and postfertile women. Is there nothing suspicious about passionately locating one's orthodoxy in an area where one will never be personally challenged or inconvenienced?

Prohibition was wrong because it attempted to impose a private moral position on a pluralistic society. The prohibition of abortion is wrong for the same reason. Society must allow for the debate of valid issues, and then for freedom of choice, not coercion. Some moral positions are not within the pale of respectability, and we properly use coercion to prohibit them. Refusing to educate children, denying sick children blood transfusions, keeping snakes in a church for faith-testing are not respectable options, and we forbid them. But most abortions are not in that category. Abortion is an issue deserving respectable debate.

A moral opinion merits respectable debate if it is supported by serious reasons which commend themselves to many people and if it has been endorsed by a number of reputable religious or other humanitarian bodies. Note the two requirements: *good reasons* and *reliable authorities.* The principle of respectable debate is based on some confidence in the capacity of free minds to come to the truth, and on a distrust of authoritarian short-cuts to consensus and uniformity. This principle is integral to American political thought and to the Catholic doctrine of probabilism. On the other hand, prohibition represents a despairing effort to compel those whom one cannot convince; it can only raise new and unnecessary doubts about Catholic compatibility with democratic political life.

But what of legislators who personally believe that all abortion is wrong? Those legislators must recognize that it is not their function to impose their own private moral beliefs on a pluralistic society. St. Augustine and St. Thomas Aguinas both found prostitution morally repugnant, but felt that it should be legalized for the greater good of the society. St. Thomas wryly but wisely suggested that a good legislator should imitate God, who could eliminate certain evils but does not do so for the sake of the greater good. The greater good supported by the principle of respectable debate is the good of a free society where conscience is not unduly constrained on complex matters where good persons disagree. Thus a Catholic legislator who judges all abortions to be immoral may in good conscience support the decisions of *Roe v. Wade,* since that ruling is permissive rather than coercive. It forces no one to have an abortion, while it respects the moral freedom of those who judge some abortions to be moral.

Good government insists that essential freedoms be denied to no one. Essential freedoms concern basic goods such as the right to marry, the right to a trial by jury, the right to vote, the right to some education and the right to bear *or not to bear* children. The right not to bear children includes abortion as a means of last resort. Concerning such goods, government should not act to limit freedom along income lines, and should ensure that poverty takes no essential freedoms from any citizen. Furthermore, the denial of abortion funding to poor women is not a neutral stance, but a natalist one. The government takes sides on the abortion debate by continuing to pay for births while denying poor women funds for the abortion alternative that is available to the rich. Funding cutbacks are also forcing many to have later abortions, since they have to spend some months scraping up the funds denied them by the government. The denial of funding is an elitist denial of moral freedom to the poor and a stimulus for later or unsafe abortions.

Abortion has become the Catholic orthodoxy's stakeout. In January 1983, California Bishop Joseph Madera threatened excommunication for "lawmakers who support the effective ejection from the womb of an unviable fetus." (His warning also extended to "owners and managers of drugstores" where abortion-related materials are sold.) In a bypass of due process, Sister Agnes Mary Mansour was pressured out of her identity as a Sister of Mercy because her work for the poor of Michigan involved some funding for abortions. Despite his distinguished record in working for justice and peace, Robert Drinan, S.J., was ordered out of politics by the most politically involved pope of recent memory. I am not alone in seeing a link between this and the antecedent right-wing furor over Father Drinan's position on abortion funding. The 4,000 Sisters of Mercy (who operate the second-largest hospital system in the U.S., after the Veterans Administration) were ordered, under threat of ecclesiastical penalties, to abandon their plan to permit tubal ligations in their hospitals. A Washington, D.C., group called Catholics for Free Choice had its paid advertisements turned down by *Commonweal*, the *National Catholic Reporter* and *America*. This group is not promoting abortions, but simply honestly acknowledging Catholic pluralism on the issue. (Interestingly, the only "secular" magazine to refuse their advertisement was the *National Review*.) In June 1983, Lynn Hilliard, a part-time nurse in a Winnipeg, Manitoba, clinic where abortions are performed, had her planned marriage in a Catholic parish peremptorily canceled by Archbishop Adam Exner two weeks before the event, even though the archbishop admitted he did not know whether Ms. Hilliard was formally responsible for any abortions. In the face of all this injustice, Catholic theologians remain remarkably silent; they exhibit no signs of anger. Seven hundred years ago, Thomas Aquinas lamented that we had no name for the virtue of anger in our religious lexicon. He quoted the words of St. John Chrysostom, words that are still pertinent today: "Whoever is without anger, when there is cause for anger, sins."

POSTSCRIPT

Is Abortion Wrong?

Although both the Hebrew Bible and the Christian New Testament speak of the shedding of "innocent blood" as a sin (King James Version, Deut. 19:10 and Matt. 27:4) and contain the command "thou shalt not kill" (KJV, Exod. 20:13 and Rom. 13:9), there is controversy over whether or not the Bible specifically forbids abortion. One of the oft-debated verses is found in the words of the Hebrew prophet Moses:

> If men strive, and hurt a woman with child, so that her fruit depart *from her*, and yet no mischief follow: he shall be surely punished, according as the woman's husband will lay upon him; and he shall pay as the judges *determine*. And if *any* mischief follow, then thou shalt give life for life.
>
> — KJV, Exod 21:22–23; italics added

It is clear that if someone caused a miscarriage, a fine was imposed. If a person caused a miscarriage and death resulted, the perpetrator had to give up his life. The controversy comes in determining whose death the guilty person is paying for. Is the death penalty imposed because of the death of the mother, the infant, or both?

The same question appears in the Qur'an as well. While Islamic texts speak of life as sacred and contain many statements against murder, it can be debated whether or not abortion is specifically addressed.

Most statements on abortion from religious leaders are found in writings outside of Scripture. What follows are statements from a variety of religious traditions that represent the diversity of opinion that exists.

Though Buddhists have a fairly clear orientation against abortion and for protecting the life of the unborn child for members of their own faith, they take a pluralistic position toward the religious beliefs of others. Buddhism is particularly open to individuals making their own decisions based on their own circumstances. The XIV Dalai Lama, leader of the Tibetan Vajrayana branch of Buddhism, is quoted by T. Gyasto in "Kindness, Clarity and Insight," in L. Steffen, ed., *Abortion: A Reader* (Pilgrim, 1996) as having stated:

> With the basic understanding of all humans as brothers and sisters, we can appreciate the usefulness of different systems and ideologies that can accommodate different dispositions, different tastes. For certain people under certain conditions, a certain ideology or cultural heritage is more useful. Each person has the right to choose whatever is most suitable. This is the individual's business.

A Greek Orthodox perspective is stated by The Greek Orthodox Archdiocese of North and South America in "A Statement of Abortion," in L. Steffen, ed., *Abortion: A Reader* (Pilgrim 1996):

> When the unborn child places the life of its mother in jeopardy, then and only then can this life be sacrificed for the welfare of its mother. To move beyond this exception would be transgressing man's duty in the protection of human life as understood and interpreted by the Orthodox Church.

While known by many as the "Mormon Church," the LDS Church is more accurately known as The Church of Jesus Christ of Latter-day Saints. The Latter-day Saint position on abortion is stated in "The First Presidency," *Ensign* (March 1991):

> The Church of Jesus Christ of Latter-day Saints has consistently opposed elective abortion.... We have repeatedly counseled people everywhere to turn from the devastating practice of abortion for personal or social convenience. The Church recognizes that there may be rare cases in which abortion may be justified—cases involving pregnancy by incest or rape; when the life or health of the woman is adjudged by competent medical authority to be in serious jeopardy; or when the fetus is known by competent medical authority to have severe defects that will not allow the baby to survive beyond birth. But these are not automatic reasons for abortion. Even in these cases, the couple should consider abortion only after consulting with each other, and their bishop [church leader], and receiving divine confirmation through prayer.

Is abortion wrong under any circumstance? If there are circumstances where an abortion is legitimate, what are they? Who establishes the criteria? The controversy over abortion is as ancient as it is modern. If the moral debates of the past indicate something of what we will face in the future, we will undoubtably see abortion continue to be one of the great moral dilemmas of the twenty-first century.

Suggested Readings

E. Batchelor, Jr., ed., *Abortion: The Moral Issues* (Pilgrim Press, 1982).

M. J. Gorman, *Abortion and the Early Church: Christian, Jewish and Pagan Attitudes in the Greco-Roman World* (Wipf & Stock Publishers, 1998).

D. Maquire, *Sacred Choices: The Right to Contraception and Abortion in Ten World Religions, Sacred Energies Series* (Fortress, 2001).

T. Shannon, *Abortion and Catholicism: The American Debate* (Crossroad, 1988).

ISSUE 10

Is Capital Punishment Wrong?

YES: Glen H. Stassen, from "Biblical Teaching on Capital Punishment," in Glen H. Stassen, ed., *Capital Punishment: A Reader* (The Pilgrim Press, 1998)

NO: Jacob J. Vellenga, from "Is Capital Punishment Wrong?" in Glen H. Stassen, ed., *Capital Punishment: A Reader* (The Pilgrim Press, 1998)

ISSUE SUMMARY

YES: Glen H. Stassen, professor of Christian ethics at the Fuller Theological Seminary in Pasadena, California, argues that although the practice of capital punishment has biblical roots, God does not intend the penalty of death to be carried out in most cases.

NO: Former associate executive of the United Presbyterian Church Jacob J. Vellenga provides an overview of the scriptural teachings in favor of capital punishment from both Hebrew and Christian Scriptures. He maintains that capital punishment is one of the consequences God instituted to punish the perpetrator and prevent the same kinds of acts among others.

While it appears that the majority of religions are officially opposed to capital punishment, the greater percentage of the American public supports the death penalty. It is surprising to note that religion seemingly does not exert a major influence on the public opinion about capital punishment. A 1999 Gallup poll reveals that 7 out of 10 adults in America support capital punishment. Additionally, capital punishment is supported as much by those who say religion is important to them as by those who report that religion is not a significant part of their lives.

As is the case with many other controversial moral issues, the issue of capital punishment reaches far back into the historical past. Originally the word "capital" meant "relating to the head." Historically, one way of carrying out the death penalty was to sever the head from the body—hence the term "capital punishment." The decapitation of John the Baptist is a scriptural example of this practice.

The first biblical reference to capital punishment occurs in Genesis: "Whoso sheddeth man's blood, by man shall his blood be shed: for in the image of God made he man" (King James Version, Gen. 9:6). Jacob J. Vellenga, believes this verse to be a clear indication that capital punishment is the divine penalty for murder. Glen H. Stassen, taking an opposite view, believes Genesis 9:6 to be a description of what generally happens to those who shed innocent blood—that violence begets violence. A significant detail affecting the interpretation of this verse is that it was given before the Law of Moses was instituted, suggesting that capital punishment was not only a part of the "lesser law" given to Moses, but a part of the teachings given by God to Adam, Enoch, Noah, Abraham, Isaac, and Jacob. Genesis 9:6 and a host of other verses in Jewish, Christian, and Muslim Scripture have been studied and debated for thousands of years by theologians, clergy, and laypeople alike in an attempt to understand God's instruction concerning the taking of life as a penalty for sin.

Hebrew Scripture contains at least 40 different sins for which death is the penalty. This list of offenses ranges from murder (Lev. 24:17) and adultery (Lev. 20:10) to gluttony and excessive drinking (Deut. 21:20). While some theologians interpret Romans 12:17–21 (KJV) as clear evidence against capital punishment, others argue that the text simply provides a warning against personal vengeance. Supporters of capital punishment offer these verses from Paul as a statement that endorses capital punishment as long as it is carried out by those with legitimate legal authority:

> Let every soul be subject unto the higher powers [government authority]. For there is no power but of God: the powers that be are ordained of God. . . . For rulers are not a terror to good works, but to the evil. Wilt thou then not be afraid of the power? do that which is good, and thou shalt have praise of the same: For he is the minister of God to thee for good. But if thou do that which is evil, be afraid; for he beareth not the sword in vain: for he is the minister of God, a revenger to *execute* wrath upon him that doeth evil.
>
> — KJV, Rom. 13:1, 2–4

Stassen and Vallenga provide persuasive arguments for each opposing view. Stassen argues that although the justification for capital punishment is found in Scripture, God does not intend the death penalty to be carried out in most cases but used only as a warning about the sanctity of life. He provides extensive examples from Hebrew and Christian Scripture, writings from the Mishnah (the basis of the Jewish Talmud), and arguments from Christian and Jewish scholars to make his case against capital punishment.

Vellenga originally wrote "Is Capital Punishment Wrong?" for publication in *Christianity Today* in 1959. While recognizing that capital punishment is "a controversial issue upon which good people are divided," he states that Scripture should be our primary source of truth, and that Scripture is clearly supportive of the penalty of death for those who commit capital crimes.

Glen H. Stassen

 **YES**

Biblical Teaching on Capital Punishment

This biblical study was written at the request of Rev. Joe Doss, then Rector of St. Mark's Episcopal Church in Palo Alto, California, Dr. James Bresnahan, S.J., a member of the Society of Christian Ethics—both of whom are lawyers as well as practicing clergy—and Colleen Rohan, Deputy State Public Defender in California. They requested it because prosecuting attorneys in California and elsewhere were making strong closing arguments that the Bible favors the death penalty and therefore jurors should impose the death penalty in the case at hand. Doss, Bresnahan, and Rohan asked me to write a study of biblical teaching on capital punishment that could be authoritative, and widely supported by leaders of the Society of Christian Ethics—who are trained in careful teaching in Christian ethics.

I wrote briefly so it could be read quickly; simply and concretely so lawyers or juries would find it useful; and fairly basically without developing highly original argument so it might get widespread support from scholars of different denominations and persuasions. All twelve most recent presidents of the Society of Christian Ethics at the time of writing signed the statement, as well as many other members present at the annual meeting in 1992. The Society of Christian Ethics is the professional society of teachers of Christian Ethics in theological schools, colleges, and universities in the United States and Canada.

The statement was then distributed by the Most Reverend Edmond L. Browning, Presiding Bishop of the Episcopal Church, in 1992, and made available to others for their use.

The Hebrew Scriptures—The Old Testament

It may seem odd that the Torah (the first five books of the Old Testament) prescribes the death penalty even for children who curse their parents, and for adults who have sex during menstruation, but forbids the death penalty for the prototype of all murderers, Cain, who killed his brother, Abel, premeditated and unprovoked.

From Glen H. Stassen, "Biblical Teaching on Capital Punishment," in Glen H. Stassen, ed., *Capital Punishment: A Reader* (The Pilgrim Press, 1998). Originally published in *Review and Expositor*, vol. 93 (Fall 1996). Copyright © 1996 by *Review and Expositor*. Reprinted by permission of *Review and Expositor* and the author.

On the one hand, the Torah authorizes (or perhaps only predicts) the death penalty for murder (Gen. 9:6);[1] for owning an animal that kills people (Exod. 21:14, 29); kidnapping (Exod. 21:16; Deut. 24:7); giving false witness against a defendant in a death penalty trial (Deut. 18:18–21); for a stubborn son's disobedience to his mother or father, or a child's cursing or striking a parent (Exod. 21:15, 17; Lev. 20:9; Deut. 21:18–21); incest, adultery, bestiality, homosexual practice, rape, and having sex during a woman's menstrual period (Exod. 22:19; Deut. 22:21, 24, 25; Lev. 20:10–14; 21:18); for witchcraft and sorcery (Exod. 22:18; Lev. 20:27); Sabbath-breaking (Exod. 31:14; Num. 15:32–36); child sacrifice (Lev. 21:9); false claim to be a prophet (Deut. 13:5, 10); blasphemy (Lev. 24:15–16); and for a non-Levite who enters the sacred place (Num. 1:51, 3:10, 38; 18:7).[2]

On the other hand, Cain is the father of all murderers. He murders his own brother, out of premeditated jealousy. Found out, he cries out, "I shall be a restless wanderer on the earth, and whoever finds me will kill me." But the Lord said to him, "Not so!" . . . Then the Lord put a mark on Cain, so that no one who found him would kill him (Gen. 4:14–15). Claus Westermann, the Old Testament scholar who has written what is widely recognized as the most authoritative commentary on Genesis, explains this means "no human being has the right to step in and execute God's prerogative."[3] Similarly, Moses is seen in the act of murder, and instead of receiving the death penalty, is chosen by God to deliver his people from slavery (Exod. 2:11 ff.). David not only committed adultery with the beautiful Bathsheba while she was still having her period, but then had Bathsheba's husband killed. Nathan the prophet confronted him, saying, "You have smitten Uriah the Hittite with the sword, and have taken his wife to be your wife." David confessed, saying, "I have sinned against the Lord.' And Nathan said to David, 'The Lord has put away your sin; you shall not die" (2 Sam. 11–12). Accused of adultery, Tamar admits she has committed adultery with her father-in-law, an act specifically requiring the death penalty. She is allowed to live, and her adultery produces an ancestor of David and Jesus (Gen. 38; Matt. 1:3; Luke 3:33). The book of Hosea tells how Gomer commits adultery repeatedly, and Hosea, not without great pain, forgives her, welcoming her back into their covenant relationship. In this adultery and forgiveness Hosea sees the picture of God's way of forgiving his people for their whoring with other gods.

The Old Testament rule of retaliation—a life for a life, an eye for an eye, a tooth for a tooth (Exod. 21:24, 25)—is intended not to require vengeance, but to limit it. Otherwise angry family members might take seven or more lives for a life, as Lamech boasted (Gen. 4:23), and as the Hatfields and the McCoys tried to do. The rules of a life for a life and an eye for an eye are supplemented by rules defining acceptable substitutions, which continue to be elaborated down through Jewish history so that by the time of Jesus most of these penalties could be absolved through payments of money. Just as the law of Moses in Deut. 24 does not mean to approve of divorce, but only, as a concession to the hardness of human hearts, to regulate the separations which were already taking place, so the law of retaliation does not command, but rather limits vengeance as a concession.[4]

The Mishnah is the record of authoritative oral interpretation of the written law of the Torah by the Jewish religious leaders from about 200 B.C.E. to about 200 C.E. It makes the death penalty almost impossible. Death penalty trials required 23 judges. The biblical law (Deut. 19:15) requiring at least two eye witnesses to the commission of the crime "prevented many cases from being brought to trial at all, since such crimes are seldom committed with so much publicity." The testimony of near relatives, women, slaves, or people with a bad reputation is not admitted. If the judges find a witness testified falsely with malicious intent, the witness gets the penalty that would have gone to the defendant, as Deut. 19:16 ff. prescribes. "It is clear that with such a procedure conviction in capital cases was next to impossible, and that this was the intention of the framers of the rules is equally plain."[5] The Mishnah brands a court which executes one man in seven years as "ruinous" or "destructive." It summarizes the teaching of authoritative Rabbis: "Rabbi Eliezar ben Azariah says: Or one in even seventy years. Rabbi Tarfon and Rabbi Akiba say: Had we been in the Sanhedrin none would ever have been put to death.[6] . . .

So the death penalty is prescribed for an unworkably long list of crimes and moral, sexual, and religious transgressions, but either unenforced or made almost impossible to enforce even though eyewitnesses were present and the perpetrator admitted the crime.

To understand this seeming contradiction, we have to understand that the Torah is affirming two moral principles. One is profound moral seriousness about obeying God's will. Disobedience may not be taken lightly. The other is profound seriousness about the sacredness of human life, created in the image of God (Gen. 1:26 f.). Killing people to punish them must be avoided if there is another morally serious way to punish crime. Therefore, in practice, the death penalty becomes increasingly rare. One almost never hears of it in the Prophets and the Writings (the parts of the Old Testament written after the oldest law codes of the first five books were formulated). The Mishnah frowns on it. Modern Israel has never had capital punishment, which shows something of present-day Jewish understanding of the meaning of the tradition. The American Jewish Congress says "capital punishment degrades and brutalizes the society which practices it; and . . . is cruel, unjust, and incompatible with the dignity and self respect of men."[7]

Any effort to interpret biblical teaching on the death penalty without emphasizing the Bible's moral seriousness about disobedience and injustice will fail. Any effort to interpret it without taking seriously its commitment to human life, and to mercy, and its preference for avoiding the death penalty, will likewise fail.

Jesus Rejected the Retaliation of "Life for Life" or "Death for Death"

Once these two principles are fully understood, along with the developing trend to abolish the death penalty in favor of other penalties, the New Testament may be understood as a continuation or further development of the tradition. Jesus was certainly serious about moral obedience. And he especially emphasized the mercy of God and the value of human life: "Be ye merciful, even as your Father is merciful" (Luke 6:36). Not only should we not kill, but even continuing to be angry with one's brother or insulting him leads to judgment (Matt. 5:21 ff.). So Jesus commanded that we take an initiative with someone we are angry with: go talk and seek to make peace (Matt. 5:21 ff.).

Jesus came down firmly on the mercy side of the equation. In Leviticus 19:15 ff., in the Old Testament, the death penalty was justified but limited as "life for life, eye for eye." Jesus named this method explicitly, and changed it to merciful transforming initiatives that avoid vengeance or violence but instead confront the offender and seek repentance:

> "You have heard that it was said, 'an eye for an eye and a tooth for a tooth.' But I say to you, do not set yourself in violent or revengeful resistance against an evildoer.[8] But if any one strikes you on the right cheek, turn the other also; and if any one wants to sue you and take your coat, give your cloak as well; and if any one forces you to go one mile, go also the second mile. Give to anyone who begs from you, and do not refuse anyone who wants to borrow from you" (Matt. 5:38 ff.).

If "life for life" is understood as a limiting of revenge by killing only the killer and not also the killer's family, then Jesus is here taking a further leap in the same direction, limiting it all the way down to zero. If "life for life" is understood as justifying or requiring the death penalty, then Jesus directly opposes it. Either way, Jesus opposes taking a life as retribution for a life. The Apostle Paul makes this clear in Romans 12:19, which most New Testament scholars believe quotes or echoes Jesus' teaching against retaliation: "Beloved, never avenge yourselves, but leave it to the wrath of God; for it is written, 'Vengeance is mine, I will repay, says the Lord.'"

Jesus does not only oppose life-for-life retaliation. He points to a "third way," a way of "transforming initiatives," that moves away from vicious cycles of retaliation into creative confrontation and constructive community-building.[9]

Jesus was confronted by the death penalty directly in John 8. The scribes and Pharisees made a woman stand before him to be judged. "Teacher, this woman was caught in the very act of adultery. In the law Moses commanded us to stone such women. Now what do you say? . . . They said this to test him, so that they might have some charge to bring against him." If he replied flatly, "God's mercy forbids the death penalty," they could charge him with the blasphemy of disagreeing with Moses and stone him. Jesus answered, "Let anyone among you who is without sin throw the first stone." Whey they heard this, they went away one by one, and Jesus was left with the woman standing before him. He said to her, "Woman, where are they? Has no one condemned you?" She said, "No one, sir." Jesus said, "Neither do I condemn you. Go your way, and from now on do not sin again."

Raymond E. Brown, the widely respected scholar who specializes in the Gospel of John, praises the beauty of this story with "its succinct expression of the mercy of Jesus." Brown concludes: "The delicate balance between the justice of Jesus in not condoning the sin and his mercy in forgiving the sinner is one of the great gospel lessons."[10] Here Dr. Brown is pointing to the two principles we saw in the Old Testament: moral seriousness about sin, and mercy toward sinners. Disobedience may not be taken lightly. But mercy and the sacredness of human life require us to avoid killing criminals if there is a morally serious alternative. Jesus releases her from the death penalty. But he admonishes her not to commit adultery again.

Bishop Lowell Erdahl says the accusers "were convicted of their own sins and accepted the fact that there is no justification for the vengeful execution of one sinner by another. If all Christians had followed their example, there would have been no blessing of capital punishment in Christian history."[11] He points out that this fits Jesus' consistent character and teaching. "The woman's accusers knew enough about Jesus to expect that he might oppose her execution. We too are not surprised.... We would be shocked if Jesus had said, ' ...Go ahead and kill this wretched sinner."

Jesus' Crucifixion Was Unjust

Jesus confronted the death penalty one other time. He himself was the victim of capital punishment. Crucifixion was state terrorism. It was given only to slaves and rebels. They were tortured and then killed in full public view to terrorize other slaves and potential rebels, to coerce them into docility in spite of unjust imperialism.[12]

The gospel accounts make clear that Jesus was falsely accused and unjustly condemned (for example, John 18:38). Ironically, Barabbas, who was actually guilty of the crime of insurrection that Jesus was falsely accused of, was freed in Jesus' place. This was clearly unjust. Jesus said from the cross, "Father, forgive them, for they know not what they do" (Luke 23:34). The reason they needed forgiveness is that they were doing terrible wrong. The New Testament witness is that God used their wrong to bring forgiveness and redemption, but this does not alter the fact that it was unjust. Christians who remember their Lord was unjustly and cruelly given the death penalty have a hard time being enthusiastic about imposing the death penalty on others. The cross on Christian churches signifies not that we should advocate more crosses for others, but that we all need mercy. We are not to seek vengeance (Rom. 12:19). We are to love our enemies, and seek to do mercy (Luke 6:35–36).

Here an odd argument is made by William H. Baker.[13] He refers to a conversation in John 19 between Jesus and the Roman colonial government authority, Pilate, as Pilate is about to sentence Jesus to death. Pilate asserts he has authority to crucify Jesus. Jesus answers, "You would have no authority over me, unless it had been given you from above; for this reason he who delivered me up to you has the greater sin."

Jesus is clearly saying that what Pilate is doing is wrong, a sin. Yet Baker argues this shows God approves of capital punishment and governmental authority to order the death penalty. Baker and Pilate both *think* the conversation is about Pilate's secular authority. But read in context, John is clearly showing Pilate misunderstands what the topic is.

The theme of ironic misunderstanding runs throughout the Gospel of John, and this passage is a good example. Jesus is speaking of God's power to bring about the hour of redemption, when he will die so that we will live. Pilate plays a role in *this* death only because God is allowing it. And he misses the point, thinking the topic is his power to command legions and kill people. Jesus is speaking of God's gift of redemption, not engaging in a discussion of whether God approves of capital punishment.[14] As Raymond Brown says, "No one can take Jesus' life from him; he alone has power to lay it down. However, now Jesus has voluntarily entered 'the hour' appointed by his father (12:37) when he will lay down his life. In the context of 'the hour' therefore, the Father has permitted men to have power over Jesus' life."[15]

The gospels make clear that the governmental authorities acted unjustly in sentencing Jesus to death. By no means do they teach that giving capital punishment to Jesus was justice. Baker himself admits "that Pilate allowed a miscarriage of justice to take place." To use this miscarriage of justice as an argument for the rightness of the death penalty suggests desperation to find a New Testament rationalization for a preconceived interest.

All Death Penalties in the New Testament Are Unjust

Baker makes a similar argument concerning Acts 25:11, although he admits the passage does not have "the express purpose of teaching anything about the subject of capital punishment."[16] The point of the passage is the Apostle Paul's defense against accusers who want to kill him. Paul says: "*if* I ... have committed anything worthy of death. ..." He knows he does not deserve the death penalty. The authorities twice explicitly declare they have found that "he had done nothing deserving of death" (Acts 25:25; 26:31).

What Paul says is not that he approves of capital punishment, but that he is not afraid to die. This is a point he makes elsewhere, writing, for example, "For me to live is Christ and to die is gain" (Phil. 1:21). His defense tells how he had once voted for the death penalty for Christians as blasphemers, and how he has now repented for his action (Acts 26:10 ff.).

An individual passage should not be (mis)interpreted as an isolated prooftext. It should be understood in the context of the many instances of capital punishment mentioned in the New Testament. Otherwise it is too easy to read one's own bias into a single passage. The New Testament describes many instances of the death penalty being threatened or imposed. Nowhere do the followers of Jesus advocate the death penalty. Every instance of the death penalty mentioned by the New Testament is clearly presented as an injustice: the beheading of John the Baptist (Matt. 14:9 ff.); the crucifixion of Jesus (John 18:38 and Luke 23:34); the stoning of Stephen (Acts 7); the stoning of other Christians (Matt. 21:35; 23:37; John 10:31 f; Acts 14:5); the threatened death penalty for Paul (Acts 25:11, 25:25, and 26:31); the persecution of Christians in the Book of Revelation. Furthermore, in the Letter to Philemon, Paul writes persuasively "to save the life of the escaped slave, Onesimus, who under Roman law was liable to execution."[17]

Romans 13 Concerns the Authority to Tax, Not Capital Punishment

Some have argued that the authority of the Roman government to impose capital punishment is specifically endorsed in Romans 13: "Let every person be subject to the governing authorities.... For the authority does not bear the sword in vain.... For the same reason you also pay taxes, for the authorities are God's servants, busy with this very thing. Pay to all what is due them—taxes to whom taxes are due, revenue to whom revenue is due...."

The authoritative study of this passage was written by a team of well-known New Testament scholars in Germany.[18] They point out Paul is urging his readers to pay the Roman taxes and not to participate in a rebellion against Nero's new tax. An insurrection against taxes had recently occurred and had gotten Christians kicked out of Rome. Another one was brewing. The Greek in Romans 13:4 translated "sword" (*machairan*) does not name the instrument used in capital punishment. It names the symbol of authority carried by the police who accompanied tax collectors. Paul was urging Christians to make peace, pay Nero's new tax, and not rebel. He was not arguing for capital punishment. He was arguing *against* violence.

The Central Biblical Themes of Justice and Redemption Define the Context

These discussions of specific scripture passages concerning (or not concerning) the death penalty should be understood in the overall context of fundamental themes that are central to the Bible and that are critically important to the death penalty in its actual practice. One is: "Do not slay the innocent." But errors are made. The death penalty is the one penalty that does not allow reinstatement after it is carried out. Another is the central emphasis on justice for the poor, the powerless, and the oppressed. This is emphasized from the Exodus of the oppressed Jews from Egypt through the redemption of the persecuted followers of the Lamb in the Book of Revelation. "You shall not afflict any widow or orphan. If you do afflict them, and they cry out to me, I will surely hear their cry, and my wrath will burn.... You shall not pervert the justice due to your poor in their suit. Keep far from a false charge, and do not slay the innocent and righteous, for I will not acquit the wicked" (Exod. 22:22 f. and 23:6 f.). Walter Berns, in his book arguing for capital punishment, admits that no affluent person ever has been given the death penalty in U.S. history.[19] It goes primarily to the poor who cannot afford extensive legal help. African American murderers are given the death penalty much more often than Caucasian murderers, and the ratio soars if the victims were white. As in the Roman Empire, where the death penalty was reserved for slaves and rebels, so in the U.S. it is reserved for the poor and the black.

Central to the biblical story is the emphasis on redemption, even of one's enemies.

"Which of you, having a hundred sheep, and having lost one of them, will not leave the ninety-nine in the wilderness, and go after the one which is lost, until it is found?... There will be more joy in heaven over one sinner who repents than over ninety-nine righteous persons who need no repentance" (Luke 15:4–7).

The death penalty terminates the chance for repentance. "What hope is there for a dead man's redemption or reformation?"[20]

In sum, the Bible affirms two profound principles. One is profound moral seriousness about obeying God's will. Disobedience may not be taken lightly. The other is profound seriousness about the sacredness of human life. Killing people to punish them must be avoided if there is another morally serious way to punish crime. Therefore, in practice, the death penalty becomes increasingly rare. One almost never hears of it in the Prophets and the Writings, and every mention of it in the New Testament concerns an unjust death penalty. Other penalties develop, and the death penalty is avoided. Mercy becomes central. Vengeance is ruled out: "Beloved, never avenge yourselves, but leave it to the wrath of God; for it is written, 'Vengeance is mine, I will repay,' says the Lord" (Rom. 12:19; Lev. 19:18; Deut. 32:35; Heb. 10:30). And the Bible again and again emphasizes justice for the poor, the powerless, the oppressed, and the innocent. Furthermore, it rejects whatever blocks the possibility of repentance and redemption.

The Way to Deliverance From Homicide's Devastation of Families

But what then of taking the victims seriously? And the devastation to the victims' families? How can we reverse the trend toward ever more murders, a trend which has continued during recent years after the death penalty was reinstated and advocated enthusiastically by national leaders? [Author's note: Since 1991, the U.S. murder rate has decreased each year.]

In the Sermon on the Mount (Matt. 5–7), Jesus did not simply oppose evils such as killing, lying, and hating the enemy; *Jesus consistently emphasized a transforming initiative that could deliver us from the vicious cycle of violence or alienation.*

Simply to oppose the death penalty is unlikely to be effective. Many people feel too much anger about the victims of murder to give up the death penalty if there is not an alternative that takes injustice seriously and does something about the murderous violence in our society. The biblical clue is to look for transforming initiatives that can begin to deliver us from the cycles of violence that we experience.

Otherwise we are back in the days when bloodletting was the known cure for fever and pneumonia. Someone who simply opposed the treatment would encounter great anger: "My father died of pneumonia, and now my brother may too. Why are you telling us not to treat him?" Merely opposing bloodletting because it was ineffective or bad for the patient would be unpersuasive unless you could offer a better alternative. We have to take the injustice of murder with profound moral seriousness.

Scientific studies[21] show capital punishment does not reduce homicide rates and may increase them. They also show what *does* reduce homicides: catching and convicting murderers more promptly and efficiently; governmental example in opposing killing (homicides increase when governments kill, make war, or spread guns); a culture that opposes violence (vs. television violence and ready access to guns); working to achieve equal-opportunity justice for those who are being denied rights and equality; funding drug rehabilitation programs; and developing neighborhood communities rather than depersonalized cities.

Many nations have remarkably fewer murders than the United States does. Some cities and states have fewer than others do. Comparisons are possible. Comparisons across time are also possible. Comparative studies suggest the above actions are in fact effective in decreasing murder rates.[22] That is where our emotions and energies should be directed.

This means as long as people's emotions are diverted into advocating capital punishment as the cure for murder, they are being led to neglect the initiatives that can make a difference. Like the pre-scientific practice of bloodletting, misdirected emotion drives people into vengeful and diversionary destruction and away from constructive and effective action.

The constructive action that is effective in decreasing homicides, as indicated by scientific studies, closely resembles the effective action advocated by biblical ethics: take initiatives to convert the people and change the culture from being pro-violence to anti-violence (Rom. 12:17–21; Isa 60:17b–20); invest yourselves in remedial justice and equal rights for the poor and the outcasts (Isa. 61:1–4 and 8–11); don't seek a cure by shedding blood, but by compassionate justice for those who need it (Jer. 22:1–5 and 22:13–17); do punish criminals justly (Exod. 23:6 ff.; Isa. 5:22–23; Jer. 12:1); seek the welfare of your city's neighborhoods, not false escapes (Jer. 29:4–9); persuade the government to take steps that make peace rather than war (Jer. 4:19 ff.; 6:13 ff.; 22:3–17; Luke 19:41 ff.). This is the way of deliverance.

Notes

1. Genesis 9:4–6 says we shall not eat meat with any blood still in it; emphasizes that we are made in God's own image and our life is sacred; and says "whoever sheds the blood of man, by man shall his blood be shed." This should probably be interpreted as a realistic prediction that violence causes violence, which is the way Jesus interprets it (Matt. 26:52). Lewis Smedes shows the unworkability and violent extremes we would be led into if we took Genesis 9:6 out of context as a command to execute everyone who kills someone, regardless of motive, circumstance, or accident. It is not a universal moral command for us and all time, but is probably to be understood in its context "as a shrewd observation of what usually happens to killers." Lewis Smedes, *Mere Morality: What God Expects from Ordinary People* (Grand Rapids, Mich.: Eerdmans, 1983), 119–21. Claus Westermann argues that Genesis 9:6 belongs to *sacral* rules of worship which are no longer binding (sacrificing animals on an altar—Gen. 8:20–9:6), and is not intended as a *moral* command, anymore than the command not to eat meat with any blood

in it is a moral command for us. See Westermann, *Genesis 1–11: A Commentary* (Minneapolis: Augsburg Publishing House, 1984), 463 ff.

2. I am grateful for the insights and collegiality of my students Gene Gladney, Aubrey Williams, and Michael Westmoreland-White, as well as my colleagues Henlee Barnette and Paul Simmons, each of whom has written papers on capital punishment from which I have learned.

3. Westermann, *Genesis 1–11: A Commentary*, 312.

4. John Howard Yoder, *The Christian and Capital Punishment* (Newton, Kans.: Faith and Life Press, 1961), 6–7.

5. George Foot Moore, *Judaism in the First Centuries of the Christian Era* (New York: Shocken Books, 1971 edition), vol. II, 184–87. See also George Horowitz, *The Spirit of Jewish Law* (New York: Central Book Company, 1963), 165–70 and 176.

6. Herbert Danby, trans., *The Mishnah* (London: Oxford University Press, 1933), 403; Makkoth, 1.10.

7. American Jewish Congress, "Statement on Capital Punishment," adopted at the 66th Annual Meeting, May 6, 1972.

8. The usual English translation of the Greek as "do not resist evil" is inadequate, as is shown by Walter Wink in his book *Violence and Nonviolence: Jesus' Third Way* (Philadelphia and Santa Cruz: n.p., 1987), 13 ff.; and in his well-documented "Beyond Just War and Pacifism: Jesus' Nonviolent Way," *Review and Expositor* 89:2 (spring 1992): 197–214. The Greek means continuous, violent or vengeful resistance. Paul shows this in Romans 12:19, when he reports the teaching as "Never avenge yourselves." Both Jesus and Paul resisted evildoers, but they never advocated vengeance or violence, never the death penalty.

9. See Pinchas Lapide, *The Sermon on the Mount* (Maryknoll, N.Y.: Orbis, 1986), chapters 10, 13 and 14; and the two pieces by Walter Wink cited above.

10. Raymond E. Brown, S.S., *The Gospel According to John* (Garden City, N.Y.: Doubleday, 1966), vol. I, 336 f.

11. Lowell Erdahl, *Pro-Life/Pro-Peace* (Minneapolis: Augsburg, 1986), 114.

12. Martin Hengel, *Crucifixion in the Ancient World and the Folly of the Message of the Cross* (Philadelphia: Fortress, 1977).

13. William H. Baker, *On Capital Punishment* (Chicago: Moody Press, 1973, 1985), 57 ff.

14. Alan Culpepper, *Anatomy of the Fourth Gospel* (Philadelphia: Fortress Press, 1983), 161 and 172. Cf. Brown, *The Gospel According to John*, 892.

15. Brown, *The Gospel According to John*, 893.

16. Baker, *On Capital Punishment*, 62 ff.

17. Henlee Barnette, *Crucial Problems in Christian Perspective* (Philadelphia: Westminster Press, 1970), 129.

18. Johannes Friedrich, Wolfgang Pöhlmann, and Peter Stuhlmacher, "Zur historischen Situation and Intention von Röm 13, 1–7," *Zeitschrift für Theologie und Kirche* (1976), 131 ff. See also John Howard Yoder, *Politics of Jesus* (Grand Rapids, Mich.: Eerdmans, 1976), 206.

19. Walter Berns, *For Capital Punishment* (New York: Basic Books, 1979), 33 ff.

20. Barnette, *Crucial Problems in Christian Perspective*, 129.

21. A highly sophisticated regression analysis is Brian E. Forst, "The Deterrent Effect of Capital Punishment: A Cross-State Analysis of the 1960's," *Minnesota Law Review* (May 1977), 743 ff. In the two months following an execution the number of homicides and the brutality with which they are executed increases dramatically in the immediate area and increases significantly throughout the area where the

execution was publicized. See William Browers's research, in Kenneth Haas and James Inciardi, eds., *Challenging Capital Punishment: Legal and Social Science Approaches* (Beverly Hills, Calif.: Sage Publishing, 1988), 49–90; and Ted Gurr, *Why Do Men Rebel?*, passim.

22. Ibid.; and especially the carefully analyzed transnational and longitudinal statistical research of Dane Archer and Rosemary Gartner, *Violence and Crime in Cross-National Perspective (New Haven, Conn.: Yale University Press, 1984*, 64 ff., 86, 104, 115, 136 f., 159; Ted Gurr, *Why Men Rebel*, which won the annual award of the American Political Science Association. The Archer and Gartner and Gurr research is extremely helpful in pointing toward effective corrective action, and should be widely read and extensively applied.

NO ⬅

Jacob J. Vellenga

Is Capital Punishment Wrong?

The church at large is giving serious thought to capital punishment. Church councils and denominational assemblies are making strong pronouncements against it. We are hearing such arguments as: "Capital punishment brutalizes society by cheapening life." "Capital punishment is morally indefensible." "Capital punishment is no deterrent to murder." "Capital punishment makes it impossible to rehabilitate the criminal."

But many of us are convinced that the church should not meddle with capital punishment. Church members should be strong in supporting good legislation, militant against wrong laws, opposed to weak and partial law enforcement. But we should be sure that what we endorse or what we oppose is intimately related to the common good, the benefit of society, the establishment of justice, and the upholding of high moral and ethical standards.

There is a good reason for saying that opposition to capital punishment is not for the common good but sides with evil; shows more regard for the criminal than the victim of the crime; weakens justice and encourages murder; is not based on Scripture but on a vague philosophical system that makes a fetish of the idea that the taking of life is wrong, under every circumstance, and fails to distinguish adequately between killing and murder, between punishment and crime.

Capital punishment is a controversial issue upon which good people are divided, both having high motives in their respective convictions. But capital punishment should not be classified with social evils like segregation, racketeering, liquor traffic, and gambling.

Those favoring capital punishment are not to be stigmatized as heartless, vengeful, and lacking in mercy, but are to be respected as advocating that which is the best for society as a whole. When we stand for the common good, we must of necessity be strongly opposed to that behavior which is contrary to the common good.

Old Testament on Capital Punishment

From time immemorial the conviction of good society has been that life is sacred, and he who violates the sacredness of life through murder must pay the supreme penalty. This ancient belief is well expressed in Scripture: "Only you shall not eat flesh with its life, that is, its blood. For your lifeblood I will surely require a reckoning; of every beast I will require it and of man; of every man's brother I will require the life of man. Whoever sheds the blood of man, by man shall his blood be shed; for God made man in his own image" (Gen. 9:4–6, RSV). Life is sacred. He who violates the law must pay the supreme penalty, just because life is sacred. Life is sacred since God made man in His image. There is a distinction here between murder and penalty.

Many who oppose capital punishment make a strong argument out of the Sixth Commandment: "Thou shalt not kill" (Exod. 20:13). But they fail to note the commentary on that Commandment which follows: "Whoever strikes a man so that he dies shall be put to death.... If a man willfully attacks another to kill him treacherously, you shall take him from my altar that he may die" (Exod. 21:12, 14). It is faulty exegesis to take a verse of Scripture out of its context and interpret it without regard to its qualifying words.

The Exodus reference is not the only one referring to capital punishment. In Leviticus 24:17 we read: "He who kills a man shall be put to death." Numbers 35:30–34 goes into more detail on the subject: "If any one kills a person, the murderer shall be put to death on the evidence of witnesses; but no person shall be put to death on the testimony of one witness. Moreover you shall accept no ransom for the life of a murderer who is guilty of death; but he shall be put to death.... You shall not thus pollute the land in which you live; for blood pollutes the land, and no expiation can be made for the land, for the blood that is shed in it, except by the blood of him who shed it. You shall not defile the land in which you live, in the midst of which I dwell; for I the Lord dwell in the midst of the people of Israel." (Compare Deut. 17:6–7 and 19:11–13.)

Deuteronomy 19:4–6, 10 distinguishes between accidental killing and willful murder: "If any one kills his neighbor unintentionally without having been at enmity with him in time past ... he may flee to one of these cities [cities of refuge] and save his life; lest the avenger of blood in hot anger pursue the manslayer and overtake him, because the way is long, and wound him mortally, though the man did not deserve to die, since he was not at enmity with his neighbor in time past ... lest innocent blood be shed in your land which the Lord your God gives you for an inheritance, and so the guilt of bloodshed be upon you."

The cry of the prophets against social evils was not only directed against discrimination of the poor, and the oppression of widows and orphans, but primarily against laxness in the administration of justice. They were opposed to the laws being flouted and criminals not being punished. A vivid expression of the prophet's attitude is recorded in Isaiah: "Justice is turned back, and righteousness stands afar off; for truth has fallen in the public squares, and uprightness cannot enter.... The Lord saw it and it displeased him that there was no justice. He saw that there was no man, and wondered that there was no one to intervene; then his own arm brought him victory, and his righteousness upheld him. He put on righteousness as a breastplate, and a helmet of salvation upon his head; he put on garments of vengeance for clothing and wrapped himself in a fury as a mantle. According to their deeds, so will he repay, wrath to his adversaries, requital to his enemies" (Isa. 59:14–18).

New Testament on Capital Punishment

The teachings of the New Testament are in harmony with the Old Testament. Christ came to fulfill the law, not to destroy the basic principles of law and order, righteousness and justice. In Matthew 5:17–20 we read: "Think not that I have come to abolish the law and the prophets; I have come not to abolish them but to fulfill them. For truly, I say to you, till heaven and earth pass away, not an iota, not a dot, will pass from the law until all is accomplished.... For I tell you, unless your righteousness exceeds that of the scribes and Pharisees, you will never enter the kingdom of heaven."

Then Christ speaks of hate and murder: "You have heard that it was said to the men of old, 'You shall not kill; and whoever kills shall be liable to judgment [capital punishment].' But I say to you that everyone who is angry with his brother shall be liable to judgment [capital punishment]" (Matt. 5:21–23). It is evident that Jesus was not condemning the established law of capital punishment, but was actually saying that hate deserved capital punishment. Jesus was not advocating doing away with capital punishment but urging his followers to live above the law so that law and punishment could not touch them. To live above the law is not the same as abrogating it.

The church, the Body of Christ, has enough to do to evangelize and educate society to live above the law and positively to influence society to high and noble living by maintaining a wide margin between right and wrong. The early Christians did not meddle with laws against wrong doing. Paul expresses this attitude in his letter to the Romans: "Therefore, he who resists the authorities resists what God has appointed, and those who resist will incur judgment. For rulers are not a terror to good conduct, but to bad ... for he is God's servant for your good. But if you do wrong, be afraid, for he does not bear the sword in vain; he is the servant of God to execute his wrath on the wrongdoer" (13:2–4).

The early Christians suffered many injustices and were victims of inhuman treatment. Many became martyrs because of their faith. Consequently, they were often tempted to take the law in their own hands. But Paul cautioned them: "Beloved, never avenge yourselves, but leave it to the wrath of God; for it is written, 'Vengeance is mine, I will repay, says the Lord.' No, 'if your enemy is hungry, feed him; if he is thirsty, give him drink; for by so doing you will heap burning coals upon his head' " (Rom. 12:19–21).

There is not a hint of indication in the New Testament that laws should be changed to make it lenient for the wrongdoer. Rather the whole trend is that the church leave matters of justice and law enforcement to the government in power. "Let every person be subject to the governing authorities. For there is no authority except from God, and those that exist have been instituted by God" (Rom. 13:1). Note the juxtaposition of love to enemies with a healthy respect for government. The Christian fellowship is not to take law in its own hands, for God has government in his economy in order to take care of matters of justice.

Jesus' words on loving one's enemies, turning the other cheek, and walking the second mile were not propaganda to change jurisprudence, but they were meant to establish a new society not merely made up law-abiding citizens but those who lived a life higher than the law, so that stealing, adultery, and murder would become inoperative, but not annulled. The law of love, also called the law of liberty, was not presented to do away with the natural laws of society, but to inaugurate a new concept of law written on the heart where the mainsprings of action are born. The church is ever to strive for superior law and order, not to advocate a lower order that makes wrongdoing less culpable.

Love and mercy have no stability without agreement on basic justice and fair play. Mercy always infers a tacit recognition that justice and rightness are to be expected. Lowering the standards of justice is never to be a substitute for the concept of mercy. The Holy God does not show mercy contrary to his righteousness but in harmony with it. This is why the awful Cross was necessary and a righteous Christ had to hang on it. This is why God's redemption is always conditioned by one's heart attitude. There is no forgiveness for anyone who is unforgiving. "Forgive us our debts, as we forgive our debtors" (Matt. 6:12). There is no mercy for anyone who will not be merciful. "Blessed are the merciful for they shall obtain mercy" (Matt. 5:7). There is striking similarity to these verses in Psalm 18:25–26: "With the loyal thou dost show thyself loyal; with the blameless man thou dost show thyself blameless; with the pure thou dost show thyself pure; and with the crooked thou dost show thyself perverse."

Professor C. S. Lewis in his recent book *Reflections on the Psalms* deals with the difficult subject of the spirit of hatred which is in some of the psalms. He points out that these hatreds had a good motivation. "Such hatreds are the kind of thing that cruelty and injustice, by a sort of natural law, produce.... Not to perceive it at all—not even to be tempted to resentment—to accept it as the most ordinary thing in the world—argues a terrifying insensibility. Thus the absence of anger, especially that sort of anger which we call indignation, can, in my opinion, be a most alarming symptom.... If the Jews cursed more bitterly than the Pagans this was, I think, at least in part because they took right and wrong more seriously."

Vindictiveness is a sin, but only because a sense of justice has gotten out of hand. The check on revenge must be in the careful and exact administering of justice by society's government. This is the clear teaching of Scripture in both the Old and New Testaments. The church and individual Christians should be active in their witness to the Gospel of love and forgiveness and ever lead people to the high law of love of God and our neighbors as ourselves; but meanwhile wherever and whenever God's love and mercy are rejected, as in crime, natural law and order must prevail, not as extraneous to redemption but as part of the whole scope of God's dealings with man.

The argument that capital punishment rules out the possibility of repentance for crime is unrealistic. If a wanton killer does not repent when the sentence of death is upon him, he certainly will not repent if he has 20 to 50 years of life imprisonment ahead of him.

We, who are supposed to be Christian, make too much of physical life. Jesus said, "And do not fear those who kill the body but cannot kill the soul;

rather fear him who can destroy both soul and body in hell" (Matt. 10:28). Laxness in law tends to send both soul and body to hell. It is more than a pious remark when a judge says to the condemned criminal: "And may God have mercy on your soul." The sentence of death on a killer is more redemptive than the tendency to excuse his crime as no worse than grand larceny.

It is significant that when Jesus voluntarily went the way of the Cross he chose the capital punishment of his day as his instrument to save the world. And when he gave redemption to the repentant thief he did not save him from capital punishment but gave him Paradise instead which was far better. We see again that mercy and forgiveness are something different than being excused from wrongdoing.

No one can deny that the execution of a murderer is a horrible spectacle. But we must not forget that murder is more horrible. The supreme penalty should be exacted only after the guilt is established beyond the shadow of a doubt and only for wanton, willful, premeditated murder. But the law of capital punishment must stand, no matter how often a jury recommends mercy. The law of capital punishment must stand as a silent but powerful witness to the sacredness of God-given life. Words are not enough to show that life is sacred. Active justice must be administered when the sacredness of life is violated.

It is recognized that this article will only impress those who are convinced that the Scriptures of the Old and New Testament are the supreme authority of faith and practice. If one accepts the authority of Scripture, then the issue of capital punishment must be decided on what Scripture actually teaches and not on the popular, naturalistic ideas of sociology and penology that prevail today. One generation's thinking is not enough to comprehend the implications of the age-old problem of murder. We need the best thinking of the ages on how best to deal with crime and punishment. We need the Word of God to guide us.

POSTSCRIPT

Is Capital Punishment Wrong?

While conservative religious groups tend to be supportive of capital punishment, the more traditional Catholic and mainline Protestant churches are opposed to such a practice. Among the specific denominations opposing capital punishment are Roman Catholicism, the Methodist Church, American Baptist, Eastern Orthodox, Evangelical Lutheran, Conservative Judaism, Presbyterian, Episcopal, Reformed, and the United Church of Christ. Among those denominations supportive of capital punishment are the Southern Baptists, the Lutheran Church (Missouri Synod), Islam, and Orthodox Judaism. Interestingly, several denominations are divided on the issue—the Baptists, Lutherans, and those espousing Judaism have groups within their general traditions who support capital punishment as well as groups who do not.

It is somewhat of an irony that Martin Luther and the Catholic Church (in which he was a priest) parted company over the question of man's involvement in his own salvation. The Catholic Church taught that the good works that a man did and did not do played a part in salvation. Luther believed humankind was saved by the grace of Christ alone. If the faith traditions that sprang from these original beliefs were true to their theology, why wouldn't the Catholic Church be anxious for a murderer to do his own part to be forgiven by giving his own life for his sins? Conversely, why would many Protestants favor the death penalty when they believe that there is nothing a man can do to influence his salvation but accept Christ?

Suggested Readings

G. C. Hanks, *Capital Punishment and the Bible* (Herald, 2002).

C. D. Marshall, *Beyond Retribution: A New Testament Vision for Justice, Crime, and Punishment* (Eerdmans, 2001).

J. J. Megivern, *The Death Penalty: An Historical and Theological Survey* (Paulist Press, 1997).

A. Scalia, "God's Justice and Ours," *First Things* (May 2002).

ISSUE 11

Does the Bible Forbid Same-Sex Relationships?

YES: Richard B. Hays, from "Awaiting the Redemption of Our Bodies: The Witness of Scripture Concerning Homosexuality," in Jeffrey S. Siker, ed., *Homosexuality in the Church: Both Sides of the Debate* (Westminster John Knox Press, 1994)

NO: Victor Paul Furnish, from "The Bible and Homosexuality: Reading the Texts in Context," in Jeffrey S. Siker, ed., *Homosexuality in the Church: Both Sides of the Debate* (Westminster John Knox Press, 1994)

ISSUE SUMMARY

YES: Richard B. Hays, New Testament professor at the Duke Divinity School in Durham, North Carolina, provides evidence from both Hebrew and Christian Scripture prohibiting the practice of homosexuality. Hays argues that the prohibition against homosexual relations has continued from ancient times to the present.

NO: Victor Paul Furnish, New Testament professor at Southern Methodist University in Dallas, Texas, reasons that the arguments made against homosexual behavior found in the Bible are generally taken out of context and should not be interpreted as prohibitions against the practice.

Same-sex attraction (homosexuality) has become one of the great controversies of the religious as well as the secular world. Advocates both for and against the legitimacy of same-sex relationships have looked to religion for direction and theological understanding in the formulation and support of their positions. Almost every religious organization has taken or is in the process of taking a stand concerning the morality of same-sex relationships. As one would expect, even among the religious groups whose leaders have issued a formalized policy, dissenting opinions exist within the general church membership. While a small minority of religious organizations accepts homosexual predisposition, attitude, and behavior, the great majority does not allow a person to engage in homosexual behavior and remain in full fellowship. The Hebrew

Bible, Christian New Testament, and Islamic Qur'an all provide prohibitions against same-sex relationships, but as illustrated by the following selections, each scriptural reference is subject to a variety of interpretations.

Richard B. Hays discusses each of the major biblical verses dealing with same-sex attraction. He then addresses such questions as, Should the church support civil rights for homosexuals? Can homosexual persons be members of the Christian Church? Is it appropriate for homosexual Christians to maintain a homosexual lifestyle? Should the church sanction homosexual unions? Should homosexual Christians be expected to change their orientation? Should homosexuals be ordained?

Victor Paul Furnish argues that the various scriptural prohibitions against homosexuality are taken out of context and interpreted incorrectly. He does not believe biblical teachings should be generalized from the past to the present but that each statement has application only to a specific person or situation at a given moment in time. In the following selection, Furnish identifies each biblical incident related to alleged illicit homosexual contact and discusses how each passage functioned in its "original, multidimensional context."

Richard B. Hays

 **YES**

Awaiting the Redemption of Our Bodies: The Witness of Scripture Concerning Homosexuality

This article originally appeared in the July 1991 *Sojourners* as one part of a forum on the subject of gay and lesbian sexuality and the churches' response. Contributors to the forum were chosen because of their differing perspectives and life experiences, and they represent a spectrum of voices in the debate on gay and lesbian sexuality throughout the churches. The purpose of the forum was to encourage respectful, informed, and humble dialogue on all sides. *Sojourners* did not take a position in this forum, and no single article is intended to represent an editorial position on the part of *Sojourners*.

What Does the Bible Say?

A theological discussion of homosexuality must proceed through a series of widening circles. Beginning at the center, we must consider the biblical texts that explicitly say something about homosexuality. Then we must consider how these texts are to be assessed within a wider biblical framework and in relation to other factors (scientific evidence, changing social realities, etc.). Finally, we must ask what the church should do in light of scripture and in response to the issues confronting us.

The Bible hardly ever discusses homosexual behavior. There are perhaps half a dozen brief references to it in all of scripture. In terms of emphasis, it is a minor concern, in contrast, for example, to economic injustice. What the Bible does say should be heeded carefully, but any ethic that intends to be biblical will seek to get the accents in the right places. (Would that the passion presently being expended in the church over the question of homosexuality were devoted instead to urging the wealth to share with the poor! Some of the most urgent champions of "biblical morality" on sexual matters become strangely equivocal when the discussion turns to the New Testament's teachings about possessions.)

From Richard B. Hays, "Awaiting the Redemption of Our Bodies: The Witness of Scripture Concerning Homosexuality," in Jeffrey S. Siker, ed., *Homosexuality in the Church: Both Sides of the Debate* (Westminster John Knox Press, 1994). Originally published in *Sojourners* (July 1991), pp. 17–21. Copyright © 1991 by *Sojourners*. Reprinted by permission of *Sojourners*, 800 714-7474. http://www.sojo.net.

Genesis 19:1–29

The notorious story of Sodom and Gomorrah—often cited in connection with homosexuality—is actually irrelevant to the topic. The "men of Sodom" come pounding on Lot's door, apparently with the intention of gang-raping Lot's two visitors, who, as we readers know, are actually angels. The angels rescue Lot and his family and pronounce destruction of the city. The gang-rape scenario exemplifies the wickedness of the city, but there is nothing in the passage pertinent to a judgment about the morality of consensual homosexual intercourse. Indeed, there is nothing in the rest of the biblical tradition, save an obscure reference in Jude 7, to suggest that the sin of Sodom was particularly identified with sexual misconduct of any kind. In fact, the clearest statement about the sin of Sodom is to be found in an oracle of the prophet Ezekiel: "This was the guilt of your sister Sodom: She and her daughters had pride, excess of food, and prosperous ease, but did not aid the poor and needy" (Ezek. 16:49).

Leviticus 18:22; 20:13

The few biblical texts that do address the topic of homosexual behavior, however, are unambiguously and unremittingly negative in their judgment. The Holiness Code in Leviticus explicitly prohibits male homosexual intercourse: "You shall not lie with a male as with a woman; it is an abomination" (Lev. 18:22). In Lev. 20:10–16, the same act is listed as one of a series of sexual offenses—along with adultery, incest, and bestiality—that are punishable by death. It is worth noting that the *act* of "lying with a male as with a woman" is categorically proscribed: motives for the act are not treated as a morally significant factor.

Quoting a law from Leviticus, of course, does not settle the question for Christian ethics. The Old Testament contains many prohibitions and commandments that have, ever since the first century, generally been disregarded or deemed obsolete by the church, most notably rules concerning circumcision and dietary practices. Some ethicists have argued that the prohibition of homosexuality is similarly superseded for Christians: it is merely part of the Old Testament's ritual "purity rules" and therefore morally irrelevant today.

The Old Testament, however, makes no systematic distinction between ritual law and moral law. The same section of the Holiness Code also contains, for instance, the prohibition of incest (Lev. 18:6–18). Is that a purity law or a moral law? Leviticus makes no distinction in principle. In each case, the church is faced with the task of discerning whether Israel's traditional norms remain in force for the new community of Jesus' followers.

1 Corinthians 6:9; 1 Timothy 1:10

The early church did, in fact, consistently adopt the Old Testament's teaching on matters of sexual morality and on homosexual acts in particular. In 1 Cor. 6:9 and 1 Tim. 1:10, we find homosexuals included in lists of persons who do things unacceptable to God.

In 1 Corinthians 6, Paul, exasperated with the Corinthians—some of whom apparently believe themselves to have entered a spiritually exalted state in which the moral rules of their old existence no longer apply to them (cf. 1 Cor. 4:8, 5:1–2, 8:1–9)—confronts them with a blunt rhetorical question: "Do you not know that wrongdoers will not inherit the kingdom of God?" He then gives an illustrative list of the sorts of persons he means: "fornicators, idolaters, adulterers, *malakoi, arsenokoitai,* thieves, the greedy, drunkards, revilers, robbers."

I have left the terms pertinent to the present issue untranslated, because their translation has been disputed recently by [John] Boswell and others. The word *malakoi* is not a technical term meaning "homosexuals" (no such term existed either in Greek or in Hebrew), but it appears often in Hellenistic Greek as pejorative slang to describe the "passive" partners—often young boys—in homosexual activity. The other word, *arsenokoitai,* is not found in any extant Greek text earlier than 1 Corinthians. Some scholars have suggested that its meaning is uncertain, but Robin Scroggs[1] has shown that the word is a translation of the Hebrew *mishkav zakur* ("lying with a male"), derived directly from Lev. 18:22 and 20:13 and used in rabbinic texts to refer to homosexual intercourse. The Septuagint (Greek Old Testament) of Lev. 20:13 reads, "Whoever lies with a man as with a woman (*meta arsenos koitēn gynaikos*), they have both done an abomination." This is almost certainly the idiom from which the noun *arsenokoitai* was coined. Thus, Paul's use of the term presupposes and reaffirms the Holiness Code's condemnation of homosexual acts.

In 1 Cor. 6:11, Paul asserts that the sinful behaviors catalogued in the vice list were formerly practiced by some of the Corinthians. Now, however, since they have been transferred into the sphere of Christ's lordship, they ought to have left these practices behind: "This is what some of you used to be. But you were washed, you were sanctified, you were justified in the name of the Lord Jesus Christ and in the Spirit of our God." The remainder of the chapter (1 Cor. 6:12–20) counsels the Corinthians to glorify God in their bodies because they belong now to God and no longer to themselves.

The 1 Timothy passage includes *arsenokoitai* in a list of "the lawless and disobedient," whose behavior is specified in a vice list that includes everything from lying to murdering one's parents, under the rubric of actions "contrary to sound teaching according to the glorious gospel." Here again, the Old Testament prohibition is presupposed, but the context offers little discussion of sexual morality as such.

Romans 1:18–32

The most crucial text for Christian ethics concerning homosexuality remains Romans 1, because this is the only passage in the New Testament that places the condemnation of homosexual behavior in an explicitly theological context.

> Therefore God gave them up in the lusts of their hearts to impurity, to the degrading of their bodies among themselves, because they exchanged the truth about God for a lie and worshiped and served the creature rather than the Creator.... For this reason God gave them up to degrading passions.

Their women exchanged natural intercourse for unnatural, and in the same way also the men, giving up natural intercourse with women, were consumed with passion for one another. Men committed shameless acts with men and received in their own persons the due penalty for their own error (Rom. 1:24–27).

(This is, incidentally, the only passage in the Bible that refers to lesbian sexual relations.)

Because the passage is often cited and frequently misunderstood, an examination of its place in Paul's argument is necessary. The aim of Romans 1 is not to teach a code of sexual ethics; nor is the passage a warning of God's judgment against those who are guilty of particular sins. Rather, Paul is offering a *diagnosis* of the disordered human condition: he adduces the fact of widespread homosexual behavior as evidence that human beings are indeed in rebellion against their creator. The fundamental human sin is the refusal to honor God and give God thanks (1:21); consequently, God's wrath takes the form of letting human idolatry run its own self-destructive course. Homosexuality, then, is not a *provocation* of "the wrath of God" (Rom. 1:18); rather, it is a *consequence* of God's decision to "give up" rebellious creatures to follow their own futile thinking and desires. The unrighteous behavior catalogued in Rom. 1:26–31 is a list of *symptoms*: the underlying sickness of humanity as a whole, Jews and Greeks alike, is that they have turned away from God and fallen under the power of sin (cf. Rom. 3:9).

When this context is kept clearly in view, several important observations follow:

1. Paul is not describing the individual life histories of pagan sinners; not every pagan has first known the true God of Israel and then chosen to turn away into idolatry. When Paul writes, "they exchanged the truth about God for a lie," he is giving a global account of the universal fall of humanity. This fall is manifested continually in the various ungodly behaviors listed in vv. 24–31.
2. Paul singles out homosexual intercourse for special attention because he regards it as providing a particularly graphic image of the way in which human fallenness distorts God's created order. God the creator made man and woman for each other, to cleave together, to be fruitful and multiply. When human beings engage in homosexual activity, they enact an outward and visible sign of an inward and spiritual reality: the rejection of the Creator's design. They *embody* the spiritual condition of those who have "exchanged the truth about God for a lie."
3. Homosexual acts are not, however, specially reprehensible sins; they are no worse than any of the other manifestations of human unrighteousness listed in the passage (vv. 29–31), no worse in principle than covetousness or gossip or disrespect for parents.
4. Homosexual activity will not *incur* God's punishment: it is its own punishment, an "anti-reward." Paul here simply echoes a traditional Jewish idea. The Wisdom of Solomon, an intertestamental writing that has

surely influenced Paul's thinking in Romans 1, puts it like this: "Therefore those who in folly of life lived unrighteously [God] tormented through their own abominations" (Wisd. Sol. 12:1).

Repeated again and again in recent debate is the claim that Paul condemns only homosexual acts committed promiscuously by heterosexual persons—because they "*exchanged* natural intercourse for unnatural." Paul's negative judgment, so the argument goes, does *not* apply to persons who are "naturally" of homosexual orientation. This interpretation, however, is untenable. The "exchange" is not a matter of individual life-decisions; rather, it is Paul's characterization of the fallen condition of the pagan world. In any case, neither Paul nor anyone else in antiquity had a concept of "sexual orientation." To introduce this concept into the passage (by suggesting that Paul disapproves only of those who act contrary to their individual sexual orientations) is to lapse into an anachronism.[2] The fact is that Paul treats *all* homosexual activity as prima facie evidence of humanity's tragic confusion and alienation from God the Creator.

One more thing must be said: Rom. 1:18–32 performs a homiletical sting operation. The passage builds a crescendo of condemnation, declaring God's wrath upon human unrighteousness, using rhetoric characteristic of Jewish polemic against Gentile immorality. It whips the reader into a frenzy of indignation against others: those believers, those idol worshippers, those immoral enemies of God. But then, in Rom. 2:1, the sting strikes: "Therefore you have no excuse, whoever you are, when you judge others; for in passing judgment on another you condemn yourself, because you, the judge, are doing the very same things."

We all stand without excuse under God's judgment. Self-righteous judgment of homosexuality is just as sinful as the homosexual behavior itself. That does not mean that Paul is disingenuous in his rejection of homosexual acts and all the other sinful activities mentioned in Romans 1; all the evils listed there remain evils. But no one should presume to be above God's judgment; all of us stand in radical need of God's mercy. That warning must temper the tone of our debate about homosexuality.

The Wider Biblical Framework

Though only a few biblical texts speak of homoerotic activity, all of them express unqualified disapproval. In this respect, the issue of homosexuality differs significantly from matters such as slavery or the subordination of women, concerning which the Bible contains internal tensions and counterposed witnesses. No theological consideration of homosexuality can rest content, however, with a short list of passages that treat the matter explicitly. We must consider how Scripture frames the discussion more broadly. To place the prohibition of homosexual activity in a canonical context, we should keep in mind at least the following factors in the biblical portrayal of human existence before God.

1. God's creative intention for human sexuality. From Genesis 1 onwards, scripture affirms repeatedly that God has made man and woman for one another and that our sexual desires rightly find fulfillment within heterosexual marriage (see, for instance, Mark 10:2–9, 1 Thess. 4:3–8, 1 Cor. 7:1–9, Eph. 5:21–33, Heb. 13:4). This picture of marriage provides the positive backdrop against which the Bible's few emphatic negations of homosexuality must be read.

2. The fallen human condition. The biblical analysis of the human predicament, most sharply expressed in Pauline theology, offers a subtle account of human bondage to sin. As great-grandchildren of the Enlightenment, we like to think of ourselves as free moral agents, choosing rationally among possible actions, but Scripture unmasks that cheerful illusion and teaches us that we are deeply infected by the tendency to self-deception. Romans 1 depicts humanity in a state of self-affirming confusion: *"They became futile in their thinking, and their senseless minds were darkened. Claiming to be wise, they became fools.... They know God's decree, that those who practice such things deserve to die—yet they not only do them but applaud others who practice them"* (Rom. 1:21–22, 32). Once in the fallen state, we are not free not to sin; we are "slaves of sin" (Rom. 6:17), which distorts our perceptions, overpowers our will, and renders us incapable of obedience (Romans 7). *Redemption* (a word that means "being emancipated from slavery") is God's act of liberation, setting us free from the power of sin and placing us within the sphere of God's transforming power for righteousness (Rom. 6:20–22, 8:1–11, cf. 12:1–2).

Thus we must reject the apparently common-sense assumption that only freely chosen acts are morally culpable. Quite the reverse: The very nature of sin is that it is not freely chosen. That is what it means to live "in the flesh" in a fallen creation. We are in bondage to sin but still accountable to God's righteous judgment of our actions. In light of this theological anthropology, it cannot be maintained that a homosexual orientation is morally neutral because it is involuntary.

3. The eschatological character of Christian existence. The Christian community lives in a time of tension between "already" and "not yet." Already we have the joy of the Holy Spirit; already we experience the transforming grace of God. But at the same time, we do not yet experience the fullness of redemption: we walk by faith, not by sight. The creation groans in pain and bondage, "and not only the creation, but we ourselves, who have the first fruits of the Spirit, groan inwardly while we wait for adoption, the redemption of our bodies" (Rom. 8:23). This means, among other things, that Christians, set free from the power of sin through Christ's death, must continue to struggle to live faithfully in the present time. The "redemption of our bodies" remains a future hope; final transformation of our fallen physical state awaits the resurrection. Consequently, in the interim some may find disciplined abstinence the only viable alternative to disordered sexuality.

4. Demythologizing the idolatry of sex. The Bible undercuts our cultural obsession with sexual fulfillment. Scripture, along with many subsequent generations of faithful Christians, bears witness that lives of freedom, joy, and service are possible without sexual relations. Indeed, however odd it may seem to contemporary sensibilities, some New Testament passages (Matt. 19:10–12, 1 Corinthians 7) clearly commend the celibate life as a way of faithfulness.

Biblical Authority and Other Voices

But what about the authority of the Bible? Are Leviticus and Paul the apostle trustworthy guides on sexual ethics? We must still consider how the Bible's teaching is to be weighted in relation to other sources of moral wisdom. An adequate discussion of this problem would be very long indeed. For the present, I offer only some brief reflections as places to start the discussion.

1. The Christian tradition.   Far more emphatically than scripture itself, the moral teaching tradition of the Christian church has for more than nineteen hundred years declared homosexual behavior to be contrary to the will of God. Only within the past twenty years has any serious question been raised about the church's universal prohibition of such conduct. If anything, a passage like Romans 1 might serve to moderate the tradition's harsh judgments. (John Chrysostom, for example, a brilliant and influential theologian of the fourth century, declared that homosexual intercourse was a sin worse than fornication, worse even than murder. Surely the biblical passages give no support to such a claim.) In any case, it is impossible to construct an argument for acceptance of homosexuality by juxtaposing the authority of tradition to the authority of Scripture. The result of the juxtaposition is to strengthen the Bible's prohibitions.

2. Reason and scientific evidence.   Here the picture is cloudy. Some studies have claimed that as much as 10 percent of the population is inclined to same-sex erotic preference, and some theorists hold that homosexual orientation is innate (or formed by a very early age) and unchangeable. This is the opinion espoused by most advocates of full acceptance of homosexuality in the church: If homosexual orientation is a genetically determined trait, so the argument goes, then any disapproval of it is a form of discrimination analogous to racism.

Others, however, regard homosexual orientation as a form of developmental maladjustment or "symbolic confusion." Some therapists claim significant clinical success rates in helping homosexual persons develop a heterosexual orientation; others challenge such claims. A major cross-cultural study recently published by David F. Greenberg,[3] professor of sociology at New York University, contends that homosexual identity is socially constructed rather than inborn. According to Greenberg, the "essentialist" view of sexual orientation is a fallacy.

In one sense, however, the etiology of homosexual orientation is not a significant factor for the formation of normative Christian ethics. We need not take sides in the debate of nature versus culture. Even if it could be shown that same-sex preference is somehow genetically programmed, that would not necessarily make homosexual behavior morally appropriate. Surely Christian ethics does not want to hold that all inborn traits are good and desirable. The analogy of alcoholism, while only an analogy, is perhaps helpful: A considerable body of evidence suggests that some people are born with a predisposition to alcoholism. Once exposed to alcohol, they experience an attraction so powerful that it can be counteracted only by careful counseling, community support, and total abstinence. We now conventionally speak of alcoholism as a disease and carefully distinguish our disapproval of the behavior associated with it from our loving support of the person afflicted by it. Perhaps homoerotic attraction should be treated similarly.

The argument from statistical incidence of homosexual behavior is even less useful in normative ethical deliberation. Even if 10 percent of the people in the United States should declare themselves to be of homosexual orientation (and that figure is a doubtful one), that would not settle the *normative* issue; it is impossible to argue simply from an "is" to an "ought." If Paul were shown the poll results, he would reply sadly, "Indeed, the power of sin is rampant in the world."

3. The experience of the community of faith.   This is the place where the advocates of homosexuality in the church have their most serious case. Scroggs argues that the New Testament's condemnation of homosexuality applies only to a certain "model" of exploitative pederasty that was common in Hellenistic culture; hence, it is not applicable to the modern world's experience of mutual, loving homosexual relationships. I think that Scroggs's position fails to reckon adequately with Romans 1, where the relations are not described as pederastic and where Paul's disapproval has nothing to do with exploitation.

But the fact remains that there are numerous homosexual Christians— like . . . some of my ablest students at Yale—whose lives show signs of the presence of God, whose work in ministry is genuine and effective. How is such experiential evidence to be assessed? Should we, like the earliest Jewish Christians who hesitated to accept "unclean" Gentiles into the community of faith, acknowledge the work of the Spirit and say, "Who are we to stand in the way of what God is doing" (cf. Acts 10:1–11:18)? Or should we see this as one more instance of a truth that all of us in ministry know sadly about ourselves: "We have this treasure in earthen vessels"? God gives the Spirit to broken people and ministers grace even through us sinners, without thereby endorsing our sin.

In view of the considerable uncertainty surrounding the scientific and experiential evidence, in view of our culture's present swirling confusion about gender roles, in view of our propensity for self-deception, I think it prudent and necessary to let the univocal testimony of Scripture and the Christian tradition order the life of the church on this painfully controversial matter. We must affirm that the New Testament tells us the truth about ourselves as sinners and as God's sexual creatures: Marriage between man and woman is the normative form for human sexual fulfillment, and homosexuality is one among many tragic signs that we are a broken people, alienated from God's loving purpose.

Practical Consequences: Living Under the Cross

How then shall we respond in the church to the pastoral and political realities of our time? Having said that we cannot condone homosexual behavior, we still find ourselves confronted by complex problems that demand rigorous and compassionate solutions. Those who uphold the biblical teaching against homosexuality must remember Paul's warning in Rom. 2:1–3: We are all "without excuse"; we all stand or fall under God's judgment and mercy. The second thing to be said—as a presupposition for all that follows—is that the church is called to be a fellowship of committed believers, knowing itself to have an identity and vocation distinct from the world.

In what follows, I pose several key issues and venture some discernments. These opinions—based on the exegesis and theological reflections already set forth in this essay—should be taken as proposals offered to the community of faith, to be judged in light of Scripture and the community's prayerful corporate wisdom.

1. Should the church support civil rights for homosexuals? Yes. Any judgment about the church's effort to influence Caesar's social policies requires complex reasoning. There is no reason, however, for the church to single out homosexual persons for malicious discriminatory treatment. Insofar as Christians have done so in the past, we must repent and seek instead to live out the gospel of reconciliation.

2. Can homosexual persons be members of the Christian church? This is rather like asking, "Can envious persons be members of the church?" (cf. Rom. 1:29) or "Can alcoholics be members of the church?" Unless we think that the church is a community of sinless perfection, we will have to acknowledge that persons of homosexual orientation (granting, as I am willing to do, that there is such a thing) are welcome along with other sinners in the company of those who trust in the God who justifies the ungodly (Rom. 4:5). If they are not welcome, I will have to walk out the door along with them, leaving in the sanctuary only those entitled to cast the first stone.

3. Is it Christianly appropriate for homosexual Christians to maintain a homosexual lifestyle? No. The only one who was entitled to cast a stone instead charged the recipient of his mercy to "go and sin no more." It is no more appropriate for homosexual Christians to persist in a homosexual lifestyle than it would be for heterosexual Christians to maintain a lifestyle of fornication or adultery. (Insofar as the church fails to teach clearly about heterosexual chastity outside of marriage, its disapproval of homosexual coupling will appear arbitrary and biased.) Unless they are able to change their orientation and enter a heterosexual marriage relationship, homosexual Christians should seek to live lives of disciplined sexual abstinence.

Despite the smooth illusions perpetrated by American mass culture, sexual gratification is not a sacred right, and celibacy is not a fate worse than death. Here the Catholic tradition has something to teach those of us raised in Protestant communities. While mandatory priestly celibacy is unbiblical, a life of sexual abstinence can promote "good order and unhindered devotion to the Lord" (1 Cor. 7:35). It is worth noting that 1 Cor. 7:8–9, 25–40 commends celibacy as an option for everyone, not just for a special caste of ordained leaders. Within the church, we should work diligently to recover the dignity and value of the single life.

My friend Gary, in his final letter to me, wrote urgently of the imperatives of discipleship: "*Are homosexuals to be excluded from the community of faith? Certainly not. But anyone who joins such a community should know that it is a place of transformation, of discipline, of learning, and not merely a place to be comforted or indulged.*" The community demands that its members pursue holiness, while it also sustains the challenging process of character formation that is necessary for Jesus' disciples. The church must be a community whose life together provides true friendship and emotional support for persons seeking an alternative to the gay subculture, as well as for heterosexually oriented single persons. In this respect, as in so many others, the church can fulfill its vocation only by living as a countercommunity in the world.

4. Should the church sanction and bless homosexual unions?   No. The church should continue to teach—as it always has—that there are two possible ways for God's human sexual creatures to live well-ordered lives of faithful discipleship: heterosexual marriage and sexual abstinence.

5. Should homosexual Christians expect to change their orientation?   This tough question must be answered in the critical framework of New Testament eschatology. On the one hand, the transforming power of the Spirit really is present in our midst; the testimonies of those who claim to have been healed and transformed into a heterosexual orientation should be taken seriously. "He breaks the power of canceled sin; he sets the prisoner free." If we do not continue to live with that hope, we may be hoping for too little from God. On the other hand, the "not yet" looms large; the testimonies of those . . . who pray and struggle in Christian community and seek healing unsuccessfully for years must be taken with no less seriousness. Perhaps for many the best outcome attainable in this time between the times will be a life of disciplined abstinence, free from obsessive lust. (Exactly the same standard would apply for unmarried persons of heterosexual orientation.) . . .

6. Should homosexuals be ordained?   I save this question deliberately for last, where it belongs. It is unfortunate that the battle line has been drawn in the denominations at the question of ordination of homosexuals. The ensuing struggle has had the horrible effect of reinforcing a double standard for "clergy" and "lay" morality; it would be far better to articulate a single set of moral norms that apply to all Jesus' followers. Strictures against homosexuality belong in the church's moral catachesis, not in its ordination requirements. It is arbitrary to single out homosexuality as a special sin that precluded ordination. (Certainly the New Testament does not do this.) The church has no analogous special rules to exclude from ordination the greedy or the self-righteous.

Such matters are left to the discernment of the bodies charged with examining candidates for ordination; these bodies must determine whether the individual candidate has the gifts and graces requisite for ministry. In any event, a person of homosexual orientation seeking to live a life of disciplined abstinence would clearly be an appropriate candidate for ordination.

We live, then, as a community that embraces sinners as Jesus did, without waiving God's righteousness. We live confessing that God's grace claims us out of confusion and alienation and sets about making us whole. We live knowing that wholeness remains a hope rather than an attainment in this life. The homosexual Christians in our midst may teach us something about our true condition as people living between the cross and the final redemption of our bodies.

In the midst of a culture that worships self-gratification and a church that preaches a false Jesus who panders to our desires, those who seek the narrow way of obedience have a powerful word to speak. Just as Paul saw in pagan homosexuality a symbol of human fallenness, so ... I have seen in ... homosexual friends and colleagues, a symbol of God's power made perfect in weakness (2 Cor. 12:9). . . . Thus [they] embod[y] the "sufferings of this present time" of which Paul speaks in Romans 8: living in the joyful freedom of the "first fruits of the Spirit," even while groaning along with a creation in bondage to decay.

Notes

1. Robin Scroggs, *The New Testament and Homosexuality* (Philadelphia: Fortress Press, 1984), 106–08.

2. The expression *para physin* ("contrary to nature"), used here by Paul, is the standard terminology in dozens of ancient texts for referring to homoerotic acts. Readers interested in technical details and citations of pertinent ancient sources should see my article "Relations Natural and Unnnatural: A Response to John Boswell's Exegesis of Romans 1" in the *Journal of Religious Ethics* 14/1 (Spring 1986): 184–215.

3. David F. Greenberg, *The Construction of Homosexuality* (Chicago: University of Chicago Press, 1989).

NO

Victor Paul Furnish

The Bible and Homosexuality: Reading the Texts in Context

Introduction

The question "What does the Bible say about homosexuality?" is misleading in several ways. First, it fails to take into account the fact that the ancient world had no word for or concept of "homosexuality." Second, it overlooks the fact that the Bible is actually a collection of writings, representative of many different authors, times, and places. It is therefore wrong simply to presume that "the Bible says" just *one* thing about any given subject. Third, those who ask this question often fail to realize that determining *what* the biblical writings say is only part of their task. It is also necessary to ask *why* these writings say what they do. This requires a careful examination of each text in all of its appropriate contexts—literary, cultural, and theological. And for anyone who regards the biblical writings as authoritative (as "Scripture"), there is a fourth critical question: How, if at all, may these ancient texts inform our understanding and give us moral guidance in today's world?

In dealing with these matters, it is important to examine, in turn, each of the biblical passages that are most often cited when the topic of homosexuality is discussed. Our objective, in each case, will be to understand how the given passage functioned in its original, multidimensional context. Then it will be possible, in conclusion, to consider how the Bible can—and cannot—inform those who come to it seeking guidance about homosexuality.[1]

The Texts in Their Ancient Contexts

Before we begin our survey of passages, two points need to be noted about terminology. First, "sexuality" is an abstract concept for which we are indebted to modern psychological investigations and theories. The same is of course true for the concepts of "heterosexuality," "homosexuality," and "bisexuality." There were no such concepts and no terms for them in the ancient world. It was universally presupposed that everyone was "heterosexual" in the sense of being inherently ("naturally") constituted for physical union with the opposite sex. Thus there is no biblical passage about "homosexuality" understood as a "condition" or "orientation."[2]

Second, the word "sodomite" appears nowhere in the Hebrew text of the Old Testament, not even to mean a "resident of Sodom." The Hebrew term that was translated as "sodomite" in the King James Version (Deut. 23:17–18; 1 Kings 14:22–24; 15:12; 22:46; 2 Kings 23:7; Joel 3:3) refers to a (male) temple prostitute, as virtually every modern English version properly recognizes. Nor does the word "sodomite" ever appear in the Greek text of the New Testament, although the English word is employed twice in the New Revised Standard Version [NRSV] (1 Cor. 6:9; 1 Tim. 1:10).

These observations should remind us that translations can sometimes be misleading and that the exact meaning of a word always depends in part on the context in which it appears. It is for this reason that every text must be set as fully as possible within its own context.

The Men of Sodom (Genesis 19:1–25)

The story about the men of Sodom is the one that most people think of when the topic of the Bible and homosexuality is discussed. However, this is not a story about homosexual behavior in general—and certainly not a story about homosexual acts performed by consenting adults. It is a story about the intent to do violence to strangers, who ought rather to have been accorded protection. It is only incidental to the story that, had the attack succeeded, it would have meant the rape of Lot's two male visitors by a mob of other males. It appears that the men of Sodom were "out for a 'wilding,' " and that Lot's vulnerable guests happened along as a handy target.[3]

Significantly, not one of the biblical references to the story makes a point of the homosexual character of the intended rape. For example, in Ezekiel 16 Sodom's sin is described as her greed and her indifference to those in need: "This was the guilt of your sister Sodom: she and her daughters had pride, excess of food, and prosperous ease, but did not aid the poor and needy" (16:49). In Matt. 10:12–15 and the parallel in Luke 10:10–12. Sodom's sin is identified with inhospitality in general, without any sexual reference at all; and the reference in Matt. 11:23–24 to the city's destruction serves as a reminder of what happens to those who disobey God's will. Nor does the comment in Jude 7 about Sodom's "sexual immorality" (reworded by a later writer, 2 Peter 2:10) have "homosexuality" in view. The Greek text says, literally, that Sodom and Gomorrah "went after *strange flesh*" (NRSV footnote; italics added), an allusion to the fact that Lot's guests, unbeknown even to the host himself, were actually angels disguised as men. Thus here, Sodom's sin is viewed not as males violating other males but as mortals violating immortals.[4]

A Levitical Rule (Leviticus 18:22 and 20:13)

Two formulations of a rule against a male having sex with another male occur in the so-called Holiness Code of Lev. 17–26. This code, which had achieved its present form by the time of the Exile (sixth century B.C.E.), is probably a compilation of several originally different collections of laws and regulations.[5]

The two versions of the prohibition about male "homosexuality" stand in two distinct collections within this code, and each has its own history of transmission. Overall, the code as we have it reflects ancient Israel's concern for *purity*, which was understood quite objectively as the state of being clean and whole as opposed to unclean and polluted. To be "pure" meant to be an unblemished specimen of one's kind, unmixed with any other kind (which would be pollution). Within this context, therefore, "defilement" does not mean *moral* defilement but uncleanness in a literal, physical sense. This is why the Holiness Code prohibits such things as breeding animals "with a different kind," sowing a field "with two kinds of seeds," and wearing a garment that is "made of two different materials" (Lev. 19:19).

This is the cultural background against which the prohibitions of Lev. 18:22 and 20:13 must be understood. They condemn sex between two males because in any such act one partner is required—as the Hebrew literally says —to "lie the lyings of a woman." With this, according to the ancient Hebrew conception, that partner's maleness has been compromised; he is no longer an unblemished specimen of his kind. Because he is defiled, the whole act is unclean—and the other partner, too.

It is important to observe that this Levitical rule takes no specific account of what is "good" or "just" or "loving." The single concern is for *purity*, understood in an objective, literal sense. This is also why the prohibition is so absolute and unqualified. It does not matter who the males might be, how old they are, what their relationship, or whether there has been mutual consent. It matters only that one of them will be physically polluted by taking the part of a female and will thus defile the act itself and his partner.

The Creation Accounts (Genesis 1:26–28 and 2:24–25)

There are two accounts of creation in Genesis: the earlier, so-called Yahwistic account in Genesis 2 and 3, and the later, so-called Priestly account in Genesis 1. They have entered into the discussion of homosexuality because of what they say about God's creation of "male and female" and about the sexual union of man and woman. . . .

Summary
It is sometimes argued that the creation accounts present heterosexuality as intrinsic to the created order, God's intention for humankind, and at least part of what it means to have been created in the image of God. It has been concluded from this that any kind of a homosexual relationship is fundamentally evil, a perversion of the created order, and contrary to God's will. The texts themselves, however, do not support this interpretation. Although the creation accounts presume and explain heterosexual behavior, they do not command it. They are not about God's will for individual members of the species but only about what is typical of the species as a whole. For this reason, they take no account whatever of the physically or mentally impaired, the celibate, the impotent—or of those who in modern times have come to be described as "homosexual."

The Jesus Traditions

Our primary access to Jesus' own teaching is through traditions about Jesus that have been incorporated into the Synoptic Gospels (Matthew, Mark, and Luke). Although these traditions include teachings on a number of specific topics, the matter of "homosexual" relationships or practice is not among them. For example, the Levitical prohibition of sex between males is neither cited nor alluded to in the Jesus traditions; and, as noted above, the references to Sodom (Matt. 10:12–15, parallel Luke 10:10–12; Matt. 11:23–24) do not specify the nature of the city's sinfulness.

According to Mark 10:6–9 (parallel Matt. 19:4–6), Jesus did cite the comment in Gen. 1:27 about God's creation of "male and female" and also the statement in Gen. 2:24 about man and woman becoming "one flesh." However, the topic of this tradition is not "heterosexuality" but divorce, and the conclusion is not about "homosexuality" but that divorce is in every case a perversion of the created order and thus always contrary to God's will (Mark 10:11–12; the parallel in Matt. 19:7–9 allows for one exception: a man may divorce his wife if she has been unfaithful). Nor does the saying about "eunuchs" in Matt. 19:11–12 have anything to do with "homosexuality." It is presented as Jesus' response to his disciples' suggestion that it may be "better not to marry" (v. 10). On the contrary, says Jesus, in addition to those who lack the needed sexual organs or have become sexually disabled, singleness is appropriate only for those [males] to whom celibacy is "given" (v. 11) for the purpose of serving God's kingdom more fully (v. 12).

This silence of the Jesus traditions about same-sex practices does not mean that Jesus had nothing to say on the subject. It does suggest, however, that Jesus had nothing distinctive to say about it, and that "homosexuality" was not a matter of special concern within the church that preserved and applied his sayings.

The Letters of Paul

There are only three explicit references to anything like "homosexuality" in the whole of the New Testament. Two of these occur in Paul's letters (Romans and 1 Corinthians), and the third stands in a letter penned by a later writer in Paul's name (1 Timothy).

1 Corinthians 6:9; 1 Timothy 1:10

In 1 Cor. 6:9–10 Paul has identified a number of types of people who, in his view, will not be allowed to enter the kingdom of God. Similar lists of disapproved behaviors or people are found rather often in first-century works on morality, pagan and Jewish as well as Christian. Other Pauline examples of such lists include Rom. 1:29–31, Gal. 5:19–21, and 1 Cor. 5:11. Despite some overlapping of terms (especially of those in 1 Cor. 5:11 and 1 Cor. 6:9–10), no two of Paul's lists are identical. Moreover, none of them was meant to be either comprehensive or definitive, and none of them was formulated with any specific cases of immoral conduct in view.

Two terms appear in 1 Cor. 6:9 that refer to males who have sex with other males. The first of these (in Greek, *malakoi*) means literally, "soft ones." In Paul's day, this term was often used negatively to describe men who, in the eyes of others, appeared to be somehow "effeminate." It was also applied to the more passive male in a same-sex relationship, and—more specifically—to adolescent boys who sold themselves for sex with older men (hence the NRSV translation, "male prostitutes"). The second word has been translated in the NRSV as "sodomites," but the term actually used (*arsenokoitai*) is a combination of two Greek words meaning, respectively, "male" and "bed." Since this is the earliest occurrence of the word discovered so far, it is theoretically possible that Paul himself coined it. However, it is also possible that it had already been coined by other Hellenistic Jews, who would have been acquainted with the Greek version of Lev. 18:22 and 20:13, where the words "male" and "bed" (meaning "intercourse") both appear. In combination, then, the words seem to mean, "a male who has intercourse [with another male]." The same word, with the same meaning, is listed among the vices identified in 1 Tim. 1:9–10.

It is unclear whether, in 1 Cor. 6:9, Paul was thinking particularly of male prostitutes and their customers or of "homosexual" acts between any two males. Whichever the case, he disapproved, as did the anonymous author of 1 Timothy. But "homosexuality" is not the topic in either passage, and neither writer provides any reason for condemning it. Both of them simply list it as one of the behaviors that their readers regard as "obviously" evil.

Romans 1:26–27

This is the only place in the New Testament where there is as much as one complete sentence about same-sex intercourse—and the only place in the entire Bible where female relationships, as well as male, come into view. The following adaptation of the NRSV translation will give a better idea than most English versions of how this sentence reads in Paul's Greek:

> [26]For this reason God gave them up to degrading passions, for just as their women exchanged natural intercourse for unnatural, [27]so also the men, abandoning natural intercourse with women, were consumed with passion for one another, men committing shameless acts with men and receiving in their own persons the penalty required by their error.

This sentence contains no specific moral instruction or commandment, nor is "homosexual" practice the topic. The subject of the sentence is *God* (see v. 26a), and it stands in a passage where Paul is commenting on "the revealing of God's wrath" within the Gentile world (1:18–32). In the wider context (1:18–3:20), the topic is the human predicament and, consequently, humanity's need for the saving grace of God. The "bottom line" is summed up by the apostle himself when he emphasizes that "there is no distinction" between Jew and Gentile, meaning humankind as a whole, because all have sinned and fall short of God's glory (3:22b–23). In these chapters, Paul is not trying to specify what Christians should or should not do. His specific moral instructions and appeals come at the end of Romans, in chapters 12–15.

Paul's comments about the Gentiles in Rom. 1:18–32, and again in 2:12–16, bear the imprint of his Hellenistic-Jewish heritage, especially as this is evident in the Wisdom of Solomon, a book of the late first century B.C.E. which the church regarded as scriptural. According to this tradition, idolatry leads inevitably to various forms of "sexual immorality" (Wisd. Sol. 14:12), including the "interchange of sex roles" (Wisd. Sol. 14:26), and thus to same-sex intercourse. The belief expressed by Paul in Romans that such intercourse is "unnatural" and an expression of "degrading passions" accords with certain presuppositions about "homosexuality" that were widespread in the Greco-Roman world. Paul himself does not identify these presuppositions, but they are evident enough in a number of other first-century works, both Jewish and pagan. . . .

The Theological Context of Paul's Remarks

The references to same-sex intercourse in 1 Cor. 6:9, 1 Tim. 1:10, and Rom. 1:26–27 simply presume, without argument, that "homosexual" practice is contrary to God's will. However, it is apparent from both the wording and the content of Paul's remark in Romans that he shared the common Hellenistic-Jewish view of "homosexuality." There is nothing distinctively Pauline, or even Christian, about that remark. Philo himself could have written it—and so could any number of pagan moralists, given just a few changes.

Paul meant his comment in Rom. 1:26–27 to help demonstrate the reality of the human predicament, as he discusses this in 1:18–3:20, and thus to help prepare for his exposition of the gospel, which begins in 3:21 and continues through chapter 8. What he has said about "homosexual" practices in 1:26–27 must not be isolated from this wider theological context. Two points in particular have to be borne in mind.

First, Paul wishes to demonstrate the brokenness of life apart from God. This is his point in Rom. 1:18–3:20, which he recapitulates in 3:22b–23 as he opens a new phase of the discussion: "There is no distinction, because all humanity has sinned and come short of God's glory" (author's translation). What Paul understands by *sin* is evident from 1:18–21, although the word itself is not used there. Humanity can know God through what God has created (1:18–20), yet knowing God is not enough. God must also be acknowledged as the One from whom all life has come and by whom all life is claimed. "Sin" is the refusal to do this, the refusal to glorify [NRSV: "honor"] God and to give God thanks (1:21).[13] Sin means trying to go it alone without God, refusing to let God be God, seeking to be one's own god, attempting to live out of one's own finite resources. Sin is the presumption that one exists as a self-generated and self-sustaining individual. It is the refusal to accept one's creatureliness—one's own *humanity*—as a gift from God. This is the folly that Paul sees manifested in pagan idolatry (Rom. 1:22–23); those who fashion the idols, refusing to acknowledge their own mortality, end up worshiping lifeless images that are inferior even to themselves. Thus, in Rom. 1:24–32 Paul is not enumerating specific "sins" but listing some representative consequences of sin. Here it is evident that he shares several Hellenistic-Jewish ideas: that "one is punished by the very things by which one sins" (Wisd. Sol. 11:16), that the failure to acknowledge God leads to a fundamental "confusion" about right and wrong (e.g., Wisd. Sol. 14:26), and that sexual immorality is an especially telling symptom of this confusion (e.g., Wisd. Sol. 15:15–17). In short, humanity's refusal to let God be God sets "Murphy's Law" in operation; everything that can go wrong does go wrong. Alienation from God brings the breakdown and de-formation of every other relationship. And Paul makes it clear that this is not the case only among the Gentiles; the Jews as well have come short of God's glory (Rom. 2:23–24). Far from singling out any particular group or practice for special criticism, the apostle is insisting that when people condemn others they are also condemning themselves (Rom. 2:1).

This "bad news" about the human condition is followed in Rom. 3:21–8:39 with the "good news" about God. Here is the second point that needs to be kept in mind about the context of Paul's remark in Rom. 1:26–27. Having completed his description of the human predicament, he goes on to proclaim that the source of humanity's salvation is God's grace as that has been disclosed and established in Christ. Moreover, he emphasizes that this saving grace is bestowed as a sheer gift (e.g., 3:24), with absolutely no conditions (e.g., 5:6, 8). Clearly, he had not written the earlier paragraphs in order to "condemn sinners," to frighten them into repenting, or to specify what one should and should not do. He had written them in order to demonstrate that the whole of humanity shares a common plight, and that all people are equally dependent on the One from whom they have received life and by whose grace their lives are renewed and enriched.

What, then, have we learned about the remark in Rom. 1:26–27 about same-sex intercourse? While it is true that this is the only biblical reference to same-sex practice that stands within a specifically theological context, the point of view that it represents has no distinctively Christian roots. Rather, it is nourished by presuppositions that were widespread in ancient culture, including Hellenistic Judaism. Nor is there any evidence that Paul's thinking on this subject was specifically informed either by the rule of Leviticus 18 and 20 or by the story about the men of Sodom. Some interpreters do argue that his description of same-sex intercourse as "unnatural" is based on a reading of the Genesis creation accounts, which he understood to affirm that "heterosexuality" is intrinsic to God's created order.[6] Perhaps Paul did believe this, but it can scarcely be documented from Romans 1. Three points are worth noting.

First, Rom. 1:18–32 contains neither a quotation from Genesis 1–3 nor a single identifiable allusion to any part of those creation accounts. Creation is of course in view, but not because Paul wants to emphasize *what* God brought into being or God's *intentions* for creation. Rather, in this passage his emphasis is almost entirely on *God as the Creator* because his concern is to show the folly of pagan idolatry. For this purpose, he seems to be relying mainly on Wisdom of Solomon 13–15; behind these chapters lie not the accounts of creation in Genesis 1–3 but such passages as Psalm 115 (esp. vv. 1–8), Isaiah 40 (esp. vv. 18–26, 28), and Isaiah 44 (esp. vv. 9–20).

Second, the Hellenistic-Jewish texts that are roughly contemporary with Paul's letters almost never invoke an argument from the order of creation.[7] Homoerotic acts are usually condemned for the same kinds of reasons given by non-Jewish authors of the period. We have already seen that these texts generally refer to "homosexuality" as unnatural because it was thought to "confuse" the roles of male and female and because it was regarded as a threat to the continuance of the human species.

Finally, no such "creation theology" as that alleged for Rom. 1:26–27 is evident in any of Paul's other references to what is "natural" or "unnatural." The most significant of these (with respect to the present topic) occurs in 1 Cor. 11:2–16, where the apostle is trying to show why women who pray or prophesy during worship should do so with their long hair neatly bound up on the top of their heads, like a covering.[8] In this passage, his appeal to what "nature itself" teaches (vv. 13–15) is nothing more than an appeal to social convention—to the practice with which he himself is familiar and that he therefore regards as self-evidently "proper."[9]

Summary Observations

This survey of the biblical texts most often discussed in connection with homosexuality yields the following general observations.

1. There is nothing in the Bible about homosexuality understood as a "condition," since the ancient world had no conception of anything like sexual orientation.
2. There are only a few biblical references or allusions to same-sex acts, and in no case is there any extended discussion of these. The subject seems not to have been a major concern of any biblical writer or tradition.
3. Each reference or allusion stands within its own particular literary, cultural, and theological context. Except for the rule in Lev. 18:22 and 20:13, same-sex acts are not the topic as such in any of these instances.
4. Every biblical reference or allusion to same-sex intercourse presumes that it is wrong, but no specific arguments, theological or otherwise, are offered to explain why. These must be inferred from the literary, cultural, and theological contexts of each reference.
5. The most comprehensive and important biblical reference to same-sex intercourse is Rom. 1:26–27, where Paul, like many other ancient critics of the practice, describes it as "unnatural." Such a description presupposed that everyone is "naturally" attracted only to the opposite sex, that all same-sex intercourse is intrinsically lustful, that same-sex intercourse compromises what patriarchal societies regard as the properly dominant role of males over females, and that same-sex intercourse could lead eventually to the extinction of the human species.

The Texts in Modern Contexts

Can the Bible in any way inform our understanding and give us moral guidance about homosexuality today? At least for the church, which accepts the writings of the Old and New Testaments as scriptural, this question cannot be avoided. Given the limited scope of the present essay, it is not possible to explore this question in any detail. As a start, however, the following points are offered for consideration:

1. The specific laws, rules, and moral teachings of the Bible are all more or less culturally conditioned. They generally presuppose beliefs about the physical world, human beings, and social relationships that we can no longer presuppose. This is especially true of what the various biblical traditions and writers have to say about sex and sexual relationships. For one thing, their views of sex were profoundly conditioned by the patriarchalism that pervaded ancient society. In addition, they were formulated without any knowledge of the complex origins of one's sexual identity and sexual orientation.

2. The specific moral rules, teachings, and advisories of Scripture reflect the effort of God's people, in the midst of the vicissitudes and contingencies of particular times and places, to be faithful to the One by whom their existence as human beings has been graced and claimed. It is therefore not surprising that the specific laws and moral counsels of the Bible are very diverse, often in tension with one another, sometimes even contradictory. This is not a "flaw" in Scripture but evidence of the moral seriousness of the faith communities within which the biblical writings were produced. To be specifically relevant, a moral directive or appeal has to address the particular situation; to be intelligible and credible, it has to be expressed in a way that is meaningful within the particular social and cultural setting. Since the situations and settings of the biblical writings were varied, so are the specific moral directives and appeals they contain.

3. To the extent that the specific teachings of Scripture are specific to the times and places for which they were variously formulated, they cannot be taken over automatically as God's will for all other times and places. In cases like this, one must be aware of what may be called "the law of diminishing relevancy": The *more specifically applicable* an instruction is to the situation for which it was originally formulated, the *less specifically applicable* it is to every other situation.

4. At the core of the scriptural witness, received and affirmed by the church, is what it attests about God's saving grace and what it affirms about Christ as the one through whom God's grace is bestowed. In Christ, the church has experienced the grace of God both as an unconditional gift and as an unconditional claim. It is by this word of grace that the church historically has been guided in its considerations about good and evil, right and wrong. To be graced and claimed by God's love revealed in Christ is to be called to manifest that love in one's own life. For the Christian community, then, the ethical question comes down to this: Which decisions, actions, and relationships give scope to God's grace, and which do not?

5. Finally, Scripture provides access to the apostolic witness of faith, wherein the believing community finds the norm by which appropriately *Christian* faith and conduct, including sexual conduct, may be

ascertained. It would be a simple matter if this norm could be found in what Scripture provides by way of specific rules, teachings, and advisories concerning "homosexual" practices. But that is not the case. However pertinent they may have been for the various times and circumstances within which they were originally formulated, the biblical injunctions and teachings on this topic presume much that can no longer be presumed about human sexuality.

Therefore, it is not "what the Bible says" about homoerotic acts that constitutes the witness of Scripture on this topic. Rather, in this instance as in every other, the witness of Scripture is that human existence, like the whole of creation, is the gift of a sovereign, just, benevolent, and caring God; that God's purposes are shaped and accomplished by God's love, over which nothing in all creation (including humanity's rebelliousness) can finally prevail; that the people of God are repeatedly summoned to walk in the same love from and in which, by God's grace, they properly "live and move and have their being"; that the claim inherent in God's love is no less boundless than the gift; and that it is in Christ that women and men of faith will find, at last, both the saving power of God's gift of love and the strength to follow where it leads.

Notes

1. Except as noted, all quotations from the Bible (including the Apocrypha) are from the New Revised Standard Version. Other ancient texts are cited either from translations in the *Loeb Classical Library* (Cambridge: Harvard University Press, various dates), designated as LCL, or from translations in *The Old Testament Pseudepigrapha*, ed. James H. Charlesworth (2 vols.; Garden City, N.Y.: Doubleday, 1983), designated as *OTP*.

2. The word "homosexual" was not coined until 1869, when a Hungarian physician (Karoly M. Benkert), writing in German, used it with reference to "male or female individuals" who "from birth" are erotically oriented toward their own sex. According to the *Oxford English Dictionary*, the word appeared for the first time in English only in 1912. Its earliest use in an English Bible was in 1946, in the first edition of the Revised Standard Version (1 Cor. 6:9).

3. See Simon B. Parker, "The Hebrew Bible and Homosexuality," *Quarterly Review* 11/3 (1991), 6.

4. Richard Bauckham, *Jude, 2 Peter*, Word Biblical Commentary (Dallas: Word Books, 1983), 54.

5. David Winston, trans., *The Wisdom of Solomon*, Anchor Bible, 43 (Garden City, N.Y.: Doubleday, 1979), 269, 280. This tradition also taught that "one is punished by the very things by which one sins" (Wisd. Sol. 11:16), which explains Paul's remarking that God "gave up" the Gentiles to their own wicked ways (Rom. 1:24, 26, 28).

6. Richard B. Hays provides an unusually well-informed and carefully reasoned argument to this effect in "Relations Natural and Unnatural: A Response to John Boswell's Exegesis of Romans 1," *Journal of Religious Ethics* 14 (1986): 184–215, esp. 191–194. Compare Stott, "Homosexual Partnerships?" 233.

7. Testament of Naphtali 3:4 is a significant exception, but it is not entirely certain that "homosexuality" is what the author has in view. The reference may be to the crossing of the line between earthly (the men of Sodom) and heavenly (Lot's angelic visitors), as in the very next sentence (3:5, which alludes to Gen. 6:1).

8. Perhaps the Corinthians' interpretation of the affirmation that in Christ "there is no longer male or female" (Gal. 3:28) had led some of them to adopt certain practices (in dress, hairstyles, etc.) that Paul thought inappropriate.

9. To be sure, in 1 Cor. 11:2–16 there are allusions to the creation accounts—specifically, to Gen. 1:27a; 2:18; 2:22–23. But Paul has not based his argument here on God's creation of two different sexes ("heterosexuality"). The terms for "male" and "female" do not occur in the passage (he uses them only in Rom. 1:26–27 and Gal. 3:28), nor is there any allusion to God's creation of such. Rather, Paul has based his argument on the fact that man was created *before* woman and that woman was then created *from* man.

POSTSCRIPT

Does the Bible Forbid Same-Sex Relationships?

Inasmuch as Hays and Furnish have addressed the question of same-sex attraction from a Christian perspective, the following statements from other religious traditions provide a broader perspective.

Islam While a diversity of opinion exists within Islam concerning same-sex attraction, the overall judgment, especially from Islamic scripture, appears to be in opposition to it. From the Qur'an we read the following passages:

> Do ye commit lewdness such as no people in creation (ever) committed before you? For ye practice your lusts on men in preference to women: ye are indeed a people transgressing beyond bounds. (7:80–81)

> If any of your women are guilty of lewdness, Take the evidence of four (Reliable) witnesses from amongst you against them; and if they testify, confine them to houses until death do claim them, or God ordain for them some (other) way. (*The Noble Qur'an*, 4:15)

Judaism Within Judaism, like Christianity and Islam, a wide-ranging spectrum of perspectives exists on same-sex attraction, ranging from conservative to liberal. Orthodox and conservative congregations generally oppose homosexual behavior, while reform and reconstructionist groups are more accepting. Orthodox Jews interpret the following verse from the Torah literally: "Thou shalt not lie with mankind, as with womankind: it *is* abomination" (King James Version, Lev. 18:22). More liberal Jews believe this passage to simply mean that neither male homosexual partner should assume a submissive (womanly) role in the relationship, and they are not opposed to same-sex relationships.

The Bahai Faith The Bahai are accepting of all religions as having come from the same divine origin, and they believe all faiths have truth. The Bahai perspective on same-sex attraction is not as accepting. The following statement, which can be found at http://www.bahai=library.org, is taken from the National Spiritual Assembly of the Bahais of the United Kingdom:

> Bahais believe that the sexual impulse is a God-given one, and the source of great joy and fulfilment if expressed in the intended way. The appropriate circumstance for this is within marriage, the legally, socially, and spiritually sanctioned union of two adults of the opposite sex. Other expressions are neither valid nor to be encouraged.

The Zoroastrian Faith   Zoroastrianism, the religion of ancient Persia (modern Iran), is purportedly one of the oldest religions of the world. Zoroastrian scripture (the Avesta), said to be the writings of Zarathustra, prohibits the practice of homosexual relations:

> The man that lies with mankind as man lies with womankind, or as woman lies with mankind, is the man that is a Daeva; this one is the man that is a worshipper of the Daevas, that is a male paramour of the Daevas, that is a female paramour of the Daevas, that is a wife to the Daeva; this is the man that is as bad as a Daeva, that is in his whole being a Daeva; this is the man that is a Daeva before he dies, and becomes one of the unseen Daevas after death: so is he, whether he has lain with mankind as mankind, or as womankind.

> — *The Vendidad*, Fargard 8, chapter 5, paragraph 32

Unitarian Universalism   Unitarian Universalism is an example of a religion that is open to those of almost any belief system or—for the purpose of this debate—any gender orientation. Unitarian Universalists are completely open to gay or lesbian belief or practice. According to the Unitarian Universalist Association of Congregations' Web site at `http://www.uua.org/aboutuu/newcomerfaq.html#4`:

> One could not be considered a Unitarian Universalist and believe that subscription to specific doctrines or creeds are necessary for access to God or spirituality or membership in our congregations. Unitarian Universalists could not believe that God favors any group of people based on any inherent qualities, such as skin color, gender, sexual orientation, physical ability, etc.—or that any group of people is more worthy of access to opportunities than any other as a result of these qualities.

It is clear from the various arguments discussed by Hays and Furnish that there is a wide variety of beliefs among the various religions concerning same-sex attraction and homosexual relationships. However, there is one theme common to almost all of the religions that have made statements on this issue —the importance of treating all people, without regard to sexual preference, as sons and daughters of God, worthy of compassion and understanding.

Suggested Readings

S. L. Jones and M. A. Yarhouse, *Homosexuality: The Use of Scientific Research in the Church's Moral Debate* (InterVarsity Press, 2000).

C. L. Seow, ed., *Homosexuality and Christian Community* (Westminster John Knox, 1996).

M. L. Soards, *Scripture and Homosexuality: Biblical Authority and the Church Today* (Westminster John Knox, 1995).

W. Wink, ed., *Homosexuality and Christian Faith: Questions of Conscience for the Churches* (Fortress, 1999).

On the Internet ...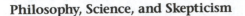

Philosophy, Science, and Skepticism

The Philosophy, Science, and Skepticism site was created in response to many of the scientific assertions made in support of theistic creation. This Web site includes an article entitled, "Frequently Encountered Criticisms in Evolution vs. Creationism: 2002 Edition," as well as links to other articles and papers.

http://www.vuletic.com/hume/cefec

Creationism.org

Creationism.org is a Web site that contains basic information on the tenets and supporting arguments for creationism. Included is a link on creation science articles as well as links on geology and speciation, among others.

http://www.creationism.org

The Psychology of Religion Pages

The Psychology of Religion Pages Web site is an introductory site that offers various approaches to the relationship between psychology and religion.

http://www.psychwww.com/psyrelig/index.htm

PART 4

Religion and Science Issues

*T*his part explores the tentative relationship that religion and science share. As science progresses and changes, religion often responds in kind. As religion presents more compelling arguments for its own validity, science attempts to provide counterexplanations for its own worth. What is the more legitimate explanation for human experience? What is the most satisfying for individuals?

- Does the Theory of Evolution Explain the Origins of Humanity?

- Does Religious Commitment Improve Mental Health?

ISSUE 12

Does the Theory of Evolution Explain the Origins of Humanity?

YES: Daniel C. Dennett, from *Darwin's Dangerous Idea: Evolution and the Meanings of Life* (Simon & Schuster, 1995)

NO: John MacArthur, from *The Battle for the Beginning: The Bible on Creation and the Fall of Adam* (W Publishing Group, 2001)

ISSUE SUMMARY

YES: Daniel C. Dennett, professor of arts and sciences at Tufts University in Medford, Massachusetts, argues against a God being involved in creation. He maintains that Darwin's theory of evolution is the strongest and most elegant explanation for the creation of the universe and humankind.

NO: Featured teacher of the radio ministry *Grace to You* and president of The Master's College in Santa Clarita, California, John MacArthur argues for divine creation. MacArthur believes that faithful Christians are being deceived by the naturalistic philosophy of evolution, and he provides conservative, scriptural arguments supporting a God-directed creation.

$\mathbf{F}$ew issues have proven more controversial than the recurring debate concerning creation and evolution. Since Charles Darwin published *On the Origin of Species* in 1859, the debate has raged on many fronts but particularly between theologians and scientists. Tradition holds that the first formal debate occurred in 1860 between Charles Darwin's colleague Thomas Henry Huxley and the Church of England's bishop of Oxford. It is reported that the bishop of Oxford inquired whether Huxley preferred to think of himself descending from an ape on his grandfather's or his grandmother's side of the family. Huxley retorted that he would rather have descended from an ape than a bishop. While the historical accuracy of this anecdote is another matter of debate, it nevertheless illustrates the rancor that exists, even to the present, surrounding the debate over evolution.

Society's conflict and concern over the theory of evolution during the nineteenth century is the same concern and contention experienced at present for this theory can be interpreted as a direct challenge to the existence of God. Evolutionary biologist Richard Dawkins states in *The Blind Watchmaker* (W. W. Norton, 1996), "Although atheism might have been logically tenable before Darwin, Darwin made it possible to be an intellectually fulfilled atheist."

William B. Provine, professor of biology at Cornell University, candidly affirmed in a debate at Stanford University in April 1994 that the religious implications of Darwinian atheism are: "no life after death; no ultimate foundation for ethics; no ultimate meaning for life; no free will."

Some people tend to dichotomize the evolution/creation debate into an either/or proposition. From this perspective, one either believes that God is the creator or that all creation was, in the words of agnostic philosopher Bertrand Russell, "a curious accident in a backwater." Others have accepted evolution as a divine principle of creation used by God to bring about divine purposes.

According to a 1997 Gallup poll, ten percent of the American public believes in evolution to the extent that "God had no part in [the] process." Forty-four percent of the respondents believes God created "human beings pretty much in their present form at one time within the last 10,000 years." Thirty-nine percent believes "human beings have developed over millions of years . . . but God has guided the process."

This debate deals with the fundamental issue of divine creation versus naturalistic evolution. In the first selection, Daniel C. Dennett argues that Darwin's theory of evolution makes obsolete any religious explanation of creation. The title of the book from which the following selection has been taken, *Darwin's Dangerous Idea*, represents the serious consequences of Dennett's arguments.

In the second selection, John MacArthur, argues for divine creation. He provides a defense of divine creationism based on a literal interpretation of the Bible. MacArthur believes that many Christians, non-Christians, as well as atheists have been deceived in various ways. He boldly asserts, "The notion that natural evolutionary processes can account for the origin of all living species has never been and never will be established as fact."

Daniel C. Dennett

 **YES**

Darwin's Dangerous Idea:
Evolution and the Meanings of Life

We used to sing a lot when I was a child, around the campfire at summer camp, at school and Sunday school, or gathered around the piano at home. One of my favorite songs was "Tell Me Why." ...

> Tell me why the stars do shine,
> Tell me why the ivy twines,
> Tell me why the sky's so blue.
> Then I will tell you just why I love you.
> Because God made the stars to shine,
> Because God made the ivy twine,
> Because God made the sky so blue.
> Because God made you, that's why I love you.

This straightforward, sentimental declaration still brings a lump to my throat—so sweet, so innocent, so reassuring a vision of life!

And then along comes Darwin and spoils the picnic. Or does he? ... From the moment of the publication of *Origin of Species* in 1859, Charles Darwin's fundamental idea has inspired intense reactions ranging from ferocious condemnation to ecstatic allegiance, sometimes tantamount to religious zeal. Darwin's theory has been abused and misrepresented by friend and foe alike. It has been misappropriated to lend scientific respectability to appalling political and social doctrines. It has been pilloried in caricature by opponents, some of whom would have it compete in our children's schools with "creation science," a pathetic hodgepodge of pious pseudo-science.[1]

Almost no one is indifferent to Darwin, and no one should be. The Darwinian theory is a scientific theory, and a great one, but that is not all it is. The creationists who oppose it so bitterly are right about one thing: Darwin's dangerous idea cuts much deeper into the fabric of our most fundamental beliefs than many of its sophisticated apologists have yet admitted, even to themselves.

The sweet, simple vision of the song, taken literally, is one that most of us have outgrown, however fondly we may recall it. The kindly God who lovingly fashioned each and every one of us (all creatures great and small) and sprinkled the sky with shining stars for our delight—*that* God is, like Santa Claus, a myth of childhood, not anything a sane, undeluded adult could literally believe in. *That* God must either be turned into a symbol for something less concrete or abandoned altogether.

Not all scientists and philosophers are atheists, and many who are believers declare that their idea of God can live in peaceful coexistence with, or even find support from, the Darwinian framework of ideas. Theirs is not an anthropomorphic Handicrafter God, but still a God worthy of worship in their eyes, capable of giving consolation and meaning to their lives. Others ground their highest concerns in entirely secular philosophies, views of the meaning of life that stave off despair without the aid of any concept of a Supreme Being—other than the Universe itself. Something *is* sacred to these thinkers, but they do not call it God; they call it, perhaps, Life, or Love, or Goodness, or Intelligence, or Beauty, or Humanity. What both groups share, in spite of the differences in their deepest creeds, is a conviction that life does have meaning, that goodness matters.

But can *any* version of this attitude of wonder and purpose be sustained in the face of Darwinism? From the outset, there have been those who thought they saw Darwin letting the worst possible cat out of the bag: nihilism. They thought that if Darwin was right, the implication would be that nothing could be sacred. To put it bluntly, nothing could have any point. Is this just an overreaction? What exactly are the implications of Darwin's idea—and, in any case, has it been scientifically proven or is it still "just a theory"?

Perhaps, you may think, we could make a useful division: there are the parts of Darwin's idea that really are established beyond any reasonable doubt, and then there are the speculative extensions of the scientifically irresistible parts. Then—if we were lucky—perhaps the rock-solid scientific facts would have no stunning implications about religion, or human nature, or the meaning of life, while the parts of Darwin's idea that get people all upset could be put into quarantine as highly controversial extensions of, or mere interpretations of, the scientifically irresistible parts. That would be reassuring.

But alas, that is just about backwards. There are vigorous controversies swirling around in evolutionary theory, but those who feel threatened by Darwinism should not take heart from this fact. Most—if not quite all—of the controversies concern issues that are "just science"; no matter which side wins, the outcome will not undo the basic Darwinian idea. That idea, which is about as secure as any in science, really does have far-reaching implications for our vision of what the meaning of life is or could be.

In 1543, Copernicus proposed that the Earth was not the center of the universe but in fact revolved around the Sun. It took over a century for the idea to sink in, a gradual and actually rather painless transformation. (The religious reformer Philipp Melanchthon, a collaborator of Martin Luther, opined that "some Christian prince" should suppress this madman, but aside from a few such salvos, the world was not particularly shaken by Copernicus himself.) The Copernican Revolution did eventually have its own "shot heard round the world": Galileo's *Dialogue Concerning the Two Chief World Systems*, but it was not published until 1632, when the issue was no longer controversial among scientists. Galileo's projectile provoked an infamous response by the Roman Catholic Church, setting up a shock wave whose reverberations are only now dying out. But in spite of the drama of that epic confrontation, the idea that our planet is not the center of creation has sat rather lightly in people's minds. Every schoolchild today accepts this as the matter of fact it is, without tears or terror.

In due course, the Darwinian Revolution will come to occupy a similarly secure and untroubled place in the minds—and hearts—of every educated person on the globe, but today, more than a century after Darwin's death, we still have not come to terms with its mind-boggling implications. Unlike the Copernican Revolution, which did not engage widespread public attention until the scientific details had been largely sorted out, the Darwinian Revolution has had anxious lay spectators and cheerleaders taking sides from the outset, tugging at the sleeves of the participants and encouraging grandstanding. The scientists themselves have been moved by the same hopes and fears, so it is not surprising that the relatively narrow conflicts among theorists have often been not just blown up out of proportion by their adherents, but seriously distorted in the process. Everybody has seen, dimly, that a lot is at stake.

Moreover, although Darwin's own articulation of his theory was monumental, and its powers were immediately recognized by many of the scientists and other thinkers of his day, there really were large gaps in his theory that have only recently begun to be properly filled in. The biggest gap looks almost comical in retrospect. In all his brilliant musings, Darwin never hit upon the central concept, without which the theory of evolution is hopeless: the concept of a *gene*. Darwin had no proper *unit* of heredity, and so his account of the process of natural selection was plagued with entirely reasonable doubts about whether it would work. Darwin supposed that offspring would always exhibit a sort of blend or average of their parents' features. Wouldn't such "blending inheritance" always simply average out all differences, turning everything into uniform gray? How could diversity survive such relentless averaging? Darwin recognized the seriousness of this challenge, and neither he nor his many ardent supporters succeeded in responding with a description of a convincing and well-documented mechanism of heredity that could combine traits of parents while maintaining an underlying and unchanged identity. The idea they needed was right at hand, uncovered ("formulated" would be too strong) by the monk Gregor Mendel and published in a relatively obscure Austrian journal in 1865, but, in the best-savored irony in the history of science, it lay there unnoticed until its importance was appreciated (at first dimly) around 1900. Its triumphant establishment at the heart of the "Modern Synthesis" (in effect, the synthesis of Mendel and Darwin) was eventually made secure in the 1940s, thanks to the work of Theodosius Dobzhansky, Julian Huxley, Ernst Mayr, and others. It has taken another half-century to iron out most of the wrinkles of that new fabric.

The fundamental core of contemporary Darwinism, the theory of DNA-based reproduction and evolution, is now beyond dispute among scientists. It demonstrates its power every day, contributing crucially to the explanation of planet-sized facts of geology and meteorology, through middle-sized facts of ecology and agronomy, down to the latest microscopic facts of genetic engineering. It unifies all of biology and the history of our planet into a single grand story. Like Gulliver tied down in Lilliput, it is unbudgeable, not because of some one or two huge chains of argument that might—hope against hope—have weak links in them, but because it is securely tied by hundreds of thousands of threads of evidence anchoring it to virtually every other area of human knowledge. New discoveries may conceivably lead to dramatic, even "revolutionary" *shifts* in the Darwinian theory, but the hope that it will be "refuted" by some shattering breakthrough is about as reasonable as the hope that we will return to a geocentric vision and discard Copernicus.

Still, the theory is embroiled in remarkably hot-tempered controversy, and one of the reasons for this incandescence is that these debates about scientific matters are usually distorted by fears that the "wrong" answer would have intolerable moral implications. So great are these fears that they are carefully left unarticulated, displaced from attention by several layers of distracting rebuttal and counter-rebuttal. The disputants are forever changing the subject slightly, conveniently keeping the bogeys in the shadows. It is this misdirection that is mainly responsible for postponing the day when we can all live as comfortably with our new biological perspective as we do with the astronomical perspective Copernicus gave us.

Whenever Darwinism is the topic, the temperature rises, because more is at stake than just the empirical facts about how life on Earth evolved, or the correct logic of the theory that accounts for those facts. One of the precious things that is at stake is a vision of what it means to ask, and answer, the question "Why?" Darwin's new perspective turns several traditional assumptions upside down, undermining our standard ideas about what ought to count as satisfying answers to this ancient and inescapable question. Here science and philosophy get completely intertwined. Scientists sometimes deceive themselves into thinking that philosophical ideas are only, at best, decorations or parasitic commentaries on the hard, objective triumphs of science, and that they themselves are immune to the confusions that philosophers devote their lives to dissolving. But there is no such thing as philosophy-free science; there is only science whose philosophical baggage is taken on board without examination.

The Darwinian Revolution is both a scientific and a philosophical revolution, and neither revolution could have occurred without the other. As we shall see, it was the philosophical prejudices of the scientists, more than their lack of scientific evidence, that prevented them from seeing how the theory could actually work, but those philosophical prejudices that had to be overthrown were too deeply entrenched to be dislodged by mere philosophical brilliance. It took an irresistible parade of hard-won scientific facts to force thinkers to take seriously the weird new outlook that Darwin proposed. Those who are still ill-acquainted with that beautiful procession can be forgiven their continued allegiance to the pre-Darwinian ideas. And the battle is not yet over; even among the scientists, there are pockets of resistance.

Let me lay my cards on the table. If I were to give an award for the single best idea anyone has ever had, I'd give it to Darwin, ahead of Newton and

Einstein and everyone else. In a single stroke, the idea of evolution by natural selection unifies the realm of life, meaning, and purpose with the realm of space and time, cause and effect, mechanism and physical law. But it is not just a wonderful scientific idea. It is a dangerous idea. My admiration for Darwin's magnificent idea is unbounded, but I, too, cherish many of the ideas and ideals that it *seems* to challenge, and want to protect them. For instance, I want to protect the campfire song, and what is beautiful and true in it, for my little grandson and his friends, and for their children when they grow up. There are many more magnificent ideas that are also jeopardized, it seems, by Darwin's idea, and they, too, may need protection. The only good way to do this—the only way that has a chance in the long run—is to cut through the smokescreens and look at the idea as unflinchingly, as dispassionately, as possible.

On this occasion, we are not going to settle for "There, there, it will all come out all right." Our examination will take a certain amount of nerve. Feelings may get hurt. Writers on evolution usually steer clear of this apparent clash between science and religion. Fools rush in, Alexander Pope said, where angels fear to tread. Do you want to follow me? Don't you really want to know what survives this confrontation? What if it turns out that the sweet vision— or a better one—survives intact, strengthened and deepened by the encounter? Wouldn't it be a shame to forgo the opportunity for a strengthened, renewed creed, settling instead for a fragile, sickbed faith that you mistakenly supposed must not be disturbed?

There is no future in a sacred myth. Why not? Because of our curiosity. Because, as the song reminds us, *we want to know why.* We may have outgrown the song's answer, but we will never outgrow the question. Whatever we hold precious, we cannot protect it from our curiosity, because being who we are, one of the things we deem precious is the truth. Our love of truth is surely a central element in the meaning we find in our lives. In any case, the idea that we might preserve meaning by kidding ourselves is a more pessimistic, more nihilistic idea than I for one can stomach. If that were the best that could be done, I would conclude that nothing mattered after all. . . .

·◄❂►·

At what "point" does a human life begin or end? The Darwinian perspective lets us see with unmistakable clarity why there is no hope at all of *discovering* a telltale mark, a saltation in life's processes, that "counts." We need to draw lines; we need definitions of life and death for many important moral purposes. The layers of pearly dogma that build up in defense around these fundamentally arbitrary attempts are familiar, and in never-ending need of repair. We should abandon the fantasy that either science or religion can uncover some well-hidden fact that tells us exactly where to draw these lines. There is no "natural" way to mark the birth of a human "soul," any more than there is a "natural" way to mark the birth of a species. And, contrary to what many traditions insist, I think we all do share the intuition that there are gradations of value in the ending of human lives. Most human embryos end in spontaneous abortion—fortunately, since these are mostly *terata,* hopeless monsters whose lives are all but impossible. Is this a terrible evil? Are the mothers whose bodies abort these embryos guilty of involuntary manslaughter? Of course not. Which is worse, taking "heroic" measures to keep alive a severely deformed infant, or taking the equally "heroic" (if unsung) step of seeing to it that such an infant dies as quickly and painlessly as possible? I do not suggest that Darwinian thinking gives us answers to such questions; I do suggest that Darwinian thinking helps us see why the traditional hope of solving these problems (finding a moral algorithm) is forlorn. We must cast off the myths that make these old-fashioned solutions seem inevitable. We need to grow up, in other words.

Among the precious artifacts worth preserving are whole cultures themselves. There are still several thousand distinct languages spoken daily on our planet, but the number is dropping fast (Diamond 1992, Hale et al. 1992). When a language goes extinct, this is the same kind of loss as the extinction of a species, and when the culture that was carried by that language dies, this is an even greater loss. But here, once again, we face incommensurabilities and no easy answers.

I began . . . with a song which I myself cherish, and hope will survive "forever." I hope my grandson learns it and passes it on to his grandson, but at the same time I do not myself believe, and do not really want my grandson to believe, the doctrines that are so movingly expressed in that song. They are too simple. They are, in a word, wrong—just as wrong as the ancient Greeks' doctrines about the gods and goddesses on Mount Olympus. Do you believe, literally, in an anthropomorphic God? If not, then you must agree with me that the song is a beautiful, comforting falsehood. Is that simple song nevertheless a valuable meme? I certainly think it is. It is a modest but beautiful part of our heritage, a treasure to be preserved. But we must face the fact that, just as there were times when tigers would not have been viable, times are coming when they will no longer be viable, except in zoos and other preserves, and the same is true of many of the treasures in our cultural heritage.

The Welsh language is kept alive by artificial means, just the way condors are. We cannot preserve *all* the features of the cultural world in which these treasures flourished. We wouldn't want to. It took oppressive political and social systems, rife with many evils, to create the rich soil in which many of our greatest works of art could grow: slavery and despotism ("enlightened" though these sometimes may have been), obscene differences in living standards between the rich and the poor—and a huge amount of ignorance. Ignorance is a necessary condition for many excellent things. The childish joy of seeing what Santa Claus has brought for Christmas is a species of joy that must soon be extinguished in each child by the loss of ignorance. When that child grows up, she can transmit that joy to her own children, but she must also recognize a time when it has outlived its value.

The view I am expressing has clear ancestors. The philosopher George Santayana was a Catholic atheist, if you can imagine such a thing. According to Bertrand Russell (1945, p. 811), William James once denounced Santayana's ideas as "the perfection of rottenness," and one can see why some people would be offended by his brand of aestheticism: a deep appreciation for all the formulae, ceremonies, and trappings of his religious heritage, but lacking the faith.

Santayana's position was aptly caricatured: "There is no God and Mary is His Mother." But how many of us are caught in that very dilemma, loving the heritage, firmly convinced of its value, yet unable to sustain any conviction at all in its truth? We are faced with a difficult choice. Because we value it, we are eager to preserve it in a rather precarious and "denatured" state—in churches and cathedrals and synagogues, built to house huge congregations of the devout, and now on the way to being cultural museums. There is really not that much difference between the roles of the Beefeaters who stand picturesque guard at the Tower of London, and the Cardinals who march in their magnificent costumes and meet to elect the next Pope. Both are keeping alive traditions, rituals, liturgies, symbols, that otherwise would fade.

But hasn't there been a tremendous rebirth of fundamentalist faith in all these creeds? Yes, unfortunately, there has been, and I think that there are no forces on this planet more dangerous to us all than the fanaticisms of fundamentalism, of all the species: Protestantism, Catholicism, Judaism, Islam, Hinduism, and Buddhism, as well as countless smaller infections. Is there a conflict between science and religion here? There most certainly is.

Darwin's dangerous idea helps to create a condition in the memosphere that in the long run threatens to be just as toxic to these memes as civilization in general has been toxic to the large wild mammals. Save the Elephants! Yes, of course, but not *by all means*. Not by forcing the people of Africa to live nineteenth-century lives, for instance. This is not an idle comparison. The creation of the great wildlife preserves in Africa has often been accompanied by the dislocation—and ultimate destruction—of human populations. (For a chilling vision of this side effect, see Colin Turnbull 1972 on the fate of the Ik.) Those who think that we should preserve the elephants' pristine environment *at all costs* should contemplate the costs of returning the United States to the pristine conditions in which the buffaloes roam and the deer and the antelope play. We must find an accommodation.

I love the King James Version of the Bible. My own spirit recoils from a God Who is He or She in the same way my heart sinks when I see a lion pacing neurotically back and forth in a small zoo cage. I know, I know, the lion is beautiful but dangerous; if you let the lion roam free, it would kill me; safety demands that it be put in a cage. Safety demands that religions be put in cages, too—when absolutely necessary. We just can't have forced female circumcision, and the second-class status of women in Roman Catholicism and Mormonism, to say nothing of their status in Islam. The recent Supreme Court ruling declaring unconstitutional the Florida law prohibiting the sacrificing of animals in the rituals of the Santeria sect (an Afro-Caribbean religion incorporating elements of Yoruba traditions and Roman Catholicism) is a borderline case, at least for many of us. Such rituals are offensive to many, but the protective mantle of religious tradition secures our tolerance. We are wise to respect these traditions. It is, after all, just part of respect for the biosphere.

Save the Baptists! Yes, of course, but not *by all means*. Not if it means tolerating the deliberate misinforming of children about the natural world. According to a recent poll, 48 percent of the people in the United States today believe that the book of Genesis is literally true. And 70 percent believe that "creation science" should be taught in school alongside evolution. Some recent writers recommend a policy in which parents would be able to "opt out" of materials they didn't want their children taught. Should evolution be taught in the schools? Should arithmetic be taught? Should history? Misinforming a child is a terrible offense.

A faith, like a species, must evolve or go extinct when the environment changes. It is not a gentle process in either case. We see in every Christian sub-species the battle of memes—should women be ordained? should we go back to the Latin liturgy?—and the same can also be observed in the varieties of Judaism and Islam. We must have a similar mixture of respect and self-protective caution about memes. This is already accepted practice, but we tend to avert our attention from its implications. We preach freedom of religion, but only so far. If your religion advocates slavery, or mutilation of women, or infanticide, or puts a price on Salman Rushdie's head because he has insulted it, then your religion has a feature that cannot be respected. It endangers us all.

It is nice to have grizzly bears and wolves living in the wild. They are no longer a menace; we can peacefully coexist, with a little wisdom. The same policy can be discerned in our political tolerance, in religious freedom. You are free to preserve or create any religious creed you wish, so long as it does not become a public menace. We're all on the Earth together, and we have to learn some accommodation. The Hutterite memes are "clever" not to include any memes about the virtue of destroying outsiders. If they did, we would have to combat them. We tolerate the Hutterites because they harm only themselves —though we may well insist that we have the right to impose some further openness on their schooling of their own children. Other religious members are not so benign. The message is clear: those who will not accommodate, who will not temper, who insist on keeping only the purest and wildest strain of their heritage alive, we will be obliged, reluctantly, to cage or disarm, and we will do our best to disable the memes they fight for. Slavery is beyond the pale. Child abuse is beyond the pale. Discrimination is beyond the pale. The pronouncing of death sentences on those who blaspheme against a religion (complete with bounties or rewards for those who carry them out) is beyond the pale. It is not civilized, and is owed no more respect in the name of religious freedom than any other incitement to cold-blooded murder.[2] . . .

Long before there was science, or even philosophy, there were religions. They have served many purposes (it would be a mistake of greedy reductionism to look for a single purpose, a single *summum bonum* which they have all directly or indirectly served). They have inspired many people to lead lives that have added immeasurably to the wonders of our world, and they have inspired many more people to lead lives that were, given their circumstances, more meaningful, less painful, than they otherwise could have been. . . .

Religions have brought the comfort of belonging and companionship to many who would otherwise have passed through this life all alone, without glory or adventure. At their best, religions have drawn attention to love, and made it real for people who could not otherwise see it, and ennobled the attitudes and refreshed the spirits of the world-beset. Another thing religions have accomplished, without this being thereby their *raison d'être*, is that they have kept *Homo sapiens* civilized enough, for long enough, for us to have learned how to reflect more systematically and accurately on our position in the universe. There is much more to learn. There is certainly a treasury of ill-appreciated truths embedded in the endangered cultures of the modern world, designs that have accumulated details over eons of idiosyncratic history, and we should take steps to record it, and study it, before it disappears, for, like dinosaur genomes, once it is gone, it will be virtually impossible to recover.

We should not expect this variety of respect to be satisfactory to those who wholeheartedly embody the memes we honor with our attentive—but not wor-shipful—scholarship. On the contrary, many of them will view anything other than enthusiastic conversion to their own views as a threat, even an intolera-ble threat. We must not underestimate the suffering such confrontations cause. To watch, to have to participate in, the contraction or evaporation of beloved features of one's heritage is a pain only our species can experience, and surely few pains could be more terrible. But we have no reasonable alternative, and those whose visions dictate that they cannot peacefully coexist with the rest of us will have to quarantine as best we can, minimizing the pain and damage, trying always to leave open a path or two that may come to seem acceptable.

If you want to teach your children that they are the tools of God, you had better not teach them that they are God's rifles, or we will have to stand firmly opposed to you: your doctrine has no glory, no special rights, no intrinsic and inalienable merit. If you insist on teaching your children falsehoods—that the Earth is flat, that "Man" is not a product of evolution by natural selection—then you must expect, at the very least, that those of us who have freedom of speech will feel free to describe your teachings as the spreading of falsehoods, and will attempt to demonstrate this to your children at our earliest opportunity. Our future well-being—the well-being of all of us on the planet—depends on the education of our descendants.

What, then, of all the glories of our religious traditions? They should cer-tainly be preserved, as should the languages, the art, the costumes, the rituals, the monuments. Zoos are now more and more being seen as second-class havens for endangered species, but at least they are havens, and what they preserve is irreplaceable. The same is true of complex memes and their phenotypic ex-pressions. Many a fine New England church, costly to maintain, is in danger of destruction. Shall we deconsecrate these churches and turn them into muse-ums, or retrofit them for some other use? The latter fate is at least to be preferred to their destruction. Many congregations face a cruel choice: their house of wor-ship costs so much to maintain in all its splendor that little of their tithing is left over for the poor. The Catholic Church has faced this problem for centuries, and has maintained a position that is, I think, defensible, but not obviously so: when it spends its treasure to put gold plating on the candlesticks, instead of providing more food and better shelter for the poor of the parish, it has a different vision of what makes life worth living. Our people, it says, benefit more from having a place of splendor in which to worship than from a little more food. Any atheist or agnostic who finds this cost-benefit analysis ludi-crous might pause to consider whether to support diverting all charitable and governmental support for museums, symphony orchestras, libraries, and scientific laboratories to efforts to provide more food and better living conditions for the least well off. A human life worth living is not something that can be uncontroversially measured, and that is its glory.

And there's the rub. What will happen, one may well wonder, if religion is preserved in cultural zoos, in libraries, in concerts and demonstrations? It is happening; the tourists flock to watch the Native American tribal dances, and for the onlookers it is folklore, a religious ceremony, certainly, to be treated with respect, but also an example of a meme complex on the verge of extinction, at least in its strong, ambulatory phase; it has become an invalid, barely kept alive by its custodians. Does Darwin's dangerous idea give us anything in exchange for the ideas it calls into question?

... [T]he physicist Paul Davies proclaim[ed] that the reflective power of human minds can be "no trivial detail, no minor by-product of mindless purposeless forces," and [I] suggested that being a by-product of mindless purposeless forces was no disqualification for importance. And I have argued that Darwin has shown us how, in fact, *everything* of importance is just such a product. Spinoza called his highest being God or Nature *(Deus sive Natura)*, expressing a sort of pantheism. There have been many varieties of pantheism, but they usually lack a convincing *explanation* about just how God is distributed in the whole of nature.... Darwin offers us one: it is in the distribution of Design throughout nature, creating, in the Tree of Life, an utterly unique and irreplaceable creation, an actual pattern in the immeasurable reaches of Design Space that could never be exactly duplicated in its many details. What is design work? It is that wonderful wedding of chance and necessity, happening in a trillion places at once, at a trillion different levels. And what miracle caused it? None. It just happened to happen, in the fullness of time. You could even say, in a way, that the Tree of Life created itself. Not in a miraculous, instantaneous whoosh, but slowly, slowly, over billions of years.

Is this Tree of Life a God one could worship? Pray to? Fear? Probably not. But it *did* make the ivy twine and the sky so blue, so perhaps the song I love tells a truth after all. The Tree of Life is neither perfect nor infinite in space or time, but it is actual, and if it is not Anselm's "Being greater than which nothing can be conceived," it is surely a being that is greater than anything any of us will ever conceive of in detail worthy of its detail. Is something sacred? Yes, say I with Nietzsche. I could not pray to it, but I can stand in affirmation of its magnificence. This world is sacred.

Notes

1. I will not devote any space [here to] cataloguing the deep flaws in creationism, or supporting my peremptory condemnation of it. I take that job to have been admirably done by others.

2. Many, many Muslims agree, and we must not only listen to them, but do what we can to protect and support them, for they are bravely trying, from the inside, to reshape the tradition they cherish into something better, something ethically defensible. *That* is—or, rather, ought to be—the message of multiculturalism, not the patronizing and subtly racist hypertolerance that "respects" vicious and ignorant

doctrines when they are propounded by officials of non-European states and religions. One might start by spreading the word about *For Rushdie* (Braziller, 1994), a collection of essays by Arab and Muslim writers, many critical of Rushdie, but all denouncing the unspeakably immoral "fatwa" death sentence proclaimed by the Ayatollah. Rushdie (1994) has drawn our attention to the 162 Iranian intellectuals who, with great courage, have signed a declaration in support of freedom of expression. Let us all distribute the danger by joining hands with them.

NO ↰

John MacArthur

The Battle for the Beginning

All Scripture quotations in this book, except those noted otherwise, are from the New King James Version.

Quotations marked KJV are from the King James Version of the Bible.

Introduction

Thanks to the theory of evolution, naturalism is now the dominant religion of modern society. Less than a century and a half ago, Charles Darwin popularized the credo for this secular religion with his book *The Origin of Species*. Although most of Darwin's theories about the mechanisms of evolution were discarded long ago, the doctrine of evolution itself has managed to achieve the status of a fundamental article of faith in the popular modern mind. Naturalism has now replaced Christianity as the main religion of the Western world, and evolution has become naturalism's principal dogma.

Naturalism is the view that every law and every force operating in the universe is natural rather than moral, spiritual, or supernatural. Naturalism is inherently antitheistic, rejecting the very concept of a personal God. Many assume naturalism therefore has nothing to do with religion. In fact, it is a common misconception that naturalism embodies the very essence of scientific objectivity. Naturalists themselves like to portray their system as a philosophy that stands in opposition to all faith-based world-views, pretending that it is scientifically and intellectually superior precisely because of its supposed non-religious character.

Not so. *Religion* is exactly the right word to describe naturalism. The entire philosophy is built on a faith-based premise. Its basic presupposition—a rejection of everything supernatural—requires a giant leap of faith. And nearly all its supporting theories must be taken by faith as well.[1]

Consider the dogma of evolution, for example. The notion that natural evolutionary processes can account for the origin of all living species has never been and never will be established as fact. Nor is it "scientific" in any true sense of the word. Science deals with what can be observed and reproduced by experimentation. The origin of life can be neither observed nor reproduced in any laboratory. By definition, then, true science can give us no knowledge what-soever about where we came from or how we got here. Belief in evolutionary theory is a matter of sheer faith. And dogmatic belief in any naturalistic theory is no more "scientific" than any other kind of religious faith.

Modern naturalism is often promulgated with a missionary zeal that has powerful religious overtones. The popular fish symbol many Christians put on their cars now has a naturalist counterpart: a fish with feet and the word *Darwin* embossed into its side. The Internet has become naturalism's busiest mission field, where evangelists for the cause aggressively try to deliver benighted souls who still cling to their theistic presuppositions. Judging from the tenor of some of the material I have read seeking to win converts to naturalism, naturalists are often dedicated to their faith with a devout passion that rivals or easily exceeds the fanaticism of any radical religious zealot. Naturalism is clearly as much a religion as any theistic world-view.

The point is further proved by examining the beliefs of those naturalists who claim to be most unfettered by religious beliefs. Take, for example, the case of Carl Sagan, perhaps the best-known scientific celebrity of the past couple of decades. A renowned astronomer and media figure, Sagan was overtly antago-nistic to biblical theism. But he became the chief televangelist for the religion of naturalism. He preached a world-view that was based entirely on naturalistic assumptions. Underlying all he taught was the firm conviction that everything in the universe has a natural cause and a natural explanation. That belief—a matter of faith, not a truly scientific observation—governed and shaped every one of his theories about the universe.

Sagan examined the vastness and complexity of the universe and con-cluded—as he was bound to do, given his starting point—that there is nothing greater than the universe itself. So he borrowed divine attributes such as infini-tude, eternality, and omnipotence, and he made them properties of the universe itself.

"The cosmos is all that is, or ever was, or ever will be" was Sagan's trade-mark aphorism, repeated on each episode of his highly rated television series, *Cosmos*. The statement itself is clearly a tenet of faith, not a scientific con-clusion. (Neither Sagan himself nor all the scientists in the world combined could ever examine "all that is, or ever was, or ever will be" by any scien-tific method.) Sagan's slogan is perfectly illustrative of how modern naturalism mistakes religious dogma for true science.

Sagan's religion was actually a kind of naturalistic pantheism, and his motto sums it up perfectly. He deified the universe and everything in it—insisting that the cosmos itself is that which was, and is, and is to come (cf. Revelation 4:8). Having examined enough of the cosmos to see evidence of the Creator's infinite power and majesty, he imputed that omnipotence and glory to creation itself—precisely the error the apostle Paul describes in Romans 1:20–22:

> For since the creation of the world His invisible attributes are clearly seen, being understood by the things that are made, even His eternal power and Godhead, so that they are without excuse, because, although they knew God, they did not glorify Him as God, nor were thankful, but became futile in

their thoughts, and their foolish hearts were darkened. Professing to be wise, they became fools.

Exactly like the idolaters Paul was describing, Sagan put creation in the Creator's rightful place.

Carl Sagan looked at the universe, saw its greatness, and concluded nothing could possibly be greater. His religious presuppositions forced him to deny that the universe was the result of intelligent design. In fact, as a devoted naturalist, he had to deny that it was created at all. Therefore he saw the universe as eternal and infinite, so it naturally took the place of God in his thinking....

Sagan's religion included the belief that the human race is nothing special. Given the incomprehensible vastness of the universe and the impersonality of it all, how could humanity possibly be important? Sagan concluded that our race is not significant at all....

In a book published near the end of his life, Sagan wrote, "Our planet is a lonely speck in the great enveloping cosmic dark. In our obscurity, in all this vastness, there is no hint that help will come from elsewhere to save us from ourselves."[2]

Although Sagan resolutely tried to maintain a semblance of optimism to the bitter end, his religion led where all naturalism inevitably leads: to a sense of utter insignificance and despair. According to his world-view, humanity occupies a tiny outpost—a pale blue speck in a vast sea of galaxies. As far as we know, we are unnoticed by the rest of the universe, accountable to no one, and petty and irrelevant in a cosmos so expansive. It is fatuous to talk of outside help or redemption for the human race. No help is forthcoming. It would be nice if we somehow managed to solve some of our problems, but whether we do or not will ultimately be a forgotten bit of cosmic trivia. That, said Sagan, is a perspective well worth pondering.

All of this underscores the spiritual barrenness of naturalism. The naturalist's religion erases all moral and ethical accountability, and it ultimately abandons all hope for humanity. If the impersonal cosmos is all there is, all there ever was, and all there ever will be, then morality is ultimately moot. If there is no personal Creator to whom humanity is accountable and if the survival of the fittest is the governing law of the universe, all the moral principles that normally regulate the human conscience are ultimately groundless—and possibly even deleterious to the survival of our species.

Indeed, the rise of naturalism has meant moral catastrophe for modern society. The most damaging ideologies of the nineteenth and twentieth centuries were all rooted in Darwinism. One of Darwin's earliest champions, Thomas Huxley, gave a lecture in 1893 in which he argued that evolution and ethics are incompatible. He wrote that "the practice of that which is ethically best—what we call goodness or virtue—involves a course of conduct which, in all respects, is opposed to that which leads to success in the cosmic struggle for existence."[3]

Philosophers who incorporated Darwin's ideas were quick to see Huxley's point, conceiving new philosophies that set the stage for the amorality and genocide that characterized so much of the twentieth century.

Karl Marx, for example, self-consciously followed Darwin in the devising of his economic and social theories. He inscribed a copy of his book *Das Kapital* to Darwin, "from a devoted admirer." He referred to Darwin's *The Origin of Species* as "the book which contains the basis in natural history for our view.[4]

Herbert Spencer's philosophy of "Social Darwinism" applied the doctrines of evolution and the survival of the fittest to human societies. Spencer argued that if nature itself has determined that the strong survive and the weak perish, this rule should govern society as well. Racial and class distinctions simply reflect nature's way. There is therefore no transcendent moral reason to be sympathetic to the struggle of the disadvantaged classes. It is, after all, part of the natural evolutionary process and society will actually be improved by recognizing the superiority of the dominant classes and encouraging their ascendancy. The racialism of such writers as Ernst Haeckel (who believed that the African races were incapable of culture or higher mental development) was also rooted in Darwinism.

Friedrich Nietzsche's whole philosophy was based on the doctrine of evolution. Nietzsche was bitterly hostile to religion, and particularly to Christianity. Christian morality embodied the essence of everything Nietzsche hated; he believed Christ's teachings glorified human weakness and were detrimental to the development of the human race. He scoffed at Christian moral values such as humility, mercy, modesty, meekness, compassion for the powerless, and service to one another. He believed such ideals had bred weakness in society. Nietzsche saw two types of people: the "master-class," an enlightened, dominant minority; and the "herd," sheeplike followers who were easily led. And he concluded that the only hope for humanity would be when the master-class evolved into a race of Übermenschen (supermen), unencumbered by religious or social mores, who would take power and bring humanity to the next stage of its evolution.

It's not surprising that Nietzsche's philosophy laid the foundation for the Nazi movement in Germany. What is surprising is that at the dawn of the twenty-first century, Nietzsche's reputation has been rehabilitated by philosophical spin-doctors, and his writings are once again trendy in the academic world. Indeed, his philosophy—or something very nearly like it—is what naturalism must inevitably return to.

All of these philosophies are based on notions that are diametrically opposed to a biblical view of the nature of man, because they all start by embracing a Darwinian view of the origin of humanity. They are rooted in anti-Christian theories about human origins and the origin of the cosmos, and therefore it is no wonder that they stand in opposition to biblical principles at every level.

The simple fact of the matter is that all the philosophical fruits of Darwinism have been negative, ignoble, and destructive to the very fabric of society. Not one of the major twentieth-century revolutions led by post-Darwinian philosophies ever improved or ennobled any society. Instead, the chief social and political legacy of Darwinian thought is a full spectrum of evil tyranny with Marx-inspired communism at one extreme and Nietzsche-inspired fascism at the other. The moral catastrophe that has disfigured modern Western society is also directly traceable to Darwinism and the rejection of the early chapters of Genesis.

At this moment in history, even though most of modern society is already fully committed to an evolutionary and naturalistic world-view, our society still benefits from the collective memory of a biblical world-view. People in general still believe human life is special. They still hold remnants of biblical morality, such as the notion that love is the greatest virtue (1 Corinthians 13:13), service to one another is better than fighting for personal dominion (Matthew 20:25–27), and humility and submission are superior to arrogance and rebellion (1 Peter 5:5). But to whatever degree secular society still holds those virtues in esteem, it does so entirely without any philosophical foundation. Having already rejected the God revealed in Scripture and embraced instead pure naturalistic materialism, the modern mind has no grounds whatsoever for holding to any ethical standard, no reason for whatsoever for esteeming "virtue" over "vice," and no justification whatsoever for regarding human life as more valuable than any other form of life. Modern society has already abandoned its moral foundation.

As humanity enters the twenty-first century, an even more frightening prospect looms. Now even the church seems to be losing the will to defend what Scripture teaches about human origins. Many in the church are too intimidated or too embarrassed to affirm the literal truth of the biblical account of creation. They are confused by a chorus of authoritative-sounding voices who insist that it is possible—and even pragmatically necessary—to reconcile Scripture with the latest theories of the naturalists.

Of course, theological liberals have long espoused theistic evolution. They have never been reluctant to deny the literal truth of Scripture on any issue. The new trend has also influenced some evangelicals who contend that it is possible to harmonize Genesis 1–3 with the theories of modern naturalism without doing violence to any essential doctrine of Christianity. They affirm evangelical statements of faith. They teach in evangelical institutions. They insist they believe the Bible is inerrant and authoritative. But they are willing to reinterpret Genesis to accommodate evolutionary theory....

The result is that over the past couple of decades, large numbers of evangelicals have shown a surprising willingness to take a completely non-evangelical approach to interpreting the early chapters of Genesis. More and more are embracing the view known as "old-earth creationism," which blends some of the principles of biblical creationism with naturalistic and evolutionary theories, seeking to reconcile two opposing world-views. And in order to accomplish this, old-earth creationists end up explaining away rather than honestly exegeting the biblical creation account.

A handful of scientists who profess Christianity are among those who have led the way in this revisionism—most of them lacking any skill whatsoever in biblical interpretation. But they are setting forth a major reinterpretation of Genesis 1–3 designed specifically to accommodate the current trends of naturalist theory. In their view, the six days of creation of Genesis 1 are long ages, the chronological order of creation is flexible, and most of the details about creation given in Scripture can be written off as poetic or symbolic figures of speech.

Many who should know better—pastors and Christian leaders who defend the faith against false teachings regularly—have been tempted to give up the battle for the opening chapters of Genesis. An evangelical pastor recently approached me after I preached. He was confused and intimidated by several books he had read—all written by ostensibly evangelical authors—yet all arguing that the earth is billions of years old. These authors treat most of the evolutionists' theories as indisputable scientific fact. And in some cases they wield scientific or academic credentials that intimidate readers into thinking their views are the result of superior expertise, rather than naturalistic presuppositions they have brought to the biblical text. This pastor asked if I believed it possible that the first three chapters of Genesis might really be just a series of literary devices—a poetic saga giving the "spiritual" meaning of what actually occurred through billions of years of evolution.

I answered unapologetically, *No, I do not*. I am convinced that Genesis 1–3 ought to be taken at face value—as the divinely revealed history of creation. Nothing about the Genesis text itself suggests that the biblical creation account is merely symbolic, poetic, allegorical, or mythical. The main thrust of the passage simply cannot be reconciled with the notion that creation occurred via natural evolutionary processes over long periods of time. And I don't believe a faithful handling of the biblical text, by any acceptable principles of hermeneutics, can possibly reconcile these chapters with the theory of evolution or any of the other allegedly scientific theories about the origin of the universe.

Furthermore, much like the philosophical and moral chaos that results from naturalism, all sorts of theological mischief ensues when we reject or compromise the literal truth of the biblical account of creation and the fall of Adam.

I realize, of course, that some old-earth creationists do hold to the literal creation of Adam and affirm that Adam was a historical figure. But their decision to accept the creation of Adam as literal involves an arbitrary hermeneutical shift at Genesis 1:26–27 and then again at Genesis 2:7. If everything around these verses is handled allegorically or symbolically, it is unjustifiable to take those verses in a literal and historical sense. Therefore, the old-earth creationists' method of interpreting the Genesis text actually undermines the historicity of Adam. Having already decided to treat the creation account itself as myth or allegory, they have no grounds to insist (suddenly and arbitrarily, it seems) that the creation of Adam is literal history. Their belief in a historical Adam is simply inconsistent with their own exegesis of the rest of the text.

But it is a necessary inconsistency if one is to affirm an old earth and remain evangelical. Because if Adam was not the literal ancestor of the entire human race, then the Bible's explanation of how sin entered the world makes no sense. Moreover, if we didn't fall in Adam, we cannot be redeemed in Christ, because Christ's position as the Head of the redeemed race exactly parallels Adam's position as the head of the fallen race: "For as in Adam all die, even so in Christ all shall be made alive" (1 Corinthians 15:22)....

So in an important sense, everything Scripture says about our salvation through Jesus Christ hinges on the literal truth of what Genesis 1–3 teaches about Adam's creation and fall. There is no more pivotal passage of Scripture.

What old-earth creationists (including, to a large degree, even the evangelical ones) are doing with Genesis 1–3 is precisely what religious liberals have always done with all of Scripture—spiritualizing and reinterpreting the text allegorically to make it mean what they want it to mean. It is a dangerous way to handle Scripture. And it involves a perilous and unnecessary capitulation to the religious presuppositions of naturalism—not to mention a serious dishonor to God.

Evangelicals who accept an old-earth interpretation of Genesis have embraced a hermeneutic that is hostile to a high view of Scripture. They are bringing to the opening chapters of Scripture a method of biblical interpretation that has built-in antievangelical presuppositions. Those who adopt this approach have already embarked on a process that invariably overthrows faith. Churches and colleges that embrace this view will not remain evangelical long.

One popular view held by many old-earth advocates is known as the "framework hypothesis." This is the belief that the "days" of creation are not even distinct eras, but overlapping stages of a long evolutionary process. According to this view, the six days described in Genesis 1 do not set forth a chronology of any kind, but rather a metaphorical "framework" by which the creative process is described for our finite human minds.

This view was apparently first set forth by liberal German theologians in the nineteenth century, but it has been adopted and propagated in recent years by some leading evangelicals, most notably Dr. Meredith G. Kline of Westminster Theological Seminary....

Naturally, advocates of this view accept the modern scientific theory that the formation of the earth required several billion years. They claim the biblical account is nothing more than a metaphorical framework that should overlay our scientific understanding of creation. The language and details of Genesis 1 are unimportant, they say; the only truth this passage aims to teach us is that the hand of divine Providence guided the evolutionary process. The Genesis creation account is thus reduced to a literary device—an extended metaphor that is not to be accepted at face value.

But if the Lord wanted to teach us that creation took place in six literal days, how could He have stated it more plainly than Genesis does? The length of the days is defined by periods of day and night that are governed after day four by the sun and moon. The week itself defines the pattern of human labor and rest. The days are marked by the passage of morning and evening. How could these not signify the chronological progression of God's creative work?

The problem with the framework hypothesis is that it employs a destructive method of interpretation. If the plain meaning of Genesis 1 may be written off and the language treated as nothing more than a literary device, why not do the same with Genesis 3? Indeed, most theological liberals do insist that the talking serpent in chapter 3 signals a fable or a metaphor, and therefore they reject that passage as a literal and historical record of how humanity fell into sin. Where does metaphor ultimately end and history begin? After the Flood?

After the Tower of Babel? And why there? Why not regard all the biblical miracles as literary devices? Why could not the Resurrection itself be dismissed as a mere allegory? In the words of E. J. Young, "If the 'framework' hypothesis were applied to the narratives of the Virgin Birth or the Resurrection or Romans 5:12 ff., it could as effectively serve to minimize the importance of the context of those passages as it now does the content of the first chapter of Genesis."[5]

Young points out the fallacy of the framework hypothesis:

> The question must be raised, "If a nonchronological view of the days be admitted, what is the purpose of mentioning six days?" For, once we reject the chronological sequence which Genesis gives, we are brought to the point where we can really say very little about the content of Genesis one....

The simple, rather obvious fact is that no one would ever think the time-frame for creation was anything other than a normal week of seven days from reading the Bible and allowing it to interpret itself. The Fourth Commandment makes no sense whatsoever apart from an understanding that the days of God's creative work parallel a normal human work week.

The framework hypothesis is the direct result of making modern scientific theory a hermeneutical guideline by which to interpret Scripture. The basic presupposition behind the framework hypothesis is the notion that science speaks with more authority about origins and the age of the earth than Scripture does. Those who embrace such a view have in effect made science an authority over Scripture. They are permitting scientific hypotheses—mere human opinions that have no divine authority whatsoever—to be the hermeneutical rule by which Scripture is interpreted.

There is no warrant for that. Modern scientific opinion is not a valid hermeneutic for interpreting Genesis (or any other portion of Scripture, for that matter). Scripture is God-breathed (2 Timothy 3:16)—inspired truth from God. "[Scripture] never came by the will of man, but holy men of God spoke as they were moved by the Holy Spirit" (2 Peter 1:21). Jesus summed the point up perfectly when He said, "Thy word is truth" (John 17:17 KJV). The Bible is supreme truth, and therefore it is the standard by which scientific theory should be evaluated, not vice versa.

And Scripture always speaks with absolute authority. It is as authoritative when it instructs us as it is when it commands us. It is as true when it tells the future as it is when it records the past. Although it is not a textbook on science, wherever it intersects with scientific data, it speaks with the same authority as when it gives us moral precepts. Although many have tried to set science against Scripture, science never has disproved one jot or tittle of the Bible and it never will.

It is therefore a serious mistake to imagine that modern scientists can speak more authoritatively than Scripture on the subject of origins. Scripture is God's own eyewitness account of what happened in the beginning. When it deals with the origin of the universe, all science can offer is conjecture. Science has proven nothing that negates the Genesis record. In fact, the Genesis record answers the mysteries of science....

Evolution was introduced as an atheistic alternative to the biblical view of creation. According to evolution, man created God rather than vice versa. And as we have seen, the evolutionists' ultimate agenda is to eliminate faith in God altogether and thereby do away with moral accountability.

Intuition suggests a series of questions to the human mind when we contemplate our origin: Who is in control of the universe? Is there Someone who is sovereign—a Lawgiver? Is there a universal Judge? Is there a transcendent moral standard to live by? Is there Someone to whom we will be accountable? Will there be a final assessment of how we live our lives? Will there be any final judgment?

Those are the very questions evolution was invented to avoid.

Evolution was devised to explain away the God of the Bible—not because evolutionists really believed a Creator was unnecessary to explain how things began, but because they did not want the God of Scripture as their Judge. Marvin L. Lubenow writes:

> The real issue in the creation/evolution debate is not the existence of God. The real issue is the nature of God. To think of evolution as basically atheistic is to misunderstand the uniqueness of evolution. Evolution was not designed as a general attack against theism. It was designed as a specific attack against the God of the Bible, and the God of the Bible is clearly revealed through the doctrine of creation. Obviously, if a person is an atheist, it would be normal for him to also be an evolutionist. But evolution is as comfortable with theism as it is with atheism. An evolutionist is perfectly free to choose any god he wishes, as long as it is not the God of the Bible. The gods allowed by evolution are private, subjective, and artificial. They bother no one and make no absolute ethical demands. However, the God of the Bible is the Creator, Sustainer, Savior, and Judge. All are responsible to him. He has an agenda that conflicts with that of sinful humans. For man to be created in the image of God is very awesome. For God to be created in the image of man is very comfortable.

To put it simply, evolution was invented in order to eliminate the God of Genesis and thereby to oust the Lawgiver and obliterate the inviolability of His law. Evolution is simply the latest means our fallen race has devised in order to suppress our innate knowledge and the biblical testimony that there is a God and that we are accountable to Him (cf. Romans 1:28). By embracing evolution, modern society aims to do away with morality, responsibility, and guilt. Society has embraced evolution with such enthusiasm because people imagine that it eliminates the Judge and leaves them free to do whatever they want without guilt and without consequences.

The evolutionary lie is so pointedly antithetical to Christian truth that it would seem unthinkable for evangelical Christians to compromise with evolutionary science in any degree. But during the past century and a half of evolutionary propaganda, evolutionists have had remarkable success in getting evangelicals to meet them halfway. Remarkably, many modern evangelicals—perhaps it would even be fair to say most people who call themselves evangelicals today—have already been convinced that the Genesis account of creation is not a true historical record. Thus they have not only capitulated to evolutionary doctrine at its starting point, but they have also embraced a view that undermines the authority of Scripture at its starting point.

So-called theistic evolutionists who try to marry humanistic theories of modern science with biblical theism may claim they are doing so because they love God, but the truth is that they love God a little and their academic reputations a lot. By undermining the historicity of Genesis they are undermining faith itself. Give evolutionary doctrine the throne and make the Bible its servant, and you have laid the foundation for spiritual disaster.

Scripture, not science, is the ultimate test of all truth. And the further evangelicalism gets from that conviction, the less evangelical and more humanistic it becomes.

Scripture cautions against false "knowledge" (1 Timothy 6:20)—particularly so-called "scientific" knowledge that opposes the truth of Scripture. When what is being passed off as "science" turns out to be nothing more than a faith-based world-view that is hostile to the truth of Scripture, our duty to be on guard is magnified....

I am convinced the correct interpretation of Genesis 1–3 is the one that comes naturally from a straightforward reading of the text. It teaches us that the universe is relatively young, albeit with an appearance of age and maturity, and that all of creation was accomplished in the span of six literal days.

To those who will inevitably complain that such a view is credulous and unsophisticated, my reply is that it is certainly superior to the irrational notion that an ordered and incomprehensibly complex universe sprung by accident from nothingness and emerged by chance into the marvel that it is.

Scripture offers the only accurate explanations that can be found anywhere about how our race began, where our moral sense originated, why we cannot seem to do what our own consciences tell us is right, and how we can be redeemed from this hopeless situation.

Notes

1. Michael Ruse is an evolutionist who testified in the 1980s at the infamous Arkansas creationism trial (*McLean v. Arkansas*). During the trial, he claimed that creationism is a religion because it is grounded in unproven philosophical assumptions. But Darwinism is a science, he said, because it requires no philosophical or religious presuppositions. Ruse has since admitted that he was wrong, and he now acknowledges that evolution "is metaphysically based"—grounded in unproven beliefs that are no more "scientific" than the set of beliefs on which creationism is based. See Tom Woodward, "Ruse Gives Away the Store: Admits Evolution Is a Philosophy." Found at http://www.origins.org/real/ri9404/ruse.html.

2. Carl Sagan, *Pale Blue Dot* (New York: Random House, 1994), 9.

3. Thomas Huxley, "Evolution and Ethics," The Romanes Lecture, 1893. Huxley nonetheless went on to try to justify ethics as a positive result of humanity's higher rational functions, and he called upon his audience neither to imitate "the cosmic process" nor to run away from it, but rather to combat it—ostensibly by maintaining some semblance of morality and ethics. But what he could not do—what he and other philosophers of his era did not even bother attempting to do—was offer any justification for assuming the validity of morality and ethics per se on purely naturalistic principles. Huxley and his fellow naturalists could offer no moral compass other than their own personal preferences, and predictably,

their philosophies all opened the door wide for complete moral subjectivity and ultimately amorality.

4. Stephen Jay Gould, *Ever Since Darwin* (New York: Norton, 1977), 26.

5. Edward J. Young, *Studies in Genesis One* (Phillipsburg, N.J.: Presbyterian & Reformed, n.d.), 99.

POSTSCRIPT

Does the Theory of Evolution Explain the Origins of Humanity?

The Book of Genesis reads, "In the beginning God created the heaven and the earth" (King James Version, Gen. 1:1). British philosopher C. S. Lewis, commenting on this text in *Miracles* (Touchstone, 1996), states, "No philosophical theory which I have yet come across is a radical improvement on the words of Genesis." It is obvious from evidence in his selection that Dennett would strongly disagree with Lewis, believing Darwin's theory of evolution to be just such an improvement. However, MacArthur would agree with Lewis, insisting that the creation story in Genesis should be interpreted literally. Although Dennett's perspective is atheistic and would likely not be supported by most who profess a belief in God, MacArthur's views on creation may be too literal for some believers as well. Dennett and MacArthur's conflicting positions may lead one to ask, Is there a third option?

As mentioned in the introduction to this issue, 39 percent of the American public believes that "human beings have developed over millions of years ... but God has guided the process." The formal description of this third option is "theistic evolution." While some of Darwin's statements appear to be somewhat agnostic, much of what he wrote concerning the relationship between God and evolution leads one to conclude that he believed evolution to be the means God used to initiate life. From *On the Origin of Species* we read:

> There is grandeur in this view of life; with its several powers having been originally breathed by the Creator into a few forms or into one; and that, whilst this planet has gone cycling on according to the fixed law of gravity, from so simple a beginning endless forms most wonderfully and most beautifully have been, and are being evolved.

— As cited in *Finding Darwin's God* (Cliff Street Books, 2002), p. 292

A recent scientific development that supports the existence of God in creation has been termed *the anthropic principle*. Stephen Hawking, renowned scientist and professor at Cambridge University, provides the following description in *A Brief History of Time* (Bantam, 1988):

> The laws of science, as we know them at present, contain many fundamental numbers, like the size of the electric charge of the electron and the ratio of the masses of the proton and the electron [etc.].... The remarkable fact is that the values of these numbers seem to have been very finely adjusted to make possible the development of life.

256

Is divine evolution the best answer to the question concerning creation or evolution? Perhaps the best answer to this question is to admit we do not know all that we would like to know. Scientists express confidence in *how* some things were done but cannot answer *why*. Most theologians are confident *why* God is our creator, but most will acknowledge that they do not know *how* it was done. Clearly, there is much about creation and evolution that is yet to be understood.

Suggested Readings

N. Broom and W. A. Dembski, *How Blind Is the Watchmaker? Nature's Design & the Limits of Naturalistic Science* (InterVarsity Press, 2001).

R. Dawkins, *The Blind Watchmaker: Why the Evidence of Evolution Reveals a Universe Without Design* (W. W. Norton, 1996).

L. R. Godfrey, ed., *Scientists Confront Creationism* (W. W. Norton, 1984).

J. P. Moreland, J. M. Reynolds, and J. J. Davis, eds., *Three Views on Creation and Evolution* (Zondervan, 1999).

ISSUE 13

Does Religious Commitment Improve Mental Health?

YES: David B. Larson, from "Have Faith: Religion Can Heal Mental Ills," *Insight* (March 6, 1995)

NO: Albert Ellis, from "Dogmatic Devotion Doesn't Help, It Hurts," *Insight* (March 6, 1995)

ISSUE SUMMARY

YES: Psychiatrist and president of the International Center for the Integration of Health and Spirituality in Rockville, Maryland, David B. Larson argues that religious affiliation, belief, and practice are positively related to mental health.

NO: Psychologist and founder of rational-emotive therapy and president of the Institute for Rational-Emotive Therapy, located in New York City, Albert Ellis counters that religion is a contributor to emotional disturbance.

The relationship between religion and mental health has long been an issue in both the religious and academic worlds. Long before the development of psychology and psychiatry, people suffering from various problems identified both causes and solutions to their ills as spiritual. Sickness was generally thought to be caused by sin and/or demonic possession, and healing was brought about by the power of God. Sacred writings from several religions contain multiple examples of people suffering from what clinicians would now diagnose as psychiatric or psychological problems. Two of the many examples in the Hebrew Bible are Hannah's depression and anxiety described in 1 Samuel, chapter 1, and King Nebuchadnezzar's apparent break with reality (psychosis) in Daniel, chapter 4.

While some have criticized and discounted the religious perspective on mental illness because it appears to them to be based purely on supernatural phenomena, a review of Scripture reveals that at least some of the ancients may have been more savvy than has been supposed. Contrary to popular belief, Scripture describes various illnesses as having natural as well as supernatural causes and treatments. One such example is found in the gospel of Matthew, where Jesus heals "all sick people that were taken with divers diseases and torments, *and* those which were possessed with devils, *and* those which were lunatick, and those that had the palsy; and he healed them" (King James Version, Matt. 4:24; italics added).

The apostle Paul counsels his protege Timothy to "use a little wine for thy stomach's sake and thine often infirmities" (KJV, 1 Tim. 5:23). Apparently, Paul did not simply tell Timothy to have faith and "call him in the morning." From these verses we may conclude that some of the early religious authorities recognized that people's souls were composed of both the spirit *and* the body.

The Age of Reason brought an intellectual and academic skepticism of religion, which has continued to the present. The pendulum has swung from viewing health problems as spiritual concerns to dismissing the spiritual connection completely in favor of purely naturalistic explanations for both the cause and the treatment.

David B. Larsen offers research evidence favoring the positive benefits of religious affiliation, belief, and practice with increased mental and physical health. He also offers specific evidence linking the religious life with lower incidences of teenage suicide, alcohol and drug abuse, depression, and divorce rates. Larsen shows how religion is positively linked to a reduction in recovery time from surgery and to an increased sense of well-being.

Albert Ellis counters Larsen's argument with the assertion of religious bias. He believes that most of the research on the relationship between religion and mental health is biased in favor of religion. He argues that for the most part, the studies were conducted by researchers who were looking for results favoring religion. Ellis also argues that the subjects in the research studies were mostly religious and were biased because they desired their religious faith to be viewed in a positive light.

David B. Larson

 **YES**

Have Faith: Religion Can Heal Mental Ills

If a new health treatment were discovered that helped to reduce the rate of teenage suicide, prevent drug and alcohol abuse, improve treatment for depression, reduce recovery time from surgery, lower divorce rates and enhance a sense of well-being, one would think that every physician in the country would be scrambling to try it. Yet, what if critics denounced this treatment as harmful, despite research findings that showed it to be effective more than 80 percent of the time? Which would you be more ready to believe—the assertions of the critics based on their opinions or the results of the clinical trials based upon research?

As a research epidemiologist and board-certified psychiatrist, I have encountered this situation time and again during the last 15 years of my practice. The hypothetical medical treatment really does exist, but it is not a new drug: It is spirituality. While medical professionals have been privately assuming and publicly stating for years that religion is detrimental to mental health, when I actually looked at the available empirical research on the relationship between religion and health, the findings were overwhelmingly positive.

Just what are the correlations that exist between religion and mental health? First, religion has been found to be associated with a decrease in destructive behavior such as suicide. A 1991 review of the published research on the relationship between religious commitment and suicide rates conducted by my colleagues and I found that religious commitment produced lower rates of suicide in nearly every published study located. In fact, Stephen Stack, now of Wayne State University, showed that non-church attenders were four times more likely to kill themselves than were frequent attenders and that church attendance predicted suicide rates more effectively than any other factor including unemployment.

What scientific findings could explain these lower rates of suicide? First, several researchers have noted that the religiously committed report experiencing fewer suicidal impulses and have a more negative attitude toward suicidal behavior than do the nonreligious. In addition, suicide is a less-acceptable alternative for the religiously committed because of their belief in a moral accountability to God, thus making them less susceptible than the nonreligious to this life-ending alternative. Finally, the foundational religious beliefs in an afterlife, divine justice and the possibility of eternal condemnation all help to reduce the appeal of potentially self-destructive behavior.

If religion can reduce the appeal of potentially self-destructive behavior such as suicide, could it also play a role in decreasing other self-destructive behavior such as drug abuse? When this question has been examined empirically, the overwhelming response is yes. When Richard Gorsuch conducted a review of the relationship between religious commitment and drug abuse nearly 20 years ago, he noted that religious commitment "predicts those who have not used an illicit drug regardless of whether the religious variable is defined in terms of membership, active participation, religious upbringing or the meaningfulness of religion as viewed by the person himself."

More recent reviews have substantiated the earlier findings of Gorsuch, demonstrating that even when employing varying measures of religion, religious commitment predicted curtailed drug abuse. Interestingly, a national survey of 14,000 adolescents found the lowest rates of adolescent drug abuse in the most "politically incorrect" religious group—theologically conservative teens. The drug-abuse rates of teens from more liberal religious groups rose a little higher but still sank below rates of drug abuse among nonreligious teens. The correlations between the six measures of religion employed in the survey and the eight measures of substance abuse all were consistently negative. These findings lead the authors of the study to conclude that the amount of importance individuals place on religion in their lives is the best predictor of a lack of substance abuse, implying that "the (internal) controls operating here are a result of deeply internalized norms and values rather than fear . . . or peer pressure." For teens living in a society in which drug rates continue to spiral, religion may not be so bad after all.

Just as religious commitment seems to be negatively correlated with drug abuse, similar results are found when examining the relationship between religious commitment and alcohol abuse. When I investigated this area myself, I found that those who abuse alcohol rarely have a strong religious commitment. Indeed, when my colleagues and I surveyed a group of alcoholics, we found that almost 90 percent had lost interest in religion during their teenage years, whereas among the general population, nearly that same percentage reported no change or even a slight increase in their religious practices during adolescence. Furthermore, a relationship between religious commitment and the nonuse or moderate use of alcohol has been extensively documented in the research literature. Some of the most intriguing results have been obtained by Acheampong Amoateng and Stephen Bahr of Brigham Young University, who found that whether or not a religion specifically proscribed alcohol use, those who were active in a religious group consumed substantially less than those who were not active.

Not only does religion protect against clinical problems such as suicide and drug and alcohol abuse, but religious commitment also has been shown to enhance positive life experiences such as marital satisfaction and personal well-being. When I reviewed the published studies on divorce and religious commitment, I found a negative relationship between church attendance and divorce in nearly every study that I located.

To what can these lower rates of divorce be attributed? Some critics argue that the religiously committed stay in unsatisfactory marriages due to religious prohibitions against divorce. However, research has found little if any support for this view. In my review I found that, as a group, the religiously committed report a higher rate of marital satisfaction than the nonreligious. In fact, people from long-lasting marriages rank religion as one of the most important components of a happy marriage, with church attendance being strongly associated with the hypothetical willingness to remarry a spouse—a very strong indicator of marital satisfaction. Could these findings be skewed because, as is believed by some in the mental-health field, religious people falsify their response to such questions to make themselves look better? When the studies were controlled for such a factor the researchers found that the religiously committed were not falsifying their responses or answering in a socially acceptable manner and truly were more satisfied in their marriages.

Although the religiously committed are satisfied with their marriages, is this level of satisfaction also found in the sexual fulfillment of married couples? Though the prevailing public opinion is that religious individuals are prudish or even sexually repressed, empirical evidence has shown otherwise. Using data from *Redbook* magazine's survey of 100,000 women in 1975, Carole Tavris and Susan Sadd contradicted the longstanding assumption that religious commitment fosters sexual dysfunction. Tavris and Sadd found that it is the most religious women who report the greatest happiness and satisfaction with marital sex—more so than either moderately religious or nonreligious women. Religious women also report reaching orgasm more frequently than nonreligious women and are more satisfied with the frequency of their sexual activity than the less pious. Thus, while surprising to many, research suggests that religious commitment may play a role in improving rather than hindering sexual expression and satisfaction in marriage.

Not only has religious commitment been found to enhance sexual satisfaction, but overall life satisfaction as well. For example, David Myers of Hope College reviewed well-being literature and found that the religiously committed have a greater sense of overall life satisfaction than the nonreligious. Religion not only seems to foster a sense of well-being and life satisfaction but also may play a role in protecting against stress, with religiously committed respondents reporting much lower stress levels than the less committed. Even when the religiously committed have stress levels that are similar to the nonreligious, the more committed report experiencing fewer mental-illness problems than do the less committed.

Mental-health status has been found to improve for those attending religious services on a regular basis. Indeed, several studies have found a significant reduction in diverse psychiatric symptomatology following increased religious involvement. Chung-Chou Chu and colleagues at the Nebraska Psychiatric Institute in Omaha found lower rates of rehospitalization among schizophrenics who attended church or were given supportive aftercare by religious homemakers and ministers. One of my own studies confirmed that religious commitment can improve recovery rates as well. When my colleagues and I examined elderly women recovering from hip fractures, we found that those women with stronger religious beliefs suffered less from depression and thus were more likely to walk sooner and farther than their nonreligious counterparts.

◆

Yet, despite the abundance of studies demonstrating the beneficial effects of religious commitment on physical and mental health, many members of the medical community seem immune to this evidence. This resistance to empirical findings on the mental-health benefits of religious commitment may stem from the anti-religious views espoused by significant mental-health theorists. For example, Sigmund Freud called religion a "universal obsessional neurosis" and regarded mystical experience as "infantile helplessness" and a "regression to primary narcissism." More recently, Albert Ellis, the originator of rational-emotive therapy, has argued that "unbelief, humanism, skepticism and even thoroughgoing atheism not only abet but are practically synonymous with mental health; and that devout belief, dogmatism and religiosity distinctly contribute to, and in some ways are equal to, mental or emotional disturbance." Other clinicians have continued to perpetuate the misconception that religion is associated with psychopathology by labeling spiritual experiences as, among other things, borderline psychosis, a psychotic episode or the result of temporal-lobe dysfunction. Even the consensus report, "Mysticism: Spiritual Quest or Psychological Disturbance," by the Group for the Advancement of Psychiatry supported the long-standing view of religion as psychopathology; calling religious and mystical experiences "a regression, an escape, a projection upon the world of a primitive infantile state."

What is perhaps most surprising about these negative opinions of religion's effect on mental health is the startling absence of empirical evidence to support these views. Indeed, the same scientists who were trained to accept or reject a hypothesis based on hard data seem to rely solely on their own opinions and biases when assessing the effect of religion on health. When I conducted a systematic review of all articles published in the two leading journals of psychiatry, the *American Journal of Psychiatry* and the *Archives of General Psychiatry,* which assessed the association between religious commitment and mental health, I found that more than 80 percent of the religious-mental health associations located were clinically beneficial while only 15 percent of the associations were harmful—findings that run counter to the heavily publicized opinion of mental-health professionals. Thus, even though the vast majority of published research studies show religion as having a positive influence on mental health, religious commitment remains at best ignored or at worst, maligned by the professional community.

The question then begs to be asked: Why do medical professionals seem to ignore such positive evidence about religion's beneficial effect on mental health? One possible source of this tension could lie in clinicians' unfamiliarity with or rejection of traditional religious expression. For example, not only do mental-health professionals generally hold levels of religious commitment that diverge significantly from the general population, but they have much higher rates of atheism and agnosticism as well. The most recent survey of the belief systems of mental-health professionals found that less than 45 percent of the members of the American Psychiatric Association and the American Psychological Association believed in God—a percentage less than half that of the general population. When asked whether they agreed with the statement, "My whole approach to life is based on my religion," only one-third of clinical psychologists and two-fifths of psychiatrists agreed with that statement—again, a percentage that is nearly half that of the U.S. population. Indeed, more than 25 percent of psychiatrists and clinical psychologists and more than 40 percent of psychoanalysts claimed that they had abandoned a theistic belief system, compared with just less than 5 percent of the general population reporting the same feelings.

Science is assumed to be a domain that progresses through the gradual accumulation of new data or study findings, yet the mental-health community seems to be stalled in its understanding of the interface between religion and mental health. If a field is to progress in its knowledge and understanding of a controversial issue such as religion, empirical data and research must be relied upon more than personal opinions and biases. At a time when the rising cost of health care is causing so much discussion in our country, no factor that may be so beneficial to health can be ignored. The continuing neglect of published research on religion prevents clinicians and policymakers from fully understanding the important role of religion in health care and deprives patients as well as themselves of improved skills and methods in clinical prevention, coping with illness and quality of care. The mental health establishment needs to begin to recognize that it is treating a whole person—mind, body and, yes, even spirit.

NO ↵

Albert Ellis

Dogmatic Devotion Doesn't Help, It Hurts

According to the psychological studies cited by David Larson, religious believers have more satisfying marriages, more enjoyable sex lives, less psychological stress, less depression and less drug and alcohol abuse than nonreligious people. Do these studies present a "true" picture of the mental health benefits of being religious? Probably not, for several reasons. First, the scientific method itself has been shown by many postmodernists to be far from "objective" and unassailable because it is created and used by highly subjective, often biased individuals. Scientists are never purely dispassionate observers of "reality" but frequently bring their own biases to their experiments and conclusions.

Second, practically all the studies that Larson cites were conducted by religious believers; some were published in religious journals. Many of the researchers were motivated to structure studies to "prove" that religionists are "healthier" than nonreligionists and only to publish studies that "proved" this.

None of the studies cited—as I noted when I read many of them myself—eliminated the almost inevitable bias of the subjects they used. I showed, in two comprehensive reviews of personality questionnaires that were published in the *Psychological Bulletin* in 1946 and 1948 and in several other psychological papers, that people often can figure out the "right" and "wrong" answers to these questionnaires and consequently "show" that they are "healthy" when they actually are not. I also showed, in an article in the *American Sociological Review* in 1948, that conservative and religious subjects probably more often were claiming falsely to have "happier" marriages on the Burgess-Locke Marriage Prediction Test than were liberal and nonreligious subjects.

This tendency of conservative, religious, job-seeking and otherwise motivated individuals to overemphasize their "good" and deemphasize their "poor" behavior on questionnaires has been pointed out by a number of other reviewers of psychological studies. Because all these studies included a number of strongly religious subjects, I would guess that many of these religionists had a distinct tendency to claim to be happier, less stressful and less addictive personalities than a good clinician would find them to be. I believe that this is a common finding of psychologists and was confirmed by my reviews mentioned previously.

Although Larson has spent a number of years locating studies that demonstrated that religious believers are healthier than nonreligious subjects, a large number of researchers have demonstrated the opposite. Several other studies have found that people who rigidly and dogmatically maintain religious views are more disturbed than less-rigid religious followers. But all these studies, once again, are suspect because none of them seem to have eliminated the problem of the biased answers of some of their subjects who consciously or unconsciously want to show how healthy they are.

Larson points out that many psychologists are sure that religionists are more disturbed than nonreligionists in spite of their having no real scientific evidence to substantiate their opinions. He is largely right about this, in view of what I have already said. Nonetheless, some reasonably good data back up the views of these psychologists that devout religionists often are disturbed.

Antiabortion killers such as Paul Hill have demonstrated that fanatical beliefs can have deadly consequences. But lesser-known fanatical religious believers have used ruthless tactics to oppose such "enlightened" views as birth control, women's liberation and even separation of church and state. Some religious zealots have jailed, maimed or even killed liberal proponents of their own religions. Nobel laureate Naguib Mahfouz is still recovering from stab wounds inflicted by Muslim extremists last October near his home in Cairo. (Mahfouz, considered by many to be a devout Muslim, frequently has ridiculed religious hypocrisy in his work.) Indian-born author Salman Rushdie has lived for seven years under a death sentence pronounced by the late Ayatollah Khomeini. Rushdie explained to the *New York Times* that dissidents within the Muslim world become "persons whose blood is unclean and therefore deserves to be spilled."

Religious persecution and wars against members of other religions have involved millions of casualties throughout human history. Islamic fundamentalists from North Africa to Pakistan have established, or done their best to establish, state religions that force all the citizens of a country or other political group to strictly obey the rules of a specific religious group.

People diagnosed as being psychotic and of having severe personality disorders frequently have been obsessed with religious ideas and practices and compulsively and scrupulously follow religious teachings.

The tragic, multiple suicides of members of the Switzerland-based Order of the Solar Temple last October is only the most recent illustration of an extremist religious cult which manipulated its adherents and induced some of them to harm and kill themselves.

Do these manifestations of religious-oriented fanaticism, despotism, cultism and psychosis prove that religious-minded people generally are more disturbed than nonreligious individuals? Of course not. Many—probably most—religionists oppose the extreme views and practices I have just listed, and some actually make efforts to counteract them. One should not conclude, then, that pious religiosity in and of itself equals emotional disturbance.

However, as a psychotherapist and the founder of a school of psychotherapy called rational emotive behavior therapy, I have for many years distinguished between people who hold moderate religious views and those who espouse devout, dogmatic, rigid religious attitudes. In my judgment, most intelligent and educated people are in the former group and temperately believe God (such as Jehovah) exists, that He or She created the universe and the creatures in it, and that we preferably should follow religious, ethical laws but that a Supreme Being forgives us fallible humans when we do not follow His or Her rules. These "moderate" religionists prefer to be "religious" but do not insist that the rest of us absolutely and completely always must obey God's and the church's precepts. Therefore, they still mainly run their own lives and rarely damn themselves (and others) for religious nonobservance. In regard to God and His or Her Commandments, they live and let live.

The second kind of religious adherents—those who are devout, absolutistic and dogmatic—are decidedly different. They differ among themselves but most of them tend to believe that there absolutely has to be a Supreme Being, that He or She specifically runs the universe, must be completely obeyed and will eternally damn all believers and nonbelievers who deviate from His or Her sacred commands.

Another devout and absolutistic group of people do not believe in anything supernatural, but do rigidly subscribe to a dogmatic, secular belief system —such as Nazism, Fascism or Communism—which vests complete authority in the state or in some other organization and which insists that nonallegiance or opposition to this Great Power must be ruthlessly fought, overthrown, punished and annihilated.

As an advocate of mental and emotional health, I have always seen "moderate" religious believers as reasonably sound individuals who usually are no more neurotic (or otherwise disturbed) than are skeptical, nonreligious people. Like nonbelievers, they are relatively open-minded, democratic and unbigoted. They allow themselves to follow and experience "religious" and "secular" values, enjoyment and commitments. Therefore, they infrequently get into serious emotional trouble with themselves or with others because of their religious beliefs and actions.

This is not the case with fanatical, pietistic religionists. Whether they are righteously devoted to God and the church or to secular organizations and cults (some of which may be atheistic) these extreme religionists are not open-minded, tolerant and undamning. Like nonreligious neurotics and individuals with severe personality disorders, they do not merely wish that other religionists and nonbelievers agree with them and worship their own Supreme Being and their churchly values. They insist, demand and command that their God's and their church's will be done.

Since the age of 12, I have been skeptical of anything supernatural or god-like. But I always have believed that undogmatic religionists can get along well in the world and be helpful to others, and I relate nicely to them. Many, if not most, of the mental-health professionals with whom I have worked in the field of rational emotive behavior therapy are religious. A surprisingly large number of them have been ordained as Protestant ministers, Catholic priests or nuns or Jewish rabbis. A few have even been fundamentalists! So some forms of psychotherapy and moderate religious belief hardly are incompatible.

The important question remains: Is there a high degree of correlation between devout, one-sided, dogmatic religiosity and neurosis (and other personality disorders)? My experience as a clinical psychologist leads me to conclude that there well may be. Some of the disturbed traits and behaviors that pietistic religionists tend to have (but, of course, not always have) include these:

A dearth of enlightened self-interest and self-direction. Pietistic religionists tend to be overdevoted, instead, to unduly sacrificing themselves for God, the church (or the state) and to ritualistic self-deprivation that they feel "bound" to follow for "sacred" reasons. They often give masochistic and self-abasing allegiance to ecclesiastical (and/or secular) lords and leaders. Instead of largely planning and directing their own lives, they often are mindlessly overdependent on religious-directed (or state-directed) creeds, rules and commandments.

Reduced social and human interest. Dogmatic religionists are overly focused on godly, spiritual and monastic interests. They often give greater service to God than to humanity and frequently start holy wars against dissidents to their deity and their church. Witness the recent murders by allegedly devout antiabortionists!

Refusal to accept ambiguity and uncertainty. In an obsessive-compulsive fashion, they hold to absolute necessity and complete certainty, even though our universe only seems to include probability and chance. They deny pliancy, alternative-seeking and pluralism in their own and other people's lives. They negate the scientific view that no hypothesis is proved indisputably "true" under all conditions at all times.

Allergy to unconditional self-acceptance. Emotionally healthy people accept themselves (and other humans) unconditionally—that is, whether they achieve success and whether all significant others approve of them. Dogmatic religionists unhealthily and conditionally accept themselves (and others) only when their God, their church (or state) and similar religionists approve of their thoughts, feelings and behaviors. Therefore, they steadily remain prone to, and often are in the throes of, severe anxiety, guilt and self-condemnation.

In rational-emotive therapy we show people that they "get" emotionally disturbed not only by early or later traumas in their lives but mainly by choosing goals and values that they strongly prefer and by unrealistically, illogically and defeatingly making them into one, two or three grandiose demands: (1) "I absolutely must succeed at important projects or I am an utterly worthless person"; (2) "Other people must treat me nicely or they are totally damnable"; (3) "Life conditions are utterly obligated to give me everything that I think I need or my existence is valueless."

When people clearly see that they are largely upsetting themselves with these godlike commandments, and when they convert them to reasonable— but often still compulsive—desires, they are able to reconstruct their disturbed thoughts, feelings and actions and make themselves much less anxious, depressed, enraged and self-hating and much more self-actualizing and happy.

Being a philosophical system of psychotherapy, rational emotive behavior therapy has much to learn from theological and secular religions. But individuals who choose to be religious also may learn something important from it, namely: Believe whatever you wish about God, the church, people and the universe. But see if you can choose a moderate instead of a fanatical form of religion. Try to avoid a doctrinal system through which you are dogmatically convinced that you absolutely must devote yourself to the one, only, right and unerring deity and to the one, true and infallible church. And try to avoid the certitude that you are God. Otherwise, in my view as a psychotherapist, you most probably are headed for emotional trouble.

POSTSCRIPT

Does Religious Commitment Improve Mental Health?

Many of the great minds of the last century have argued that religion should not only be replaced because of its obsolescence but also that it should not be practiced at all because of its negative effect on health. Sigmund Freud, the father of psychoanalysis, described religion as "the universal compulsive neurosis of humanity." Ellis states:

> Religiosity is in many respects equivalent to irrational thinking and emotional disturbance.... The elegant therapeutic solution to emotional problems is to be quite irreligious.... The less religious they are, the more emotionally healthy they will be.

> — *Journal of Consulting and Clinical Psychology* (vol. 48), p. 635

Not all academics have taken this stance. William James, referred to by some as the father of American psychology, had a much different view of the relationship between psychology and religion, a view that has been gaining favor during the past two decades. In his influential publication, *The Varieties of Religious Experience* (Modern Library, 1902), James states:

> We and God have business with each other; and in opening ourselves to His influence our deepest destiny is fulfilled. The universe, and those parts of it which our personal being constitutes, take a turn genuinely for the worse or the better in proportion as each one of us fulfills or evades God's commands.

Much of the academic research on this issue has shown a positive relationship between religion and mental health. Further, much research with all faiths has led to a similar conclusion—people of faith have higher scores on measures of mental health than those who identify themselves as agnostic or atheist.

Although many would concede that there is often a positive relationship between religion and mental health, they would argue that this does not necessarily mean that all religious beliefs and practices are equally healthy. Some cases, in fact, are not linked to pathology. Research evidence and common experience indicate that any belief or way of life if taken to a fanatical extreme can become problematic. Many individuals as well as groups have given the world tragic testimony of religion gone astray.

Suggested Readings

S. Freud, *The Future of An Illusion* (W. W. Norton, 1989) (reissue).

A. R. Fuller, ed., *Psychology and Religion: Eight Points of View* (Littlefield Adams, 1994).

H. G. Koenig, *Is Religion Good for Your Health?* (Haworth Pastoral Press, 1997).

J. F. Shumaker, *Religion and Mental Health* (Oxford University Press, 1992).

Links of Interest to Religion and Politics

The Links of Interest to Religion and Politics Web site provides links to some of the most important organizations that deal with the separation between church and state.

http://www.gustavus.edu/oncampus/academics/poli-sci/relpol/hotlist.html

Liberty Counsel

Matthew Staver's Liberty Counsel Web site serves as a sounding board for Christian perspectives on contemporary political issues.

http://www.lc.org

PART 5

Political Issues

*P*olitics have not remained unaffected by religious concerns. In fact, religion often exercises a strong influence on national and international actions. As the world becomes more interconnected and individual countries become more diverse, the beliefs held by various groups and communities will be of greater concern to policy-making bodies.

- Is War Ever Justified?

- Should There Be a Strict Separation Between Church and State?

- Does the Religious Right Threaten American Freedoms?

ISSUE 14

Is War Ever Justified?

YES: Editors of *First Things*, from "In a Time of War," *First Things* (December 2001)

NO: Walter Wink, from "Beyond Just War and Pacifism," in J. Patout Burns, ed., *War and Its Discontents: Pacifism and Quietism in the Abrahamic Traditions* (Georgetown University Press, 1996)

ISSUE SUMMARY

YES: The editors of an interreligious, nonpartisan publication entitled *First Things* provide an argument defending military action, using both historical and theological backgrounds in support of just war theory.

NO: Walter Wink, professor of biblical interpretation at Auburn Theological Seminary in New York City, argues that victims of evil should not respond to evil on its own terms but choose a form of nonviolent resistance.

$\mathbf{V}$iolence and war have been a reality since the beginning of recorded history. The Bible begins with the story of Cain killing Abel (Gen. 4:8) and ends with the apostle John's description of the final great battle at Armageddon (Rev. 16). The Book of Revelation also includes an interesting detail about a "war in heaven" before the world in which we dwell came into existence (King James Version, Rev. 12:7). Scripture clearly describes the existence of conflict from the beginning to end.

Some have argued that the war in Afghanistan, in which America is now engaged, is fundamentally religious, with the forces of the West (Christianity and Judaism) allied against the fundamentalist factions of Islam. Others, including America's president, George W. Bush, have made a concerted effort to avoid that the present conflict be viewed in religious terms. While the origin of the disastrous events of September 11, 2001, are interpreted in various ways, it is evident that religious factors play a major role in both the origin and perhaps the solution to the problems we face.

Religious groups in particular have addressed the question of the morality of war in a variety of ways, the two major contrasting views termed *just war* and *pacifism*. Although the just war theory has historical roots that run deep into Hebrew culture and Scripture, the Catholic bishop and theologian Augustine (A.D. 354–430) is generally identified as the first theologian to articulate a reasoned argument supporting a theory of just war. After Augustine's conversion to Christianity, he served as the bishop of Hippo, a city in North Africa continually invaded by barbarian tribes. It was while confronting violence and aggression in both Hippo and Rome that Augustine came to believe a point exists at which war is justified as a means of preserving peace. In response to the needs of his own people, Augustine carefully scripted what has come to be known as *jus ad bellum,* which outlines when it is permissible to wage war. Augustine also provided direction concerning *jus in bello,* which considers the limitations of the way war is to be carried out once it has been declared.

Augustine reasoned that for war to be justified it has to be conducted under the *proper authority* and for a *proper cause*. Augustine and many theologians and clergy who have followed have generally agreed that *proper authority* is limited to recognized heads of state. *Proper cause* is most often limited to (1) "protecting the innocent from unjust attack," (2) restoring "the rights wrongfully denied," and (3) reestablishing "an order necessary for decent human existence."

While pacifist priests, parishioners, and academics have existed and continue to exist in most, if not all, of the major religions, the teachings of Jesus and his apostles are generally accepted as the founding principles of pacifism. Jesus Christ taught, "Ye have heard that it hath been said, An eye for an eye, and a tooth for a tooth: But I say unto you, That ye resist not evil: but whosoever shall smite thee on thy right cheek, turn to him the other also" (KJV, Matt. 5:38–39).

In a sermon delivered in the National Cathedral on March 31, 1968, three days before his death, the Reverend Martin Luther King, Jr., argued that "the choice is no longer between violence and nonviolence. It's nonviolence or nonexistence." The events of September 11th were a sober reminder that we live in perilous times and that war and retaliation are not simply experiences associated with the historical past.

The following selections are written by Christians representing two very different views on what our position as individuals and nations should be concerning the legitimacy of war. The editors of *First Things* provide arguments in defense of just war, while Walter Wink provides a compelling defense of "overcoming evil with good" through nonviolent practices.

The *First Things* editors maintain that while the teachings of Jesus certainly propose peaceful solutions to conflict, his words also allow for the exercise of justice in the pursuit of peace. Wink supports his argument in favor of nonviolent resistance by providing examples of how if we carefully follow the teachings of Jesus, we can prevent the need for violence and appropriately address violence when it is experienced.

In a Time of War

This is war. Call it a sustained battle or campaign, if you will, but the relevant moral term is war. It is not, as some claim, a metaphorical war. Metaphorical airplanes flown by metaphorical hijackers did not crash into metaphorical buildings leaving thousands of metaphorical corpses. This is not virtual reality; this is reality. This is, for America and those who are on our side, a defensive war. The aggressor leaves no doubt that this is war. Osama bin Laden and his like do not head a sovereign state but they speak for many of our declared enemies. "We are steadfast on the path of jihad," bin Laden declares. Of the terrorists he says, "We hope that they are the first martyrs in Islam's battle in this era against the new crusade and Jewish campaign led by the big crusader Bush under the flag of the cross." Bin Laden and his counterparts lead a shadow state or, more precisely, a parasite state that lives off the states that provide them refuge and aid. As we have now learned to our remorse, the terrorist parasite state also lives off the freedom and hospitality of the nations it attacks, including the United States of America.

Steadfast clarity about this historical moment and the obligations attending requires our recalling President Bush's address to Congress on September 20 [2001]. "On September 11," he said, "enemies of freedom committed an act of war against our country." It is claimed by some that terrorist attacks are not acts of war but crimes to be punished by international tribunals. To which President Bush answers, "Whether we bring our enemies to justice or bring justice to our enemies, justice will be done." The inescapable fact is that they are *our* enemies, and the rule of justice is that it is the first duty of the State to protect its citizens. There are no credible instruments of international force that can fulfill that duty or see that justice is done. The United States must lead, in the hope that those who understand that an attack on us is an attack on them will follow. "Every nation in every region now has a decision to make," said President Bush. "Either you are with us or you are with the terrorists. From this day forward, any nation that continues to harbor or support terrorism will be regarded by the United States as a hostile regime."

In response to aggression, America does not appeal to the so-called court of international opinion. Rather, by its response, and invitation to others to join in that response, it intends to create a court of international opinion—and a coalition for international action. More than two centuries ago, in another time of testing, Americans declared that "a decent respect to the opinions of mankind requires that they should declare the causes which impel them [to action]." We have again declared the causes, and the response to this declaration is revealing who does and who does not have not only a decent respect for the opinions of mankind but a decent respect for mankind. Determined hostility to a parasite state bent upon the mass murder of innocents is a minimal definition of decency.

"Our enemy," said President Bush, "is a radical network of terrorists and every government that supports them." Congress, with but one dissenting vote, has given him authority to prosecute this war to its end, which almost certainly will not be soon. "It will not end," the President declared, "until every terrorist group of global reach has been found, stopped, and defeated." That is the declared aim of the war. Then these bold words: "We will rally the world to this cause by our efforts, by our courage. We will not tire, we will not falter, and we will not fail." In the coda of that historic speech, boldness is touched by humility: "The course of this conflict is not known, yet its outcome is certain. Freedom and fear, justice and cruelty, have always been at war. And we know that God is not neutral between them. We will meet violence with patient justice, assured of the rightness of our cause and confident of the victories to come. In all that lies before us, may God grant us wisdom and may He watch over the United States of America."

A Nation Under God

In such words some claim to detect not humility but hubris, an uncritical identification of our purposes with the purposes of God. Let them make the case that between freedom and fear, between justice and cruelty, God *is* neutral. Let them make the case that those who have declared war against us do *not* intend to instill fear by inflicting cruelty. Assured as we are and must be of the rightness of our cause, the President submits that cause in prayer to a higher authority. In a time of grave testing, America has once again given public expression to the belief that we are "one nation under God"—meaning that we are under both His protection and His judgment. That is not national hubris. Confidence that we are under His protection is faith; awareness that we are under His judgment is humility. This relationship with God is not established by virtue of our being Americans, but by the fact that He is the Father of the common humanity of which we are part. Most Americans are Christians who understand the mercy and justice of God as revealed in the gospel of Jesus Christ. Recognizing the danger that the motto "For God and country" can express an idolatrous identity of allegiances, most Americans act in the hope that it represents a convergence of duties. All Americans, whatever their ultimate beliefs, have reason to hope that reality is not neutral in this war against the evil of terrorism.

We have witnessed a remarkable upsurge of a patriotism that some thought was lost beyond recovery. Many thought its loss a very good thing. If patriotism can be the last refuge of a scoundrel, and it can be, contempt for patriotism can be the refuge of gnostics who, in their presumed superiority to the particulars of time and place and people, would evade their duty. Planted in the beginnings of Christianity is a distinction that its adherents will probably never get just exactly right: "Render to Caesar what is Caesar's, and to God what is God's." It is agreed by all that the emphasis falls on the second injunction —do not render to Caesar what is God's. Whether with respect to patriotism, wealth, family, or anything else, it is always a matter of the right ordering of our loves and loyalties. The meaning of that is set forth by the anonymous author of *The Letter to Diognetus*, written in the second century to explain to a pagan reader the way it is with these odd people called Christians:

> Christians are not distinguished from the rest of humanity by either coun-
> try, speech, or customs. They do not live in cities of their own; they use
> no peculiar language, they do not follow an eccentric manner of life. They
> reside in their own countries, but only as alien citizens; they take part in
> everything as citizens, and endure everything as foreigners. Every foreign
> country is their homeland, and every homeland a foreign country. They
> obey the established laws, but in their own lives they go beyond the law. In
> a word: what the soul is in the body, that Christians are in the world. The
> soul dwells in the body, but does not belong to the body; just so Christians
> live in the world, but are not of the world.

Over the centuries, these "alien citizens," still far from their true home in the New Jerusalem that is history's promised consummation, have followed the course of Christian fidelity in accepting responsibility for the well-being of what is their home in time before the End Time. One product of that fidelity is the doctrine of just war associated with St. Augustine in the fourth and fifth centuries and further developed in what is aptly called the Great Tradition of Christian thought to the present day. In this teaching, just war, although occa-sioned by evil, is not itself an evil; nor is it even, as is commonly said today, a necessary evil. It is, if just, a positive duty, the doing of which, while it may entail much suffering, is to be counted as a good.

A War That Is Just

In this Christian teaching, the criteria of just war are divided into two categories —*ius ad bellum* and *ius in bello*. The first have to do with the reasons that justify going to war, the second with how a just war is to be conducted. According to the first set of criteria, a just war is *defensive*, aimed at protecting the innocent against unjust aggression. It must be undertaken with the *right intention* of establishing a just peace, and a reasonable expectation that the means employed will be *proportionate* to the ends sought. A just war is a *last resort*, undertaken when it is reasonably determined that there are not alternative ways to resolve the conflict, and when there is a reasonable *probability of success* in achieving the aims of the war. Such, all too briefly, are the criteria pertinent to the decision to go to war—*ius ad bellum*. By these criteria, the decision of the United States to wage war against terrorism is amply justified.

The second set of criteria, *ius in bello*, is quite distinct, and must be kept so. Distinctions can be multiplied, but the *ius in bello* criteria are essentially two: *proportionality* and *discrimination*. The first requires the use of no more force than is necessary to vindicate the just cause. The second pertains to what is called "noncombatant immunity," meaning that there must be no intentional killing of innocent civilians. Put differently, *ius ad bellum* deals with the "cause" of war and *ius in bello* with the "conduct" of war. The present war is just in its cause and, we may reasonably hope, will be just in its conduct. A war against the parasite state of terrorism will, we are told, be conducted in an often furtive and secretive manner. It seems likely that unjust acts will be committed, also by our side, and when they are known they must be condemned. Known or unknown, they are wrong.

The duty to engage in just war is undertaken in the awareness that its conduct and costs cannot always be anticipated or controlled. The decisions pertinent to *ius ad bellum* are reasoned and principled. The decisions pertinent to *ius in bello*, while they are to be held accountable to reason and principle, are contingent and sometimes improvised under severe pressures. Those who do their duty in waging war to protect the innocent should have no illusions. Even the most just war entails great horror. The words of General Sherman must be kept ever in mind: "It is only those who have neither fired a shot nor heard the shrieks and groans of the wounded who cry aloud for blood, more vengeance, more desolation. War is hell." Just war teaching never countenances the cry for blood, vengeance, and desolation. That is the cry of our enemies who have forced this war upon us. Blood, vengeance, and desolation is their aim, as is now evident to all but the willfully blind. They are our enemies. They have repeatedly declared so in venomous words and murderous deeds. We must pray that one day they will not be our enemy. At present, and perhaps for a long time into the future, it is our moral duty to see to it that they are "found, stopped, and defeated." If we allow ourselves to be paralyzed by the uncertainties entailed in the conduct and outcome of war, we surrender to the certain triumph of great injustice.

Coalitions and Moral Legitimacy

Toward that end, America must unapologetically take the lead. In recent years, the idea has spread that unilateral action is not morally legitimate. That idea is not grounded in sound moral reasoning. Sometimes the choice is between unilateral action or no action at all. In every dimension of prosecuting this war—diplomatic, policing, intelligence, financial, and military—the U.S. will of course welcome the cooperation of others, but there is no moral requirement for necessary action to be held hostage to the veto power of a coalition in which the most timorous member calls the plays....

Because we are a democracy, we will tolerate a large measure of dissent from our national purpose in this war—some of it honorable, much of it contemptible. Our morally debilitated professoriat in particular often seems to be a breed apart, going on endlessly about how violence breeds violence and how we must address the root causes of resentment, etc., etc. They are inveterate complexifiers, offering detailed analyses of the seven sides of four-sided questions while declaring their achingly superior sensitivities that make them too sensitive for decent company. They test the patience of ordinary Americans who view reality from the moral pinnacle of common sense, but so far Americans have passed the test and they will likely continue to do so.

Pacifisms

Then there are the pacifists, real and fraudulent. The refusal to resist aggression, and thus the refusal to participate in war, has a long and venerable history in the Christian tradition. That refusal, along with the discipline of celibacy and poverty, is institutionalized in monasticism. Among the other services rendered by monastics, their pattern of radical discipleship is a powerful reminder of the call to be "in but not of the world." Such communities of heroic virtue are proleptic outposts of the Peaceable Kingdom that is not yet. Among Protestants, too, there are, for instance, the Mennonites, followers of the sixteenth-century Menno Simons, who are pledged to nonresistance as an article of faith. Our laws make provision also for those individuals who, for reasons they find compelling, decide that they cannot in good conscience participate in war. We rightly respect their decision, even as we may be unpersuaded by their reasons.

Fraudulent pacifism, which is now making a noisy reappearance, is something else. Proponents of "nonviolent resistance" are not pacifists. Pacifists embrace not nonviolent resistance but nonresistance. Nonviolent resistance to the aggression we face is simply a proposed tactic that most sensible people find implausible. The proposal that aggression should be resisted by hugging a terrorist is not idealistic; it is simply dumb. The "pacifist" proponents of nonviolent resistance do not, as many seem to think, occupy the moral high ground while the rest of us are prepared to get our hands dirty in "the real world." They live in an unreal world of utopian fantasy that has no basis in Christian faith. Yes, they may be intensely sincere, and that can be touching, but they are also monumentally wrong. The difference is not between idealism and realism, nor between moral purity and moral compromise. The difference is a disagreement in discerning one's duty in the face of a challenge not of one's choosing. In a time of patriotic fervor, it may take a measure of courage to be in a minority advocating nonviolent resistance, but the advocates of that course are also comfortably refusing the call to service with its risk of killing or of being killed.

Some ask, What would Jesus do? Can you imagine, it is asked, Jesus flying a stealth bomber or joining in a commando raid? One might as well ask if you can imagine Jesus driving a bus, editing a magazine, or being a tenured professor in a religious studies department. The question is not what Jesus would do but what he would have us do. Real pacifists answer that question one way. Other faithful disciples answer that, in obedience to the command to love the neighbor, it is their duty to defend the innocent by engaging in a just war against a murderous aggressor. One matter that has been morally muddied in recent decades should now be clarified: those who in principle oppose the use of military force have no legitimate part in the discussion about how military force should be used. They only make themselves and their cause appear frivolous by claiming that military force is immoral and futile, and, at the same time, wanting to have a political say in how such force is to be employed. The morally serious choice is between pacifism and just war. Here, too, sides must be taken. . . .

Tocqueville's America

If there is such a thing as a national character, and we think there is, the character of America is now being tested as perhaps it has not been since 1941, and an awful lot has happened to us as a people over those sixty years. The question everyone is asking is whether the current level of national resolve can be sustained for the duration, which is likely to be a long time. Obviously, nobody knows. In a country that is said to be bent upon entertaining itself to death, the media have to date, with few exceptions, been commendably steady in their focus on the war. But in the absence of televised spectacles of great successes or great defeats in battle—or, God forbid, of new and more terrible attacks on the homeland—interest may wane. It is neither possible nor desirable to maintain a sense of crisis at fever pitch. Yet the country is, perhaps unavoidably, being subjected to confusing messages: be vigilant but not afraid; be prepared to sacrifice, but do your patriotic duty by going on a shopping spree; everything is different now, but defy the enemy by returning to business as usual. It is much too early to say how all this will sort itself out in the months and years ahead.

Many have remarked on the spontaneous resurgence of religion in public life. Some who had managed to convince themselves that ours is a secular or rapidly secularizing society expressed surprise. There is no reason for surprise. Whether this is, as some claim, the portent of another Great Awakening we do not know. More likely, the resurgence is simply giving public expression to what has been there all along in an overwhelmingly Christian nation rooted, albeit sometimes tenuously, in the Judeo-Christian moral tradition. It is noteworthy that, following the attack, the first gathering of national leadership and the first extended, and eloquent, address by the President was in a cathedral. And that Irving Berlin's "God Bless America" is getting equal time, at least, with the less religiously explicit national anthem. And that children in public schools gather in the classroom for prayer. And that the fallen beams of the World Trade Center, forming a cross, are blessed as the semi-official memorial to the victims. Intellectuals are forever in search of "the real America." The weeks following the attack of September 11 provided one answer to that search. It is an America that [Alexis] Tocqueville would recognize, even if it surprised, and no doubt offended, many intellectuals.

World Politics Reconfigured

September 11 did not change everything, but it did reconfigure world politics. That reconfiguration has already happened, and there is now no undoing of it. At the center of that reconfiguration is the world-historical role of Islam. For more than a decade, a few prescient scholars have been warning about the coming conflict, now commonly referred to by Samuel Huntington's phrase "the clash of civilizations." This journal has been attacked by Muslim organizations for drawing attention to that warning. This touches on questions of daunting delicacy and complexity. President Bush has repeatedly said that this is not a war with Islam and that the Muslims among us are not to be held responsible for what has happened. That is exactly the right thing for him to say, even though it is not the whole truth. The American war strategy is to split off the terrorist fanatics from the great majority of Muslims in the world. That is exactly the right thing to attempt, even though it may not succeed.

Returning from their holiday from history, Americans are surprised to discover that there are a billion Muslims in the world, most of whom, if they do not hate us, resent us very deeply. Nobody should have been surprised. It is not simply a few Palestinian teenagers who danced in joy as they watched the hijacked aircraft fly into the twin towers. Throughout the Muslim world, and not only in the Middle East, there were expressions of supreme satisfaction that America was at last getting what it deserved. It is not only the Osama bin Ladens who speak of a world divided into two camps, "the camp of the faithful and the camp of the infidel," or of America as "leading the crusade of the infidels." That is the fevered language heard daily in newspapers and broadcasts, frequently under government auspices, in large parts of the Muslim world. It is, for instance, the language of the main government newspaper in Egypt, a country that the U.S. supports with three billion dollars per year.

In the last ten years, the Islamist regime in Khartoum has killed or enslaved more than two million Christians and animists in its declared war against the infidels. In Nigeria, Muslims are fomenting a brutal civil war in order to establish Sharia as the law of the land, and similar movements are to be found as far away as East Timor and parts of the Philippines. Samuel Huntington does not exaggerate when, surveying conflicts all over the world, he speaks of "the bloody borders of Islam." Then there is the Middle East itself, where, in one of the exquisite ironies of history, radical Muslims view the State of Israel as the forward salient of Christendom and make no secret of their determination to drive it into the sea. Perhaps we will succeed in splitting off the fanatics from their host culture, or in simply crushing their networks of global reach, but that does not necessarily mean the culture will be transformed. More likely, angry Muslims will temporarily back off to seethe in impotent rage until an opportune time for vengeance. We must brace ourselves for the duration, and the duration is a prospect that stretches far into the future. . . .

It is for Christians, Jews, and other non-Muslims to call for tolerance and understanding toward Muslims in this country. It is not for them to explain what is and is not "authentic Islam." That is a task for Muslims; not for secularized academics who happen to be Muslim by background but for Muslims who can speak believably from the heart of Muslim faith and life. It may seem unfair that Muslims, especially those who are American citizens, are required to demonstrate that they have really chosen our side, but then there are those terrorists who are aided and abetted by Muslims in this country, and there are those bodies that were buried, and some still buried, beneath the towers only a mile or so south of here, and there is a jihad declared and prosecuted by Muslims in the name of Islam, all adding up to yet another occasion for observing that life is unfair. When Islam is believably interpreted as a religion compatible with, and even supportive of, democratic freedoms and justice for all, there will no doubt be great relief in this country and the world. We may expect a boom in Islamic studies on our campuses, and a new generation inclined to a sympathetic understanding of Islam. That is a welcome prospect, provided the Islam that is presented is not Islam as we would wish it to be but Islam as believed and practiced by the Muslims of this country and the world.

Islam and the War of Centuries

President Bush is right to insist that this is not a war of religion, even if that may be more wish than fact. We of the West definitively put wars of religion behind us with the Treaty of Westphalia in 1648. But that was a piece of the story of the West of which Islam was not part and for which Islam has no counterpart. Like it or not, and we decidedly do not like it, we are engaged in a war that can be defined in many ways, but is also and inescapably a war of religion. After September 11 many American pundits and editorialists asked, Why do they hate us so? One after another, they answered that they hate us because "America is free, rich, powerful, and good." There is something in that, but for the most part it is smug self-delusion. They hate us because they believe that the West, now indisputably led by America, has marginalized, exploited, and oppressed them for centuries. They hate us for the cultural decadence that we export and that many of them hate themselves for enjoying. They hate us because we have troops on their sacred soil, and they hate us because we support what they view as the alien State of Israel on their land. Intertwined with all the reasons they hate us, they hate us because we are the infidel who has for years beyond numbering in ways beyond numbering humiliated the chosen people of God.

Bernard Lewis of Princeton, one of the most astute students of Islam, has long been urging us to understand that, when Muslims speak of the West, they mean the Christian West. They mean Christendom. Many in the West want to believe that ours is a secularized culture, but Lewis reminds us that most Muslims view secularization itself as a form of specifically Christian decadence. Today many in the West are asking, Who are they? We cannot ask Who are they? without also asking Who are we? More and more, as this war continues, we may come to recognize that we are, however ambiguously, who they think we are, namely, the Christian West.

The memory of wars of religion, and the fear of their revival, make some commentators understandably hesitant to emphasize the religious dimension of the contest in which we are engaged. A few acknowledge that the contest is most importantly about religion, but then go on to trivialize that reality by saying we are at war with all forms of "fundamentalism," including the "religious right" in this country. There are many things wrong with that, not least the use of "fundamentalist" to describe any belief system we do not like. Fundamentalism refers to a very specific form of Protestantism that arose in America in the early twentieth century and has thoughtful, if theologically wrongheaded, proponents both here and elsewhere. Its use as a term of general opprobrium only confuses ourselves and those whom we should be trying to understand. Bin Laden and his like are not fundamentalists. Scholars urge upon us the distinction between Islam and Islamism, the latter denoting the militant faith and theocratic aspirations now arrayed against us. Call them militant Muslims, radical Muslims, monistic Muslims, or even fanatical Muslims. They call themselves faithful Muslims.

They are other. A welcome consequence of the war may be the collapse of the multiculturalism that has dominated the academy in recent years. The doctrine of multiculturalism is that all cultures, except our own, are equal, and we should celebrate the otherness of the other. In fact, multiculturalism in most of its forms refuses to let the other be other. They are not just like us. With respect to freedom, human rights, and the dignity of the person, their difference is not a diversity to be celebrated but a threat to be opposed. The terrorists have now unmistakably underscored their otherness, and with it the otherness of Islam. Ten years ago in the *Atlantic*, Bernard Lewis published an article, "The Roots of Muslim Rage," that now seems eerily prescient. "Islam," he wrote,

> has brought comfort and peace of mind to countless millions of men and women. It has given dignity and meaning to drab and impoverished lives. It has taught people of different races to live in brotherhood and people of different creeds to live side by side in reasonable tolerance. It inspired a great civilization in which others besides Muslims lived creative and useful lives and which, by its achievement, enriched the whole world. But Islam, like other religions, has also known periods when it inspired in some of its followers a mood of hatred and violence. It is our misfortune that part, though by no means all or even most, of the Muslim world is now going through such a period, and that much, though again not all, of that hatred is directed against us.

Lewis described the fourteen centuries of history apart from which we cannot begin to understand the conflict of today. He ended on the note that not all Muslims conflate their faith with hatred of the West. "There are others, more tolerant, more open, that helped to inspire the great achievements of Islamic civilization in the past, and we may hope that these other traditions will in time prevail. But before this issue is decided there will be a hard struggle, in which we of the West can do little or nothing. Even the attempt might do harm, for these are issues that Muslims must decide among themselves." That was ten years ago. Ten years later, we do not have the option of doing little or nothing. We are at war. Pray that our cause will prevail. Pray that those other traditions in Islam will in time prevail. Pray that the one outcome does not preclude the other.

NO ◄

Walter Wink

Beyond Just War and Pacifism

For over four centuries, the peace churches have kept alive the Gospel's witness against war.[1] During that period, roughly 140 million people have been killed in war, most of them in this century.[2] Two-thirds of these casualties were in "Christian" Europe.

Parallel to the escalation of violence, and, no doubt, in response to it, we are also seeing an increase in the use of nonviolence. In 1989 alone, thirteen nations experienced nonviolent revolutions, all but one of them (China) successful. These nonviolent struggles involved 1.7 billion people, almost a third of humanity (32 percent). If we add the other nonviolent revolutions waged in this century, the figure reaches 3.3 billion—a staggering 64 percent of humanity![3]

No one can say any longer that nonviolence "doesn't work." It has been working remarkably. It was only supposed to be effective against "genial" opponents like the British or the whites in the American South, but not against the brutal Communists. Now we have seen it succeed in one Communist nation after another. Given the near monopoly governments have on weaponry, and the enormous increase in firepower, nonviolence is virtually the only way left to an unarmed people. Paradoxically, it has been the exponential increase in violence in our century that has persuaded people to choose nonviolence.

These new international developments need to be met by new thinking on our part. Theology has been particularly slow to respond to the new possibilities. Many pacifists still base their opposition to violence and warfare on a misunderstanding of the teaching of Jesus, and many just war theorists do so as well.

The text in question is the famous passage in Matthew 5:38–41, where Jesus commands his followers not to resist evil, but to turn the other cheek, give the second garment, or walk the second mile. Many pacifists interpreted "resist not" as teaching nonresistance to evil—an odd conclusion, given the fact that Jesus himself resisted evil with every fiber of his being.[4]

Augustine also agreed that the Gospel teaches nonresistance, and therefore declared that a Christian must under no circumstances attempt self-defense. However, he noted, if someone is attacking *my neighbor*, then the love commandment requires me to defend my neighbor, by force of arms if necessary.[5]

From Walter Wink, "Beyond Just War and Pacifism," in J. Patout Burns, ed., *War and Its Discontents: Pacifism and Quietism in the Abrahamic Traditions* (Georgetown University Press, 1996). Adapted and reprinted from Walter Wink, *Engaging the Powers* (Augsburg Fortress, 1992). Copyright © 1992 by Augsburg Fortress. Reprinted by permission.

With that deft stroke, Augustine opened the door to just war theory, the military defense of the Roman Empire, and the use of torture and capital punishment. Following his lead, Christians have ever since been declaring as "just" wars fought for nothing more than greed, revenge, or bravado.

Jesus on Nonviolence

But the Gospel does not teach nonresistance to evil. The Greek word translated as "resist" in Matt. 5:39 ("Do not resist one who is evil") is *antistenai*, meaning literally to stand (*stenai*) against (*anti*).[6] The translation, "resist," creates the impression that only two alternatives exist, resistance and nonresistance. Since Jesus clearly forbids resistance, nonresistance alone remains. What this has frequently meant in practice is passivity, withdrawal, submissiveness in the face of evil, an unwillingness to stand up for one's rights or the rights of others, and supine cowardice.

What the translators have overlooked is that *antistenai* is most often used in the Greek version of the Old Testament as a technical term for warfare (44 out of 71 times). "Stand against" referred to the practice of marching one's army up against the opponent's until the two fell upon each other in battle. The same usage characterizes Josephus' use of the word (15 out of 17 times). Ephesians 6:13 reflects precisely this imagery: "Therefore take up the whole armor of God, so that you may be able to withstand (*antistenai*) on that evil day, and having done everything, to stand firm (*stenai*)."[7] The image is not of a punch-drunk boxer somehow managing to stay on his feet, but of standing one's ground, keeping ranks, refusing to flee.

Jesus is not, therefore, telling us to capitulate to evil, but rather to refuse to oppose it on its own terms. He is urging us to avoid mirroring evil, to refuse to let the opponent dictate the methods of our opposition.[8] The correct translation would be the one still preserved in the earliest version of this saying: "Do not repay evil for evil."[9] The Scholars Bible brilliantly renders the phrase, "Don't react violently against the one who is evil."

The examples that follow confirm this reading. "If anyone strikes you on the right cheek, turn the other also."[10] Readers generally imagine this as a blow with the right fist. But such a blow would fall on the *left* cheek. To hit the right cheek with a fist would require the left hand. But the left hand was reserved only for unclean tasks; at Qumran, even to gesture with the left hand meant exclusion from the meeting and penance for ten days.[11] The only conceivable blow is a right-handed backhand.[12]

The backhand was not a blow to injure, but to insult, humiliate, degrade. It was not administered to an equal, but to an inferior. Masters backhanded slaves; husbands, wives; parents, children; Romans, Jews. The whole point of the blow was to force someone who was out of line back into his or her normal social station.[13]

Notice Jesus' audience: "If anyone strikes *you*." These are people used to being degraded. He is saying to them, "Refuse to accept this kind of treatment anymore. If they backhand you, turn the other cheek." By turning the cheek, the servant makes it impossible for the master to use the backhand again. The left cheek now offers a perfect target for a blow with the right fist; but only equals have fistfights,[14] and the last thing the master wishes to do is to establish this underling's equality. Logistically, the superior is deprived of any way to make his point. The servant has irrevocably conveyed the message: I am not a "thing," I am a human being, and nothing you do from now on can deprive me of that status. I refuse to be humiliated any longer. I am your equal. I am a child of God.

Such defiance is no way to avoid trouble. Meek acquiescence is what the master wants. Such "cheeky" behavior may call down a flogging or worse. But the defiance has had its effect. The Powers That Be have lost their power to make this person submit. And when large numbers begin behaving thus (and Jesus was addressing a crowd), you have the makings of a social revolution.[15]

How different this is from the usual view that this passage teaches us to turn the other cheek so our assailant can simply pummel us again! How often that interpretation has been fed to battered wives and children. And it was never what Jesus intended in the least. To such victims he advises, "Stand up for yourselves, take control of your responses, don't answer the oppressor in kind, but find a new, third way that is neither cowardly submission nor violent reprisal." . . .

One could easily misuse Jesus' advice vindictively; that is why it must not be separated from the command to love one's enemies integrally connected with it in both Matthew and Luke. But love is not averse to taking the law and using its oppressive momentum to throw the soldier into a region of uncertainty and anxiety where he has never been before.

To those whose lifelong pattern has been to cringe before their masters, Jesus offers a way to liberate themselves from servile actions and a servile mentality. And he asserts that they can do this *before* there is a revolution. There is no need to wait until Rome has been defeated, or peasants are landed and slaves freed. They can begin to behave with dignity and recovered humanity *now*, even under the unchanged conditions of the old order. Jesus' sense of divine immediacy has social implications. The reign of God is already breaking into the world, and it comes not as an imposition from on high but as the leaven slowly causing the dough to rise.[16] Jesus' teaching on nonviolence is thus of a piece with his proclamation of the dawning of the reign of God.

In the conditions of first-century Palestine, a political revolution against the Romans could only be catastrophic, as the events of 66–70 C.E. would prove. Jesus does not propose armed revolution. But he does lay the foundations for a social revolution, as Richard A. Horsley has pointed out. And a social revolution becomes political when it reaches a critical threshold of acceptance; this in fact did happen to the Roman empire as the Christian church subverted it from below.[17]

The logic of Jesus' examples in Matthew 5:39b–41 goes beyond both inaction and overreaction, capitulation and murderous counterviolence, to a new response, fired in the crucible of love, that promises to liberate the oppressed from evil even as it frees the oppressor from sin. "Do not react violently to evil, do not counter evil in kind, do not let evil dictate the terms of your opposition, do not let violence draw you into mimetic rivalry"—this is the revolutionary principle, recognized from earliest times, that Jesus articulates as the basis for nonviolently engaging the Powers.[18]

From a situation of powerlessness, Jesus in all three examples shows his hearers how to take command of the situation, using the momentum of the system to throw it, judo-like. This is not "nonresistance" to evil. It is active nonviolence. It is not passivity. It is proactive, aggressive, and courageous.

Jesus' teaching on nonviolence forms the charter for a way of being in the world that breaks the spiral of violence. Jesus here reveals a way to fight evil with all our power without being transformed into the very evil we fight. It is a way—the only way possible—of not becoming what we hate. "Do not counter evil in kind"—this insight is the distilled essence, stated with sublime simplicity, of the experience of those Jews who had, in Jesus' very lifetime, so courageously and effectively practiced nonviolent direct action against Rome.[19]

Jesus, in short, abhors both passivity and violence. He articulates, out of the history of his own people's struggles, a way by which evil can be opposed without being mirrored, the oppressor resisted without being emulated, and the enemy neutralized without being destroyed. Those who have lived the nonviolent way—Leo Tolstoy, Mohandas K. Gandhi, Martin Luther King, Jr., Abraham Heschel, Dorothy Day, César Chavez, Adolpho Pérez Esquivel—point us to a new way of confronting evil whose potential for personal and social transformation we are only beginning to grasp today.[20]

Just War, or Just War?

The new reality Jesus proclaimed was nonviolent. That much is clear not just from the Sermon on the Mount but from his entire life and teaching and, above all, the way he faced his death. His was not merely a tactical or pragmatic nonviolence seized upon because nothing else would have "worked" against the Roman Empire's near monopoly on violence. Rather, he saw nonviolence as a direct corollary of the nature of God and of the new reality emerging in the world from God. In a verse quoted more than any other from the New Testament during the church's first four centuries, Jesus taught that God loves everyone, and values all, even those who make themselves God's enemies. We are therefore to do likewise.[21] The reign of God, the peaceable kingdom, is (despite the monarchical terms) an order in which the inequity, violence, and domination characteristic of oppressive societies are superseded. Thus nonviolence is not just a means to the kingdom of God; it is a quality of the kingdom itself. Those who live nonviolently are already manifesting the transformed reality of the divine order now, even under the conditions of the domination system.

For three centuries the church remained steadfastly nonviolent.[22] It saw the Roman Empire as the acute manifestation of the domination system and opposed it with the message of God's domination-free order. With the "conversion" of Constantine, however, the empire assumed from the church the role of God's providential agent in history. Once Christianity became the religion of the empire, its success was linked to the success of the empire, and preservation of the empire became the decisive criterion for ethical behavior. The church no longer saw the demonic as lodged in the empire, but in the empire's enemies.

Augustine (d. 430) made the accommodation of Christianity to its new status as a privileged religion in support of the state. As was stated earlier, Augustine believed that Christians had no right to defend themselves from violence. But he identified a problem that no earlier theologian had faced: what Augustine regarded as the loving obligation to use violence if necessary to defend the innocent against evil. Drawing on Stoic just war principles, he articulated the position that was to dominate church teaching from his time right up to the present.

Though most Christians, Catholic or Protestant, will, if questioned, claim that they support the use of violence in certain cases on the basis of just war thinking, they do nothing of the sort. Just war theory is a very rigorous and complex ethical discipline. It has never been taught to the average church member or even to most clergy. The vast majority of professional theologians would be at a loss to list the seven or more criteria used in just war decisions. What most people call "just war" is really something else. Some mean by it the entirely different idea of the *holy war* or *crusade*, which knows no limits and admits no ethical quandaries. Holy wars are total wars aimed at the utter subjugation or extermination of any enemy.[23] Others who believe they are advocates of just war are in reality supporting a *political war*, or a *war of national interests*.[24] These are military interventions made by nations into the affairs of other nations for purely pragmatic political and economic reasons. These wars have frequently been "justified" by religious sycophants, but they are driven purely by the necessities of power politics. And finally, others call "just" those wars that are pursued for the sake of *machismo or pride*, such as the personalization of the Gulf War by Saddam Hussein and George Bush.

Just war theory is quite distinct from these three types of war, though it is endlessly confused with them. Every war that Christians of the world's nations have engaged in has been either a holy war crusade, a war of national interests, or an affair of machismo. No authoritative Christian body has ever, prior to the commencement of fighting, decreed that one side or the other is justified in warfare on the basis of just war criteria. Instead, the sorry record reveals that Christian churches have usually simply endorsed the side on which they happened to find themselves. Significant parts of the population have even opposed a war, as in the case of the Mexican-American War, the U.S. Civil War, and the Vietnam War. But I know of no national church body (and very few significant Christian leaders) that, at the inception of hostilities, ever denounced a war of national interest fought by its own nation. (For the first time, in advance of a war, many prominent Christian leaders, the Pope included, declared that war in the Persian Gulf did *not* meet just war criteria.)[25]

Most Christians assume that any war that they *feel* is just, or merely necessary and unavoidable, *is* just. The just war criteria, however, are extraordinarily demanding. They presuppose that no Christian should be involved in a war unless it meets all or at least most of the criteria.[26] The burden of proof is *always* on those who resort to violence.

Just war theory assumes that initiating war is generally a crime and that only one party, usually not the aggressor, can be just.[27] Just war theory never assumes that survival is an overriding consideration for either the individual or the state. It anticipates situations where victory cannot be gained without the use of indefensible means, and renounces them, accepting defeat as an honorable outcome.

Various writers present slightly different lists, but the essential conditions that must be met before a decision to go to war is considered justified (*jus ad bellum*) are these:

1. The war must have a *just cause*.
2. It must be waged by a *legitimate authority*.
3. It must be *formally declared*.
4. It must be fought with a *peaceful intention*.
5. It must be a *last resort*.
6. There must be reasonable *hope of success*.
7. The means used must possess *proportionality* to the end sought.

Three additional conditions must be met for the permissible conduct of war (*jus in bello*):

1. *Noncombatants* must be given immunity.
2. *Prisoners* must be treated humanely.
3. *International treaties and conventions* must be honored.

These general rules can be extremely difficult to apply in concrete situations.[29] What constitutes a legitimate authority—say, in a guerrilla insurgency aimed at overthrowing a dictator? How do we distinguish between an "offensive" and a "defensive" war or determine who really started it? Who are noncombatants in the age of democracies and total war? What happens when *both* sides believe they can construct a valid case for a just war? Do some criteria outweigh others? Must they all be met? Are they still applicable in the nuclear age, or in the face of the unparalleled firepower now available to assailants? Are the criteria too punctiliar, ignoring as they do the factors leading up to actual combat? And why should these criteria be regarded as authoritative?

Despite the casuistic cast of these criteria and the difficulty in applying them, I believe they are indispensable in the struggle to mitigate the violence of war. It is not the criteria themselves that are problematic, but the fact that they have been subordinated to the myth of redemptive violence: the belief that violence saves. In that mythic context, the just war criteria have normally been used simply to justify wars that are unjustifiable. Freed from that context, and subordinated to the church's vocation for nonviolence, these criteria can play a critical role in preventing wars and in reducing the level of violence in wars that cannot be averted.

Just war theorists have often bristled at the perfectionism of pacifists, whose concern for ethical means sometimes seems to obscure the demand for justice. Pacifists have often criticized just war theorists for functioning as a propaganda arm of the war machine, providing moral legitimacy for military interventions motivated by the needs of empire. Pacifists have seemed irresponsible. Just war theorists have appeared accommodating. Is there not a third way here as well, one that affirms the pacifist's nonviolence and the just war theorist's concern for moral accountability even in war? I believe that there is, but that it involves a prior commitment to nonviolence and a far more rigorous use of the just war criteria than has often been the case.[30]

Just war theory has taken seriously the possibility of making ethical judgments about the use of violence by or against a state. It assumes that we live in a morally coherent universe in which all human actions, even under duress, are susceptible to moral evaluation.[31] But it has been profoundly discredited because so many of the professional ethicists identified with just war theory supported the Vietnam War, even after its barbarity was evident for everyone to see. Paul Ramsey, John Courtney Murray, and Reinhold Niebuhr supported the Cold War and nuclear deterrence, further discrediting just war theory with the peace movement around the world.

What causes the gravest misgivings about just war theory and practice is that, for all its intellectual rigor, it often appears morally slack. To live a moral life means to form binding intentions and to act on them, even in the face of adverse circumstances.[32] Just war theory often seems more intent on finding a way around the binding intentions in the teaching of Jesus, and it tends to do so in the name of the bloodiest ideology of our time: nationalism. By their very nature, moral principles need to be highly resistant to the making of exceptions. Just war theory, by contrast, is notorious for the ease with which some of its proponents have made exceptions. Hence the impression that it is nothing more than casuistry in the service of the god Mars.

According to the criterion of noncombatant immunity, for example, civilians should be protected against direct attack. But this prohibits only "the deliberate human act of intentionally aiming at civilians, not their foreseeable destruction collateral to aiming at legitimate and important military targets," according to Paul Ramsey, one of the leading proponents of just war theory.[33] "There *is* no rule against *causing* the death of noncombatants, but only against intending to target them directly."[34] If guerrillas choose to hide among civilians, then it is legitimate to blow up civilians along with them. "No Christian and no moralist should assert that it violates the moral immunity of noncombatants from direct, deliberate attack to direct the violence of war upon vast Vietcong strongholds whose destruction unavoidably involves the collateral deaths of a great many civilians."[35] It was the incapacity of peasants in Vietnam to understand the "Christian" and "moral" rightness of their being napalmed and bombed that cost America their support in that war. But is the criterion flawed, or only its interpretation by Ramsey?

Ramsey believed that we may perform an act that we know will kill many civilians as long as we do not intend to kill them. This notion is ethically bankrupt. In practice it leads to the acceptance of civilian casualty rates so astronomical as to render the criterion of civilian *immunity* absurd. When this criterion was promulgated, the idea was that *no* civilians were to be killed. But if we include in civilian casualties those deaths made inevitable by war's disruption of farming, sanitation, and food distribution, we arrive at an average of 50 percent civilian deaths for all wars since 1700. Significantly, there has been virtually no fluctuation in the average of civilian casualties from 1700 until recently. This means that anyone planning war can be fairly certain that civilian casualties will be at least 50 percent, and, given modern firepower, more likely far higher. In the decade of the 1980s, the proportion of civilian deaths jumped to 74 percent, and in 1990 it appears to have been close to 90 percent. On this basis alone, very few wars in the last three centuries have not violated the criterion of civilian immunity.[36]

What these statistics fail to show is the enormous increase in *total* casualties in our century:

- 1500s—1,600,000 killed
- 1600s—6,100,000
- 1700s—7,000,000
- 1800s—19,400,000
- 1900s—107,800,000[37]

At a constant 50 percent, civilian deaths increased over five centuries from 800,000 in the 1500s to 53,900,000 in the 1900s. As if that level of casualties were not enough to forever banish war beyond the pale of morality, some just war theorists justified nuclear deterrence, despite the certainty that civilian deaths would number in the tens or hundreds of millions. If one agrees that the killing of civilians is prohibited, by what distorted logic is one able to justify casualties of such magnitude? Even if we inflate the probable total casualties from war for *all* the centuries since domination states arose (ca. 3000 B.C.E.), *more people will have been killed in war in our century than in all the preceding 5,000 years combined.* And yet there are still Christian ethicists soberly pondering the question of justifying certain wars!

Now the Persian Gulf War has blurred the distinction between nuclear and conventional warfare, since tens of thousands of Iraqi soldiers were killed by nonnuclear bombing in only a matter of days. The distinction between civilian and military casualties also becomes indistinct, since conscription amounts to involuntary servitude. Those Kurdish and Shi'ite soldiers whom Saddam Hussein placed on the front lines in order to liquidate them as internal threats to his regime did not die willingly.

Or take the criterion of "last resort." Theoretically, just war theorists are committed to the use of every feasible nonviolent alternative before turning to war. In fact, I know of only one just war theorist—James F. Childress—who devotes any space at all to nonviolent alternatives.[34] The rest focus on what constitutes last resort. This focus has the effect, however, of shrinking the ethical field. "Last resort" becomes "timely resort," as in the writings of Ramsey; and we soon find ourselves discussing "preemptive strikes," the assassination of heads of state, and even Pentagon doublespeak like "anticipatory retaliation." In our war with Iraq, did we allow enough time for sanctions to work? Was that war truly a "last resort"?

The other just war criteria are as easily manipulated. A just war must be declared by a "legitimate authority," but the Vietnam War never was declared on the American side by the sole agency entrusted with that power: the American Congress. Yet this fact did not cause many just war theorists to declare that war unjust. No nuclear war could be "won" without a surprise attack; but that completely obviates the "formal declaration" required by traditional just war theory.[39]

War has to have a "just cause"; but how is the public really to know if the cause is just when the first casualty of war is truth? The Gulf of Tonkin incident off North Vietnam was apparently *staged* in order to gain congressional support for the war.

Again, the means used in a war must be *proportionate* to the end sought. But how can we know in advance what level of destruction will follow armed conflict? Even beyond casualties, ruined cities, a gutted economy, women raped or reduced to prostitution, children dying from malnutrition and intestinal diseases, how does one measure into the future the continuing hazard of exploding landmines and bombs, drug addiction, alcoholism, mental illness, physical crippling, suicide? How can this be weighed before or even during a war?[40]

Yet when all these objections to just war theory are analyzed, they come down to one point: Just war theory is objectionable only when it is captive to the myth of redemptive violence.

Perhaps charity requires a distinction between just war theory and some of its advocates, who during the Cold War period were wed to an interventionist credo. Perhaps, too, we should note the source of confusion built into the very phrase "just war," which implies that there *are* wars that are just, and that the church or its moral theologians have the ability and authority to discern which they are. Many would deny that *any* war can be just. This has caused some to jettison just war theory in its entirety. *But even they will be found using just war criteria to explain their rejection of the notion of a just war.* The fact is that just war criteria are indispensable in attempting to prevent or mitigate the hellishness of war.[41]

I propose that we terminate all talk of "just wars." Even as the word "pacifism" sounds too much like "passivity," "just war" sounds too much like "war is justifiable." The very term "just war" is saturated with illusions about the rightness of war that are no longer tenable. Those who regard all wars as criminal can scarcely avail themselves of these helpful criteria when they are forced to discuss them with nomenclature that is intrinsically inadequate.[42]

Christians can no more speak of just war than of just rape, or just child abuse, or just massacres (and all of these are inevitably drawn into the train of war). But we also cannot wish away a world of bewildering complexity, in which difficult decisions are forced on us by the violence of others, and where nonviolent solutions are not always forthcoming.

Violence Reduction Criteria

Instead, I suggest that we rename the just war criteria "violence-reduction criteria." That, after all, is what most of us are after. We are not seeking a rationale for legitimating particular wars, but ways of avoiding warfare before it starts, and of decreasing its horrors once it begins. Perhaps both just war theorists and advocates of nonviolence can find common ground for attempting to restrain bellicosity in the phrase "violence-reduction criteria."

After all, both nonviolence and just war theory agree on several key points:

1. Both acknowledge that nonviolence is preferable to violence.
2. Both agree that the innocent must be protected as much as possible.
3. Both reject any defense of a war motivated solely by a crusade mentality or national security interests or personal egocentricity.
4. Both wish to persuade states to reduce the levels of violence.
5. Both wish to hold war accountable to moral values, both before and during the conflict.[43]

Violence-reduction criteria might provide prudential moral leverage on political leaders for whom the language of the Gospel carries no conviction. Some nations have already taken steps to limit war and to allow moral resistance to it: by laws allowing conscientious objection to military service; recognition of the legitimacy of civil disobedience; establishing war-crime tribunals; and acknowledgment of the right of soldiers to refuse to carry out illegal orders.

What is being proposed here is nothing more than a return to the ancient position of the church, antedating Augustine's adaptation of Stoic just war theory. Early Christians, who opposed all wars, nevertheless made distinctions between wars, arguing that humane treatment of the enemy was superior to cruelty.[44]

Beyond Pacifism and Just War

Some pacifists, literally interpreting Matthew 5:38–41 as rejecting all resistance to evil, have refused to join in nonviolent direct actions or civil disobedience because they believed such actions constituted resistance to evil and were coercive. We now see that this position was based on false exegesis. The nonviolence Jesus teaches *is* coercive. But it is not lethal or injurious.[45]

But just war theorists have also justified their position on the same misreading of Matthew 5 as nonresistance. Of course we are to resist evil! But we are to do so nonviolently. Jesus was not counseling nonresistance, but nonviolence. And his kind of nonviolence was a good deal more aggressive than some pacifists might have liked. Jesus did not hesitate to use shame, condemnation, ridicule, and other forms of "tough love" (consider the cleansing of the temple episode!) in order to free both the oppressed from oppression and the oppressors from sin.

It appears that we are now in a position to move beyond the old arguments between pacifism and just war. Jesus is clearly against violence and domination in all their forms. As Gandhi observed, "The only people on earth who do not see Christ and His teachings as nonviolent are Christians."[46] It is now high time that Christians of every stripe recognize and embrace the nonviolence that is at the heart of the Gospel. Jesus teaches a new way that forswears both passivity and war. We must abandon the idea that there can be just wars. Perhaps then we might also retire the word "pacifist," with its hopeless entanglement with "passivity" and its inadequate foundation in Scripture. Instead of calling themselves pacifists, Christians should insist that they are simply Christians, committed to the coming of God's domination-free order.

From the "peace church" heritage, the position proposed here affirms nonviolence as a fundamental tenet of the Gospel of God's inbreaking new order. The church cannot then justify any violence or war as "good" or "just." And from the "just war" heritage, the just war criteria can be turned into "violence-reduction criteria" and used in an attempt to lessen the devastation of a given war from a position of principled nonviolence.[47]

Just war theory has been not so much mistaken as mis-married to the ideology of redemptive violence. Its pagan roots were never sufficiently purged of their origin in the domination system. Freed from their misuse as justifications for wars of national interest, or holy war crusades, or egotistical face-offs, these criteria can now be focused on preventing or mitigating the barbarities of war from a committed nonviolent perspective. Christians today can no longer regard war as an extension of policy, but must see it as a dangerous anachronism, destined for oblivion in the new, nonviolent order of God.

Notes

1. The material in this paper is fully discussed in my book *Engaging the Powers* (Minneapolis: Fortress Press, 1992), where documentation in support of these arguments can be found. These notes direct the reader to the appropriate pages in the book (hereafter referred to as *Powers*) and offer information from the notes found there.

2. *Powers*, p. 221, citing Ruth Leger Sivard, *World Military and Social Expenditures, 1991* (Washington, D.C.: World Priorities, 1991), p. 20.

3. *Powers*, pp. 228, 389, n. 73.

4. *Powers*, p. 175.

5. *Powers*, pp. 212, 227, citing Augustine, *Sermon on the Mount* 1.19.56–68; *Reply to Faustus the Manichee* 22.76; *On Lying* 27; *Letter* 47.5. Reinhold Niebuhr exactly mirrored this view in *Christianity and Power Politics* (New York: Charles Scribner's Sons, 1940), p. 10, and *An Interpretation of Christian Ethics* (New York: Harper and Brothers, 1935), pp. 50, 62–83.

6. *Powers*, pp. 184–85.

7. *Powers*, p. 185.

8. *Powers*, p. 186.

9. Rom. 12:17; 1 Thes. 5:15; 1 Pet. 3:9.

10. Matt. 5:39.

11. The Dead Sea Scrolls, 1 QS 7.

12. *Powers*, pp. 175–76.

13. *Powers*, p. 176.

14. See the Mishnah, *Baba Kamma* 8:1–7.

15. *Powers*, pp. 176–77.

16. Matt. 13:33, parallel Luke 13:20–21.

17. *Powers*, p. 183, citing Richard A. Horsley, *Jesus and the Spiral of Violence* (San Francisco: Harper & Row, 1987), pp. 318–26.

18. *Powers*, p. 186.

19. *Powers*, p.189. See Josephus, *War* 2.169–74; *Ant.* 18.55–59; *War* 2.229–31; Philo, *Leg.* 299–305; and later, Josephus, *Ant.* 18.261–309, and Philo, *Leg.* 225–29; and Horsley's excellent discussion in *Spiral of Violence*, pp. 90–120.

20. I have attempted to apply Jesus' teaching on the "third way" to the situation in South Africa in *Violence and Nonviolence in South Africa* (Philadelphia: New Society Publishers, 1987).

21. Matt. 5:45; cf. Luke 6:35.

22. *Powers*, p. 209. C. J. Cadoux fills 160 pages with quotations from the New Testament and the early theologians expressing Christian disapproval of participation in war; see *The Early Christian Attitude toward War* (London: George Allen & Unwin, 1940).

23. *Powers*, p. 212. The Islamic *jihād* is not a "holy war" in our sense, in that it has sometimes acted as a brake on violence as well as a cause of it. The very term *jihād* was an attempt to restrict religious resort to war to a very limited set of cases (David Little, in a personal conversation).

24. *Powers*, p. 213, citing John Howard Yoder, *When War is Unjust* (Minneapolis: Augsburg, 1984), p. 21.

25. *Powers*, p. 213.

26. *Powers*, p. 214, citing Paul Ramsey, with Stanley Hauerwas, *Speak Up for Just War or Pacifism* (University Park: Pennsylvania State University Press, 1988), p. 71.

27. Bernard T. Adeney, *Just War, Political Realism, and Faith,* American Theological Library Association Monograph Series, 24 (Metuchen, N.J.: American Theological Library Association, 1988), p. 98.

28. Stanley Hauerwas, *Against the Nations* (Minneapolis: Winston Press, 1985), pp. 138–39. According to George Weigel, the just war tradition regards conflict as the political manifestation of original sin, and war as a legitimate but not inevitable means of resolving conflict. War is thus a just means for defending a legitimate political community and human rights, and not simply another expression of human fallenness; see *Tranquillitas Ordinis* (New York: Oxford University Press, 1987), p. 329. I argue just the opposite. War is a consequence of original sin, as is the violence system generally. War is the epitome of fallenness.

29. *Powers*, p. 215. Using the same just war criteria, James Turner Johnson argued that the Persian Gulf War was just, and Alan Geyer that it was unjust, in "Just War Tradition and the War in the Gulf," *Christian Century* 108 (February 6–13, 1991): 134–35. Their differences do not invalidate the criteria, but illustrate that their use is conditioned by one's starting assumptions.

30. *Powers*, p. 215.

31. *Powers*, p. 220, citing George Weigel, "Religion and Peace: An Argument Complexified," Conference on Conflict Resolution in the Post-Cold War Third World, United States Institute of Peace, Washington, D.C., October 3–5, 1990; see *Resolving Third World Conflict: Challenges for a New Era*, ed. Sheryl J. Brown and Kimber M. Schraub (Washington: United States Institute of Peace Press, 1992), pp. 171–92.

32. *Powers*, p. 220, citing Barrie Paskins and Michael Dockrill, *The Ethics of War* (London: Duckworth, 1979), p. 232.

33. *Powers*, p. 220, citing Paul Ramsey, *Speak Up*, p. 53.

34. *Powers*, p. 220, citing Ramsey, *Speak Up*, p. 102.

35. *Powers*, p. 220, citing Ramsey, *The Just War* (New York: Lanham, 1981), p. 503.

36. *Powers*, p. 221.

37. *Powers*, p. 221.

38. *Powers*, p. 222. See James F. Childress, *Moral Responsibility in Conflicts: Essays on Nonviolence, War and Conscience* (Baton Rouge: Louisiana State University Press, 1982).

39. *Powers*, p. 222.

40. *Powers*, p. 222. Augustine added another criterion that modern just war theorists have, mercifully, dropped: Every act of war must be conducted in love. The drift of Jesus' commandment seems to be loving our enemies *instead* of killing them, not loving them *as* we kill them. Augustine, however, grasped the implications of just war theory: Once killing is justified, it must somehow be integrated into the rest of the gospel of love and nonviolence.

41. *Powers*, p. 223.

42. *Powers*, p. 223.

43. *Powers*, pp. 223–24.

44. *Powers*, p. 226.

45. *Powers*, p. 227.

46. *Powers*, p. 216, citing Dale W. Brown, *Biblical Pacifism* (Elgin, Ill: Brethren Press, 1986), p. ix.

47. *Powers*, p. 228. Glen Stassen has also proposed a third way between just war theory and pacifism in *Just Peacemaking* (Louisville, Ky.: Westminister/John Knox Press, 1992).

POSTSCRIPT

Is War Ever Justified?

The British philosopher C. S. Lewis wrote in *Mere Christianity* (Scribner, 1952): "He [the devil] always sends errors into the world in pairs—pairs of opposites. And he always encourages us to spend a lot of time thinking which is the worse. You see why, of course? He relies on your extra dislike of the one error to draw you gradually into the opposite one." Could it be that extreme views pertaining to either pacifism or patriotism are equally destructive? In another book written during World War II, Lewis makes the following argument from the position of a league of devils attempting to destroy humankind:

> Consider whether we [a league of devils] should make the patient [the person being tempted] an extreme patriot or an extreme pacifist. All extremes except devotion to the Enemy [Christ] are to be encouraged. Not always, of course, but at this period. Some ages are lukewarm and complacent, and then it is our business to soothe them fast asleep. Other ages such as the present one are unbalanced and prone to faction, and it is our business to inflame them.... Whichever he adopts [pacifism or patriotism] your main task will be the same. Let him begin by treating the Patriotism or the Pacifism as a part of his religion. Then let him, under the influence of the partisan spirit, come to regard it as the most important part. Then quietly and gradually nurse him into the stage at which religion becomes merely part of the "cause" and his [faith] is valued chiefly for the excellent arguments it can produce in favour of the British war effort or of Pacifism.... Once you have made the world an end, and faith the means, you have almost won your man.... Provided that meetings, pamphlets, policies, movements, causes, and crusades mean more to him than prayer and sacraments and charity, he is ours—and the more "religious" on those terms the more securely ours.

> — *The Screwtape Letters* (Penguin, 1988), pp. 26–28

Is it possible to reconcile just war theory with the arguments of pacifism? The Hebrew Bible states, "Justice and judgment *are* the habitation of thy throne: mercy and truth shall go before thy face" (KJV, Psalms 89:14). Most religious traditions describe God as being *both* just and merciful. The New Testament describes Jesus casting some people from the temple while healing others during the same incident (see Matthew 21:12–14). God's expression of both justice and mercy represents the great paradox of war and peace.

Suggested Readings

J. T. Johnson and J. Kelsay, *Cross, Crescent, and Sword: The Justification and Limitation of War in Western and Islamic Tradition* (Greenwood Press, 1990).

M. Juergensmeyer, *Terror in the Mind of God: The Global Rise of Religious Violence* (University of California Press, 2000).

R. Niebuhr, *Christianity and Power Politics* (Archon, 1969).

W. Wink, *Peace Is the Way: Writings on Nonviolence From the Fellowship of Reconciliation* (Orbis, 2000).

ISSUE 15

Should There Be a Strict Separation Between Church and State?

YES: Richard Davis, from "Should There Be a Strict Separation Between Church and State? Yes," An Original Essay Written for This Volume (2002)

NO: Mathew D. Staver, from "Separation of Church and State," Liberty Counsel, http://www.lc.org/OldResources/separation. html (2000)

ISSUE SUMMARY

YES: Richard Davis, professor of political science at Brigham Young University in Provo, Utah, argues for a strict interpretation of the Constitution concerning church and state issues. He states that history has demonstrated that when there is not a strict separation, the civil government, religion, and especially the people suffer.

NO: Mathew D. Staver, a Christian attorney specializing in religious liberty law and founder of Liberty Counsel, contends that a strict separation between church and state is not what the founding fathers had in mind when they established the Constitution. He presents evidence supporting the assertion that strict separation should exist on the federal but not the state level of government.

The Constitution serves as the basic law of the United States of America. It was written in 1787 and amended in 1791 to include the Bill of Rights. This historical document specifically mentions religion twice: in Article XI of the Constitution, which contains a clause outlawing any "religious test" as criterion for public office, and in the First Amendment of the Bill of Rights. It is the First Amendment that has consistently remained at the center of the debate concerning the separation of church and state. The First Amendment reads as follows:

> Congress shall make no law respecting an establishment of religion, or prohibiting the free exercise thereof; or abridging the freedom of speech, or of the press; or the right of the people peaceably to assemble, and to petition the government for a redress of grievances.

The first 16 words of this amendment comprise the foundation on which every church/state debate builds: "Congress shall make no law respecting an establishment of religion, or prohibiting the free exercise thereof." Those arguing against a strict separation between church and state maintain that the founding fathers wrote this clause solely to prevent the establishment of a state-sponsored religion. They believe that this literal interpretation of the Constitution does not prohibit appropriate governmental support of religion. An example of appropriate governmental support, according to those who support this position, is preserving the words "In God We Trust" on American currency.

Those in favor of a strict separation make a much broader interpretation of the First Amendment, an interpretation that not only bans a state-sponsored religion but also prohibits the establishment or countenancing of any religious belief or practice by government. Generally, these supporters of strict separation argue against such practices as prayer in schools, the posting of the Ten Commandments, and/or displaying other religious symbols in state-sponsored institutions. They would also oppose government funding for religiously sponsored relief agencies, such as President George W. Bush's controversial "faith-based initiative."

Obviously, not all religions or religious individuals can fit their position neatly into one of these two categories. Many differing interpretations and applications exist among individuals and groups concerning church-state issues.

The following selections provide a striking contrast of perspectives concerning the separation of church and state. It is important to note that both Richard Davis and Mathew D. Staver are Christians who are active in their faith. The fact that they are men of faith and maintain opposing views underscores the reality that the church-state issue is not simply a debate between religious and nonreligious individuals.

In addition to providing statements from the founding fathers on the importance of the separation of church and state, Davis documents several historical incidences where failure to maintain a division led to destructive consequences. He includes examples such as the Spanish Inquisition, the experience of the Puritans in England, and the present problems in Northern Ireland. Davis also outlines the benefits to both churches and the state when a strict separation is maintained.

Staver argues his position from the writings of the Continental Congress: "Religion, morality and knowledge, being necessary to good government and the happiness of mankind, schools and the means of education shall be forever encouraged." His strongest reasoning is that while some of the arguments for a strict division between church and state are legitimate, they apply to the federal and not the state governments.

Richard Davis  **YES**

Should There Be a Strict Separation Between Church and State? Yes

T he first amendment to the U.S. Constitution reads "Congress shall make no law respecting an establishment of religion." Unlike some passages in the Constitution, this sentence, known as the religious establishment clause, avoids vagueness. It is clear in its opposition to use government to promote religious preference. Although the amendment specifically applies to the Congress, the U.S. Supreme Court has extended such a prohibition over the establishment of religion to the states.[1]

Given the powerful role of religion in American life, why was this provision placed in the Constitution and how is it applicable to our lives today? Those are the questions this essay will answer.

Early American Political Leaders Intended for the Separation of Church and State

Although many of the early American political leaders were church-goers themselves, they were concerned about the role of religion in the new nation. Unlike many today who advocate integration of religion and the state, they understood what happens when state and church intermingle. The dangers of that combination were much more real for them than they are for us because fairly recent historical events for them were still fresh in their memory.

Some examples:

- The Spanish inquisition was still under way at the Founders' time. The inquisition was an effort by the Catholic Church and the state to purge Spain of Protestants, Jews, and other non-Christians by violent means.[2]
- Recent English history had been the story of a struggle over which church would dominate (Roman Catholic or Protestant) with intense persecution of those religionists who ended up on the losing side.[3]
- The Puritans had abandoned England precisely because of their inability to practice their religious beliefs.[4]

- Religious minorities such as Quakers were subject to intense religious persecution. In England, many were imprisoned and tortured for their beliefs.[5]

Nor had all of the religious persecution existed on the other side of the Atlantic. Many of the colonists proved to be just as intolerant of religious diversity as their European counterparts. The Puritans established their religious haven in the Plymouth Colony but then proceeded to use governmental power to oppress religious dissenters such as Roger Williams and Anne Hutchinson. Citizens of some colonies were forced to pay taxes to churches they did not belong to. Connecticut law, for example, tolerated "all denominations of Christians" but excluded non-Christians.[6]

Even though more toleration of minority faiths had emerged in some parts of Europe and the United States by the late 1700s, there was still a governmental bias toward a single denomination or faith. The bias ranged from tax money paid out to certain churches to government control over the faith's clergy. When the Framers met in Philadelphia in 1787, most of the colonies still offered legal status to certain established churches such as Congregationalist churches in New England and Anglican churches in the mid-Atlantic states.[7]

Given this history of the intersection of government and religion, it is not surprising that one of the questions arising from the formation of a new national government was the role of religion. What role should religion play in the new government? Which of the variety of denominations extant at the time should become the nation's established church?

The Framers essentially ignored these questions. Only one provision of the Constitution even mentions religion. That is the prohibition on a religious test for national office in Article VI.[8] Such tests were not uncommon in the individual states as religious majorities attempted to impose yet another discrimination on those in the religious minority. The effect of the constitutional prohibition was the inability of a religious majority to determine who could or could not serve in office in the national government. Had that provision not been inserted in the Constitution, it is not far fetched to believe that adherents of minority religions such as Catholics, Jews, Mormons, or Seventh Day Adventists may have been unable to serve in the executive, legislative, or judicial branches of the United States for much of our history.

The establishment clause was not a part of the original constitution. It came about because of opposition to its absence in the original document and an unwillingness by some states to ratify it without such guarantees.[9]

Yet, its presence in the Constitution signalled a new and distinctive direction for the nation. There would be no established church. For people in the late 1700s this was a radical notion. Established religions dominated throughout Europe. England supported Anglicanism, France and Italy were Catholic nations, while Scandinavian countries adopted Lutheranism.

There was a pragmatic side to the establishment clause, as well. By promising to add it, along with the free exercise clause ("or prohibiting the free exercise thereof"), supporters of ratification of the Constitution could appeal to the variety of religious groups within the new nation such as Catholics in Maryland, Congregationalists in New England, Anglicans in Virginia, or Quakers in Pennsylvania.

By offering no preference for any religious organization, and banning religious tests for office, the amended Constitution created a nation where individual believers could worship privately but they could not use the national government as a vehicle for legal preferences for themselves. Churches with large numbers of adherents and those with but a few would enjoy the same political rights. Government would not support one religion over another.

Supreme Court Decisions Enforcing the Establishment Clause Protect Our First Amendment Rights

Despite the First Amendment's explicit provisions on the establishment of religion, various governments in the United States have continued to attempt to mandate religious practices. States or local governments have passed laws or enacted policies requiring Bible reading, the saying of the Lord's prayer in classrooms, or the placing of the Ten Commandments in school rooms. Simultaneously, others have prohibited preaching in a public park by ministers from minority religions or other activities common to minority faiths seeking converts such as door-to-door solicitation and the distribution of literature in public places.

Writing about the relationship between government and religion, Thomas Jefferson coined a famous phrase describing the ideal connection between the two:

> Believing . . . that religion is a matter which lies solely between man and his God, that he owes account to none other for his faith or his worship, that the legitimate powers of government reach actions only, and not opinions, I contemplate with sovereign reverence that act of the whole American people which declared that their Legislature should "make no law respecting an establishment of religion, or prohibiting the free exercise thereof," thus building a wall of separation between Church and State.[10]

Taking the lead from Thomas Jefferson, who first coined the phrase in 1802, the U.S. Supreme Court began interpreting the religious establishment clause in order to install a wall of separation between church and state. According to the Supreme Court, it is not enough for the government not to endorse a specific religion. Rather, it is the duty of government to remain neutral on religion.

In the case of *Everson v. Board of Education,* Justice Black wrote for the majority of the Court:

> The "establishment of religion" clause of the First Amendment means at least this: Neither a state nor the Federal Government can set up a church. Neither can pass laws which aid one religion, aid all religions, or prefer one religion over another. . . .

> Neither a state nor the Federal Government can, openly or se-
> cretly, participate in the affairs of any religious organizations
> or groups and vice versa. In the words of Jefferson, the clause
> against establishment of religion by law was intended to erect
> "a wall of separation between Church and State."[11]

The recent landmark case in this interpretation process was *Lemon v. Kurtzman* (1971).[12] The Court's decision created what is known as the Lemon Test, which is designed to help judges determine the constitutionality of laws regarding religion. The Lemon Test has three parts:

1. The law must have a secular purpose.

    For example, if a state provides financial assistance for parochial schools who treat special education, the purpose must be to promote the education of these children rather than support of the religious institution.

2. The primary effect of the law must be to neither advance nor inhibit religion.

    For example, a state or local government can provide tax deductions to those who make contributions to a religious organization, but the law must apply to all charitable organizations not just religious ones.

3. The law must avoid excessive government entanglement with religion.

    The government must not be closely interacting with a religious organization such as determining the content of religious instruction in a parochial school.

Obviously, the religious nature of the American public (60 percent of Americans say they belong to a church or synagogue and four in ten say they attend church regularly) and overt efforts by some groups, particularly on the religious right to provide governmental preference for their religious beliefs, leads to conflict over application of the establishment clause.[13]

One issue is the placing of religious symbols on public property. The Supreme Court has struck down placing nativity scenes on government property, but not Christmas and Hanukkah symbols together. The context of symbols is important. Christmas symbols alone, especially religious ones, have the primary effect of advancing the cause of a single religion, i.e. Christianity. But the placement of differing religious symbols neither advances nor inhibits any religion.

The courts have been faced with cases involving a weakening of a strict interpretation of the establishment clause. In one case, a judge in Alabama posted the Ten Commandments on the wall in his courtroom and invited prayers to be said prior to each session, as long as they were Christian prayers. Another issue is the constitutionality of vouchers or credits for families of children attending religious schools. Still another involves federal funding for religious institutions who perform charitable work but also prosletyze.

The best means for handling these conflicts is to maintain a strict separation between the government and religious organizations. Such an approach will benefit both the church and the state.

A Strict Separation Benefits Both Church and State

The government's role as a neutral arbiter among religions as well as between the religious and nonreligious is preferable to one of government role as advocate. A strict separation between the power of government and religious belief and activity aids both parties.

Benefits for Churches and Believers

One undeniable benefit to the church is the absence of concern about the state dictating religious doctrines and practices to the church and its believers. For example, if the government began providing funding to religious organizations, how much control does the government possess over those organizations' practices? President George W. Bush's faith-based initiative program bogged down early in his administration because groups such as the Salvation Army and the Catholic Church objected to federal requirements that they not discriminate in employment of church employees on the basis of sexual orientation.

Another issue would be the implementation of government-sponsored school prayer, which invariably means group involvement. It is most likely that the method of prayer employed by the group will be the one held by the majority. How does an individual believer who does not subscribe to the majority's method of religious observance handle the expectation of a religious exercise as part of a government-mandated activity such as school attendance? Do they change their religious practices to conform to the majority's? Wouldn't that be a violation of the religious exercise clause?

A recent example of this problem was the school district policy in Rhode Island of inviting a member of the clergy to offer a prayer during high school graduation ceremonies. The clergy members were given pamphlets "containing guidelines for the composition of public prayers at civic ceremonies" and were advised that "the prayers should be nonsectarian."[14] The government, then, goes into the business of determining the kind of prayer that a religious believer can offer.

Religious differences have existed in the United States since colonists of differing faiths came to American shores to start new lives. The differences across faiths are not minor. Within Christianity, Catholics and Protestants adopt contrasting doctrines. Within Protestantism, there is a wide range of beliefs and practices. Jews, Muslims, Hindus, Buddhists, and other non-Christian faiths also contrast starkly with Christian denominations and with each other.

No believer should be placed in a position of giving tacit support to a religious practice he or she may not approve of. Yet, religious activity under the aegis of government can do just that.

The movement toward nonsectarianism in public religious activity may be suitable for some believers. But for many others it is an unacceptable watering down of their religious practices. Believers should not be expected to participate in others' religious practices as a part of their normal interactions with government. Religion is a highly personal exercise. It is "too precious to be either proscribed or prescribed by the State."[15]

In a case involving state-sponsored graduation prayer, Justice Kennedy wrote for the Court:

> It is beyond dispute that, at a minimum, the Constitution guarantees that government may not coerce anyone to support or participate in religion or its exercise, or otherwise act in a way which "establishes a [state] religion or religious faith, or tends to do so."

Even believers can rest assured that, when there is strict separation of church and state, they will not be coerced to participate in a religious exercise because they attend a high school graduation, enroll their children in school, or show up for a public meeting.

The power of the state is intentionally significant. When the state intervenes in religious matters, it invariably takes sides. That is the reason for the historic wall of separation.

If government takes sides, its preference will be for religious majorities because they are also political majorities. Such bias will harm minority religions, who are vulnerable to majority rule. We have already seen this vulnerability in the past. States have passed laws requiring Jehovah's Witnesses children to salute the flag, an act which violates the basic tenets of their religion.

Those members of religious minorities—both Christian and non-Christian —are the most vulnerable to the power of the state. Since they must interact with government in their responsibilities as citizens and their children must attend school (and should not be forced to choose between a private school or maintaining their religious beliefs), laws relating to religion that provide for group religious exercise within government meetings or public school sessions place such individuals in an awkward position.

Unfortunately, too many of the advocates of school prayer or the posting of the Ten Commandments or other religious displays in classrooms seem ignorant of the rich diversity of religious life in the United States today and the potential effects of these efforts to force a majority religious view on people who strive to maintain their religious faith in sometimes hostile social environments.

Let me make clear that separation of church and state does not preclude religious groups from acting like other interested parties in lobbying government on policy matters. For example, the Catholic Church's efforts to ban abortion or end the death penalty fall squarely within the First Amendment's guarantee that citizens (regardless of their religious affiliation) can "petition the government for a redress of grievances."

In such cases, religious groups act as outsiders who seek to influence government policy. That is a wholly different matter than a situation where religious organizations acquire a quasi-official status allowing them to promote their views or practices over those of others such as organizations who seek to declare the United States a "Christian nation" or attempt to mandate religious activity in public settings such as prayer in public schools.

Benefits for Nonbelievers

Nonbelievers also benefit because their tax dollars are not used to support religions they do not support. Nor are they required to participate in religious exercises they do not believe in. That fact cannot be overemphasized. The role of the government is not to impose or even attempt to persuade nonbelievers that they should be believers. Attempts to break down the wall of separation between church and state such as school prayer, religious displays on public property (including schools), or prayer at government meetings are not directed primarily at believers who can receive these messages in their religious gatherings, but at nonbelievers. That should not be the business of government.

Benefits for the State

Not only does the church benefit from strict separation; so does the state. The state benefits by not having to make choices among varying religious doctrines and practices. Government can focus on the myriad of other responsibilities it has.

This is not an insignificant point. When New York state devised a prayer to be said in schools, it had to determine the wording of the prayer. The prayer had to be religious, but not offensive. The state of Rhode Island provided pay supplements to teachers in parochial schools who did not teach religion classes or "any subject matter expressing religious teaching, or the morals or forms of worship of any sect."[16] It then would become the business of the state to examine the curriculum of parochial school teachers to assure that there was no such discussion. Should the state do such a thing?

More recently, some local governmental bodies have initiated the practice of beginning their meetings with prayer. But when one resident attempted to use the prayer to make a statement against government-sponsored religious activity, the city council had to judge whether the person's prayer was really a prayer.[17]

Similarly, when the government places religious displays on public property, it has to decide what symbols represent what religions. Is Christmas best represented by a Santa Claus figure or by a creche? Is a Wicca figure a religious symbol? Government should not be in the business of making the decision about what is religious and what is not. The best approach is for government to limit its interaction with religion, since such interaction inevitably will result in harm to either church or state or both.

Over thirty years after the addition of the religious establishment clause to the Constitution, James Madison praised its virtue in maintaining separation between the church and the state and the value of such a separation.

> Every new and successful example, therefore, of a *perfect separation between the ecclesiastical and civil matters, is of importance;* and I have

no doubt that every new example will succeed, as every past one has done, in showing that religion and Government will both exist in greater purity the less they are mixed together.[18]

Madison's words are still meaningful today. The wall of separation of church and state is still as essential today as it was two hundred years ago.

Notes

1. See, for example, *West Virginia State Board of Education v. Barnette* 319 U.S. 624 (1943); *Murdock v. Commonwealth of Pennsylvania*, 319 U.S. 105 (1943); *Everson v. Board of Education of Ewing TP.*, 330 U.S. 1 (1947); *Engel v. Vitale*, 370 U.S. 421 (1962); *Abington School District v. Schempp*, 374 U.S. 203 (1963); *Lemon v. Kurtzman*, 403 U.S. 602 (1971); *Stone v. Graham*, 449 U.S. 39 (1980); *Wallace v. Jaffree*, 472 U.S. 38 (1985); and *Lee v. Weisman*, 505 U.S. 577 (1992).

2. See, for example, Henry Kamen, *The Spanish Inquisition*, New Haven: Yale University Press, 1998, pp. 189–213; and Jean Plaidy, *The Spanish Inquisition: Its Rise, Growth, and End*, New York: Citadel Press, 1967, pp. 104–123.

3. See Doreen Rosman, *From Catholic to Protestant: Religion and People in Tudor England*, London: UCL Press, 1996.

4. John Spurr, *English Puritanism, 1603–1689*, New York: St. Martin's Press, 1998; and Edward H. Bloomfield, *The Opposition to the English Separatists, 1570–1625*, Washington: University Press of America, 1981, pp. 35–40.

5. Adrian Davies, *The Quakers in English Society, 1655–1725;* and Hugh Barbour, *The Quakers in Puritan England*, New Haven, Yale University Press, 1964, pp. 207–233.

6. Leonard Levy, *The Establishment Clause*, 2nd ed., Chapel Hill, N.C.: University of North Carolina, 1994, pp. 1–51.

7. Levy, *op cit.*

8. "... no religious test shall ever be required as a qualification to any office or public trust under the United States." (Article VI, U.S. Constitution).

9. Levy, pp. 83–93.

10. "Letter to Danbury Baptists, 1802," *The Writings of Thomas Jefferson*, vol. 16, Washington, D.C.: The Thomas Jefferson Memorial Association, 1904, pp. 281–282.

11. Everson v. Board of Education of Ewing TP. 330 U.S. 1 (1947).

12. Lemon v. Kurtzman, 403 U.S. 602 (1971).

13. See Gallup Organization, "Easter Season Finds a Religious Nation: More than Six in 10 Americans Think Religion 'Can Answer All or Most of Today's Problems,'" April 13, 2001, at http://www.gallup.com/poll/releases/pr010413.asp.

14. Lee v. Weisman, 505 U.S. 577 (1992).

15. Lee v. Weisman, 505 U.S. 577 (1992).

16. Lemon v. Kurtzman, 403 U.S. 602 (1971).

17. Joe Costanzo, "Decision Stems From Suit Over a Prayer to 'Mother in Heaven,'" *Deseret News* (Salt Lake City, Utah), September 12, 1997, p. A1.

18. "Letter to Edward Livingston, July 10, 1822," in Roberts S. Alley, ed., *James Madison on Religious Liberty*, New York: Prometheus Books, 1985, pp. 82–83.

Mathew D. Staver

Separation of Church and State

This country was established upon the assumption that religion was essential to good government. On July 13, 1787, the Continental Congress enacted the Northwest Ordinance, which stated: "Religion, morality and knowledge, being necessary to good government and the happiness of mankind, schools and the means of education shall be forever encouraged."[1] The First Amendment prohibited the federal government from establishing a religion to which the several states must pay homage. The First Amendment provided assurance that the federal government would not meddle in the affairs of religion within the sovereign states.

In modern times groups like the American Civil Liberties Union (ACLU) and Americans United for Separation of Church and State have attempted to create an environment wherein government and religion are adversaries. Their favorite phrase has been "separation of church and state." These groups have intoned the mantra of "separation of church and state" so long that many people believe the phrase is in the Constitution. In Proverbs Chapter 18, verse 16, the Bible says, "He who states his case first seems right until another comes to challenge him." I'm sure you have seen legal arguments on television where the prosecution argues to the jury that the defendant is guilty. Once the prosecution finishes the opening presentation, you believe that the defendant is guilty. However, after the defense attorney completes the rebuttal presentation of the evidence, you may be confused, or at least you acknowledge that the case is not clear cut.

The same is true with the phrase "separation of church and state." The ACLU and the liberal media have touted the phrase so many times that most people believe the phrase is in the Constitution. Nowhere is "separation of church and state" referenced in the Constitution. This phrase was in the former Soviet Union's Constitution, but it has never been part of the United States Constitution.

Justice Oliver Wendell Holmes once said, "It is one of the misfortunes of the law that ideas become encysted in phrases, and thereafter for a long time cease to provoke further analysis."[2] The phrase, "separation of church and state," has become one of these misfortunes of law.

In 1947 the Supreme Court popularized Thomas Jefferson's "wall of separation between church and state."[3] Taking the Jefferson metaphor out of context, strict separationists have often used the phrase to silence Christians and to limit any Christian influence from affecting the political system. To understand Jefferson's "wall of separation," we should return to the original context in which it was written. Jefferson himself once wrote:

> On every question of construction, [we must] carry ourselves back to the time when the constitution was adopted, recollect the spirit manifested in the debates, and instead of trying what meaning may be squeezed out of the test, or invented against it, conform to the probable one in which it was a part.[4]

Thomas Jefferson was inaugurated as the third President on March 4, 1801. On October 7, 1801, a committee of the Danbury Baptist Association wrote a congratulatory letter to Jefferson on his election as President. Organized in 1790, the Danbury Baptist Association was an alliance of churches in Western Connecticut. The Baptists were a religious minority in the state of Connecticut where Congregationalism was the established church.[5]

The concern of the Danbury Baptist Association is understandable once we understand the background of church-state relations in Great Britain. The Association eschewed the kind of state sponsored enforcement of religion that had been the norm in Great Britain.

The Danbury Baptist Association committee wrote to the President stating that, "Religion is at all times and places a Matter between God and Individuals —that no man ought to suffer in Name, person or affects on account of his religious Opinions."[6] The Danbury Baptists believed that religion was an unalienable right and they hoped that Jefferson would raise the consciousness of the people to recognize religious freedom as unalienable. However, the Danbury Baptists acknowledged that the President of the United States was not a "national Legislator" and they also understood that the "national government cannot destroy the Laws of each State."[7] In other words, they recognized Jefferson's limited influence as the federal executive on the individual states.

Jefferson did not necessarily like receiving mail as President, but he generally endeavored to turn his responses into an opportunity to sow what he called "useful truths" and principles among the people so that the ideas might take political root. He therefore took this opportunity to explain why he as President, contrary to his predecessors, did not proclaim national days of fasting and prayer.

Jefferson's letter went through at least two drafts. Part of the first draft reads as follows:

> Believing with you that religion is a matter which lies solely between man & his god, that he owes account to none other for his faith or his worship, that legitimate powers of government reach actions only and not opinions, I contemplate with sovereign reverence that act of the whole American people which declared that their legislature should make no law respecting an establishment of religion, or prohibiting the free exercise thereof; thus

building a wall of separation between church and state. Congress thus inhibited from acts respecting religion, and the Executive authorized only to execute their acts, I have refrained from prescribing even occasional performances of devotion...[8]

Jefferson asked Levi Lincoln, the Attorney General, and Gideon Granger, the Postmaster General, to comment on his draft. In a letter to Mr. Lincoln, Jefferson stated he wanted to take the occasion to explain why he did not "proclaim national fastings & thanksgivings, as my predecessors did."[9] He knew that the response would "give great offense to the New England clergy" and he advised Lincoln that he should suggest necessary changes.[10]

Mr. Lincoln responded that the five New England states have always been in the habit of "observing fasts and thanksgivings in performance of proclamations from the respective Executives" and that this "custom is venerable being handed down from our ancestors."[11] Lincoln therefore struck through the last sentence of the above quoted letter about Jefferson refraining from prescribing even occasional performances of devotion. Jefferson penned a note in the margin that this paragraph was omitted because "it might give uneasiness to some of our republican friends in the eastern states where the proclamation of thanksgivings" by their state executives is respected.[12]

To understand Jefferson's use of the wall metaphor in his letter to the Danbury Baptist Association, we must compare his other writings. On March 4, 1805, in Jefferson's Second Inaugural Address, he stated as follows:

> In matters of religion, I have considered that its free exercise is placed by the Constitution independent of the powers of the General [i.e., federal] Government. I have therefore undertaken, on no occasion, to prescribe the religious exercises suited to it; but have left them, as the Constitution found them, under the direction and discipline of State or Church authorities acknowledged by the several religious societies.[13]

Then on January 23, 1808, Jefferson wrote in response to a letter received by Reverend Samuel Miller, who requested him to declare a national day of thanksgiving and prayer:

> I consider the government of the United States as interdicted by the Constitution from intermeddling with religious institutions, their doctrines, discipline, or exercises. This results not only from the provisions that no law shall be made respecting the establishment or free exercise of religion [First Amendment], but from that also which reserves to the States the powers not delegated to the United States [Tenth Amendment]. Certainly no power to prescribe any religious exercise, or to assume authority in religious discipline, has been delegated to the General [i.e., federal] Government. It must then rest with the States, as far as it can be in any human authority.[14]
>
> I am aware that the practice of my predecessors may be quoted. But I have every belief, that the example of State executives led to the assumption of that authority by the General Government, without due examination, which would have discovered

that what might be a right in State government, was a violation of that right when assumed by another.... [C]ivil powers alone have been given to the President of the United States, and no authority to direct the religious exercises of his constituents.[15]

Comparing these two responses to his actions in the state government of Virginia show the true intent of Jefferson's wall metaphor. As a member of the House of Burgesses, on May 24, 1774, Jefferson participated in drafting and enacting a resolution designating a "Day of Fasting, Humiliation, and Prayer."[16] This resolution occurred only a few days before he wrote "A Bill for Establishing Religious Freedom." In 1779, while Jefferson was governor of Virginia, he issued a proclamation decreeing a day "of publick and solemn thanksgiving and prayer to Almighty God." In the late 1770's, as chair of the Virginia committee of Revisers, Jefferson was the chief architect of a measure entitled, "A Bill for Appointing Days of Public Fasting and Thanksgiving." Interestingly, this bill authorized the governor, or Chief Magistrate with the advice of Counsel, to designate days of thanksgiving and fasting and, required that the public be notified by proclamation. The bill also provided that "[e]very minister of the gospel shall on each day so to be appointed, attend and perform divine service and preach a sermon, or discourse, suited to the occasion, in his church, on pain of forfeiting fifty pounds for every failure, not having a reasonable excuse."[17] Though the bill was never enacted, Jefferson was its chief architect and the sponsor was none other than James Madison.

So what did Jefferson mean when he used the "wall" metaphor? Jefferson undoubtedly meant that the First Amendment prohibited the federal Congress from enacting any law respecting an establishment of religion or prohibiting the free exercise thereof. As the chief executive of the federal government, the President's duty was to carry out the directives of Congress. If Congress had no authority in matters of religion, then neither did the President. Religion was clearly within the jurisdiction of the church and states. As a state legislator, Jefferson saw no problem with proclaiming days of thanksgiving and prayer, and even on one occasion prescribed a penalty to the clergy for failure to abide by these state proclamations. Jefferson believed that the Constitution created a limited government and that the states retained the authority over matters of religion not only through the First Amendment but also through the Tenth Amendment.[18] The federal government had absolutely no jurisdiction over religion, as that matter was left where the Constitution found it, namely with the individual churches and the several states.

In summary, the First Amendment says more about federalism than religious freedom. In other words, the purpose of the First Amendment was to declare that the federal government had absolutely no jurisdiction in matters of religion. It could neither establish a religion, nor prohibit the free exercise of religion. The First Amendment clearly erected a barrier between the federal government and religion on a state level. If a state chose to have no religion, or to have an established religion, the federal government had no jurisdiction one way or the other. This is what Thomas Jefferson meant by the "wall of separation." In context, the word "state" really referred to the federal government. The First Amendment did not apply to the states. It was only applicable as a restraint against the federal government. The problem arose in 1940[19] and then again in 1947[20] when the Supreme Court applied the First Amendment to the states. This turned the First Amendment on its head, and completely inverted its meaning.[21] The First Amendment was never meant to be a restraint on state government. It was only applicable to the federal government. When the Supreme Court turned the First Amendment around 180 degrees and used Jefferson's comment in the process, it not only perverted the First Amendment, but misconstrued the intent of Jefferson's letter.

There is nothing wrong with the way Jefferson used the "wall of separation between church and state" metaphor. The problem has arisen when the Supreme Court in 1947 erroneously picked up the metaphor and attempted to construct a constitutional principal. While the metaphor understood in its proper context is useful, we might do well to heed the words of the United States Supreme Court Justice William Rehnquist:

> The "wall of separation between church and State" is a metaphor based on bad history, a metaphor which has proved useless as a guide to judging. It should be frankly and explicitly abandoned.[22]

Jefferson used the phrase "wall of separation between church and state" as a means of expressing his republican view that the federal or general government should not interfere with religious matters among the several states. In its proper context, the phrase represents a clear expression of state autonomy.

Accordingly, Jefferson saw no contradiction in authoring a religious proclamation to be used by state officials and refusing to issue similar religious proclamations as president of the United States. His wall had less to do with the separation of church and *all* civil government than with the separation of federal and state governments.[23]

The "wall of separation between church and state" phrase as understood by Jefferson was never meant to exclude people of faith from influencing and shaping government. Jefferson would be shocked to learn that his letter has been used as a weapon against religion. He would never countenance such shabby and distorted use of history.

Notes

1. Ord. or 1789, July 13, 1787, Art. A III, *reprinted in Documents Illustrative of the Formation of the Union of American States* 52 (1927).

2. *Hyde v. United States*, 225 U.S. 347, 384 (1912) (Holmes, J., dissenting).

3. *See Everson v. Bd. of Educ.*, 330 U.S. 1 (1947). *See also McCollum v. Bd. of Educ.*, 333 U.S. 203, 211 (1948).

4. Thomas Jefferson to Messers. Nehemiah Dodge, Ephraim Robbins and Stephen S. Nelson, a Committee of the Danbury Baptist Association in the State of Connecticut, January 1, 1802, Presidential Papers Microfilm, *Thomas Jefferson Papers*, Manuscript Division, Library of Congress, Ser. I, reel 25, November 15, 1801–March 31, 1802; Jefferson to William Johnson, June 12, 1823, Presidential Papers Microfilm, *Thomas Jefferson Papers*, Manuscript Division, Library of Congress, Ser. I, reel 70. The letters referenced below can be found at this citation.

5. Daniel Dreisbach, *"Sowing Useful Truths and Principles": The Danbury Baptists, Thomas Jefferson, and the "Wall of Separation,"* 39 Journal of Church and State 455, 459 (1997).

6. *Id.* at 460.

7. *Id.*

8. *Id.* at 462.

9. *Id.* at 463 n. 16.

10. *Id.* at 465.

11. *Id.* at 466.

12. *Id.* at 462 n. 13.

13. Thomas Jefferson to the Reverend Samuel Miller, January 23, 1808, in Andrew A. Lipscomb et al., eds., *The Writings of Thomas Jefferson* 11:428; Jefferson, Second Inaugural Address, March 4, 1805, in Andrew A. Lipscomb et al., eds., *The Writings of Thomas Jefferson* 3:378.

14. Thomas Jefferson to the Reverend Samuel Miller, January 23, 1808, in *The Writings of Thomas Jefferson* 11:428.

15. *Id.* at 11:430.

16. J. Body, ed., *The Papers of Jefferson* 1:105.

17. Report of the *Committee of Revisors Appointed by the General Assembly of Virginia in MDCCLXXVI* (Richmond, Va., 1984) 59-60; Julian P. Boyd, et al., eds., *The Papers of Thomas Jefferson* 2:556.

18. In the Kentucky-Virginia Resolutions of 1798, Jefferson wrote that the powers not delegated to the United States are reserved to the States and that "no power over the freedom of religion, freedom of speech, or freedom of the press being delegated to the United States by the Constitution, nor prohibited by it to the States, all lawful powers respecting the same did of right remain, and were reserved to the States, or to the people... [and are] withheld from the cognizance of federal tribunals." *The Kentucky-Virginia Resolutions and Mr. Madison's Report of 1799* 2-3.

19. *See Cantwell v. Connecticut,* 310 U.S. 296 (1940).

20. *See Everson,* 330 U.S. at 1.

21. One of the early Supreme Court Justices, Joseph Story, wrote that "the whole power over the subject of religion is left exclusively to the state governments, to be acted upon according to their own sense of justice, and the state constitutions..." J. Story, *Commentaries on the Constitution* § 1879 (1833).

22. *Wallace v. Jaffree,* 472 U.S. 38, 106 (Rehnquist, J., dissenting).

23. Daniel Dreisbach, *Thomas Jefferson and the Danbury Baptists Revisited,* 56:4 William and Mary Quarterly 805, 812 (1999).

POSTSCRIPT

Should There Be a Strict Separation Between Church and State?

While Davis and Staver provide strong political and historical arguments for and against a strict separation of church and state, they do not address the theology upon which their arguments are based. One of the basic tenets of the Protestant Reformation is the concept that God created two separate forms of authority, the temporal and the spiritual, to bring about different purposes. Spiritual authority was given by God to oversee the salvation of souls, and the temporal (civic) authority was provided to ensure order in the physical world. The words of Jesus concerning Roman law and submission to Caesar could be interpreted as an example of this separateness:

> Then went the Pharisees, and took counsel how they might entangle him in *his* talk. And they sent out unto him their disciples with the Herodians, saying, Master, we know that thou art true, and teachest the way of God in truth, neither carest thou for any *man*: for thou regardest not the person of men. Tell us therefore, What thinkest thou? Is it lawful to give tribute unto Caesar, or not? But Jesus perceived their wickedness, and said, Why tempt ye me, *ye* hypocrites? Shew me the tribute money. And they brought unto him a penny. And he saith unto them, Whose *is* this image and superscription? They say unto him, Caesar's. Then saith he unto them, Render therefore unto Caesar the things which are Caesar's; and unto God the things that are God's.

> — KJV, Matt. 22:15–21

Before and during much of the time of the Reformation, church and state were not separate. For the most part, religious and civil authority were consolidated into the hands of a single ruler. The Holy Roman Empire is an example of such a consolidation. Many of the great civilizations of the world, such as those in Egypt, Assyria, Babylon, and Persia, were similar in their religious and civil governance. In fact, this traditional type of government was so prevalent, it could be argued that it was not until what began with the Reformation and continued with the eventual founding of the United States of America that a workable and advantageous relationship between church and state existed.

The theological roots of the church-state controversy in America extend back to the debates between two of America's early religious leaders, Roger Williams and John Cotton. Both were religious leaders in the Massachusetts Bay Colony, and both agreed on the importance of having separate leaders of church and state with differing responsibilities, but they differed greatly in their opinions of the proper relationship between civil and ecclesiastical law. Cotton believed that it was necessary for civil authorities to enforce religious law because he felt that all truth was God's truth. Williams believed that the state should not have authority over the first four of the Ten Commandments dealing with the relationship between God and man but could settle questions dealing with the last six commandments with regard to human relationships. Williams was eventually banished from the Boston area because of his separationist beliefs and eventually assisted in the founding of Rhode Island—a colony that became well known for religious tolerance and separation between church and state.

Some would say that perhaps the tension between church and state does not need to be resolved. Just as justice and mercy, faith and reason, obedience and selfhood are all paradoxical by design, perhaps the relationship between church and state exists in the same way—as two opposing powers that serve to balance one another.

Suggested Readings

R. Boston, *Why the Religious Right Is Wrong: About Separation of Church and State* (Prometheus Books, 1994).

S. L. Carter, *God's Name in Vain: The Wrongs and Rights of Religion in Politics* (Basic Books, 2001).

J. Eidsmore, *Christianity and the Constitution: The Faith of Our Founding Fathers* (Baker Books, 1987).

P. Hamburger, *Separation of Church and State* (Harvard University Press, 2002).

ISSUE 16

Does the Religious Right Threaten American Freedoms?

YES: John B. Judis, from "Crosses to Bear," *The New Republic* (September 12, 1994)

NO: Fred Barnes, from "Who Needs the Religious Right? We All Do," *Crisis* (September 1994)

ISSUE SUMMARY

YES: John B. Judis, senior editor of *The New Republic*, argues against the Religious Right using the political process to force its morally conservative political agenda on the American public. He maintains that government should be allowed to operate independently of the Religious Right's influence.

NO: Fred Barnes, cofounder of the weekly magazine *The Standard*, argues in support of the Religious Right keeping traditional moral issues alive in the public debate. He asserts that morality plays a vital role in the success of America, and without the influence of religious conservatism, the nation's freedom may be in jeopardy.

Historically, religion played a central role in the founding of the United States of America. The dominant factor motivating many of America's founders was a quest to practice their Protestant faith without the corruption that existed between the church and state in England. The Pilgrims who came to the Americas in 1620 were known as Separatists; they had become disillusioned with the corruption in the Church of England and wanted to disengage and establish a separate church. The Puritans, another group who came to America from Europe, agreed with the Pilgrims that the Church of England had become corrupt, but they believed that it was their mission to maintain their membership and attempt to "purify" the church from within. The Puritans intended to establish a "holy commonwealth" by constituting a state religion and conducting it strictly according to the gospel principles as outlined in the Bible. Even though the Pilgrims came to America before the Puritans, by 1700 the Pilgrims were outnumbered and became, for the most part, assimilated into Puritan culture.

While many settlers evolved into Puritans, Roger Williams, an ordained priest in the Church of England, went in the opposite direction. Williams came to America in 1631 as a Puritan, soon became a Separatist, established the first Baptist church in America, and later became a Seeker—not recognizing any religion as having authority from God. During this time, he founded Rhode Island, basing the colony on complete religious toleration and a separation of church and state. Many other faiths, including Judaism and the Religious Society of Friends (Quakers), were attracted to Rhode Island because of the tolerance that existed there.

Williams's separation from Puritanism prefigures the movement of those in present-day America who believe religion and politics should be separate. On the other hand, there are individuals and religions who believe that it is their responsibility to *purify* the American culture through religious influence. As one can see, religion has been polarized nearly from the beginning of the American culture.

America has been heavily influenced by Protestantism, even to the extent that some scholars like E. W. Smith have identified the reformer John Calvin as the "virtual founder of America." Although Protestantism, Catholicism, Judaism, and other religions have many theological differences, for the most part they have provided a moral consensus for many generations of American citizens. This moral consensus, however, began to be seriously challenged in the early 1960s. Conservative factions battled more liberal factions. Many Protestant denominations adapted to the new ways of thinking, but groups that were fundamental and evangelical did not. Conservative factions have come to be known as the Religious Right and are seen by some as the only hope for a culture in moral decay. Others, including John B. Judis, consider the Religious Right to be a hazard to America's constitutional principles. Judis argues that the Religious Right is a threat because of the movement's agenda to use the political process as a vehicle to impose its conservative religious views on others.

Taking the opposing view, Fred Barnes describes America's need for the Religious Right's role in keeping alive moral issues and traditional values important to most Americans. He also provides evidence against the assertion made by some that the Religious Right has overtaken the Republican party.

John B. Judis  **YES**

Crosses to Bear

*Some people have the idea that the [Young Communist Leaguer] is po-
litically minded, that nothing outside of politics means anything. Gosh
no. They have a few simple problems. There is the problem of getting
good men on the baseball team this spring, of opposition from ping-pong
teams, of dating girls, etc. We go to shows, parties, dances and all that.
In short, the YCL and its members are no different from other people
except that we believe in dialectical materialism as the solution to all
problems.*

— Young Communist League pamphlet, circa 1938

In October 1980, when I was covering the South Dakota Senate race
between George McGovern and Republican challenger James Abdnor, I inter-
viewed the Rev. Donald Tottingham, the leader of the state's Moral Majority
chapter and a prime opponent of McGovern's. Tottingham told me how his political activity flowed from his conviction, gleaned from the Bible, that a Satanic
one-world government was imminent. I had similarly extensive, though not
as bizarre, conversations in 1986 with the Rev. Don Lynch, a Muncie, Indiana,
Republican congressional candidate, and in 1992 with W. E. "Bob" McClellan,
a Southern California car dealer and member of the Christian Coalition, who
had been elected to the San Diego City Council the year before. It didn't surprise me that evangelical Christians wanted to talk about the relationship of
their religious beliefs to politics: bringing the "good news" of the gospel to the
unconverted and unconvinced was central to their faith.

But during the last two years, when I've asked leaders of religious right
organizations such as the Christian Coalition about the relationship of religion
to politics, I've gotten hard glances and vague, noncommittal answers. After
staring me down, Steve Sheffler, the field director of the Christian Coalition in
Iowa, responded that the organization's overall goal is "some positive change
in the way the country is going." A prominent national leader of the religious
right would only discuss the relevance of religion to politics if his views were
off the record. Moreover, public spokesmen such as Ralph Reed, the director of
the Christian Coalition, now insist that their organizations are not part of the
"religious right" but of the "pro-family movement."

Has the movement changed so fundamentally in the last two years that it cannot even be called the religious or Christian right? I don't think so. Rather, what seems to have happened is that the Christian Coalition and smaller organizations of the religious right have come up against the same sort of limits all sectarian movements encounter. They have been forced to recognize that the very principles that bring members into their fold also limit wider public appeal. In response, the religious right's leaders have attempted to change its public face while retaining its private religious attraction.

Such a change has helped the movement gain influence in states such as Texas and Iowa, but in the long run it doesn't resolve the crisis that lies at its heart. Movements that draw a distinction between their private and public discourse inevitably risk schism, on the one hand, and co-optation, on the other. They risk either losing members or losing meaning. Creating a different public face also doesn't resolve the more basic question of what the relationship should be between religion and politics. Ralph Reed's pro-family movement sounds more benign than Tottingham's crusade, but it is probably no less a hazard to America's constitutional principles.

The religious right, defined as a fusion of conservative Christianity and political conservatism, goes back at least to the 1930s and the anti-New Deal crusades of Gerald B. Winrod and Gerald L. K. Smith. The movement's current incarnation, however, dates from the late '70s. It was initially organized by Southern evangelical ministers who wanted to prevent the Internal Revenue Service from removing the tax exemption on the segregated Christian academies they had set up in response to *Brown v. Board of Education.* More broadly, the religious right coalesced in response to Supreme Court decisions limiting school prayer and liberalizing abortion, and to the dramatic changes in American family life and leisure that spurred feminism, gay rights, teenage sexuality and, of course, MTV.

Two kinds of religious organizations emerged from this crucible. The first, epitomized by the Rev. James Dobson's Focus on the Family, defined itself primarily as an educational organization concerned with family issues that were relevant to evangelical Christians, including sex education and abortion. Focus on the Family lobbies the government, but only on these issues, and it does not back candidates. In political terms, it resembles Jewish, Catholic and mainline Protestant pressure groups.

The second kind of organization, more properly termed the "religious right," is typified by the Rev. Jerry Falwell's Moral Majority and the Rev. Pat Robertson's Freedom Council and Christian Coalition. Of these, the coalition is currently the most important, with nearly 1 million registered members, 900 chapters and a $13 million annual budget. All these groups function like political movements and parties—implicitly or explicitly running and endorsing candidates, and even participating as a political faction within the Republican Party. (Many of these organizations are registered as nonprofit with the IRS and must use artful dodges like grading candidates on issues through "Christian scorecards" to get around restrictions on open political endorsements.)

Initially, this new religious right was divided along denominational lines. Anti-Darwinian fundamentalists, who believed the Bible was literally true, gravitated toward Falwell's Moral Majority; Pentecostals and other charismatic Christians, who believed, in addition, that Jesus granted mortals the power to speak in tongues and perform miracles, joined Robertson's Freedom Council. Through the Christian Coalition, Robertson and Reed, to their great credit, have united what Robertson calls "biblical Christians" in a single organization.

Reed tries to portray the coalition as a garden-variety lobby. "We really see ourselves as a kind of faith-based Chamber of Commerce, a kind of League of Women Voters, if you will, for people of faith," he told National Public Radio in June. But if he's looking for an analogy, he's looking in the wrong place. The new religious right doesn't resemble the Chamber of Commerce or other business interests so much as it does the old Socialist and Communist parties. Its members are united by conviction rather than by function or employment; and its goal is not merely to defend certain discrete interests but to win political power on behalf of a broad agenda.

···

Like the older leftwing parties, the religious right also draws on a semiorganized base that is many times larger than itself. Many religious activists don't belong to any organized group, but they still take their cues from ministers affiliated with the Christian Coalition; those who belong to smaller Christian organizations, such as the American Family Association, often follow the coalition's lead. At June's Texas Republican convention, for instance, the Christian Coalition was credited with organizing Tom Pauken's victory as state party chairman, even though the coalition probably had an estimated 400 active members among the 6,000 delegates.

The Christian Coalition doesn't have an explicit membership test, but as its name implies, it is for Christians and its organizing functions make clear that it is primarily for those who take the Bible literally. At a founding seminar for the New Jersey Christian Coalition last spring, organizer Clay Mankamyer told the new recruits, "There is no doctrinal statement. Just the principle that we will go by the infallible word of God. Anybody who agrees with that is welcome." The coalition and other organizations of the religious right also take positions that are clearly derived from sectarian biblical political premises. In Iowa and Texas, the Christian Coalition and other groups have gotten the GOP to endorse planks calling for the teaching of "creation science" in the public schools—an invention of fundamentalist Protestants that was meant to replace the theory of evolution. It not only has no scientific backing from biologists, but it has no religious credence outside of a few Protestant sects. . . .

···

When the Constitution was written, there were, of course, competing views of the relationship between religion and politics. Some Americans believed the state should actively encourage Protestant religious worship and observance as a means of sustaining a moral and virtuous republic. A few states, such as

Massachusetts and New Hampshire, even maintained religious tests for holding office. But Thomas Jefferson and James Madison, the two leading architects of American democracy, believed that the realm of government should be set apart from that of religion. They maintained that the basic premises of society could be deduced from religion, but could be derived more suitably from natural law and reason. Framing belief in terms of reason allowed public discussion of differing views. By contrast, framing belief and law in religious terms led inevitably to the preference of one religious group over another and to the creation of religious tests for office. More generally, fusing politics and religion could thwart democracy, which depends on reasoned debate. It could also encourage the kind of religious wars that had torn Europe apart.

Jefferson and Madison did not deny that religion played a useful role in inculcating virtue and morality. Jefferson argued that Jesus's "system of morality was the most benevolent and sublime that has been ever taught." Nevertheless, he and Madison thought religious belief would be more likely to flourish if removed from state jurisdiction. And they were right. The United States, as Reinhold Niebuhr once wrote, continues to be "at once the most secular and the most religious of Western nations."

To the consternation of many Americans, the emergence of the religious right has encouraged the trends that Madison and Jefferson feared. At the Texas Republican convention in June [1994], candidates announced their church affiliations. At the Iowa Republican convention the same month, Christian Coalition members made Christian belief a basis for backing a candidate. (Iowa Governor Terry Branstad, the Christian Coalition's Ione Dilley declared, is a politician "who does acknowledge his creator.")

In several states, religious right candidates have been turning school board races into religious contests. [In spring 1994] in a Dallas suburb Christian right candidates, facing two Jewish incumbents, emphasized their church affiliation and religious beliefs at candidate forums. Afterward, Rebecca Morris, one of the defeated incumbents, told an interviewer, "I never know how to deal with the issue 'I'm a Christian and you're not.'" Protestants and Catholics also feel the burden. Said Republican Mary Bennett of the Texas party's elections to choose delegates, "If you didn't say, 'I am a Christian and I attend a certain church,' you were excluded."

In each presidential election since 1980, religious right leaders have argued for supporting the Republicans against the Democrats on religious grounds. In 1992 Operation Rescue founder Randall Terry wrote in his newsletter that "to vote for Bill Clinton is to sin against God." Later, Reed told a conference sponsored by the Center for Ethics and Public Policy that Terry's statement "presented a harsh side of religious belief that is simply inappropriate in a political context." Reed did not say that Terry's views were inappropriate because they imposed a religious test on candidates. They were inappropriate because they were "harsh."

In building its movement, the religious right has run up against another even more formidable wall than that separating church and state. In 1989 the Gallup Poll asked people to rate whom they would like to have as neighbors. Near the bottom, well behind Catholics, Jews, blacks, Koreans, Hispanics, Vietnamese, Russians, and unmarried couples, were "religious fundamentalists." Only members of religious cults were less popular. The poll was about fundamentalists, but the result touches on what bothers many people about the religious right: the suspicion that it is a threat to privacy.

In the last thirty years the Supreme Court has claimed that the right to privacy exists under the "penumbras" of the Bill of Rights. Yet the concept has been a practical part of American life ever since a booming early-twentieth-century economy made it possible for large numbers of citizens to enjoy the kind of education and leisure—including a prolonged period of adolescence—hitherto reserved for the upper classes. This new realm of personal freedom became the basis for new kinds of consumer products, as well as sexual experimentation and novel social arrangements.

The religious right arose, however, partly in response to the trends that emerged from this freedom, and its agenda has consisted of seeking to restrict and regulate personal life. The religious right wants to prohibit abortion; allow employers to hire and fire based on a person's sexual practices; maintain criminal statutes against homosexuality and some kinds of heterosexual practices; and force television networks and stations not to show programs that it deems immoral. Jeff Fisher, the director of the Texas branch of the American Family Association, boasted to me that his group had succeeded in forcing thirteen of seventeen ABC affiliates to take the acclaimed "NYPD Blue" off the air.

While Americans certainly sympathize with some of the religious right's causes—a majority probably opposes taxpayer financing of abortions and insurance coverage of the "domestic partners" of public employees—it's no surprise that they see the movement's overall agenda as an assault on their privacy. They see in the religious right's obsession with homosexuality and soft-core pornography an unruly intolerance that flows from a repressed discomfort with any kind of sexuality. They see in its attempts to dictate television programming a desire to turn every network into Robertson's Family Channel, which intersperses the televangelist's "700 Club" with "Lassie," "Gunsmoke" and "Rin Tin Tin" reruns. . . .

✦

To see the religious right's limits, all you have to do is look at its role in the GOP. The coalition and its allies have taken over the party apparatus in some states, but they have not taken over candidate selection or won the hearts of primary or general election voters. They have yet to elect one of their own to the Senate or governor's office. They have won control of some suburban and rural school boards around the country, and also some state legislative races. That's not much of a takeover, though. And, as in San Diego, these victories often have been followed by reversals.

The movement's greatest political successes have come in Southern and border states that have a high percentage of evangelicals and that, because of their homogeneous religious population, enjoy a much closer relation locally between church and state. Suburban voters in Georgia don't share the same fear of fundamentalism as voters in Portland, Oregon, or Alexandria, Virginia.

In states where Catholics, Jews, mainline Protestants and nonbelievers make up a large percentage of the population, and where there are growing numbers of young middle-class suburbanites, the religious right has proved a divisive force. It has succeeded in taking over Republican Party organizations, but at the expense of participation by moderate voters. The right has cost Republicans dearly in Virginia, Minnesota, Washington, Oregon and California. . . .

⋞◎⋟

Some conservatives, who are uncomfortable with the religious right's quest for a Christian America, still contend that the movement has served a useful purpose by dramatizing the dissolution of the family and the decline of schools. I'd argue the contrary. Because of its reliance on religious explanations, the Christian right has most often slighted these problems. The solutions it has proffered are either harmful or irrelevant.

Take the schools. The religious right candidates I've observed have stood for the reinstitution of school prayer, the elimination or drastic modification of sex education and the introduction of creation science. These are not issues on which the future of our young rests. School prayers are either blatantly discriminatory or meaningless; sex education is, well, complicated; and creation science is bunkum. . . .

⋞◎⋟

Is today's religious right injecting a Christian spirit of compassion and selflessness into American politics? The only group that seems to elicit its compassion is the unborn; it does not display similar compassion, for instance, toward the poor or the victims of AIDS—two obvious groups for which a modern-day Christian might be expected to express concern. Robertson, who in his youth worked among the poor, now has contempt for their suffering. Asked about the welfare system, he quotes Paul's advice on how to deal with disorderly Thessalonians, "If anyone will not work, neither let him eat." And why is the Christian Coalition against community rating of insurance premiums? Reed warns that there will be "massive cross-subsidies from intact, two-parent families with children who lead *healthy* lifestyles to those who do not." Iowa coalition official Steve Sheffler, a former insurance agent, puts it more clearly: families of the healthy will have to pay higher premiums to cover AIDS patients.

It is not a question of what policy government should finally adopt. Perhaps welfare should be eliminated and community rating discouraged. Rather, it is a question of the spirit with which Americans—and Christians—should regard the poor and the terminally ill. The Christian right is, in fact, a perfect example of what happens when the founding principles of church and state are violated. What Jefferson and Madison understood . . . is that Christianity does not provide a political agenda but rather an underlying social conscience with which to approach politics. Religion plays its most constructive role precisely when church and state are separate.

When the two are fused, however, when organizations acting in the name of Christianity seek political power, then religion becomes subordinate to politics. It becomes infected with the darker egoism of group and nation; it no longer softens and counters our ungenerous impulses but clothes them in holy righteousness.

NO ←

Fred Barnes

Who Needs the Religious Right?
We All Do

Three things about the Religious Right's influence on the 1992 election and in American politics are of particular interest to me. First, a myth that grew out of the 1992 Republican Convention in Houston. Second, the surprising gains that the Religious Right has made, particularly in the media (National Public Radio presented a fair piece on efforts by the Religious Right to expand into the black and Hispanic communities). And third, the Religious Right's role in keeping alive moral issues and traditional values important to most Americans.

I was in Houston when the myth began. The Religious Right was said to have taken over the convention and to have imposed its own religious views on the Republican Party, with the goal of imposing them on the entire nation. The myth created a media consensus on the convention: that it was intolerant, mean-spirited, exclusive, judgmental, narrow-minded, or worse. When Pat Buchanan gave his speech, I happened to be sitting next to another Washington journalist who is a bellwether of press opinion. At first he loved Buchanan's speech, but two days later his view had changed entirely as had the view of many other press people. Now he felt the convention had turned into a hate-fest because of its domination by the Religious Right. That became the conventional wisdom among reporters in Houston. No, they didn't conspire to reach this conclusion, but as they gathered to trade information and gossip, the consensus emerged that the Religious Right, if not in total control of the convention, at least had a large and pernicious influence there.

The evidence? It was the speeches by Religious Right people, like Pat Buchanan (even though he has little to do with the organized Religious Right). The mainstream press pointed to these speeches more than to the issue of homosexuality and family values. Pat Robertson's speech was cited. So was Marilyn Quayle's, though she didn't dwell on religious issues but talked about feminism and women who don't work.

There were 128 speeches at the convention, only three of which could be considered religious. Just one—Robertson's, which wasn't even given during prime time—could truly be called a Religious Right speech. Yet this was enough for the press to conclude that the Religious Right had dominated the convention.

A week after the convention, a woman television producer—married, with one child—was still furious about Marilyn Quayle's speech, because she felt it attacked women who work. Here's what Mrs. Quayle, who herself has sometimes worked full-time, actually said: "I sometimes think that the liberals are always so angry because they believe the grandiose promises of the liberation movement. They are disappointed because most women do not want to be liberated from their essential natures as women. Most of us love being mothers and wives, which gives us a richness that few men and women get from professional accomplishments alone." This was hardly a broadside against women with full-time jobs. Nonetheless many women and men in the press took it that way.

In any case, the supposed domination of the GOP by the Religious Right didn't contribute heavily to George Bush's defeat in the November election. I think Bush was defeated because he signed the 1990 budget deal. Without that, he would have been re-elected. But in the media the view lingers that the convention was a critical moment that doomed Bush and his re-election chances.

The myth is not confined to the media. Spencer Abraham, executive director of the 1992 House Republican campaign organization, ran for Republican National Chairman after the election and was defeated by Haley Barbour. Abraham talked to each of the 165 members of the Republican National Committee, because they were the electorate choosing the chairman. Amazingly, he found that a majority believed the press view of what happened at the convention, even though they themselves had been there and should have known better. Abraham was regarded as the Religious Right candidate, even though he wasn't.

Religious Right Gains

My second observation about the Religious Right is the good news that the fog hovering over it is beginning to lift. The hostility toward it has begun to soften. The 1993 races for Virginia governor, lieutenant governor, and attorney general greatly affected press opinion about the Religious Right. Since Virginia is right next door to Washington, D.C., the commercials for the races were on Washington television for national reporters to see. Clearly the Democrats overkilled in their attempts to discredit the Religious Right, trying to make it an issue not only against Michael Farris, a Religious Right favorite who was running for lieutenant governor, but also against George Allen, the Republican gubernatorial candidate. The Democrats cast Allen—who won—as a patsy for Pat Robertson, which he obviously is not.

The backlash in the press, while not sympathetic, was the beginning of a recognition that the Religious Right is a legitimate bloc in the Republican coalition. I don't want to overstate this. But after talking to ten political reporters who followed the Virginia race—Christopher Matthews of the San Francisco *Examiner*,

Gloria Borger of *U.S. News,* Brit Hume of ABC, Eleanor Clift of *Newsweek,* Carl Leubsdorf of the Dallas *Morning News,* Thomas DeFrank of *Newsweek,* syndicated columnist Robert Novak, Morton Kondracke of *Roll Call,* Paul West of the Baltimore *Sun,* and John Mushek of the Boston *Globe*—I found that most agreed the Religious Right is not an evil juggernaut, as they'd previously thought, but rather is a viable element of the Republican Party. They acknowledged that during the campaign the issue of the Religious Right changed from fear of a religious takeover to the unfairness of attacks on people for holding strong religious views. The result is a more positive view of the Religious Right, and that's a gain. The Religious Right has further enhanced its legitimacy with the secular press by tackling non-religious issues, as in the Christian Coalition's decision to air TV ads critical of the Clinton health-care plan.

Moreover, there are other voices now arguing that religious views are a legitimate source of political values and should be included in the public debate. The political left doesn't accept this, insisting that religious people want to impose their views on everyone. But President Clinton dissents from that liberal view, and so does David Wilhelm, the Democratic National Chairman. When Wilhelm spoke to the Christian Coalition, he made a significant concession. He stressed that religious values are fine and legitimate as roots of political views. That's the Religious Right position. It is not the position of most Democrats.

Clinton and Wilhelm declared that people of strong faith should not be ostracized from the public square. Christians, Jews, Muslims, and members of other faiths can properly draw on spiritual teachings to guide their political views. Wilhelm has also noted, "Let us say that while religious motivation is appropriate, it is wrong to use religious authority to coerce support in the public arena."

The Religious Right's Importance

The third thing I find interesting about the Religious Right is the notion that it is driving people away from the GOP, that most Americans want a party based on serious economic and foreign policy issues, not those horrible social issues. Here the real issue is the Republican Party's strong stand against abortion. If you are part of the élite opinion stream—where it is socially unacceptable to be opposed to abortion—you'll get flak from friends and maybe your spouse for being associated with such a party.

Richard Nixon, in an interview with William Safire, gave his opinion on abortion: "The state should stay out—don't subsidize, and don't prohibit." The view that abortion should be kept out of politics is shared by many other Republican politicians. I think this shows they are ignorant as to the party's real base. They don't understand who grassroots Republicans are.

The Republican Party does not stand a chance of becoming a majority party in America or electing another president without the Religious Right. Vast numbers of Americans are alienated from the Democratic Party, yet are leery of the Republican Party. What attracts them to the GOP is not supply-side economics or hawkishness on foreign policy but serious moral and social concerns. I understand the reluctance of millions of former Democrats to become

Republicans—the thought of being a Republican makes even me wince. But the Religious Right's cluster of issues attracts many of them.

Abortion is an issue that helped George Bush in 1992 and certainly helped George Allen win the governorship of Virginia. Millions of people were also attracted to Republican candidates because they believe in a role for religion in American life. Others became sympathetic to Republicans because they care about, for instance, the injection of gay values into the mainstream of American opinion, or about moral relativism. Whether it's the kind of multiculturalism that shows up in the Rainbow Curriculum in New York or Outcomes-based Education, only the Religious Right keeps all these values issues alive. And the beneficiary is the Republican Party.

There used to be something called the New Right, but it doesn't exist anymore. Its leaders were people like Paul Weyrich (who said in 1985 that the only serious grassroots activity in the Republican Party was religiously based—which is even more true now), Richard Viguerie, and Howard Phillips. But the New Right is now gone, leaving only the Religious Rights.

⋯◈⋯

If the Religious Right is driven out of the Republican Party, I think values issues —abortion, the role of religion in public life, gay rights, and moral relativism —will all but vanish. It is religious people who keep them on the table. Their departure would cause the Republican Party's base to shrivel dramatically. Republican élites simply do not understand this. I worry when Ralph Reed says that the Christian Coalition is not going to concentrate on opposing abortion because abortion cannot be blocked; instead, they will talk about parental consent and about other important issues like tax cuts. In truth, the Religious Right needs to emphasize the issues that brought its people into politics in the first place—basically moral issues.

The Religious Rights' issues are critical politically not only for the Republican Party but for everybody. They are more important than cutting the capital-gains tax rate or aiding the Bosnian Muslims. They involve the moral upbringing of our children, the character of our citizens and our leaders, the way we regard and treat religious faith and religious believers. If American politicians do not want to grapple with these moral issues, the overarching issues of our era, then what are they in office for?

I do not always agree with the positions of the Religious Right. I am not really concerned, for instance, whether a school-prayer amendment passes. I have also disagreed with their style, although under Ralph Reed it has gotten better. But I give them credit for forcing things onto the national agenda that are critical to the Republican Party and to the rest of us.

In 1989, when Ronald Reagan returned to California on Air Force One, he was asked what his greatest regret was after eight years as president. He said he regretted that he hadn't done more to restrict or end abortion in this country. If an entire party abandons that issue and other moral concerns and ostracizes from the party the people who want to raise those concerns, the regret will ultimately be felt by the entire nation.

POSTSCRIPT

Does the Religious Right Threaten American Freedoms?

One way to examine the potential weaknesses of a specific philosophy or theology is to ask what would happen if the principles on which it is based were taken to an extreme. If the philosophical underpinnings of the two views represented in this issue were taken to the extreme, either to the radical right or the extreme left, the result could be a political/religious relationship mirroring the Taliban in Afghanistan or the atheistic government of the former Soviet Union. Few would wish to see such forms of government in America. While Judis and Barnes have articulated their philosophical differences with regard to the Religious Right, neither of their arguments is extreme, but they serve as good introductions to the debate. Perhaps the continuing debate between these two perspectives is a part of what allows for the balanced strength of America's democracy.

Individuals and groups on both sides of the controversy over the Religious Right continue to debate these important issues. People for the American Way and the American Civil Liberties Union (ACLU) are examples of groups who closely monitor the work of the Religious Right. The Christian Coalition, Eagle Forum, and the American Family Association are examples of groups attempting to ensure that morality and religion continue to be a part of the debate in America.

It is apparent that religion will likely continue to be a part of the fabric of American culture. Perhaps there is much to understand and to learn from the religious right, left, and the moderates as well.

Suggested Readings

C. Colson and E. S. Vaughn, *Kingdoms in Conflict* (Zondervan, 1989).

W. Martin, *With God on Our Side: The Rise of the Religious Right in America* (Broadway Books, 1997).

R. C. Liebman, ed., *New Christian Right: Mobilization and Legitimation* (Aldine de Gruyter, 1983).

J. Wallis, *Who Speaks for God? An Alternative to the Religious Right—A New Politics of Compassion, Community, and Civility* (Delacorte Press, 1996).

On the Internet ...

The Church of Jesus Christ of Latter-day Saints

The official Web site of The Church of Jesus Christ of Latter-day Saints contains a summary of the church's basic beliefs as well as links to audio scripture files and information on publications.

http://www.lds.org

The Internet Public Library

The Internet Public Library Web site provides search engines for denominational themes and an index allowing the user to search for issues by religion.

http://www.ipl.org/ref/RR/static/hum80.10.00.html

Finding God in Cyberspace: A Guide to Religious Studies Resources on the Internet

Finding God in Cyberspace: A Guide to Religious Studies Resources on the Internet is a Web site that offers links to various primary Internet sources on a number of different religions. Links are provided to explore sites on Christianity, Buddhism, Judaism, and more.

http://www.fontbonne.edu/libserv/fgic/relig.htm

PART 6

Denominational Issues

*T*he study of less familiar religious movements is of particular interest today. A more pluralistic society leads to increasing contact between different faiths. Better relationships will always come when all parties have well-rounded views of the others.

- Is Mormonism Christian?

ISSUE 17

Is Mormonism Christian?

YES: Daniel K. Judd, from "Is The Church of Jesus Christ of Latter-day Saints (Mormonism) a Christian Religion?" An Original Essay Written for This Volume (2002)

NO: Craig L. Blomberg, from "Is Mormonism Christian?" in Francis J. Beckwith, Carl Mosser, and Paul Owen, eds., *The New Mormon Challenge: Responding to the Latest Defenses of a Fast-Growing Movement* (Zondervan, 2002)

ISSUE SUMMARY

YES: Daniel K. Judd, professor of ancient Scripture at Brigham Young University in Provo, Utah, reasons why The Church of Jesus Christ of Latter-day Saints (LDS) should be considered a Christian religion. He states that because the LDS Church bases its theology and practice on Jesus Christ (particularly his atonement and resurrection), it should be considered a Christian Church even though its members do not accept many of the creeds of traditional Christendom.

NO: Craig L. Blomberg, New Testament professor at the Denver Seminary in Denver, Colorado, states that Mormons are not Christian either as a church or as individuals. He bases his statement on what he interprets as inconsistencies between The Church of Jesus Christ of Latter-day Saints and the Christian Church as represented in the Bible and in early Christian creeds.

T he Church of Jesus Christ of Latter-day Saints, referred to by some as the Mormon Church, is one of the fastest growing religions in the world today. Rodney Stark, noted professor of sociology at the University of Washington in Seattle, Washington, has identified the LDS Church as the first new "world religion" to be established in 1,300 years, predicting that The Church of Jesus Christ of Latter-day Saints, the Mormons, "will soon achieve a worldwide following comparable to that of Islam, Buddhism, Christianity, Hinduism, and the other dominant world faiths." With a membership presently over 11 million, Stark projects that by the year 2080 membership in the LDS Church could reach 267,452,000. With membership increasing throughout the world, The

Church of Jesus Christ of Latter-day Saints is perceived by some as a strengthening influence in a troubled world, while others interpret the church's growth as a threat. One of the most popular debates in the religious world concerning the Latter-day Saints is whether the church is, as it professes to be, a Christian religion.

In the following selection, Daniel K. Judd presents arguments to support the notion that the LDS Church is a legitimate Christian religion. Judd describes reasons why many do not accept the Latter-day Saints as Christians, such as (1) differences over the definition of Christianity, (2) differences over doctrine, (3) disagreement over what is considered canonized Scripture, and (4) differences over Latter-day Saints not being a part of the historical Christian tradition.

Judd reasons that while Latter-day Saints may not believe and worship exactly in the same way as some other Christians, they do share a common conviction of Jesus Christ as the Son of God and Savior of the world, and a belief that besides Christ, there is "no other name given nor any other way nor means whereby salvation can come unto the children of men" (The Book of Mormon: Another Testament of Jesus Christ, Mosiah 3:17).

Craig L. Blomberg argues against the Latter-day Saint religion being included in the family of Christian religions. He cannot accept that "either Mormonism as a whole or any individual, based solely on his or her affirmation of the totality of LDS doctrine, deserves the label 'Christian' in any standard or helpful sense of the word." Blomberg bases this opinion on arguments that (1) the LDS Church is neither Roman Catholic, Protestant, nor Eastern Orthodox and therefore does not fit the definition of historic Christianity; (2) the LDS teaching of an apostasy from and a restoration of early Christianity are not supported in Scripture; (3) LDS beliefs were borrowed from Alexander Campbell and Masonic teachings of the early 1800s; and (4) statements of early LDS leaders cannot be reconciled with traditional Christian teachings. Blomberg reasons that belief in Christ alone does not make one a Christian—one must also accept the teachings of the church as represented in Scripture and in the early creeds of Christendom.

Daniel K. Judd

Is The Church of Jesus Christ of Latter-day Saints (Mormonism) a Christian Religion?

The title of this article poses a question that is the subject of some debate among scholars and lay people in the religious community. Many Latter-day Saints have a difficult time understanding why such a question would even be asked—believing the answer to be obvious in the affirmative. Others, while acknowledging the central role of Jesus Christ in Latter-day Saint theology, believe The Church of Jesus Christ of Latter-day Saints to be a non-Christian religion. Commenting on this controversy, President Gordon B. Hinckley, leader of the 11 million Latter-day Saints worldwide, recently stated:

> As a Church we have critics, many of them. They say we do not believe in the traditional Christ of Christianity. *There is some substance to what they say.* Our faith, our knowledge is not based on ancient tradition, the creeds which came of a finite understanding and out of the almost infinite discussions of men trying to arrive at a definition of the risen Christ. Our faith, our knowledge comes of the witness of a prophet [Joseph Smith, Jr.] in this dispensation who saw before him the great God of the universe and His Beloved Son, the resurrected Lord Jesus Christ. They spoke to him. He spoke with Them.... It is out of that knowledge, rooted deep in the soil of modern revelation, that we, in the words of Nephi, "talk of Christ, we rejoice in Christ, we preach of Christ, we prophesy of Christ, and we write according to our prophecies, that [we and] our children may know to what source [we] may look for a remission of [our] sins." (2 Nephi 25:26)[1]

President Hinckley acknowledges the fact that Latter-day Saints do not base their faith in Christ on the creeds, councils, customs, and teachings of fourth- and fifth-century Christianity. The Latter-day Saint doctrine of Christ is grounded in the teachings of Jesus and the Apostles as well as modern-day teachings beginning with the appearance of God the Father and His Son Jesus Christ to the prophet Joseph Smith in 1820.

The Church of Jesus Christ of Latter-day Saints is neither Catholic nor Protestant but is believed by its membership to be the *restoration* of the Savior's original church; the ecclesiastical body that He established when He was upon the earth during His mortal ministry. This restoration was necessary because of an *apostasy* from truth that occurred after the deaths of Jesus and the early apostles. The title "saints" is used today to describe the church membership individually and collectively just as the term was utilized in New Testament times (see 1 Corinthians 1:2). While Latter-day Saints recognize and affirm that their religion differs in many ways from traditional Christianity, they believe that because their faith is centered in Jesus Christ and His teachings, theirs is indeed a Christian religion.

Notwithstanding the controversy over whether the LDS Church is a Christian religion, Latter-day Saints believe in allowing and even encouraging others not of their faith to worship "how, where, or what they may."[2] The following statement from British scholar and member of the Anglican Church C. S. Lewis is consistent with the LDS perspective on judging other religions or individuals with respect to their Christianity:

> It is not for us to say who, in the deepest sense, is or is not close to the spirit of Christ. We do not see into men's hearts. We cannot judge, and are indeed forbidden to judge. It would be wicked arrogance for us to say that any man is, or is not, a Christian in this refined sense.... When a man who accepts the Christian doctrine lives unworthy of it, it is much clearer to say he is a bad Christian than to say he is not a Christian.[3]

Latter-day Saints are instructed to "contend against no church, save it be the church of the devil" (Doctrine and Covenants 18:20). The church has often taken stands against doctrines, policies, and practices it deems unholy, but the church does not publish material critical of other religions.

While LDS theology has been the subject of inaccurate and often polemic anti-Mormon publications for most of the church's history, traditional Christian scholars have recently begun to take a serious and more honest look at LDS teachings. In Francis J. Beckwith, Carl Mosser, and Paul Owen, eds., *The New Mormon Challenge: Responding to the Latest Defenses of a Fast-Growing Movement* (Zondervan, 2002), Craig L. Blomberg, professor of New Testament at the Denver Seminary, considers the question, "Is Mormonism Christian?" Professor Blomberg provides a straightforward review of the arguments of some theologians who believe that Latter-day Saints are not Christian, and he concludes with the following statement:

> I cannot... affirm with integrity that either Mormonism as a whole or any individual, based solely on his or her affirmation of the totality of LDS doctrine deserves the label "Christian" in any standard or helpful sense of the word.[4]

Professor Blomberg's justifications for excluding the LDS Church from the Christian community are similar to other criticisms of the LDS Church. Some of the most noteworthy have been summarized by professor Stephen E. Robinson as follows:

- exclusion by *definition*,
- exclusion by *misrepresentation*,
- exclusion by *ad hominem* (name calling),

- exclusion by *history*,
- *canonical* exclusion, and
- *doctrinal* exclusion.[5]

The primary purposes of this article are to (1) briefly respond to these major objections raised by Christian scholars such as Professor Blomberg; (2) provide evidence from Scripture and doctrinal teachings of church leaders that The Church of Jesus Christ of Latter-day Saints is indeed a Christian religion, though it does not necessarily fit every criterion established by the Christian clergy, creeds, and scholars; and (3) demonstrate in a general way that the central mission of the LDS Church is to assist every nation, kindred, tongue, and people to "come unto Christ, and be perfected in him" (Moroni 10:32).

Inclusion by Definition

The terms *Christian* or *Christianity* occur three times in the New Testament (Acts 11:26, 26:28, and 1 Peter 4:16). In each scriptural occurrence these terms refer to those who are followers of Jesus Christ. The *Oxford English Dictionary* describes a Christian as "one who exhibits the spirit, and follows the precepts and example, of Christ; a believer in Christ who is characterized by genuine piety." *The Book of Mormon: Another Testament of Jesus Christ* also provides a definition of what it means to be a Christian:

> And those who did belong to the church were faithful; yea, all those who were true believers in Christ took upon them, gladly, the name of Christ, or Christians as they were called, because of their belief in Christ who should come. (Alma 46:15)

Even though this reference describes a group of people who inhabited the ancient American continent, the application continues to hold true for Latter-day Saints today. When individuals are baptized into The Church of Jesus Christ of Latter-day Saints, they make covenants with God to "take upon them the name of [his] Son [Jesus Christ], and to always remember him and keep his commandments" (Doctrine and Covenants 20:77, see also the Book of Mormon, Moroni 4:3). If one can accept the definitions given in the New Testament, the *Oxford English Dictionary*, and the Book of Mormon, The Church of Jesus Christ of Latter-day Saints is, by definition, a Christian religion.

Inclusion by Name

In the past, some of the confusion over whether The Church of Jesus Christ of Latter-day Saints is a Christian religion has been a matter of misnaming. The church has been known by many of those not of the LDS faith as "the Mormon Church," instead of The Church of Jesus Christ of Latter-day Saints. Latter-day Saints are often referred to as "Mormons," and the church's doctrines and practices are sometimes referred to as "Mormonism." Church members are not generally offended by being identified by such terms, but they prefer to have their church identified as The Church of Jesus Christ of Latter-day Saints and to be known as Latter-day Saints (LDS).

In the Doctrine and Covenants, a collection of writings that Latter-day Saints accept as modern scripture, the Lord revealed to the first leader of the church, Joseph Smith, Jr., what the name of the church was to be: "Thus shall my church be called in the last days, even The Church of Jesus Christ of Latter-day Saints" (Doctrine and Covenants 115:4). The labels "Mormon," "Mormonite," and "Mormon Church" were first given to members of the LDS Church by those not of their faith. "Mormon" is actually the name of an ancient American prophet (much like Isaiah or Paul) whose writings are found in the Book of Mormon: Another Testament of Jesus Christ—an additional record viewed as scripture by Latter-day Saints. The central account in the Book of Mormon is the description of Jesus Christ's appearance to the ancient inhabitants of the Americas soon after His death and resurrection in Jerusalem. Latter-day Saints believe that the "other sheep" (KJV, John 10:16) spoken of by Jesus Christ in the Gospel of John includes the ancient American inhabitants. During Jesus' ministry in the Americas, He described His church as bearing His name and being founded upon His gospel:

> And how be it my church save it be called in my name? For if a church be called in Moses' name then it be Moses' church; or if it be called in the name of a man then it be the church of a man; but if it be called in my name then it is my church, if it so be that they are built upon my gospel. (3 Nephi 27:8)

Inclusion by Doctrine

One of the main points of disagreement between those who believe The Church of Jesus Christ of Latter-day Saints to be a Christian religion and those who do not has more to do with the doctrine of the church than with the definition of what it means to be a Christian. In the New Testament we read the words of Jesus Christ warning the people that the use of His name alone is not sufficient for salvation:

> Not every one that saith unto me, Lord, Lord, shall enter into the kingdom of heaven; but he that doeth the will of my Father which is in heaven. Many will say to me in that day, Lord, Lord, have we not prophesied in thy name? and in thy name have cast out devils? and in thy name done many wonderful works? And then will I profess unto them, I never knew you: depart from me, ye that work iniquity. (KJV Matthew 7:22–23)

These verses of Scripture introduce an area where Latter-day Saint and traditional Christian theology encounter some differences—the place of *good works* in an individual's salvation. One of the thirteen Articles of Faith, an official statement of Latter-day Saint doctrine, states: "We believe that through the Atonement of Christ, all mankind may be saved, by obedience to the laws and ordinances of the Gospel."[6] From an LDS perspective, genuine acceptance of Christ includes living a righteous life and submitting to the ordinances of salvation. Some Christians believe that this acknowledgment of the importance of good works is a blasphemous rejection of the grace of Christ. Latter-day Saints assert that the inclusion of good works in their theology is simply an expression of their belief in Jesus Christ and a desire to follow Him. Consider the following teaching from the Book of Mormon: "For we labor diligently to write, to persuade our children, and also our brethren, to believe in Christ, and to be reconciled to God; for we know that it is by grace that we are saved, after all we can do" (2 Nephi 25:23). This verse acknowledges the centrality of the grace of Christ but also includes the importance of doing our part as well. Elsewhere in the Book of Mormon the phrase "all we can do" is identified:

> And now behold, my brethren, since it has been *all that we could do,* (as we were the most lost of all mankind) to *repent* of all our sins and the many murders which we have committed, and to get God to take them away from our hearts, for it was *all we could do to repent* sufficiently before God that he would take away our stain. (Alma 24:11, italics added)

The Latter-day Saint doctrine concerning the necessity of repentance is similar to what many traditional Christian scholars espouse, including John F. MacArthur and the noted H. A. Ironside:

> Shallow preaching does not grapple with the terrible fact of man's sinfulness and guilt... we have myriads of glib-tongued professors today who give no evidence of regeneration [repentance] whatever. Prating of salvation by grace, they manifest no grace in their lives. Loudly declaring they are justified by faith alone, they fail to remember that "faith without works is dead." (KJV, James 2:20)[7]

Latter-day Saint theology embraces the doctrine that repentance—a change of heart, mind, and behavior—is necessary but not sufficient, for it is only through Jesus Christ that humankind may be granted salvation. Latter-day Saints believe that there is "no other name given nor any other way nor means whereby salvation can come unto the children of men, only in and through the name of Christ, the Lord Omnipotent" (Mosiah 3:17).

This same debate over the relationship of grace and works is also found in the history of the relationship between the Catholic and Protestant Churches. The Catholic Church (like the LDS Church) speaks of the importance of the sacraments while many Protestant denominations do not. Protestants generally accept Catholics as Christians, so why not Latter-day Saints? C. S. Lewis believed both faith and works play an important part in salvation:

> Christians have often disputed as to whether what leads the Christian home is good actions, or Faith in Christ. I have no right really to speak on such a difficult question, but it does seem to me like asking which blade in a pair of scissors is most necessary.[8]

The Doctrine of Deification

Some critics of the LDS Church argue that while the church teaches of Christ, there are other peripheral doctrines unique to the LDS Church that place it beyond the boundaries of Christendom. One such teaching is the doctrine of deification. While this doctrine is not found in the Book of Mormon or the other scriptures of the restoration, some Latter-day Saint prophets have taught that God was once mortal and that men and women can eventually become gods. Lorenzo Snow, fifth president of the LDS Church, once stated: "As man now is, God once was; as God now is, man may be."[9] While this doctrine may initially surprise the reader, consider the logic of such a teaching—was there ever a loving father who did not want his children to have all that is good? Surprising to some, the doctrine of deification is found in the New Testament (see Philippians 2:6–10 and John 10:33–42), is found throughout the writings of the early Christian fathers, and is espoused by more recent Christian theologians, as well. The second-century Christian leader Irenaeus taught, "If the Word [Christ] became man, It was so men may become gods." Consider the following quotation from C. S. Lewis:

> The command *Be ye perfect* is not idealistic gas. Nor is it a command to do the impossible. He is going to make us into creatures that can obey that command. He said (in the Bible) that we were "gods" and He is going to make good His words. If we let Him—for we can prevent Him, if we choose— He will make the feeblest and filthiest of us into a god or goddess, dazzling, radiant, immortal creature, pulsating all through with such energy and joy and wisdom and love as we cannot now imagine, a bright stainless mirror which reflects back to God perfectly (though, of course, on a smaller scale) His own boundless power and delight and goodness. The process will be long and in parts very painful; but that is what we are in for. Nothing less. He meant what He said.[10]

Latter-day Saint theology teaches that while men and women may indeed become as God is, He will always be our God and the only object of our worship. Like the Apostle Paul: "For though there be that are called gods, whether in heaven or in earth, (as there be gods many, and lords many,) But to us *there is but* one God, the Father, of whom *are* all things, and we in him; and one Lord Jesus Christ, by whom *are* all things, and we by him" (KJV, 1 Corinthians 8:5–6).

Many, if not all, Christian Churches differ on several points of doctrine as well as on policy and practice. Latter-day Saints readily acknowledge doctrinal differences with other Christian religions, but these differences are not sufficient to exclude The Church of Jesus Christ of Latter-day Saints from recognition as a Christian religion.

Space will not permit the discussion of what some consider to be other controversial Latter-day Saint doctrines and myths, but the reader can be assured that faithful members of The Church of Jesus Christ of Latter-day Saints do not practice plural marriage, persons of all races and ethnicities can be members and hold the priesthood, and Latter-day Saint men and women are considered equal partners in the marital relationship. Furthermore, Latter-day Saints do not worship Joseph Smith, Jr., nor have they replaced the Bible with one of their own.

Inclusion by Canon

Another common objection raised by some who do not accept The Church of Jesus Christ of Latter-day Saints as a Christian religion pertains to the Book of Mormon: Another Testament of Jesus Christ. The argument is that because members of the LDS Church have additional scripture outside the Christian Bible, their church cannot be Christian. One of the concluding verses of the

New Testament is often cited as scriptural authority for outlawing the Book of Mormon and other scripture of the LDS Church:

> For I testify unto every man that heareth the words of the prophecy of this book, If any man shall add unto these things, God shall add unto him the plagues that are written in this book. (KJV, Revelation 22:18)

This verse is obviously referring specifically to the Book of Revelation and not the entire Bible. Evidence for this conclusion is found in Deuteronomy, the fifth book of the Hebrew Bible:

> Now therefore hearken, O Israel, unto the statutes and unto the judgments, which I teach you, for to do them, that ye may live, and go in and possess the land which the Lord God of your fathers giveth you. *Ye shall not add unto the word which I command you, neither shall ye diminish ought from it,* that ye may keep the commandments of the Lord your God which I command you. (Deuteronomy 4:1–2, italics added)

If this verse were interpreted literally, then anything written after the fourth chapter of Deuteronomy would not qualify as Scripture. It is apparent that this verse, like its New Testament counterpart in the Book of Revelation, refers to the specific words given and not to the entire canon of Scripture.

There also exists much uncertainty about the historical sequence of the various New Testament writings. Many New Testament scholars would agree that the Book of Revelation may not have been the last book written of the New Testament writings.[11]

Latter-day Saints "believe the Bible to be the word of God as far as it is translated correctly."[12] They also believe that God's word and direction have not been limited to people having lived in lands of the Bible, but have also been given to people in other lands as well. Just as there were prophets among the ancient inhabitants of Israel such as Abraham, Isaiah, and Jeremiah, there were also prophets in the ancient Americas leading their people and recording scripture, such as Nephi, Alma, and Mormon. Latter-day Saints believe the Book of Mormon to be a second witness (the Christian Bible being the first) of God's dealings with His children as well as a source of scripture that restores "many plain and precious things taken away from the book [Christian Bible], which is the book of the Lamb of God" (1 Nephi 13:28). Above all else, the central purpose of the Book of Mormon, the "convincing of the Jew and Gentile that Jesus is the Christ" (Book of Mormon title page), stands as canonical evidence that The Church of Jesus Christ of Latter-day Saints is a Christian religion.

Inclusion by History

Because The Church of Jesus Christ of Latter-day Saints was not formally organized until April 6, 1830, it has not been a part of the historical development of Christianity. Some critics of the church believe that because LDS theology has not developed from the various councils, creeds, customs, and teachings of the early Christian leaders, then it cannot be truly Christian.

As noted earlier, The Church of Jesus Christ of Latter-day Saints is neither Catholic nor Protestant but is the *restored* Church of Jesus Christ. Latter-day

Saints believe that after the deaths of Jesus and the New Testament Apostles, the church fell into apostasy. While many of the doctrines and practices taught by Jesus and the early apostles continued, the authority of God was taken from the earth. This apostasy was foretold by many prophets and apostles in both the Hebrew Bible and the New Testament. Note the following examples of such prophecies from the writings of the prophet Amos and the apostle Paul:

> Behold, the days come, saith the Lord GOD, that I will send a famine in the land, not a famine of bread, nor a thirst for water, but of hearing the words of the LORD: And they shall wander from sea to sea, and from the north even to the east, they shall run to and fro to seek the word of the LORD, and shall not find *it*. (KJV, Amos 8:11–12)
>
> Let no man deceive you by any means: for *that day* [the Second Coming of Jesus Christ] *shall not come*, except there come a falling away first, and that man of sin be revealed, the son of perdition. (KJV, 2 Thessalonians 2:3)

The Church of Jesus Christ of Latter-day Saints is revered by its membership as the Lord's authorized church upon the earth, but LDS theology is neither pluralistic nor exclusivistic. Latter-day prophets have taught that God has revealed and continues to reveal truth to many people of many different religious and philosophical perspectives:

> The great religious leaders of the world such as Mohammed, Confucius, and the Reformers, as well as philosophers including Socrates, Plato, and others, received a portion of God's light. Moral truths were given them by God to enlighten whole nations and to bring a higher level of understanding to individuals.
>
> The Hebrew prophets prepared the way for the coming of Jesus Christ, the promised Messiah, who should provide salvation for all mankind who believed in the gospel. Consistent with these truths, we believe that God has given and will give to all peoples sufficient knowledge to help them on their way to eternal salvation, either in this life or in the life to come.[13]

Latter-day Saints acknowledge the great truth that is found and the great good that is done in other religions. President Hinckley has taught that the essence of the church's missionary work is to help people "add to" the truth they already have:

> Let me say that we appreciate the truth in all churches and the good which they do. We say to the people, in effect, you bring with you all the good that you have, and then let us see if we can add to it. That is the spirit of this work. That is the essence of our missionary program.[14]

Conclusion

Years ago I was given a publication that described The Church of Jesus Christ of Latter-day Saints as not only a non-Christian religion, but also as a "cult." The author of the pamphlet, Walter Martin, provided a list of what he termed as the "characteristics of cults"[15] and argued that Latter-day Saints fit his criteria. The Church of Jesus Christ of Latter-day Saints appears to fit the author's criteria for a "cult," but ironically, so does another church of a different time, the church of Jesus Christ of former day saints—the church Jesus established when He was upon the earth. The following list contains Walter Martin's "characteristics of cults," and a description of how The Church of Jesus Christ of Latter-day Saints and the church in the days of Jesus both fit the criteria:

- "Cults are usually started by strong and dynamic leaders." Joseph Smith, Jr. was indeed a strong and dynamic leader, as was Peter, Paul, and, above all else, the Savior Himself.
- "All cults possess some scripture that is either added to or which replaces the Bible." The Book of Mormon is additional scripture, but so were the New Testament Epistles considered "additions" to the Hebrew Bible.
- "Rigid standards for membership." Latter-day Saints are invited to not smoke tobacco or drink alcohol and are asked to pay a 10-percent tithe, etc. Jesus taught, "Ye have heard that it was said by them of old time, Thou shalt not commit adultery: But I say unto you, That whosoever looketh on a woman to lust after her hath committed adultery with her already in his heart" (Matthew 5:27–28). Jesus invited His followers to live by a higher law.
- "Cultists often become members of one cult after membership in one or more other cults." Many members of the LDS Church are converts to the Church of Jesus Christ, just as some of John the Baptist's former followers were converts in the Savior's day (see John 1:35–37).
- "Spend much of their time evangelizing new converts." The LDS Church has several hundred thousand converts each year and maintains a force of 60,000 young missionaries serving in 333 missions throughout the world. Jesus taught the disciples of His day, "Go ye therefore, and teach all nations, baptizing them in the name of the Father, and of the Son, and of the Holy Ghost" (Matthew 28:19–20).
- "Leaders . . . are not professional clergyman." The LDS Church does not have an academically trained clergy—they have a lay leadership. The early apostles Peter and John, "were unlearned and ignorant men" (Acts 4:13). Peter, James, and John were fishermen. Jesus was a carpenter.
- "A system of doctrine and practice which is in some state of flux." The LDS Church formally discontinued the practice of plural marriage in 1890. During the time of Jesus, the gospel was taught only to Israelites (see Matthew 15:22–24). After Jesus had been crucified, the policy changed when Peter was given the revelation from God to take the gospel to the Gentiles (see Acts chapter 10).
- "All cults believe that there is continual . . . communication from God." Latter-day Saints do believe that God continues to communicate to His children today. God has always communicated His will through His prophets (see Amos 3:7, Numbers 12:6, and Acts 10).
- "Cults claim to have truth not available to any other groups or individuals." The LDS Church teaches that it is the Lord's authorized church, but membership is available to anyone who is willing to genuinely accept the invitation to follow Jesus Christ. Jesus taught, "I am the way,

the truth, and the life: no man cometh unto the Father, but by me" (John 14:6). The Jews saw Jesus as a threat.

- "Cultic Vocabulary." As with any organization, the LDS Church has a vocabulary that is unique, i.e., *stake centers* (churches), *MTC* (Missionary Training Center), *baptism for the dead,* etc. First-century Christianity introduced such terms as *Millennium, Second Coming, baptism, Holy Ghost,* etc. Any organization, true or untrue, will possess a distinctive vocabulary.

From this author's perspective, The Church of Jesus Christ of Latter-day Saints is indeed a Christian religion. While arguments exist on both sides of the debate, it remains for the reader, with God's help, to make his or her own decision. While this article is not an official representation of the doctrine or policies of The Church of Jesus Christ of Latter-day Saints, the Book of Mormon: Another Testament of Jesus Christ, is. The Book of Mormon prophet Moroni provided the following regarding how to know of the truthfulness of the Book of Mormon, and, by implication, how to know if The Church of Jesus Christ of Latter-day Saints is indeed a Christian religion:

And when ye shall receive these things, I would exhort you that ye would ask God, the Eternal Father, in the name of Christ, if these things are not true; and if ye shall ask with a sincere heart, with real intent, having faith in Christ, he will manifest the truth of it unto you, by the power of the Holy Ghost. And by the power of the Holy Ghost ye may know the truth of all things. (Moroni 10:4–5)

References

1. President Gordon B. Hinckley, *Ensign,* May 2002, p. 90 (italics added).
2. Eleventh Article of Faith, found in *The Pearl of Great Price.*
3. C. S. Lewis, *Mere Christianity,* New York: Scribner (Simon & Schuster), p. xi.
4. Craig L. Blomberg (2002). "Is Mormonism Christian?" In C. Moser (ed.), *The New Mormon Challenge: Responding to the Latest Defenses of a Fast Growing Movement,* Grand Rapids: Zondervan, p. 331.
5. See Stephen E. Robinson, *Are Mormons Christians?* Salt Lake City: Bookcraft, 1991, 133 pages.
6. Third Article of Faith, found in *The Pearl of Great Price.*
7. H. A. Ironside, as cited in John F. MacArthur, *The Gospel According to Jesus,* Grand Rapids: Zondervan, 1994, p. 176.
8. C. S. Lewis, *Mere Christianity,* New York: Collier Books, Macmillan Publishing, 1952, p. 115.
9. Eliza R. Snow, *Biography and Family Record of Lorenzo Snow,* Salt Lake City: Deseret News, 1884, pp. 46–47.
10. C. S. Lewis, *Mere Christianity,* New York: Scribner (Simon & Schuster), p. 160.

11. See Feine, Behm, and Kummel, *Introduction to the New Testament,* Abingdon, 1966.
12. Eighth Article of Faith, found in *The Pearl of Great Price.*
13. First Presidency, 15 Feb. 1978, as found in General Conference Address by Elder James E. Faust, *Ensign,* May 1980, p. 12.
14. President Gordon B. Hinckley, *Ensign,* Aug. 1998, p. 72.
15. Walter Martin, *The New Cults,* Ventura (Ca.): Regal Books, 1980, pp. 17–21.

NO

Craig L. Blomberg

Is Mormonism Christian?

All Scripture quotations, unless otherwise indicated, are taken from the *Holy Bible: New International Version®.* NIV®.

With absolute incredulity Mormons often hear or read the charge that their faith is not Christian. How could it not be Christian? After all, isn't the very name of Jesus Christ in the name of their church—the Church of *Jesus Christ* of Latter-day Saints [LDS]? Isn't their Book of Mormon subtitled "Another Testament of *Jesus Christ*"? Is not the apex of its story line a record of an appearance of the resurrected Christ to the peoples inhabiting the New World? And is not the purpose of the Book of Mormon as well as the LDS Church's extensive missionary program to encourage and provide opportunity for people everywhere to "come unto Christ" (Jacob 1:7)? Moreover, Latter-day Saints worship Christ as the divine Son of God, the Messiah of Israel, and the Savior of the world. They believe that he suffered as the atonement for sin, that he bodily rose from the dead, and that he will one day return, as the New Testament teaches, to set up his kingdom on earth.

Given these and other doctrinal overlaps with historic Christianity, the average Mormon is mystified as to how any objective, rational person could cast doubt on Mormonism's Christian character. Besides, the Latter-day Saint thinks, if Mormonism is not Christian, then what is it? It is not Jewish, Islamic, Hindu, Buddhist, or the offshoot of any other world religion. Nothing is left besides "Christian." People who deny this obvious conclusion must be either hopelessly deceived or willfully dishonest.

The average evangelical Christian's perception of the Latter-day Saints, by contrast, is quite different. They have usually been taught to consider Mormonism a "cult," lumped together with as wide-ranging religious phenomena as the Jehovah's Witnesses, Transcendental Meditation, and the Branch Davidians. The "cults," in turn, are often combined with the occult, so that many evangelicals have some vaguely defined fear that it could be personally harmful to associate with Latter-day Saints, even as friends, lest something overtly satanic befall them. Not only are Mormons non-Christians in their minds, but for some, it seems that Mormons should not even receive the love and friendship Jesus commands his disciples to exhibit even to their enemies (e.g., Luke

From Craig L. Blomberg, "Is Mormonism Christian?" in Francis J. Beckwith, Carl Mosser, and Paul Owen, eds., *The New Mormon Challenge: Responding to the Latest Defenses of a Fast-Growing Movement* (Zondervan, 2002). Copyright © 2002 by Francis J. Beckwith, Carl Mosser, and Paul Owen. Reprinted by permission of Zondervan. Notes omitted.

6:27). Instead, they are shunned and at times even vilified. "Speaking the truth in love" (Eph 4:15) is thus often sacrificed by both sides in the debate.

It is thus with considerable trepidation that I write this essay. In a previous work dialoguing with Mormonism, I explicitly wrote that the book did "not intend to address the question of whether Evangelicals and Mormons are both, in certain instances, bona fide Christians, however worthwhile that issue might be to discuss." That did not stop people in both camps, however, from falsely claiming that I was indeed implying Mormonism to be Christian—some of them eventually admitting that they had not bothered to read the book in its entirety, including my disclaimer. To tackle this question directly now runs the risk of alienating everyone I did not previously alienate! I fear that my LDS friends will now accuse me of anti-Mormonism, no matter how courteous and objective I try to be. And many evangelicals may complain that I am too soft and gracious in my critique. But Ephesians 4:15 remains in my Bible, so I must proceed and hope for the best.

Uses of the Term *Christian* With Respect to a Religious Movement

Historic Christianity?

To address the question "Is Mormonism Christian?" obviously requires a New Testament definition of *Christian*. The Greek counterpart *Christianos* occurs only three times in the New Testament (Acts 11:26; 26:28; and 1 Pet 4:16), each time in a context of "outsiders" seeking a label for the fledgling Jesus movement. No formal definition of the term ever appears in the Bible. Probably the most common way the term is used in contemporary English is to denote a person who is a member of an Orthodox, Catholic, or Protestant church, the three historic divisions of the faith over the centuries of the church's existence. Thus the *World Book Encyclopedia* article on "Christianity" begins as follows: "Christianity is the religion based on the life and teachings of Jesus Christ. Most followers of Christianity, called Christians, are members of one of three major groups—Roman Catholic, Protestant, or Eastern Orthodox." Based on this definition, Mormonism is clearly not Christian, nor has it ever claimed to be so.

Indeed, the uniquely Mormon scriptures declare that all of Christendom after the apostolic age prior to 1830 was "a church which is most abominable above all other churches," whose founder is the devil (1 Nephi 13:5-6). In Doctrine and Covenants 29:21, that "great and abominable church" is called the "whore of all the earth." Joseph Smith, we are told, was commanded not to join any existing Christian denomination, "for they were all wrong," "all their creeds were an abomination in [God's] sight," their "professors were all corrupt," and their religious worship all a hypocritical pretense (Joseph Smith—History 2:19).

Restored Christianity?

Instead, the Latter-day Saints claim that their church is the restoration of the original Christianity of Jesus and the apostles. The *Encyclopedia of Mormonism* puts it this way:

> The Church of Jesus Christ of Latter-day Saints does not see itself as one Christian denomination among many, but rather as God's latter-day restoration of the fulness of Christian faith and practice. Thus, from its earliest days LDS Christians sought to distinguish themselves from Christians of other traditions. Other forms of Christianity, while bearing much truth and doing much good under the guidance of the Holy Spirit, are viewed as incomplete, lacking the authority of the priesthood of God, the temple ordinances, the comprehensive understanding of the plan of salvation, and the nonparadoxical understanding of the Godhead.

In order to support this claim, Mormons argue that the original church underwent a great apostasy as Jesus' apostles died off, produced in large measure by the corrupting influences of Hellenistic philosophy as the gospel traveled increasingly into non-Jewish territory. Thus, the major doctrinal developments of the second through sixth centuries of Christianity, culminating in the various creeds and councils, cannot be seen as the logical outworking of New Testament Christianity but are aberrant deviations from the faith. Not until the revelation given to Joseph Smith was true Christianity ever again restored.

There are several historical observations that make this reconstruction of early Christianity untenable, however. First, while it is undeniable that both Hellenistic culture in general and non-Christian philosophy in particular influenced the form of postapostolic Christianity, the amount and suddenness of transformation required to defend the Mormon view of apostasy simply cannot be elicited from the ancient sources available to us. A slow process of change over several centuries led to the emergence of the highly institutionalized Roman Catholic Church, quite different from the more informally organized churches of the New Testament, but no one event or period in early Christian history can be seen as determinative of this shift. The earliest extant post-New Testament creed, known as the Old Roman Creed, which emerged in the late second and early third centuries, was already Trinitarian in its organization, and every line in it parallels numerous New Testament texts that use almost the identical wording. The third-century Apostles' Creed, the earliest and most widely accepted of the ancient "ecumenical" creeds, differs only slightly from its Old Roman predecessor. And the fourth-century Nicene Creed simply expands on the Apostles' Creed, section by section, even as it introduces language reflective of larger debates within the Greco-Roman world. Even that language, however, is more often a critique of Hellenistic "corruption" of Christianity than a product of it.

Second, these observations are partly granted by certain recent LDS writings that, instead of trying to demonstrate how corrupt early postapostolic Christianity became, mine the preconciliar literature for supposed parallels to Mormon distinctives. They regularly build on the classic modern-era claim by

Protestant liberals of past generations of scholarship like Adolf von Harnack and Walter Bauer, who argued that what the various councils labeled heresy often predated the views that emerged as orthodoxy. Thus, they point to numerous excerpts of intertestamental Jewish apocrypha and pseudepigrapha, the writings of the mostly orthodox church fathers of the second century, and the more eccentric gnostic and New Testament apocryphal literature that demonstrate that other Jews and Christians have at times believed in such doctrines as the preexistence of souls, the corporeality of God, the ontological subordination of the Son to the Father, and so on.

Unfortunately, these discussions contain numerous fallacies. The majority of these alleged parallels come from sources themselves implicitly or explicitly influenced by Hellenistic philosophy. The Latter-day Saints cannot have it both ways. If this philosophy was primarily a corrupting influence on authentic Christianity, then it is no argument in their favor that a majority of their ancient "parallels" come from exactly that Hellenistic philosophy. Moreover, numerous studies have demonstrated that Hellenism had permeated deeply into Palestine well before the time of Christ; every portion of the New Testament Christianity was a mix of ideas that shared common ground with Jewish and Greco-Roman thought and that also differed with both arenas of thought in varying ways. Very few non-LDS scholars today, either liberal or conservative, believe that one can map out the first few centuries of Christian thought by tracing straight-line developments from orthodoxy to heresy or vice versa.

In addition, a fair number of the parallels cited by contemporary Mormons simply do not teach what it is alleged they do. For example, most of Stephen Robinson's references to early Christian belief in the corporeality of God are talking about the Incarnation—the Son taking upon himself human flesh, not the Father having a body as in the uniquely Mormon claim. So too, all of Robinson's references to divinization in the early church, mostly from *Greek* Orthodoxy, have to do with people taking on the moral characteristics of God, not his ontological distinctives. Finally, even where there are genuine conceptual parallels, they come from disparate enough sources that they do not add up to evidence for the distinctively Mormon *system* of thought (or worldview) within any *one* ancient author or branch of the church. Thus, Bickmore can cite pre-Christian Jewish sources for a fascination with an exalted angel almost parallel to God the Father, gnostic sources for esoteric rites with some similarities to various secretive LDS ceremonies, and largely "orthodox" church fathers who debated the preexistence of the soul (though usually *not* the existence of the soul prior to the creation of the earth). But one cannot find all of these beliefs in any one place, much less do they add up to any coherent doctrinal system as in modern-day Mormon thought.

Third, even if we granted the greater measure of apostasy in early postapostolic Christianity that Mormons have often claimed, with vestiges of distinctively LDS beliefs and practices scattered about, one would still have to demonstrate that these distinctives corresponded to *original* Christianity as defined by Jesus and the apostles. But such tenets are even more conspicuously absent from the New Testament than from the church fathers. Teachings about additional scriptures, the corporeality of God, deification, the premortal existence of souls, and the like find even less support (indeed, arguably, *no* support) in the New Testament than in postapostolic Christianity, and many Latter-day Saints recognize this. Hence, Joseph Smith's claim that the "abominable church" had taken away numerous "plain and precious parts of the gospel" (1 Nephi 13:34).

Now to defend this charge, Mormonism has two options. The first is to argue that the text of the New Testament itself is corrupt, substantially beyond the actual variations that textual criticism can demonstrate. This is seemingly one of the central reasons that Joseph Smith produced his own "Inspired Version" of the Bible. Unfortunately, there is almost never any manuscript evidence from antiquity to support the most theologically significant changes Smith made to the Bible; virtually all of these fall into the category of what textual critics would call the "easier readings"—changes that a scribe would introduce in copying that are designed to solve theological problems and smooth out awkward features of the text—not variants that would commend themselves as the original readings of the text. And, contrary to certain LDS claims, we have a relatively unbroken history of the transmission of the New Testament text that does not leave sizable enough gaps for sweeping changes to have been made in the copying of its documents. From the first decades of the second century, we find numerous quotes of the New Testament in the church fathers; by the late second century, we have sizable fragments of entire books preserved; and by the third and fourth centuries, hundreds of papyri and the great uncials begin to appear.

The other option is for the Latter-day Saints to concede that we do have the New Testament documents very well intact but to argue that entirely separate books have been lost from the canon. But again, there is not a shred of solid historical evidence to support this claim. Early Christian writers do occasionally quote from some lost apocryphal document, but these quotations do not contain distinctively Mormon doctrine. A large quantity of post-New Testament Christian literature, both orthodox and heterodox, still remains extant, and readers can consult this material for themselves to see how different it is from LDS theology. In answering the question "Without records how do we know what happened?" Joseph F. McConkie candidly replies, "The restoration of the gospel is the most perfect evidence." It is, in fact, the *only* evidence he cites; the circular reasoning of his argument should be obvious.

What is more, it is now widely acknowledged by biblical scholars, including not a few Roman Catholics, that the highly institutionalized forms of Christianity that created the Roman church developed *after* the apostolic age. Accounts of apostles having to appoint successors to themselves (cf. Acts 1:15–26) and to authorize the reception of the Holy Spirit (cf. Acts 8:14–17) appear only once each in the New Testament and did not become normative *patterns* of ecclesiastical practice until later centuries. Peter receiving the "keys of the kingdom" (Matt 16:19) in its original context is considerably removed from the later concept of one infallible ruler of the church. The "monarchical episcopacy" as a defining mark of "early Catholicism," so crucial to the LDS argument that the true church exists only where there are duly authorized leaders performing various sacred ceremonies, is itself a second-century corruption of pure

New Testament Christianity, not its original form. Finally, the entire argument that the distinctive beliefs and practices of Mormonism could have successfully been suppressed (or simply lost) on such a massive scale at some point in early Christian history, when we have relatively unbroken testimony of a representative cross section of early Christian belief throughout each generation of its first several centuries of existence, defies credibility.

A New Form of Christianity?

We have seen, then, that Mormonism does not fit any historic Christian option and that its claim to be a different, *restored* form of Christianity also fails. But is there, perhaps, a third way in which it might be considered Christian—not as the restoration of the original form, but as a newly revealed fourth branch of Christendom? In many respects, the LDS claims might prove more persuasive had Joseph Smith treated the Book of Mormon, not as the translation of a centuries-old work, but as brand new revelation from God, as he did with his subsequent Doctrine and Covenants. After all, a large number of LDS doctrines and practices that do find prior Christian precedent most closely parallel the broader Restorationist movement in early nineteenth-century America.

Consider, for example, the following list:

- Belief in an apostasy in the early church, which the Reformation did not adequately correct, necessitating a further Restoration.
- Belief in the necessity of believers' baptism by immersion for salvation
- Dependence on Acts 2:38 for the sequence of saving actions, which include faith, repentance, baptism, forgiveness of sins, the gift of the Holy Ghost, and appropriate good works to demonstrate persevering to the end, upon which eternal life can then be assured
- A rejection of all the historic creeds and confessions of faith of the church
- A desire to separate from all other existing forms of Christianity but to unite as the one true church of Jesus Christ
- Using a name for one's church that referred only to Christ and not to any human leaders
- Strong anti-Calvinism; against all five points of the "TULIP"—total depravity, unconditional election, limited atonement, irresistible grace, and the (guaranteed) perseverance of the saints
- Preaching against "faith only," especially in light of James 2:24
- Ambiguity as to whether or not the Holy Ghost is a person
- The necessity of weekly Communion, but avoidance of wine due to teetotalism
- Against paid clergy, clerical titles, and the factiousness caused by denominationalism
- A spirit of self-reliance, a stress on tithing, and a strong concern to care for the genuinely needy in Christian circles and elsewhere
- An emphasis on Sabbath-keeping and the restoration of morality to a church and culture widely perceived to have become antinomian

- The generation of a new translation of the Scriptures
- The ultimate harmony of science and religion
- A sharp distinction between the dispensations of the patriarchs, the law, and the gospel
- Belief in the establishment of God's kingdom in America in a more complete form than in any previous era of church history, described as "building Zion"
- A renewed missionary zeal
- A charismatic, iconoclastic founder

One might be forgiven for thinking that this list described elements of religion newly revealed to Joseph Smith, but in fact every item was a central tenet of the preaching of Alexander Campbell, from which the Disciples of Christ movement was formed. One of Campbell's brightest followers, with whom he discoursed extensively, was Sidney Rigdon, who later became Joseph Smith's "right hand man." George Arbaugh, who chronicled in detail Smith's career-long doctrinal pilgrimage increasingly away from orthodox Christianity, was even able to say that at its inception, Mormonism was a "Campbellite sect."

Of course, Campbell strictly limited his sources of authority to the Old and New Testaments. Joseph Smith had other influences for his more unparalleled "revelations." To be sure, a sizable amount of the Book of Mormon alludes to, and even explicitly quotes from, the King James Bible, including passages that subsequent textual criticism has demonstrated were not in the original manuscripts of Scripture. But Smith also became a Mason, and there are numerous parallels between the Masonic Lodge ceremonies and LDS temple rituals. He heard countless preachers from numerous denominations who passed through the Palmyra, New York, area and read voraciously from local libraries. Whether or not we will ever be able to pin down one specific literary source for the general plot of the Book of Mormon is probably irrelevant; there was enough oral and written speculation in Smith's day about the settling of the Americas by the Indians, possibilities of ancient Jewish pilgrimage to the New World, concerns over the salvation of those who had died without ever hearing the gospel (both in ancient Israel and in the Western Hemisphere), debates about the Negro race as possibly cursed by God, and hopes for America becoming a Christian Utopia (a new Israel and the site of Christ's return) that it is completely understandable that all these elements should appear in the Book of Mormon and subsequent writings by Smith. The standard LDS apologetic of how unlikely it is that the "poorly educated" (formally speaking) young Smith could have created his revelations without divine inspiration overlooks all of these clearly documented influences on his early life and thought.

Now as we speculate as to whether Mormonism could be considered Christian in the sense of simply a new nineteenth-century denomination, we must stress that this is not what the Latter-day Saints themselves claim. Nevertheless, it seems that they would be overjoyed if orthodox Christians would at least grant them that much. One obstacle to this acknowledgment, then, becomes the fact that, shorn of its Restorationist claims, Mormonism appears to relate to historic Christianity much as Christianity came to relate to Judaism: it changes enough elements to be classified better as a completely new religion.

Perhaps an analogy will help here. Suppose suddenly a group of Caucasian Swedes announced that God had given them a new work of scripture that contained many of the teachings of the Qu'ran in it. A contemporary prophet had translated it into Swedish from ancient tablets purportedly written in an otherwise unknown language called reformed Persian, but those tablets are unavailable for anyone to examine. Despite Muslim convictions about the inerrancy of the Qu'ran, this new religious movement claims that Islamic scripture is corrupt, missing many fundamental doctrines that the prophet Mohammed had in fact promulgated, including an account of Sweden being settled by middle-eastern Arabs long before the Vikings. What is more, the cardinal tenets of Islam —the monotheism of Allah and Mohammed as the prophet who brought final, definitive revelation from God—have been disproved; in fact, the Qu'ran's original views more resembled the polytheism Muslims believe Mohammed rejected than the monotheism centrally proclaimed throughout their history. While Mohammed himself was a great spokesman for Allah, there is a Swedish prophet continuing to receive revelation from God today who can supersede anything in the Qu'ran that he wishes. Meanwhile, the standard summary of Islamic religion is to be rejected as "abominable," and most of Islam's holy men are viewed as corrupt.

The analogy could, of course, be extended. But could we seriously expect any faithful Muslim today to simultaneously reject this new sect's claims to have restored original Islam and yet accept it as a legitimate expression of the Muslim faith? Presumably, the Latter-day Saints would similarly reject claims by a splinter group from within their own midst to be truly Mormon if they differed in this many fundamental ways from the larger parent organization.

There is, however, a possible way forward for Mormonism. Stephen Robinson himself draws parallels to how Roman Catholics and Protestants finally made substantial progress in interfaith dialogue in the last half-century. This became possible largely due to the historic Vatican II Council in the mid-1960s. Among other things, Catholicism toned down its claims for papal authority (mildly) and for the impossibility of salvation outside the Catholic Church (dramatically). Subsequent ecumenical gatherings of leading Catholic scholars and church authorities with both Lutherans and interdenominational groups of evangelicals have led to considerable agreement on the nature of justification by faith and Christian mission, respectively. Significantly, in each of these developments the resulting agreements more closely resemble the theology of Luther than that of the Counter-Reformation.

Most evangelicals, I am convinced, would be thrilled to observe parallel developments within Mormonism. Clearly, both the Vatican and Salt Lake City have an advantage not available to Protestants—a magisterium that can make authoritative pronouncements that supersede previous belief and practice. In both instances, this can take place very formally and suddenly, as when a pope speaks *ex cathedra* or an LDS president announces a new revelation from God. In Mormon history this had happened only twice: to cease practicing polygamy (1890), and to rescind the ban on blacks from the priesthood (1978). In each case, one by-product, whether or not intended, was to move Mormonism more in line with historic Christianity on the issue at hand. Clearly, such revelations could again move the LDS Church in what evangelicals would consider more biblical directions.

A more common kind of shift is less formal. Just as there are many segments of Western Catholicism that almost entirely disregard the still-official pronouncements of past eras of the Catholic Church about worshipping Mary or avoiding contraception (to use one theological and one moral illustration), so too the LDS authorities could simply decide not to stress those teachings that, from a historic Christian perspective, are most aberrant or offensive. If one is to believe the public persona of the LDS authorities today, this is already occurring, at least to some extent. Mormons widely perceive a movement over the last fifteen years or so, beginning with the presidency of Ezra Taft Benson, to call their church back to its roots, that is, to the Bible and the Book of Mormon. Given the orthodoxy of the Bible and the smaller amount of heterodoxy in the Book of Mormon compared with Joseph Smith's later writings, this development should be welcomed.

Similarly, the current LDS president, Gordon B. Hinckley, when asked in an interview for *Time* magazine whether the teaching of the Mormon Church today was that "God the Father was once a man like we are," replied, "I don't know that we teach it. I don't know that we emphasize it. I haven't heard it discussed for a long time in public discourse." President Hinckley's latest book, *Stand for Something,* speaks eloquently of ten cardinal virtues needed in American society today, and quotes liberally from the Old and New Testaments but not once by chapter and verse from any of the uniquely Mormon scriptures. Yet Hinckley makes his points compellingly and gives numerous illustrations from his life and that of other Mormons, including an occasional quotation from Brigham Young. Obviously this is a deliberately chosen strategy to have the greatest national impact—but if it can work so well, why not do it consistently, in-house as well as publicly? Just as renewal-movement Catholics today cite the Bible far more often than the Apocrypha or church tradition, so LDS spokespersons could substantially limit their teaching to clearly biblical texts and doctrines. (I am *not* claiming that this would be sufficient to make the LDS Church fully orthodox, merely that it would be a good first step in narrowing "the divide.")

The same could hold true for other areas that divide Mormonism from the historic Christian world. Writers like Stephen Robinson and Robert Millet are already demonstrating an acceptable diversity within LDS faith on central tenets such as the nature of God (absolutist not finite), the deification of believers (always subordinate to, and contingent on, God the Father), and salvation (by grace through faith), with frequent supporting quotations from orthodox Christian writers like C.S. Lewis and John MacArthur. And there are signs that others are starting to follow in their wake. Thus, I disagree with Francis Beckwith that changes in Mormonism must "go through" Joseph Smith and Brigham Young; that is, they must account for how those two church leaders said things are seemingly contradicted by subsequent developments in LDS circles. This was not the approach taken by Vatican II (or numerous other Catholic councils over the centuries) with respect to prior papal pronouncements. A church that believes in ongoing revelation or authoritative church tradition by definition looks to the most current form of that revelation or tradition to define its beliefs. It could actually prove counterproductive to try to stress to Catholics or Mormons (or anyone else!) that current beliefs seem to contradict former ones, if one approves of the current beliefs. Those groups might then be tempted to revert back to the older, less desirable beliefs!

I know that the scenarios I have sketched in the last five paragraphs seem far too radical to be conceivable by most current Mormons. But then Vatican II seemed impossible to Catholics even at the beginning of the 1960s. At the same time, it is important to stress that Roman Catholics already agreed with Protestants on fundamental doctrines such as the Trinity, the attributes of God, the relationship of the two natures of Christ, and so on. On much smaller scales, who would have predicted the major (though not universally accepted) changes even more recently within Seventh-Day Adventism or the Worldwide Church of God, both of which now have sizable evangelical constituencies? The Reorganized Latter Day Saints have likewise changed dramatically, largely in the direction of liberal Protestantism, and have officially renamed themselves the "Community of Christ."

Shorn of its unorthodox theology, Mormonism would still have enormous contributions to make to the contemporary religious world: a strong commitment to win people to Christ; a biblical emphasis on numerous fundamental moral values, including putting family relationships as a central priority in life; generous financial giving; a good blend of self-reliance and helping others who genuinely cannot care for themselves; all the strengths of classic Arminianism with its emphasis on human free will and responsibility; mechanisms for spiritual growth and accountability for every church member; educational institutions for all ages of people; elaborate church organization, accompanied by genuine community and warm interpersonal relationships; a desire to restore original Christianity and remove corrupting influences from it; social and political agendas often similar to evangelical counterparts; and so on. What a force for good in the world Christianity could be if historic, orthodox Christians could in good conscience link hands with a truly evangelical Mormonism! But we have not arrived at that stage yet.

Use of the Term *Christian* With Respect to an Individual

If none of the discussion thus far points to a way to label current Mormonism Christian *as an entire institution or system of thought*, what then of individual Mormons? Here LDS authors are, if anything, even more impassioned in their claims to merit the title "Christian." Peterson and Ricks, for example, return to the New Testament and conclude, "What made a person a Christian in the first century, and what makes a person a Christian today, is, simply, a commitment to Jesus Christ." Later they put it this way, "If anyone claims to see in Jesus of Nazareth a personage of unique and preeminent authority, that individual should be considered Christian." At first glance, such definitions seem eminently reasonable. But on further reflection, they are much broader than New Testament usage. The Indian Hindu Mohandas Gandhi would probably have qualified, given the sentiments he periodically expressed about Jesus as the greatest of religious teachers. More notably, these definitions would require all of the false teachers censored in the New Testament to be labeled Christian as well. Even the Judaizers in Galatia were *professing* Jewish Christians, zealously convinced that they were serving Christ as preeminent, even while requiring obedience to the Law to ensure salvation. Yet Paul twice consigns to hell anyone who continually preaches their message (Gal 1:8–9)! And Jesus speaks equally curtly of those who name him as Lord but do not do his Father's will. On Judgment Day he "will tell them plainly, 'I never knew you. Away from me, you evildoers!'" (Matt 7:23). A meaningful definition of a word must make clear what it excludes as well as what it includes.

What all this points out is that Peterson and Ricks's definitions determine only who *claims* to have Christian faith, not who is genuinely *regenerate*. Or to put it another way, when evangelicals raise the question of whether or not an individual rather than an entire religious body is Christian, they are normally asking the question "Is such a person *saved?*" Thus, the very language that Peterson and Ricks find so "idiosyncratic"—someone declaring "I have been an active and committed Lutheran since my earliest youth; I became a Christian last July"—is completely intelligible and widespread among evangelical Christians. In this kind of sentence, "Lutheran" simply means a member of a particular Lutheran church; whereas Christian means "converted." Sadly, in many liberal Protestant congregations and in even larger numbers of Catholic and Eastern Orthodox churches, it is possible to attend and be involved for years without ever hearing the message that one must personally accept Jesus as Lord and Savior and allow him to transform every area of one's life. It often requires some experience outside such congregations to lead to an individual's salvation.

Can a Mormon, then, be a Christian in this narrower, more biblical sense of "being saved" or "converted"? To answer this question, we must consider several scenarios. First, *anyone* can become a Christian by sincerely trusting in the Jesus of the New Testament as personal Lord (God and Master) and Savior and by demonstrating the sincerity of that commitment by some perceivable measure of lifelong, biblical belief and behavior. But I cannot take for granted that any given member of the LDS Church is automatically saved by virtue of church membership any more than I assume that a member of my own Baptist church is automatically saved by such membership. Probably every religious group in the history of the world has had people join it through some formal, external membership process without a corresponding internal change of heart to justify the genuineness of their professed conversions. But can an LDS Church member *become* a true Christian through genuine heartfelt conversion? The answer is "of course," and there has never been any evangelical dissent on this point.

A second question is a little harder. Can such a genuinely converted person *remain* within the LDS Church? The question is partially parallel to the question evangelicals have debated concerning converted Roman Catholics, to which today there would be a widespread (though not unanimous) consensus that again the answer is "yes," though the desirability of such a decision would be more hotly debated. Calvinist evangelicals, of course, would have to answer the question affirmatively, since they believe that the genuinely converted will necessarily persevere in their true faith. And Calvinists and Armenians alike would agree that a truly saved person does not subsequently forfeit that salvation simply because of an external matter such as church membership. But the vast majority of all evangelicals would surely also think that it would be wisest for "born-again" Mormons to change their church membership to an evangelical Protestant congregation where there would be a lesser likelihood of experiencing a mixture of true and false teaching.

Slightly different is the case of the evangelical Christian who seems to have had a genuine conversion experience and years of Christian involvement to authenticate it, and who then becomes a Mormon, a scenario that is becoming increasingly common in today's religious world. When once-active Christians simply give up all church involvement, most evangelicals refer to them as "backslidden," not as unsaved. Should evangelicals-turned-Mormon be viewed any differently? Of course, one understandable response is to declare, by definition, that anyone who makes that radical a break from their past demonstrates in so doing that they were never really saved in the first place. I have no difficulty believing that this is true for some individuals, especially in light of the close New Testament parallel described in 1 John 2:19. But experience makes it difficult for me automatically to assume that this approach accounts for all such people.

George Barna, in a poll the findings of which were publicized in 1998, surveyed a broad cross section of Americans about their religious beliefs and determined, to the extent that polls can determine such things, that 26 percent of Mormons answered the relevant questions in a way that is compatible with historic Christian belief and professed to be "born again." Barna's own explanation for how this was possible was to observe that Americans today join churches for a host of reasons other than doctrine—most notably because they have found a warm, caring fellowship of friends—and in many cases hold doctrinal beliefs inconsistent with the official teachings of the churches they join. Given that I have observed this phenomenon running rampant among evangelical churches with which I am familiar, it is hard to believe that the Latter-day Saints are exempt from similar behavior. Pursuing the analogy with evangelical churches even further, it is not difficult for me to imagine large numbers of Latter-day Saints, as in the traditional Christian world, not even knowing in detail everything their church officially teaches (especially if some of the more idiosyncratic items are seldom if ever mentioned), or not feeling any strong obligation to affirm peripheral doctrines. In our highly syncretistic world, I can readily imagine that many of the Latter-day Saints who identified themselves as "born again" are among the evangelical converts to Mormonism who, rightly or wrongly, are convinced that they can keep all of their previous beliefs and commitments and simply add some more on top of them.

A final question is the hardest to answer. Can a person who had no religious influence on his or her life except the teaching and practice of the LDS come to true, saving faith *within* the LDS Church, if he or she is exposed to the full range of official Mormon doctrine and sincerely believe all of that teaching? Regrettably, I cannot in good conscience answer affirmatively. For all the reasons discussed in the sections of *How Wide the Divide?* that I authored by myself, it seems to me that there still remain major contradictions of fundamental doctrinal issues between historic Christianity and official LDS teaching that make it impossible to *consistently* believe all of the Bible and simultaneously believe all official Mormon doctrine.

But in addition to recognizing that persons can be inconsistent without realizing it, I also recognize that many of my Mormon friends disagree with my conclusions at this point. I also want to stress that it is never appropriate for any believer to pontificate with utter certainty about the external state of another person's soul; mercifully, that role is reserved exclusively for God. Nevertheless, I feel compelled to reiterate the point that I have made repeatedly before, especially since it has so often been misquoted and misrepresented. I would love to discover at some time that a genuinely "evangelical Mormonism" existed. I have no desire to see the Latter-day Saints or any other professing Christian group as a whole or any individuals within it remain outside the fold of true Christianity. It is simply that, despite numerous encouraging signs, I do not believe we have yet reached that state of affairs. Neither am I trying to define Mormonism out of Christianity. The real problem from an evangelical perspective—or any orthodox Christian perspective—is to find a *meaningful* way to include Mormonism within Christianity. I cannot, as of this writing, therefore, affirm with integrity that either Mormonism as a whole or any individual, based solely on his or her affirmation of the totality of LDS doctrine, deserves the label "Christian" in any standard or helpful sense of the word. But my fervent prayer is that, through whatever developments God may wish to use, I will not always have to come to that conclusion.

A Final Comment

Latter-day Saint scholar Eugene England has claimed that "some Evangelicals' intolerance for Mormons has taken extreme forms, including the claim that Mormons are not Christians. But is the conclusion that Mormonism is not Christian necessarily an extreme form of intolerance? For the reasons that have been discussed [here], I do not believe it is. However, it is true that evangelicals have often made such claims in a very uncharitable manner. We do well to take to heart the following words that J. Gresham Machen penned many years ago about Protestant liberalism:

> In maintaining that liberalism in the modern Church represents a return to an un-Christian and sub-Christian form of the religious life, we are particularly anxious not to be misunderstood. 'Un-Christian' in such a connection is sometimes taken as a term of opprobrium. We do not mean it at all as such. Socrates was not a Christian, neither was Goethe; yet we share to the full the respect with which their names are regarded. They tower immeasurably above the common run of men; if he that is least in the Kingdom of Heaven is greater than they, he is certainly greater not by any inherent

superiority, but by virtue of an undeserved privilege which ought to make him humble rather than contemptuous.

It is important to apply these same sentiments, *mutatis mutandis,* to the LDS faith. When they are so applied, the claim that Mormonism is not Christian is neither intolerant nor extreme nor uncharitable.

POSTSCRIPT

Is Mormonism Christian?

From the arguments presented by Judd and Blomberg, one could conclude that The Church of Jesus Christ of Latter-day Saints could be considered a Christian religion but not in the traditional sense. Latter-day Saint leaders acknowledge these differences as well. President Gordon B. Hinckley, whom Latter-day Saints consider a modern prophet, recently stated, "As a Church we have critics, many of them. They say we do not believe in the traditional Christ of Christianity. *There is some substance to what they say.* Our faith, our knowledge is not based on ancient tradition" (*Ensign*, May 2002, p. 90; italics added). It may be that whether or not The Church of Jesus Christ of Latter-day Saints is a "Christian" church depends upon whom you ask and what criteria they use.

While it appears that many traditional Christians accept Latter-day Saints as Christians, for the most part Christian clergy and scholars do not accept the church as a Christian religion. Up to now, much of the theological dialogue between Latter-day Saints and traditional Christians has been little more than insults hurled at one another. However, the recent publication of *The New Mormon Challenge: Responding to the Latest Defenses of a Fast-Growing Movement* (Zondervan, 2002) appears to be a step toward a more "Christlike" dialogue. Though not accepting of Latter-day Saints as Christian, the editors and most authors of this publication appear to be open to the possibility of sincere dialogue.

The Church of Jesus Christ of Latter-day Saints views itself as a Christian religion but not necessarily as a part of traditional Christianity. Latter-day Saints, while respectful and accepting of the truth found in other faiths, believe their church to be the restoration of the original church that Jesus Christ established during his mortal ministry. Latter-day Saint leaders and scholars also appear to be open to dialogue with their traditional Christian colleagues.

Suggested Readings

M. Cornwall, T. B. Heaton, and L. A. Young, *Contemporary Mormonism: Social Science Perspectives* (University of Illinois Press, 1994).

T. L. Givens, *By the Hand of Mormon: The American Scripture That Launched a New World Religion* (Oxford University Press, 2002).

R. L. Millet, *The Mormon Faith: A New Look at Christianity* (Shadow Mountain, 1998).

R. N. Ostling and J. K. Ostling, *Mormon America: The Power and the Promise* (HarperSanFrancisco, 1999).

Contributors to This Volume

EDITOR

DANIEL K. JUDD is an associate professor and department chair of ancient Scripture at Brigham Young University in Provo, Utah. Judd was also professor of family science at Ricks College in Rexburg, Idaho. He received a B.S. in zoology from Southern Utah University, an M.S. in family science, and a Ph.D. in counseling psychology from Brigham Young University. Judd's research interests include the psychology of religion and the relationship of mental health and religion. He is the editor of *Religion, Mental Health, and the Latter-day Saints*, vol. 14 of *Religious Studies Center Specialized Monograph Series* (Bookcraft Publishers, 1999).

STAFF

Theodore Knight   List Manager

David Brackley   Senior Developmental Editor

Juliana Gribbins   Developmental Editor

Rose Gleich   Administrative Assistant

Brenda S. Filley   Director of Production/Design

Juliana Arbo   Typesetting Supervisor

Diane Barker   Proofreader

Richard Tietjen   Publishing Systems Manager

Larry Killian   Copier Coordinator

AUTHORS

JOHN ARTHUR is a professor of philosophy and the director of the Program in Philosophy, Politics, and Law at Binghamton University (SUNY). He is a recipient of the Chancellor Award for Excellence in Teaching. He received his Ph.D. from Vanderbilt University in 1973. He is also the editor of *Morality and Moral Controversies* (Prentice Hall, 1998), a widely used textbook for undergraduate students.

FRED BARNES is a nationally recognized journalist. He is cofounder of *The Standard*, a weekly news magazine, and he has previously written as senior editor and White House correspondent for *The New Republic*. Barnes appears as a regular panelist on *The McLaughlin Group*, a political television talk show, and *Crossfire* on CNN. He is a graduate of the University of Virginia and has appeared on *Nightline, Today, Good Morning America, Meet the Press*, and *Face the Nation*.

CRAIG L. BLOMBERG is a professor of New Testament at the Denver Seminary, where he has taught since 1986. Blomberg received a Ph.D. from Aberdeen University in Scotland and an M.A. degree in New Testament from Trinity Evangelical Divinity School in Deerfield, Illinois. He was an assistant professor of religion at Palm Beach Atlantic College and a research fellow in Cambridge, England, with Tyndale House. He has published widely in professional journals and coauthored *How Wide the Divide? A Mormon & an Evangelical in Conversation* (InterVarsity Press, 1997).

MARCUS J. BORG is a distinguished professor in religion and culture and also Hundere Endowed Chair in Religious Studies at Oregon State University. He received a Ph.D from Oxford University and is the author of two best-selling books, *Jesus: A New Vision* (HarperSanFrancisco, 1991) and *Meeting Jesus Again for the First Time* (HarperSanFrancisco, 1995). As a leading figure in contemporary Jesus scholarship, he has appeared on NBC's *Today Show*, PBS's *Newshour*, and NPR's *Fresh Air*.

RICHARD DAVIS is a professor of political science at Brigham Young University in Provo, Utah. He holds degrees in political science and mass communications from Brigham Young University and Syracuse University. He specializes in American politics. Davis is the author of many books and articles, including *The Web of Politics: The Internet's Impact on the American Political System* (Oxford University Press, 1999). His most recent book is *Campaigning Online: The Internet in U.S. Elections* (Oxford University Press, 2003).

DANIEL C. DENNETT is the distinguished arts and sciences professor at Tufts University where he is also director of the Center for Cognitive Studies. He is the author of *Brainstorms: Philosophical Essays on Mind and Psychology* (MIT Press, 1980), *Elbow Room: The Varieties of Will Worth Wanting* (MIT Press, 1984), and *Consciousness Explained* (Little, Brown, 1991).

EDITORS OF *FIRST THINGS* is published by Religion and Public Life, an interreligious, nonpartisan research and education institute. The purpose of the institute is to advance a religiously informed public philosophy for the ordering of society.

ALBERT ELLIS, founder of rational-emotive therapy, is president of the Institute for Rational-Emotive Therapy, located in New York City. He received his Ph.D. in clinical psychology from Columbia University. Ellis has authored or coauthored more than 600 articles and more than 50 books on psychotherapy, marital and family therapy, and sex therapy, including *Why Some Therapies Don't Work: The Dangers of Transpersonal Psychology* (Prometheus Books, 1989), with Raymond Yaeger.

VICTOR PAUL FURNISH is a distinguished professor of New Testament at Southern Methodist University in Dallas, Texas. Furnish received his Ph.D. in religious studies and New Testament from Yale University and has published a number of books on New Testament teachings, including *The Moral Teaching of Paul: Selected Issues* (Abingdon Press, 1985) and *The Theology of the First Letter to the Corinthians* (Cambridge University Press, 1999).

MICHAEL GOLD is a Jewish Rabbi who heads Temple Beth Torah/Tamarac Jewish Center in Tamarac, Florida. He earned his B.A. in mathematics from the University of California in San Diego and was ordained by the Jewish Theological Seminary in 1979. He lectures throughout the country on sexual ethics, infertility and adoption, and family relationships. He has served as the cochair of the Rabbinical Assembly committee on sexuality. His works include *And Hannah Wept* (Jewish Publication Society, 1994) and *The Ten Journeys of Life: Walking the Path of Abraham: A Guide to Being Human* (Health Communications, 2001).

STANLEY HAUERWAS is Gilbert T. Rowe Professor of Theological Ethics at Duke Divinity School. After graduating from Yale Divinity School in 1965 and Yale University Graduate School in 1968, he spent two years at Augustana College in Rock Island, Illinois, and then moved on to Notre Dame from 1970–1984. He has been at Duke since 1984. Hauerwas lectures widely and is a member of the Society for Christian Ethics, the American Academy of Religion, and the American Theological Society. His most recent works include *With the Grain of the Universe* (Brazos Press, 2001) and *In Good Company* (University of Notre Dame Press, 1997).

RICHARD B. HAYS is a professor of New Testament at Duke Divinity School. His book *The Moral Vision of the New Testament: Community, Cross, New Creation: A Contemporary Introduction to New Testament Ethics* (HarperSan-Francisco, 1996) was selected by *Christianity Today* as one of the 100 most important religious books of the twentieth century. As an ordained United Methodist minister, he has preached in London's Westminster Abbey. He convened the consultation on Teaching the Bible in the Twenty-First Century and has served on the editorial boards of *The Journal of Biblical Literature*, *New Testament Studies*, and *Teaching Theology and Religion*.

JOHN HICK is a world-renowned theologian and philosopher of religion, and he currently serves as a fellow of the Institute for Advanced Research in Arts and Social Sciences at the University of Birmingham. He studied at both the

University of Edinburgh and Oxford University. He has written and edited an array of influential texts, including *The Existence of God* (MacMillan, 1964) and *God Has Many Names* (Westminster John Knox Press, 1986).

KEITH E. JOHNSON received a B.S.E. in chemical engineering from the University of Michigan, an M.A. in Christian thought from Trinity Evangelical Divinity School, and a Th.M. in Christian theology from Duke Divinity School. He is currently a Ph.D. candidate in Christian theology in the Department of Religion at Duke University. Johnson's research at Duke University centers on the theological interface of Christianity and other religions in a pluralistic context. He has written several essays engaging issues of religious pluralism. An essay entitled "Theology of Religions" will be published in the (forthcoming) second edition of the *Dictionary of the Ecumenical Movement*. For the past 15 years Johnson has also served as an ordained campus minister. In this capacity he has discussed issues of religious pluralism with numerous undergraduates. His selection included in this volume emerged from those conversations.

JOHN B. JUDIS is currently a senior editor for *The New Republic* and has been a contributor since 1982. He received an M.A. from the University of California at Berkeley in 1965 and later taught philosophy there and also at the San Francisco Art Institute. He has written numerous articles, which have appeared in publications ranging from *GQ* to *Foreign Affairs*. His books include *The Paradox of American Democracy: Elites, Special Interests, and the Betrayal of Public Trust* (Taylor & Francis Group, 2001) and *Grand Illusion: Critics and Champions of the American Century* (Farrar, Straus & Giroux, 1992).

DAVID B. LARSON is president of the International Center for the Integration of Health and Spirituality in Rockville, Maryland. Larson worked for nearly 10 years at the National Institutes of Health (NIH) and is adjunct professor of psychiatry and behavioral sciences at Duke University Medical Center and Northwestern University Medical School. He has published more than 250 professional articles and is a coeditor of *Handbook of Religion and Health* (Oxford University Press, 2000).

JOHN F. MacARTHUR, JR. is the president and featured teacher of Grace to You, a nonprofit Christian ministry organization. He also currently serves as president of The Master's College, an accredited, four-year, liberal arts Christian college in Santa Clarita, California. It was mostly his work as pastor of the Grace Community Church in Sun Valley, California, where he has taught since 1969, that led to his writing and publishing of over 15 religious books. These books include *The Gospel According to Jesus* (Zondervan, 1988) and *Terrorism, Jihad, and the Bible* (World Press, 2001).

DANIEL C. MAGUIRE is a professor of ethics at Marquette University in Milwaukee, Wisconsin. He received his degree as Doctor of Sacred Theology from the Pontifical Gregorian University in Rome, and he currently serves as president of the Religious Consultation on Population, Reproductive Health, and Ethics. He has spoken to the Panel on Religious and Ethical

Perspectives on Population Issues at the International Conference on Population and Development at the United Nations. He has authored numerous books on religious ethics, including *Sacred Energies* (Fortress Press, 2000) and *Ethics for a Small Planet* (State University of New York Press, 1998).

SALLY MOREM is former president of the Humanists of Minnesota, a chapter of the American Humanist Association. She is an essayist and a reader and editor for Minnesota Clipping Service. She was a finalist in the 1996 Great American Think-Off, America's only philosophical essay and debate contest, held in New York Mills, Minnesota.

WILLIAM PALEY (1743–1805) was an influential thinker in the natural theology school that attempted to reconcile aspects of philosophy and theology. He studied for the Anglican priesthood at Christ's College, Cambridge, where he graduated in 1763. He was appointed as a fellow and tutor at Cambridge and progressed through the ranks of the Anglican Church. Paley is perhaps most well known for his formulation of the "argument from design," but he wrote numerous books on philosophy and Christianity. One of his works, *Natural Theology*, became required reading at Cambridge, where it was read by the young Charles Darwin.

CHARLES C. RYRIE is presently distinguished professor of Bible at the Philadelphia Biblical University, where he previously served as president. Ryrie has also held academic posts at the Dallas Theological Seminary and at Westmont College. His extensive list of publications includes *The Ryrie Study Bible* (Moody Press, 1986), which has been used by Christians across the world.

JOHN SANDERS is an associate professor of philosophy and religion at Huntington College in Huntington, Indiana. He received a Doctor of Theology degree from the University of South Africa and recently has written and edited a number of influential theology texts, including *No Other Name: An Investigation Into the Destiny of the Unevangelized* (Wm. B. Eerdmans Publishing, 1992) and *The God Who Risks* (InterVarsity Press, 1998).

GLEN H. STASSEN is a professor of Christian ethics at the Fuller Theological Seminary in Pasadena, California. He is the current president of the Council of the Societies for the Study of Religion and has served as president of the North American Baptist Professors of Religion. He graduated from the University of Virginia with a degree in nuclear physics and went on to earn a Ph.D. in Christian ethics, history of Christian thought, and political theory from Duke University. Following his graduate work he spent three years as a visiting scholar at Harvard University researching international relations and Christian ethics. He has written, coauthored, and edited over 40 scholarly articles on areas relating to Christian ethics and six books, including *Authentic Transformation: A New Vision of Christ and Culture* (Abingdon, 1996) and *Capital Punishment: A Reader* (Pilgrim Press, 1998).

MATTHEW D. STAVER is the founder and president of Liberty Counsel, a religious civil liberties education and legal defense organization established to preserve religious freedom. An attorney by profession, Staver also holds a master's degree in religion and is an ordained pastor. He hosts two radio programs, *Freedom's Call*, a daily commentary on religious freedom, and *Faith & Freedom*, a daily fifteen-minute program that covers recent cases and issues affecting religious liberty.

LEO TOLSTÓY is one of the most acclaimed novelists of all time and remains respected as a profound social and moral thinker. Born in 1828 at Yasnaya Polyana, the family estate south of Moscow, Tolstóy was orphaned at an early age. Under encouragement from an aunt he entered Kazan University at the age of 16, where he studied languages and law, but he left a few years later without taking a degree. Much of Tolstóy's writing centers on characters that embody class and social conflict, and he championed the cause of greater civil liberties for Russian serfs. Tolstóy married Sonya Andreyevna Bers in 1862 and wrote his two greatest novels, *War and Peace* and *Anna Karenina*, in the succeeding years while raising a large family.

THE VATICAN is associated with the Papacy and is the recognized representative of the Roman Catholic Church. Its Declarations are written from a careful referencing of papal encyclicals (official letters issued by the Pope), statements by church authorities, and academic sources from Catholic scholars.

JACOB J. VELLENGA is former associate executive of the United Presbyterian Church.

STEPHEN N. WILLIAMS is a professor of systematic theology at Union Theological College in Belfast, Ireland. He is a member of the European Editorial Board of the journal *Ethics & Medicine* and has written *Revelation and Reconciliation: A Window on Modernity* (Cambridge University Press, 1996).

WALTER WINK is a professor of biblical interpretation at Auburn Theological Seminary in New York City. He has been a parish minister and has taught at Union Theological Seminary. In 1989–1990 he was a peace fellow at the United States Institute of Peace. He has written and edited a number of works on religion and peace, including *The Powers That Be: Theology for a New Millennium* (Doubleday, 1999) and *Peace Is the Way* (Orbis Books, 2000).

N. T. WRIGHT is canon theologian of Westminster Abbey and formerly has served as dean of Lichfield Cathedral. Wright has taught in the religion departments of Cambridge, McGill, and Oxford Universities, and he is the author of a number of significant Christian works, including *Jesus and the Victory of God* (Fortress Press, 1997) and *The Original Jesus* (Wm. B. Eerdmans Publishing, 1997).

Index